Lawyers in Society

THE COMMON LAW WORLD

Lawyers in Society

VOLUME ONE
THE COMMON LAW WORLD

Edited by
RICHARD L. ABEL
and PHILIP S. C. LEWIS

UNIVERSITY OF CALIFORNIA PRESS
Berkeley / Los Angeles / London

University of California Press
Berkeley and Los Angeles, California

University of California Press, Ltd.
London, England

Library of Congress Cataloging-in-Publication Data

Lawyers in society.

Includes edited papers from a conference held in
Bellagio, Italy, July 16-21, 1984.
Bibliography: p.
Includes index.
1. Lawyers—Congresses.   I. Abel, Richard L.
II. Lewis, Philip Simon Coleman.
K117.L37   1988   340'.023   87-14302
ISBN 0-520-05603-5 (alk. paper)

Printed in the United States of America

1   2   3   4   5   6   7   8   9

Contents

Preface

This is the first of three volumes on the comparative sociology of legal professions. The present volume analyzes the legal professions of the major common law countries of the industrialized world (England and Wales, Scotland, Canada, the United States, Australia, and New Zealand) and that of the most populous common law country in the Third World (India). We made no effort to cover other common law systems in Northern Ireland and the Republic of Ireland, the Caribbean, Asia, and Africa because of limitations on our resources and our inability to identify national reporters and because the International Center for Law in Development previously produced a book on several of those countries (C. J. Dias et al., *Lawyers in the Third World* [1981]). In addition, the Commonwealth Legal Education Association currently is investigating access to legal education and the legal profession in Commonwealth countries, including those of the Third World.

The second of our three volumes contains studies of eleven civil law professions (Belgium, Brazil, the Federal Republic of Germany, France, Italy, Japan, the Netherlands, Norway, Spain, Switzerland, and Venezuela). Limited resources and the lack of national reporters also prevented us from surveying the legal professions of the socialist and the Islamic worlds (although a Yugoslav colleague did participate in early discussions). The third volume uses these national reports and other sources to draw theoretical and comparative conclusions. All three volumes are the product of the Working Group for Comparative Study of Legal Professions, which was created by the Research Committee on Sociology of Law, a constituent of the International Sociological Association.

The Working Group was formed in 1980 and met annually thereafter, in Madison (Wisconsin), Oxford, Mexico City, and Antwerp, during the conferences of the Research Committee. These meetings were devoted to discussion of theoretical approaches to the legal profession and development of an inventory of information that national reporters were to collect. Drafts of most of the chapters were presented at a week-long meeting at the Villa Serbelloni, the Rockefeller Foundation's Conference Center in Bellagio, Italy, 16–21 July 1984. They have been revised extensively since then, assisted by further discussions during meetings of the Working Group in Aix-en-Provence and New Delhi in conjunction with the annual conferences of the Research Committee.

During the course of such a lengthy project involving a large number of people, we have been assisted by many individuals and institutions. The Board of the Research Committee on Sociology of Law consistently offered moral and financial support. Stewart Field, currently on the law faculty at the University of Wales Institute of Science and Technology, Cardiff, took extensive notes on the Bellagio conference, which helped all of us revise our contributions. Pam Taylor of All Souls College, Oxford, typed those notes and retyped many of the contributions. Dorothe Brehove and Marilyn Schroeter, together with other members of the secretarial staff of UCLA Law School, also retyped contributions. We are grateful to the Rockefeller Foundation for hosting our conference and to the American Bar Foundation for financial support, which made the conference possible. Terence Halliday of the American Bar Foundation provided invaluable administrative assistance in organizing that conference and since then has taken responsibility for leading the future activities of the Working Group. Richard Abel would like to thank UCLA Law School for continuing administrative and financial support. Philip Lewis would like to thank the Trustees of the Nuffield Foundation who made possible his participation in the early stages of this project.

Richard L. Abel   Philip S. C. Lewis

UCLA Law School   All Souls College, Oxford

1
Introduction

PHILIP S. C. LEWIS

It should not be necessary to explain at length the reasons for a detailed study of legal professions. In the last one or two decades there have been dramatic increases in the professions of Western industrialized countries and even more dramatic changes in the proportion of women entrants and the size of the units in which services are produced. Challenges to these professions, mainly from within, on the basis that they have done too little for some classes of society, have been succeeded by external challenges to their professional monopolies, the limits on competition within the profession, and their powers of self-regulation. These changes and challenges have given rise to policy questions that are, to say the least, more far-reaching than any debated for many years.

Nevertheless, the importance of legal professions transcends these comparatively time-bound concerns. No matter how one approaches them, they stand between the formal legal system and those who are subject to or take advantage of it. They pass on claims from one side and statements of rights and duties from the other, sometimes modifying them in the process, and play an essential part in the enforcement or protection of rights. Insofar as the law offers generalized facilities for action, it is likely to be lawyers who structure transactions within the private sector and between the private and public sectors. In doing so they do not merely pass on messages as a telephone company transmits calls. Both in their associations and as individuals, lawyers have interests of their own, ranging from personal advantage to the organized pursuit of sectional conceptions of justice. Such interests may diminish the enforcement of particular rights or provide enhanced facilities through which certain clients may pursue their economic interests. Some bodies of law may remain as the legislature wrote them, while others—governing fields where legal representation is the norm and time or money are available for elaborated thought or argument—may be fleshed out or altered in unexpected ways. Lawyers, thus, are a significant element in legal systems, worth as much attention for what they do and how they should act as has been paid to judges and adjudication.

We hope in these volumes to provide some background to the activities of both reformers and practitioners: the first group is perhaps overly concerned with apparent defects that have excited their attention, while the second is perhaps too restricted in their outlook by the day-to-day demands of practice and the current presuppositions of professional organization. In our view there is value in a more detached approach, one that can elucidate the demographic, economic, ideological, and cultural background to the ways in which lawyers are organized and choose and carry on their work as well as to the changes that have affected or are likely to affect them. Such an approach can also show whether actions taken for apparently worthwhile motives have had unintended consequences or have been supported by those with selfish interests. Scholarly distance can help to show the limitations on or dangers of both change and inertia. Nevertheless, there are limits to the progress that can be made without the active cooperation of lawyers; so much of what they do is invisible and confidential that, without such cooperation, important material is simply not available for discussion. The scientific foundation of medicine can be used as a basis for subjecting medical practice to scientific scrutiny; except, perhaps, for arguments about justice, there is no similar basis for examining legal practice. Consequently, self-reflection tends to be postponed until either criticism of the profession's privileges or demands for justification of the expenditure of public funds brings into play other criteria altogether.

These volumes rest on two premises. The first is that lawyers should be studied in their social context and that an interdisciplinary approach is essential. The contributors have used economics, political science, history, and sociology in their efforts to understand lawyers. Nevertheless, the dominant approach is sociological (with a strong dash of history), and this seems, for the moment, likely to be particularly fruitful. The second premise is that explicit comparison of lawyers across countries will generate more understanding than will studies confined to particular countries. I deal with these points in turn.

The contribution of traditional legal studies to our understanding of lawyers has not been impressive. There has been astonishingly little discussion about the activities of lawyers, at least in the countries with which we have dealt. Even in the United States, where post-Watergate concerns for the ethical standards of lawyers gave birth to a plethora of professional responsibility courses and accompanying textbooks, only a small proportion of what has been written addresses serious issues of principle, and still less does so on the basis of any kind of ascertained fact (but see Rhode,

1981, 1985). Fears that lawyers are no more than "hired guns" have generated some philosophical discussion (Luban, 1983), and also some empirical study of the relations of lawyers to their large business clients (Rosen, 1984; Kagan and Rosen, 1984; Nelson, 1984). This sparse literature, however, represents a boundless treasure compared to legal scholarship in other countries where, except in the field of services to those who could not afford them, lawyers have been taken for granted as part of the legal landscape, raising problems roughly comparable to those presented by the court usher. In Great Britain, for example, two Royal Commissions (1979, 1980) reviewed access to legal services, and other policy issues, without considering the effects on the professions of their business and conveyancing orientation, the purposes of the legal system, or the impact on society of the professions' activities.

Comparative law has reflected this national poverty of interest. The most sophisticated recent discussion of lawyers in Western industrialized nations (Kötz, 1982) concentrates on the policy implications of broad trends such as specialization, claims to equal access, and relaxation of controls on advertising without seeking to relate them to underlying changes in the social environment or to the power of the profession vis-à-vis the state and the university. An earlier work (Johnstone and Hopson, 1967) contained many interesting comparisons and contrasts of English and American lawyers but has not been followed up.

It is very difficult to lay a proper groundwork for discussing the future organization and activities of the legal profession without understanding how change has occurred up to now and the unintended outcomes of previous decisions by interested actors. Both history and sociology address these questions, and each offers advantages. In a comparatively new and theoretically immature field, the progress of history may depend on the ability of talented individuals to formulate fruitful hypotheses and approaches; later a set of controversial questions will appear, the field will become more routine, and our understanding of particular professions will grow more profound. Sociology provides some intellectual underpinning in the form of categories for research that may be more useful to those coming fresh to the legal profession.

Experience of the history of lawyers supports these general remarks. It has certainly managed to emancipate itself from some of the unfortunate characteristics of an older legal history; contemporary work has been less inclined to trace a determinate path toward the present day, to assume that the rules governing the behavior of lawyers should be the principal concern, or to take for granted (or at its own valuation) the importance and public spirit of the profession (see, e.g., Friedman, 1985).

Significant conceptual advances have been made by Hurst (1950) and more recently by Gordon (1984), who makes very clear the differences between the work lawyers do, its economic significance, and the ideas by which lawyers justify and guide their actions. Gordon's is the latest, and intellectually the most far-reaching, of a number of recent historical studies, particularly in the United States and England but also on the Continent, some of which are beginning to adopt an explicitly comparative approach (Ranieri, 1985). However, the history of lawyers has not been intellectually isolated: it has engaged explicitly with theoretical approaches from elsewhere, not least the sociological approach underlying these volumes (Duman, 1983; Prest, 1984; Cocks, 1983: 10–11).

Law has long, though not continuously, been a subject for sociology, and for Weber the intellectual and economic concerns of specialized legal occupations played a distinctive and important part in legal development. Theoretical accounts of professions generally have been developed particularly in the Anglo-American world, where autonomous professions have most flourished (Benguigui, 1972; Rueschemeyer, 1973: 13 ff.; Freidson, 1983). Changes in thinking about professions generally have not always affected thinking about lawyers, however, and only recently has there been some fusion. A basis for this lag was pointed out by Hazard (1965) over twenty years ago: in theorizing about professions in general, the social consequences of their organization and activities are often rather shadowy compared to what can be known about their organization and modes of work. Consequently, the application of a sociological approach tends to emphasize what professions have in common and play down what is distinctive about lawyers. This is not a necessary result, but the criticism remains valid, simply because what lawyers do is not easily visible, and its social effects are methodologically and theoretically difficult to isolate.

We can distinguish between developments in the sociology of the professions generally and those relating to lawyers in particular. The former story is controversial and retold from time to time with different emphases (Dingwall, 1983; Abbott, 1986). Three strands are clear. Functionalism starts from the view that socially valuable expertise is the exclusive possession of certain occupations, which receive such privileges as monopoly, autonomy, status, and financial rewards in exchange for ensuring that this expertise is used in the interests of society. Professionalization focuses on the process by which different occupations reach the status of a profession. Research influenced by Everett Hughes (1971) emphasizes the actual conduct of occupations and the ways in which individuals enter and operate within them. The writings of Jerome Carlin (1962, 1966) are part of this last strand; the earlier book is perhaps the first on lawyers to stem from a sociological tradition.

A fourth strand might be found in the recurrent attacks on the functionalist approach as no more than a restatement of professional ideology.

The persistence of functionalist thinking, even if only as a target, suggests that it correctly poses some underlying problem that does not surrender easily to attacks on any particular formulation. It would be fruitful, therefore, to see changes in sociological thinking about the professions as one aspect of a recurrent question: "Is there a problem about the creation, use, and control of expertise in society?" Those who downplay the importance of this question or give a clear negative answer tend to address issues of professionalization and deprofessionalization; those who think that there might be such a problem may be skeptical about the solutions proposed by particular occupations but continue to borrow concepts from them. It is possible, for instance, to question the necessity for, or scope and implementation of, a particular bargain while still recognizing the value of some such bargain as a way of controlling the use of knowledge.

When one concentrates on lawyers, the terms of the discussion change. As a domain of knowledge, the legal system, the institutions based on it, and the courts that administer it have special features distinguishing them from more scientifically based fields (Rueschemeyer, 1964, 1973: 13 ff.). Legal phenomena are more obviously human-made and much more susceptible to argument about the values they embody than, say, health or structural safety. In addition, lawyers in private practice are expected to be at least somewhat partisan, and expertise at negotiation or argument and persuasion does not seem as mysterious as does knowledge of the workings of the newest drugs. This may be why the central question of controlling expertise has not seemed fruitful when those interested in lawyers have turned to sociology for enlightenment.

Mainstream sociological theory did not generate much research on lawyers apart from Carlin's work, Ladinsky's (1963) study of occupational stratification, and Parsons's essay (1954) discussing the way in which lawyers mediate between the legal system and their clients, thereby acting as agents of social control. From a different viewpoint, Berle (1933) wrote about the commercialization of law practice in "law factories," and Smigel (1964) studied the bureaucratization of Wall Street lawyers, but this kind of work had no real consequences. Similarly, Carr-Saunders and Wilson (1933) had explored controlled occupations in England, including the legal professions, as part of a general discussion of the purposes and outcomes of such controls. However, when Abel-Smith and Stevens (1967) came to write what they decribed as a "sociological" account of the legal profession and the courts, they were avowedly preoccupied with advocating specific reforms and adopted no general theoretical framework.

From the late 1960s onward, movements for political, social, and economic equality raised critical questions about the contribution of law and lawyers to social change. Critics also addressed the organization and control of the profession (Zander, 1968). Both the extent of professional autonomy and its justification have since come under scrutiny for their relevance to policy and their theoretical importance. Strangely enough, although Freidson (1970) had raised relevant questions in his work on the nature of professional knowledge and the reality of professional self-discipline, he was largely ignored by those concerned with lawyers.

Increases in state funding for legal services aroused interest in a theoretical sketch by Johnson (1972) of the situation of power in relations between client and professional and the impact on this relationship of the entry of the state as paymaster. However, although Johnson's categories were used, they seemed not to be fruitful. In spite of its theoretical perceptiveness, the work of Rueschemeyer (1964, 1973) was not taken up at all. It was not until Larson's (1977) work that progress began in earnest and those interested in lawyers took serious advantage of sociological theory.

There are many strands in Larson's work, and to disentangle them somewhat diminishes the power of the whole. Richard Abel has developed aspects of Larson's thought in essays leading up to this volume (1979, 1981). He has concentrated on the project of market control by professionals: the control of production *of* and *by* producers and, when supply control begins to fail, the stimulation of demand. These strategies, however, frequently endanger the long-run viability of the project. The principal pitfall has been the attempt to secure the cognitive status of the profession by entrusting it to the universities, which have ill repaid the trust by overproducing qualified entrants, eroding the profession's control over the production of producers. These matters are debated in this volume, and the approach has proved a fruitful starting point for elucidating much professional activity. However, as Abel has acknowledged, Larson's discussion contains more elements. She has been concerned with the persistence in professional forms of status ideas that predate the coming of the market economy and the onset of bureaucratization, thereby masking some of the underlying realities of professional existence and practice. Bureaucratization in the professions is a main theme of her work: more explicitly than her predecessors, she places it in the context of the bureaucratization of what she rightly sees as the two main pillars of the professional project, the university and the state. Some elements in her discussion have been taken up in recent studies suggesting the decline of professionalism along the lines indicated by Abel in his papers in this volume and elsewhere and disputed in comments by Freidson (1986).

Above all, Larson has brought the state back in. Johnson's earlier work (1972), with its concentration on professional–client relations, introduced the state only as a third-party paymaster, whose interests might differ from those of the parties, thereby affecting the nature of their relationship. Only in later work (Johnson, 1982) did he explore the reciprocal advantages that state and profession might draw from each other. However, Larson has emphasized the way in which supposedly autonomous professions enlisted state support to secure the market control and status position they sought, not just directly but also indirectly, through state establishment of institutions of higher education that legitimize inequality and endow professions with cognitive prestige. The essays in our second volume have much to say on state involvement in civil law countries, while other aspects of state—profession relations are discussed in the third volume. What is plain is that lawyers, whose working lives are so closely involved with state action and its consequences, have a closer connection to the state than do other professions.

The fruitfulness of these ideas can be seen in the range of the debate they have provoked. The very notion of such a project has been criticized because conscious, collective, intentional striving for the kind of goals suggested seems inherently implausible given that sectional groups pursue divergent interests. Although Larson counters arguments of this kind by postulating a general consensus underlying the apparently opposed acts of particular groups, it is difficult to see what generates the state support the project needs.

The argument also stimulates factual debate, which is reflected in this volume. The chapters on Canada and Scotland deserve special notice. In both countries the profession lacked any effective control over admissions, which was lodged, if anywhere, in the hands of individual law firms. In Scotland, until comparatively late in the profession's history, there was no national association to represent its collective interests before the state, only a number of separate associations representing competing subcategories. Similarly, the absence of state support for the barristers' profession in England and the emergence of the Bar long before industrialization have been invoked to disconnect a leading profession from some of the social and economic moorings Larson hypothesizes (Duman, 1983; Prest, 1984). Even if the argument is restricted to the Anglo-American world, as Burrage argues in the third volume, there is evidence that the professional "project" has focused on status rather than economic goals, and may even have been economically disadvantageous for all or many of its members. Similarly, in the second volume, Blankenburg and Schultz describe how German *Anwälte*, who have never been in a position to exercise supply control, have employed tactics that are not in their economic interest.

It seems, then, that the sociology of the professions provides at least a substantial starting point for research on lawyers, even though not every issue may be salient in every country, and sometimes information is simply not available. The concept of a "professional project" leads us to examine the nature of legal training and qualification and the processes by which education comes to be required and controlled, the limits of the professional monopoly and the nature of professional autonomy, and the underlying arguments concerning legal expertise and the trust to be reposed in professionals. The importance of the state in defining the monopoly and the conditions under which it can be exercised leads us to a discussion of the powers of the profession and their basis in status or expertise, while the fact that it is a market that is being controlled makes us attend to the nature of the services offered, demanded, and performed, as well as the economic determinants of the profession's organization and work.

Here we can see a possible convergence between a sociological approach and an economic one. Dingwall and Fenn (1987) have pointed out that not all economists have regarded professions as crude anticompetitive devices; Arrow (1963) thought it necessary to look at the basis of public pressure for professional restrictions, and Adam Smith considered that client trust depended on professional status. Dingwall and Fenn suggest that a sociological analysis of the need for trust could be linked with more recent economic thought on responses to consumer uncertainty about the quality of products (Arrow, 1963; Akerlof, 1970). The chapters that follow may help economists in their attempts to understand the construction of the market for legal services.

Less justification is needed for our comparative approach. The mere choice of sociology as an analytic framework argues for comparison. Regardless of whether one believes in the usefulness of establishing generalizations, any attempt to achieve greater understanding of a social phenomenon will involve the establishment of similarities and differences between it and other relevant phenomena. Comparisons among service occupations, legal occupations, or professional occupations could take place within one country. However, it is necessary to cross national boundaries if we wish to compare one legal profession with another and not simply English barristers and solicitors or French advocates and notaries. Legal professions generally have nationwide associations; are governed by a uniform national law, code of conduct, and admission qualifications; and receive entrants from a national educational system. Their subject matter, too, is likely to be a specific national legal system, and they are involved in a nationwide court system. The operations of many professionals remain local, but their background cannot easily be understood at less than a national level. Thus the nation is the most natural unit of comparison, and we have taken that as the basis of our first two volumes.

In choosing what should be compared within each nation, we weighed several alternatives, such as those who use legal knowledge in their work, those who have a legal qualification, or those who practice law privately. We have adopted a particular conception of a legal profession mainly, but not exclusively, for its relevance to the theoretical background I have sketched. In doing so we have been guided by an Anglo-American "folk-conception" (Freidson, 1983) of a lawyer, once court-centered (if no longer today), but we have treated this merely as our starting point. When one looks at particular countries or time periods, it becomes plain that such lawyers cannot be treated in isolation, even aside from the fact that private practitioners are typically still court-centered in many countries. In some countries private practitioners are being replaced or outnumbered by employed lawyers performing very similar functions, who may indeed have identical qualifications for practice and belong to the same professional associations. Even in Germany, where the number of independent practitioners is growing more rapidly than other categories, one cannot understand their position without seeing how they are located within a system of education intended for publicly employed lawyers.

In presenting the national reports, we considered possible groupings by geographic location, form of government, degree of development, and position in the world economy. The division of the first two volumes between common law and civil law countries is not unproblematic; we have grouped the national legal professions in this way in a spirit of testing the categories rather than out of any settled conviction that they are appropriate. Comparisons are most likely to be fruitful between professions that are both similar and different in important respects, and there is no a priori reason to suppose that two professions sharing a common law legal system or any of the more obviously diversified civil law systems are significantly similar. While more detailed discussion of the problems and possible outcomes of comparison is contained in our third volume, I sketch here some of the ways in which legal professions might be compared, in order to illustrate the degree to which membership in a common law system might be an important similarity.

Two different approaches intersect in comparative legal profession studies. One begins by looking at what is salient about the law and those engaged in it, such as forensic activities involving judges and advocates, as well as the giving of legal advice and the drafting of legal documents. We have decided not to discuss judges in these volumes, but the other activities will frequently be conducted by persons who claim some expertise, have recognized occupational titles, and may be identified as members of recognized local or national associations. French *avocats, avoués,* and notaries; American attorneys; and English barristers and solicitors exemplify such occupations. One can then study their origins, organization, and activities, as well as their powers in relation to their members, the members of other occupations, and the state. The difficulty is that such occupational categories differ between countries. To take only a few examples, the

notary is virtually absent in common law countries; the distinction between barrister and solicitor in terms of forensic activities does not corre-
spond to the continental division between pleading and representation;
and the varied forms of public prosecutor or other representatives of the
public interest are not found in many countries.

As a result of these differences, comparative discussion sometimes turns
to the idea of legal activities or functions, assumed to be similar in all
modern societies but performed by members of different occupations. Such
an approach can be used to explain variation in the size of occupational
categories in different countries. For instance, a lower proportion of
lawyers in private practice can be explained by the presence of notaries
who perform conveyancing functions that otherwise would fall to the
private practitioner. Work done in one country by private law firms or
qualified lawyers employed by a corporation may be performed elsewhere
by corporate employees with a law degree but without a professional legal
qualification.

These two approaches will often lead to the same questions, even if
asked with different emphases, but they can also lead in divergent directions. Historical accounts of the development of legal occupations may
seem unimportant to those concerned with the contemporary performance
of legal functions, particularly if observers assume that current social demands constitute the strongest influence on the pattern of work. Similarly,
those concerned with the development of discrete legal occupations, and
the part they have played in structuring the legal world and the division of
legal labor, may be skeptical about the assumption that societies develop a
need for legal functions to which occupations must respond. Such observers will be more conscious of the contingency of what is regarded as
legal work or work requiring legal knowledge or qualifications in a society.

Either approach must make assumptions or hypotheses about the forces
shaping legal professions. In recent discussion the two leading factors have
been the economy and the state and the sequence of developments in each.
The major comparison of legal professions in the literature (Rueschemeyer,
1973) took as the principal difference between the United States and
Germany the timing of the development of the market economy and the
state, while Luckham (1981b) relates the differences between the legal
professions in Ghana and Kenya to their forms of agricultural production.
Although changes at the level of the economy or state formation may be
especially relevant, other historical events or changes will have their effect.
Finally, and most controversially, aspects of what has been called "legal
culture" may also have an impact.

These remarks can serve as an introduction to the question as to
whether there are important relevant similarities between the common law
countries, as well as differences. Family resemblance may not be sufficient.

The idea of "families" of legal systems has been criticized (Blankenburg, 1985; but see Krislov, 1985). While David and Brierly (1985) classify legal systems by families, they give as examples of the "common law" family only England and the United States and exclude India because of the historical residue of Hindu law. They make the important point that "families" should be divided on the basis not of rules of law but of underlying principles, particularly those governing judicial reasoning. Common law countries do share such principles, as well as certain ways of doing things, such as the relationship between lawyer and judge, the structure of the adversary system, or the absence of any explicit representative of the state or the public interest. Other common features are procedure, forms of appeal, the significance of the jury, and the relationship of the courts to administrative law.

There are important differences, however, the most obvious of which is the presence of written constitutions and provisions for constitutional review for infringement of individual rights in some common law countries (the United States, India, and, recently, Canada) but not others.[1] A more general qualification is the difficulty of establishing a relation between legal professions and similarities in principles and ways of doing things. It is possible that professions could be organized on very different lines and vary widely in social, political, or economic significance and still operate in systems where the principles of procedure and those underlying judicial reasoning were similar. Only if there is reason to believe that the presence of such principles affects or is affected by the legal profession would they constitute a similarity relevant for present purposes.

There is no easy answer to this key question. Weber believed that the English legal profession (perhaps not an anachronistic term for what he saw as a "nation-wide organization") had obstructed the reception of Roman law for its own economic advantage.[2] Regardless if this is true, it seems to have been specific to its time and place; historical inheritance diffused the outcome of the struggle to other countries, but there is no reason to suppose that any other common law jurisdiction has faced similar external pressure.[3]

Mere similarity in the principles underlying the rules of law, therefore, cannot be a legitimate basis for grouping together common law countries, regardless of their differing historical backgrounds or economic or political circumstances. Yet for the common law countries this similarity is not an isolated trait, as it may be in countries such as Turkey or Japan, which consciously imported the rules and principles of a foreign legal system. It exists as a result of historical processes in which not just the rules and principles of the common law but also other legal and political institutions have been transferred, and there are ongoing cultural and intellectual links reinforced by the exchange of personnel. Such processes operate apart from the common law; Scotland is connected both with England and the Continent, and South Africa and Sri Lanka maintained links with England in spite of their Roman-Dutch systems.

English common law had different rules for settled and conquered colonies. Settlers took with them the law of England (adapted to local circumstances), while conquered colonies, although subject to the Crown (until the establishment of local representative institutions), preserved their local laws (again with various modifications if those were contrary to Christianity or "morality"). In some conquered countries, however, settlers might take with them the common law, particularly where the local law was closely connected to the prevailing religion. Thus Roman-Dutch and French law could persist in South Africa and Canada, but indigenous laws continued to be administered in some Indian courts, as Gandhi describes in this volume, while the English were govered by English rules. For all this diversity, as Holdsworth aptly remarks (1938: 251), "there is also a certain unity, which has been produced by the fact that these laws have been administered by lawyers and statesmen whose legal and political ideas have been formed by the principles and rules of English law."

The workings of the courts and the nature of local legal professions have been prime examples of Holdsworth's point. Before colonies acquired "responsible" governments[4] they were administered by the Colonial Office, which made appointments to the higher judiciary, the offices of Attorney and Solicitor-General, and the magistracy. Not surprisingly, there was a tendency to appoint those who had been born and trained and had practiced in England. Where there was responsible government, it was more likely that the higher judiciary had local origins and had practiced locally, although this was not universal: Duman (1983: 127) reports instances of the degree to which Chief Justices in Australia and New Zealand between 1865 and 1901 had been born elsewhere. The influence of English judges in perpetuating the legal profession to which they were accustomed is illustrated in Weisbrot's account of the early days of New South Wales.

Furthermore, practitioners from the "home" country (particularly barristers) came out to make their way in many colonies, although a higher proportion of practitioners were educated locally or were of local origin as the nineteenth century progressed, even if they had gone to the Inns of Court for their legal qualifications: the warnings to English practitioners not to try their luck in the colonies also became stronger. Still, in the formative years in Australia, New Zealand, South Africa, and India, British (mainly English) trained lawyers played a significant part, while Indian lawyers went to the Inns of Court for their qualifications when they could. In such a context, it is not the coincidence of common law principles that justifies treatment of these countries together but the similarity of historical influences on the development of legal administration.

Scotland, Canada, and the United States stand apart from this experience. However, the close political connection of both the Scottish legal system and some of its practitioners with those of England has exercised a considerable influence on Scottish institutions, while Canada is interesting because the slightly divergent development of its legal administration has been accompanied by a particularly faithful adoption of many English legal principles and institutions.[5] In this respect, as in many others, the United States is the odd country out. The Revolution interrupted an increase in the number of lawyers training at the Inns of Court, but England occasionally served as a source or model for legal change in the ensuing years. For a long time, scholarship and tradition treated the two legal systems as closer than they really were, and traces of these attitudes can be found today. Recently any influence has been in the other direction, and it is likely that some interaction will occur wherever two legal systems share the English language, permitting transfer of textbooks and journals, citation of cases, and the free movement of students and suggestions for reform.

This discussion has been confined to similarities within the legal systems; there may be other relevant similarities stemming from conceptions of parliamentary democracy, for instance, but it is more difficult to isolate these and identify their relevance to the legal profession. There certainly were important material links. The saying that "trade follows the flag" was reinforced by a long-lasting system of Imperial preferences; and language, as well as the relationship of primary producers to an early industrialized nation, linked the English-speaking world in trade and commerce. Since the effects of the economic system on the legal profession are not well understood even in one country, the significance of these wider links is very unclear (Luckham, 1981a, 1981b); nevertheless, they represent a possible influence on each of the professions considered in this volume.

Whether there has been a similar conception of professionalism in all these countries and whether their models of professional identity have more in common with each other than those in other countries is also important. More directly relevant is the possibility that the special sense of "profession" in the common law world may also be associated with other distinguishing features in its legal occupations. Since this notion stands in special contrast to concepts prevalent in civil law countries, it is discussed in the second volume. The size of firms and the extent to which advocates can be employed as well as the long persistence of apprenticeship as a primary form of legal education are among the possible hallmarks of common law countries.

Differences of this kind may be embodied in institutional form, but they may also remain attitudes expressed in behavior or speech, sometimes conceptualized as "legal culture." There has been controversy over whether it is meaningful or useful to study attitudes and beliefs or whether it would better to focus on actions that can be operationalized by means of cross-cultural indicators (Blankenburg, 1985).

We take the view that the attitudinal element in "legal culture" is useful for explanation as well as description. Certainly it should not be used as an all-purpose explanation, and legal culture itself requires explanation. Just as there can be local differences in patterns of medical care that seem to be related only to some local "style" of health-care delivery, however, so there can be variations—nationally, locally, or by social group—in the use of the legal system that can be explained only in terms of "cultural" attitudes.[6]

Analysts have distinguished the "internal" legal culture of officials or regular actors in the legal system from the "external" legal culture of those who use the legal system or are affected by its workings. Once we make allowance for this distinction, however, there is a temptation to treat legal culture as homogeneous within societies. To some extent this is an artifact of framing the question as to whether countries differ in their legal cultures. Rich and poor use the legal system differently, however, and a single group may have different attitudes toward such use for different purposes, while those within the legal system may be segregated by race, clientele, or place and form of practice and their attitudes affected by age, sex, or social and political background. If anything can be compared cross-nationally, it is more likely to be the mix of legal cultures and the relationships of the different groups concerned with the legal system.

For these reasons legal cultures should be used with caution as a means of classifying legal systems into groups. There is certainly room for discussing topics such as the influence of one legal culture on another, which may avoid the narrowness of comparing rules of law, although the reception of or resistance to influence may tell us something more about the society on the receiving end than about the society exercising the influence. However, influence is not transmitted through osmosis; individuals and groups pick up and promote ideas from varying motives and through channels ranging from journalism to judgments. The penetration of ideas from abroad is rarely uniform or complete, even if the receiving culture is itself homogeneous. Nor is it a package that is imported: English law centers are an amalgam of United States legal services offices with a strong streak of English egalitarianism and community orientation. The facts that in England there was no one funding source and the legal environment was less accepting of novel forms of litigation demonstrate the importance of the environment in the receiving society.

In chapter 6, on Australia, Weisbrot illustrates some of these points neatly. Although civil law systems have had divisions between lawyers who plead and lawyers who represent (in the sense of being able to bind their clients), these had vanished by the end of the eighteenth century in

Germany and were abolished in France in the 1971 reform (although other divisions remained). In the United States there was practically never any question of any official division of the profession, although it was once suggested that legal education should formally recognize the stratification that research has repeatedly revealed, at least in urban areas. A fused profession operates without question in Canada. In neither Scotland nor England, however, has there been serious pressure to fuse the two legal professions (although some English solicitors are now growing restive). But in Australia the controversy over the separation of barristers and solicitors has been a continuing sore since the early days of the colonies, with some states having de jure separation, others de facto separation, and still others de facto separation recognized by law. Solicitors could declare themselves to be barristers by fiat, and the Bar so created could enforce separation by boycott, the other face of collegiality. Weisbrot also describes how the rivalry between the two main commerical centers of Melbourne and Sydney, added to a quite striking lack of interstate mobility among lawyers, long obstructed mergers of large firms in different cities. These are aspects of the geographic and structural fragmentation of the Australian profession, in which national professional associations have played only the most limited part compared to those, say, in the United States. The underlying assumption of this argument is that uniformity does not come naturally.

It is with extreme caution, therefore, that I return to the main topic: whether there is any similarity between the legal cultures of the common law countries that might differentiate them from others. A leading candidate is the emphasis on the private practitioner as both the modal and the archetypal lawyer. In all these countries a comparatively high proportion of qualified lawyers practice privately rather than as employees in the private or public sectors. There is a problem of categorization; in India, for instance, only a very small proportion of those with law degrees become practitioners, the majority seeking rather to improve their chances of employment in nonlegal capacities. It is difficult to say whether they use their legal knowledge or regard themselves or hold themselves out as lawyers. If we take qualification to practice (perhaps confirmed by registration as a practitioner) as the dividing line, a high proportion of those so qualified in common law countries are in private practice, despite the growth in other areas. Similarly the profession's self-image is the lawyer in private practice, endowed with a substantial degree of independence, and this becomes a model of the conditions that lawyers outside private practice should enjoy. Since common law countries have been very tolerant of employment by other lawyers, such subordination is deemed not to affect the independence of the units of which they are part.

The archetypal lawyer, although a private practitioner, may no longer be an advocate. If the social significance of some litigation may have increased, the visibility of the individual advocate has declined; cases can be widely reported without the public knowing more of the lawyers than their names, if that. Perhaps, too, significant litigation as a tool in some wider economic, social, or political strategy is more amenable to the technician or tactician, members of an organized team who seek an advantageous settlement rather than put everything to a dramatic win-or-lose verdict.

Reputation within the profession can be distinguished from popular images of the successful lawyer. In common law countries, as a rule, those entering the higher judiciary are appointed from the ranks of practicing advocates. Even in the United States, where prosecutors and occasionally academic lawyers are appointed to the higher judiciary and political considerations are relevant, lack of trial experience is legitimately urged as an argument against appointment. This enhances the prestige of advocates and, more significantly, links the profession with the judiciary. The obvious contrast is with those many civil law countries in which the judiciary constitutes a separate career path. These differences are most important where the judiciary exercises control over the profession. In addition, this close relationship between the judiciary and at least part of the legal profession probably strengthens private practice in common law countries and, perhaps, although this would be difficult to prove, contributes to a similarity of approach between advocates and the judiciary, which may facilitate the working of the legal system.

In addition, the connection between the judiciary and the profession may allow each somewhat greater independence from the state than either might be able to achieve on its own. Again, this is a difficult claim to establish, but the necessity of judicial independence is strongly and successfully asserted in the common law countries (Gandhi, in chapter 8, points out some exceptions), and the state exercises relatively little control over admissions to the profession. More recently, the state has asserted an interest in supervising the processes of professional self-regulation, although it has left the issue of training and qualification to the professions and the universities to sort out between them.

Our view, then, is that considerations of history and culture justify our grouping of common and civil law countries, although a range of other political, social, or economic facts might justify some other categorization.

The varying depth and density of chapters in these volumes are an implicit statement of the degree and character of the attention that lawyers, academics, and policy-makers have paid to the legal profession in their countries. We can see not only what issues have concerned each of these groups but also the terms in which they are raised and the extent to which they are addressed by theoretical or policy arguments or by empirical inquiry. Although some of our authors have shaped the debate over the legal profession in their own countries, these chapters for the most part restate and interpret the data and views of others. Independent professions may engage in comparatively little empirical self-examination until they are challenged from outside. Legal academics have been slow to become interested in the legal profession, except with respect to education and perhaps careers (other disciplines have been slower still). Scholarship often takes the form of policy arguments that cannot be supported by facts. Similarly, public concerns may generate everything from searching official inquiry to a plethora of newspaper anecdotes. The difference between the wealth of data about lawyers in the United States and the virtual absence of such data in India is an important fact about those countries and not just about the state of scholarship. Both policy arguments and the spirit of inquiry have been strong in Australia, with the result that there is an unusual amount of data of all kinds.

Those reading these chapters should remind themselves that the United States, Canada, and Australia are federal states in which the legal profession is primarily regulated by the constituent units, and the profession has achieved a national identity or organization wholly or partially in spite of that. Although India is a federal polity, the legislation governing the profession is national and the situation is sufficiently different from the others in this volume to deserve special mention.

The Indian profession is certainly not a new one, and its real history long antedates political independence; it is as old as those in Canada or Australia and older than that of New Zealand. In each of the other countries described in this volume the national legal profession developed historically from practitioners, all of whom were governed by similar rules and practiced before similar courts. In India, however, the existence of separate court systems in the presidencies and elsewhere, as well as the ethnic differences between British and Indian lawyers, led to the development of many kinds of practitioner controlled, if at all, in very different ways; only after Independence in 1948 were they united into a single category.

What is remarkable in this story is the lack of any professionally effective formal or informal associations of Indian practitioners—political effectiveness was another matter. Although bodies of pleaders and attorney-advisers frequently grew up around courts, perhaps only in a colonial situation could courts have maintained so long the power to recognize and control grades of practitioners. India, then, received an imposed legal system and legal profession, but the diversity, which it took so long to harmonize and then unify, was not a necessary concomitant. Gandhi points out some of the undesirable consequences of the imposition of an alien system, and it is interesting to compare some recent remarks in a review of a book on Indian cricket (Bose, 1986), also an English export to the colonies, concerning the "superficial universality" and "cliches about cricket as a builder of imperial and post-imperial bridges." The reviewer (Le Quesne, 1986) points out that cricket "has in fact meant very different things for the societies in which it has taken root. Bose's book makes it quite clear that if the social history of cricket is ever to be written properly, it will have to be on a comparative basis." In Britain, the game has populist origins and a continuing strength at club and local level; in India, the game is top-heavy, "balancing precariously on a relatively weak (and almost entirely) urban popular base." It is supported for the time being by the socially mobile "middle Indians" and the current self-interest of commercial sponsors. Kidder (1979) has analyzed Indian litigation as an alien import that the indigenous population has adapted to their own purposes. Gandhi shows the lasting consequences of the fact that the legal profession was used as an avenue of personal advancement and pressure for independence. India is clearly an exceptional case: while in most of the countries dealt with here (United States, Canada, Australia, and New Zealand) the rights of native peoples have received only limited recognition, in India the maintenance of traditional law for the great majority of the population was assisted by the existence of recognizable classes of trained individuals whose claim to knowledge of it required respect.

The history of India offers an opportunity to reflect more widely on the contingent nature of diffusion. The activities of Indian lawyers in the struggle for independence influenced changes elsewhere through their impact on the British government. To avoid a repetition of the Indian experience, Britain substantially restricted the emergence of lawyers in Kenya and Tanzania by refusing bursaries to African students wishing to study law (Ghai, 1981: 148–149). This illustrates the selectivity of diffusion; the lessons are applied by one powerful party. An even more skeptical view is possible. Luckham argues (1981a: 120) that although Britain imposed its substantive rules, judicial system, and professional institutions on Ghana and maintained them through continuing contacts, these influences were far less important than the alignment of the courts and the legal profession with the national state, economy, and class structure. Furthermore, what Britain diffused throughout Third World countries was an imperial legal culture, not a municipal British one; the institutions suggested by the Colonial Office for professional development came from other colonies, not from the metropolitan profession (ibid., 117–118).

In conclusion, we should reiterate that these national accounts are not presented as definitive; they are intended to serve as a foundation, in conjunction with the papers in our third volume, for the generation of new lines of inquiry. We hope that readers find them stimulating in that sense.

NOTES

1. Both Canada and Australia have long had judicial review of matters arising out of the allocation of powers between the federal government and the legislatures of the provinces and states.

2. Weber seems to have been relying on Maitland (1901), but the latter has been doubted on this point (Elton, 1985: 79 ff.).

3. Where different legal traditions co-exist, training and social affiliations may promote adherence to one or the other (Salman, 1981). A recent example of a related process is found in Huyse's account of Belgian lawyers in the second volume; he suggests that an influx of Flemish lawyers into the Belgian profession has resulted in a shift of attention from French to Dutch and German sources.

4. My discussion here is based on Duman (1983: chapter 4), as well as the papers in this volume.

5. Apart from everything else, the Scottish and English legal systems were linked by appeals to the House of Lords, just as appeals from the colonies and dominions went to the Privy Council. This plainly led to some assimilation of English legal rules and reasoning; but without knowledge of whether practitioners are affected by the nature of their ultimate court of appeal or whether there was consciousness of the shared tradition, one cannot say whether there was any effect on the legal professions.

6. Local legal cultures are more fully described in Church (1985).

REFERENCES

Abbott, Andrew. 1986. "Jurisdictional Conflicts: A New Approach to the Development of the Legal Professions," 1986 *American Bar Foundation Research Journal* 187.

Abel, Richard L. 1979. "The Rise of Professionalism," 6 *British Journal of Law and Society* 82.

———. 1981. "Toward a Political Economy of Lawyers," [1981] *Wisconsin Law Review* 1117.

Abel-Smith, Brian, and Robert Stevens. 1967. *Lawyers and the Courts: A Sociological Study of the English Legal System*. London: Heinemann.

Akerlof, G. A. 1970. "The Market for Lemons: Qualitative Uncertainty and the Market Mechanism," 84 *Quarterly Journal of Economics* 488.

Arrow, Kenneth J. 1963. "Uncertainty and the Welfare Economics of Medical Care," 53 *American Economic Review* 941.

Benguigui, G. 1972. "La Définition des Professions," 13 *Epistémologie Sociologique* 99.

Berle, A. A. 1933. "Modern Legal Profession," 9 *Encyclopedia of the Social Sciences* 340. New York: Macmillan.

Blankenburg, Erhard. 1985. "Indikatorenvergleich der Rechtskulturen in der Bundesrepublik und den Niederlanden," 6 *Zeitschrift für Rechtssoziologie* 255.

Bose, Mihir. 1986. *A Maidan View: The Magic of Indian Cricket*. London: Allen and Unwin.

Carlin, Jerome. 1962. *Lawyers on Their Own*. New Brunswick, N. J.: Rutgers University Press.

———. 1966. *Lawyers' Ethics*. New York: Russell Sage Foundation.

Carr-Saunders, A. M., and P. A. Wilson. 1933. *The Professions*. Clarendon Press: Oxford.

Church, Thomas W. 1985. "Examining Local Legal Culture," 1985 *American Bar Foundation Research Journal* 449.

Cocks, Raymond. 1983. *Foundations of the Modern Bar*. London: Sweet and Maxwell.

David, René, and J. E. C. Brierly. 1985. *Major Legal Systems in the World Today: An Introduction to the Comparative Study of Law*, 3d ed. London: Stevens.

Dingwall, Robert. 1983. "Introduction" in Robert Dingwall and Philip Lewis, eds., *The Sociology of the Professions*. London: Macmillan.

Dingwall, Robert, and Paul Fenn. 1987. "'A Respectable Profession': Sociological and Economic Perspectives on the Regulation of Professional Services," 7 *International Review of Law and Economics* 51.

Duman, Daniel. 1983. *The English and Colonial Bars in the Nineteenth Century*. London: Croom Helm.

Elton, G. R. 1985. *F. W. Maitland*. London: Weidenfeld and Nicholson.

Freidson, Eliot. 1970. *Profession of Medicine: A Study of the Sociology of Applied Knowledge*. New York: Dodd Mead.

———. 1983. "The Theory of Professions: State of the Art," in Robert Dingwall and Philip Lewis, eds., *The Sociology of the Professions*. London: Macmillan.

———. 1986. *Professional Powers: A Study of the Institutionalization of Formal Knowledge*. Chicago: University of Chicago Press.

Friedman, Lawrence M. 1985. *History of American Law*, 2d ed. New York: Simon and Schuster.

Ghai, Yash P. 1981. "Law and Lawyers in Kenya and Tanzania: Some Political Economy Considerations," in C. J. Dias, R. Luckham, D. O. Lynch, and J. C. N. Paul, eds., *Lawyers in the Third World: Comparative and Developmental Perspectives*. Uppsala: Scandinavian Institute of African Studies and New York: International Center for Law in Development.

Gordon, Robert W. 1984. "'The Ideal and the Actual in the Law': Fantasies and Practices of New York City Lawyers, 1870–1910," in George Gawalt, ed., *The New High Priests: Lawyers in Post-Civil Law America*. Westport, Conn.: Greenwood Press.

Hazard, Geoffrey C. 1965. "Reflections on Four Studies on the Legal Profession," Supplement to Summer Issue of Social Problems 46.

Holdsworth, William. 1938. *A History of English Law*, vol. XI. London: Methuen.

Hughes, Everett. C. 1971. *The Sociological Eye* (2 vols.). Chicago: Aldine-Atherton.

Hurst, Willard. 1950. *The Growth of American Law: The Law Makers*. Boston: Little Brown.

Johnson, Terence. 1972. *Professions and Power*. London: Macmillan.

———. 1982. "The State and the Professions," in Anthony Giddens and Gavin Mackenzie, eds., *Social Class and the Division of Labour*. Cambridge: Cambridge University Press.

Johnstone, Quintin, and Dan Hopson. 1967. *Lawyers and Their Work*. Indianapolis: Bobbs-Merrill.

Kagan, Robert, and Robert Rosen. 1984. "On the Social Significance of Large Law Firm Practice," 37 *Stanford Law Review* 399.

Kidder, Robert. 1979. "Toward an Integrated Theory of Imposed Law," in Sandra Burman and Barbara Harrell-Bond, eds., *The Imposition of Law*. New York: Academic Press.

Kötz, Hein, Wolf Paul, Michel Pédamon, and Michael Zander. 1982. *Anwaltsberuf im Wandel: Rechtspflegeorgan oder Dienstleistungsgewerbe*. Frankfurt: Metzner.

Krislov, Samuel. 1985. "The Concept of Families of Law," in Adam Podgorecki, ed., *Legal Systems and Social Systems*. London: Croom Helm.

Ladinsky, Jack. 1963. "Careers of Lawyers, Law Practice and Legal Institutions," 28 *American Sociological Review* 52.

Larson, Magali Sarfatti. 1977. *The Rise of Professionalism: A Sociological Analysis*. Berkeley: University of California Press.

Le Quesne, A. L. 1986. "Other Grounds, Other Seasons," *Times Literary Supplement* 987 (September 5).

Luban, David, ed. 1983. *The Good Lawyer: Lawyers' Roles and Lawyers' Ethics*. Totowa, N. J.: Rowman and Allanfield.

Luckham, Robin. 1981a. "Imperialism, Law and Structural Dependence: The Ghana Legal Profession," in C. J. Dias, R. Luckham, D. O. Lynch, and J. C. N. Paul, eds., *Lawyers in the Third World: Comparative and Developmental Perspectives*. Uppsala: Scandinavian Institute of African Studies and New York: International Center for Law in Development.

———. 1981b. "The Political Economy of Legal Professions in the Third World: A Framework for Comparison," in C. J. Dias, R. Luckham, D. O. Lynch, and J. C. N. Paul, eds., *Lawyers in the Third World: Comparative and Developmental Perspectives*. Uppsala: Scandinavian Institute of African Studies and New York: International Center for Law in Development.

Maitland, Frederic W. 1901. *English Law and the Renaissance*. Cambridge: Cambridge University Press.

Nelson, Robert L. 1984. "Ideology, Practice and Professional Autonomy: Social Values and Client Relationships in the Large Law Firm," 37 *Stanford Law Review* 503.

Parsons, Talcott. 1954. "A Sociologist looks at the Legal Profession," in *Essays in Sociological Theory*, rev. ed. New York: Free Press.

Prest, Wilfred R. 1984. "Why the History of the Profession Is Not Written," in G. R. Rubin and David Sugarman, eds., *Law, Economy and Society 1750–1914: Essays in the History of English Law*. Abingdon: Professional Books.

Ranieri, Filippo. 1985. "Vom Stand zum Beruf: Die Professionalisierung des Juristenstandes als Forschungsausgabe der europäischen Rechtsgeschichte der Neuzeit," 13 *Ius Commune* 83.

Rhode, Deborah. 1981. "Policing the Professional Monopoly: A Constitutional and Empirical Analysis of Unauthorized Practice Prohibitions," 34 *Stanford Law Review* 1.

———. 1985. "Moral Character as a Professional Credential," 94 *Yale Law Journal* 491.

Rosen, Robert. 1984. "Lawyers in Corporate Decision Making." Ph.D. diss., University of California, Berkeley, Jurisprudence and Social Policy Program.

Royal Commission on Legal Services. 1979. *Final Report* (2 vols.). London: H.M.S.O. (Cmnd. 7648).

Royal Commission on Legal Services in Scotland. 1980. *Report* (2 vols.). Edinburgh: H.M.S.O. (Cmnd. 7846).

Rueschemeyer, Dietrich. 1964. "Doctors and Lawyers: A Comment on the Theory of the Professions," 1 *Canadian Review of Sociology and Anthropology* 17.

———. 1973. *Lawyers and Their Society: A Comparative Study of the Legal Professions in Germany and in the United States*. Cambridge: Harvard University Press.

Salman, Salman. 1981. "Legal Profession in the Sudan: A Study of Legal and Professional Pluralism," in C. J. Dias, R. Luckham, D. O. Lynch, and J. C. N. Paul, eds. *Lawyers in the Third World: Comparative and Developmental Perspectives*. Uppsala: Scandinavian Institute of African Studies and New York: International Center for Law in Development.

Smigel, Erwin. 1964. *The Wall Street Lawyer*. New York: Free Press.

Zander, Michael. 1968. *Lawyers and the Public Interest: A Study in Restrictive Practices*. London: Weidenfeld and Nicolson.

2

England and Wales

A Comparison of the Professional Projects of Barristers and Solicitors

RICHARD L. ABEL

This chapter traces the contours of the rise and decline of the English legal profession during the last century and a half. I do not use the word "decline" pejoratively—to signify a lowering of ethical standards. Rather, I view professionalism as a specific historical formation in which the members of an occupation exercise a substantial degree of control over the market for their services, usually through an occupational association. I have chosen this concept of professionalism over others that stress technical expertise, or standards of competence and ethical behavior, or altruism because it seems to me to illuminate a great deal of the history and contemporary experience of English lawyers. There can be little doubt that nineteenth century solicitors consciously and energetically sought market control, and it is painfully clear today that both branches of the profession are deeply upset about threats to their continued exercise of such control. At the same time, English lawyers offer an especially apt context for exploring fluctuations in this concept of professionalism (a cycle that is visible in other countries as well). First, English lawyers professionalized earlier than did lawyers in other common law countries and also may be deprofessionalizing sooner. Second, the divided English legal profession offers a natural laboratory for observing the choice of tactics in the professional project and their relative success or failure.

All occupations under capitalism are compelled to seek control over their markets. The only alternative is to be controlled *by* the market—a situation that is fraught with uncertainty at best and may lead to economic extinction at worst. Of course, no occupation controls its market totally, and none is wholly without influence; control is a question of degree and constantly changes. The foundation of market control is the regulation of supply. Occupations that produce goods may pursue this goal by seeking to restrict raw materials or technology, but occupations that produce services constrain supply principally by regulating the production *of* producers. Professions are distinguished from other closed occupations by their requirement of demonstrated mastery of a body of formalized knowledge. Although advocates of control invariably portray their object as improving the quality of services, we should not let this claim blind us to the fact that any improvement necessarily also limits entry. At one extreme of the spectrum of control, the profession (often backed by the state) imposes a numerus clausus—illustrated by some nineteenth century continental legal professions, notaries in certain countries today, and elite advocates, such as Queen's Counsel in England and avocats of the Conseil d'Etat and the Cour de Cassation in France. At the other extreme, entry to the occupational category is governed by market forces: demand for professional services on one hand and the distribution of ability, energy, and inclination on the other hand. Examples include gardeners in Los Angeles, drivers of non-medallion cabs in New York, or window cleaners in London. Market control is inextricably related to occupational status, not only symbolizing status but also enhancing it instrumentally, both by restricting numbers (because scarcity is an intrinsic measure of status as well as a means of increasing income) and by controlling the characteristics of entrants. Professions pursue market control and status enhancement through collective action. Having erected barriers to entry, professional associations seek to protect their members from competition, both external and internal. In order to avert external surveillance, they engage in self-regulation. This chapter will examine the contrasting careers followed by barristers and solicitors in pursuit of the professional project.

ENTRY TO THE PROFESSION

In order to trace the dramatic fluctuations in the kind and degree of supply control that English lawyers have exercised during the last century and a half, it is useful to choose as a baseline the entry barriers that prevailed at the beginning of the nineteenth century. Barristers and solicitors differed significantly in the extent to which each branch emphasized ascribed or achieved qualities—the character of the whole person or narrow technical skills—and in whether controls were formal or informal, visible or invisible.

THE PREMODERN HERITAGE

The Bar entered the nineteenth century with stringent constraints on the kind of person who might become a barrister, constraints that had been in place for several hundred years. The benchers (judges and senior barristers) who governed the four Inns of Court had complete discretion to admit or reject a student; applicants had to state their "condition in life" and provide references from two barristers. The Inns of Court extended a preference to university graduates, shortening the number of years they had to keep terms from five to three and the number of dinners they had to eat each term from six to three, so that the burden on nongraduates was more than three times as onerous. Partly for this reason, half of all barristers were university graduates at a time when this privilege was enjoyed by only a tiny fraction of the population and restricted to upper-class members of the Established Church. Once called to the Bar, the fledgling barrister was expected to serve a pupillage (apprenticeship) of one to two years with an established barrister or other legal professional. Thereafter, fully qualified barristers had to open their own chambers, for in the early nineteenth century most practiced alone.

Two things about this entry process are striking, although perhaps not immediately apparent. First, it was extremely expensive. For the majority who attended university, there was the cost of tuition and three years of maintenance. The Bar student then had to pay a fee of £30 to £40 for admission to his Inn of Court and deposit an additional £100, which was refunded without interest only after call. During his three to five years as a student, while forbidden to work at most trades, he incurred annual expenses of £5 to £10 for hall dinners, £6 to £8 for books, and about £150 for maintenance. Call fees were £70 to £80, to which must be added about 8 guineas for a wig and gown. The premium for pupillage was 200 guineas, and the pupil had to maintain himself for another two years. Once established in his own chambers, the barrister could not expect to earn enough from practice to support himself for several years (if ever), although he might make ends meet by "deviling" (salaried work for an established barrister), tutoring, marking examination papers, law reporting, or editing. A midnineteenth century estimate put the one-time costs at £300 and the annual maintenance at £250 from entering university to reaching economic self-sufficiency, which could be as long as ten years. These financial demands strongly reinforced the ascriptive criteria that influenced the university and the Inn to admit a student, the barrister to accept a pupil, and the client or solicitor to brief a fledgling barrister.

The second noteworthy feature of this lengthy and arduous process of qualifying is that it had relatively little to do with the acquisition of technical skills. Those who attended university did not study English law because it was not taught. The Inns had abandoned any pretense of education two centuries earlier. In addition, although we know little about the content of pupillage, certainly many barristers must have accepted pupils for the substantial premiums the latter paid rather than out of dedication to teaching. The Bar selected those who aspired to be "gentle-

men" (regardless of whether their fathers were landed gentry); colleague-
ship at university and within the Inns may have reinforced such gentility;
but neither selection nor training ensured technical competence in law.

Because solicitors lacked the lengthy traditions of the Bar, they initially
subjected entrants to fewer ascriptive criteria and, consequently, imposed
fewer entry barriers of any sort. Nineteenth century solicitors were not
expected to attend university; indeed, only 5 percent of enrolled solicitors
were graduates as late as the 1870s. But solicitors were required by law to
serve a five-year apprenticeship (articles). This was an ascriptive barrier in
two senses: the apprentice obtained his place through personal contacts,
often with a solicitor who was a relative, family friend, or business acquaint-
ance; and articles were expensive—about £100 for stamp duty and £200
for the premium paid to the solicitor. Yet, unlike the Bar student or pupil,
the articled clerk could minimize his expenses by living at home, since
articles were available all over England, not only in London (where all
barristers had their chambers at the beginning of the nineteenth century).
And at the end of his apprenticeship, the qualified solicitor could attain
immediate economic self-sufficiency through salaried employment with a
firm and could look forward to joining the partnership or setting up his
own practice.

Even at the beginning of the nineteenth century, barristers and solicitors
thus diverged in their exercise of supply control. The Bar used rigorous
ascriptive criteria and demanded substantial economic sacrifices, effectively
limiting numbers. Yet, these barriers were both informal (pupillage was not
a legal requirement, for instance) and invisible (no person or institution
decreed that a newly qualified barrister would fail to obtain sufficient
business). Solicitors also employed ascriptive barriers, but these were less
elaborate and seem to have been more closely related to the acquisition of
legal knowledge. Because articles lasted several times as long as pupillage
and because the supervising solicitor generally expected to employ the
apprentice thereafter, it seems plausible that the experience conferred at
least a modicum of technical skill.

CONSTRUCTING MODERN CRITERIA

These differences between the branches became considerably more pronounced during the next hundred years. The Bar retained and indeed
strengthened its ascriptive criteria. In 1829, Inner Temple (one of the four
Inns of Court) required all students who had not matriculated at university
to pass an examination in history and either Latin or Greek; although this
requirement was abandoned briefly when the other Inns failed to adopt it,
the examination had become universal by the last quarter of the nineteenth

century. In any case, almost three-quarters of all Bar students were university graduates by this time. However, the Bar moved very slowly to ensure that entrants possessed technical knowledge. It resisted the example of physicians, solicitors, and colonial lawyers, all of whom had adopted formal examinations, for the Bar feared that this might facilitate entry rather than restrain it, thereby admitting the wrong kind of person. The examination finally required in 1872 was ridiculously easy. Graduates sat it a few months after leaving university, and 80 percent to 90 percent were passing at the end of the nineteenth century. The Bar was even less interested in preparing students to practice law than in examining their competence. Although the Inns created the Council of Legal Education in the midnineteenth century, it had a minimal teaching staff and relied heavily on practitioners. It is not surprising that the majority of Bar students preferred private crammers. Thus the barriers to becoming a barrister remained much the same until after World War II: cost and the particularistic decisions of universities, pupilmasters, and (later) heads of chambers.

Solicitors pursued a very different path toward controlling the production of producers. In the absence of substantial ascriptive barriers, the number of solicitors seems to have doubled in the first third of the nineteenth century. Partly in response, one of the early acts of the Incorporated Law Society (a voluntary association formed by solicitors in the 1820s, following the demise of the Society of Gentlemen Practisers) was to impose a professional examination in 1836, nearly four decades before the "senior" branch (barristers) did so. This decision to use achievement rather than ascription as the principal entry barrier seems to have had its desired effect: the issuance of new "practicing certificates" dropped by almost a quarter over the next fifteen years, and the number of solicitors stabilized for four decades (although other factors, such as falling demand, also may have contributed to this decline). Twenty-five years after initiating professional examinations (and ten years before the first Bar Final), the Law Society added a second hurdle: the Intermediate Examination, taken by articled clerks during their apprenticeship. (Although law graduates were exempt, there were very few during this period.) Then, in 1906, the Society required a third examination in trust accounts, accounting, and bookkeeping. Although the pass rates for each examination were very high when it first was introduced, all of them declined fairly steadily and were approaching 50 percent at the beginning of World War II; since all *three* had to be passed, their cumulative effect was even greater.

The Law Society also was more serious about professional education: it instituted lectures for articled clerks in 1833, three years before the first professional examination, and progressively expanded the offerings at its Chancery Lane headquarters. Nevertheless, attendance was low: articled clerks, like Bar students, preferred private crammers; and little instruction was available outside London and a few major provincial cities. In response, the Law Society made two major changes in 1922: it required a compulsory year of lectures prior to the Intermediate Examination, and it subsidized such instruction at provincial universities.

By contrast with its concern for technical competence, the Law Society did little to raise ascriptive barriers. Individual exemptions were granted freely from the preliminary liberal arts examination imposed in 1861 (thirty years after Inner Temple had required a similar examination of Bar students), and categorical exemptions rapidly proliferated, not just for university matriculates but also for those who passed a host of other exams. The proportion of solicitors with university degrees remained small: less than a fifth of all entrants in the first decade of the twentieth century (when three-quarters of all new barristers were baccalaureates), less than a third as late as World War II. At the same time, it must be recognized that preparation for the three professional examinations itself was costly and became an important, if indirect, barrier to those who could not afford to study full time or pay the crammers.

FLUCTUATIONS IN ENTRY

How effective were the divergent strategies of barristers and solicitors in controlling the production of producers? In answering this question, it is essential to bear in mind the impact of extraneous events, the most important of which were World Wars I and II. Nearly a quarter of all solicitors served in World War I; 588 were killed and 669 seriously wounded (nearly a tenth of all practitioners). The next generation of solicitors was affected even more seriously: more than half of all articled clerks served, of whom 358 were killed and 458 seriously wounded (perhaps a third of all clerks). Although these losses were inflicted *on* the profession, it also bears some responsibility for failing to respond to them by admitting more solicitors after the war (even though pass rates on the professional examinations did increase dramatically). In addition to those killed and disabled, there was a shortfall in production of 1,700 solicitors, if the ten years beginning in 1914 are compared to the previous decade. The experience of World War II was similar: more than 500 solicitors and clerks were killed, and there was a shortfall in production of more than 1,500.

Together, professional supply control and extraneous tragedies had a dramatic effect on the number of solicitors (see table 1). The rapid increase in the production of solicitors in the first third of the nineteenth century (an annualized rate of 3.1 percent) halted abruptly in 1835—which happened to be the year before the first professional examination was administered, although it would be dangerous to infer causality. The profession remained virtually static for the next third of the century. Although there was some growth in the 1870s and 1880s, it slowed to almost nothing in the next twenty-five years. The number of solicitors declined at an annualized rate of 1.7 percent between 1913 and 1920 and remained virtually static between 1939 and 1952. As a result, solicitors entered the postwar period (1948) with almost *exactly* the same number (15,567) that had been in practice more than half a century earlier (15,090 in 1890). Statistics for the practicing strength of the Bar before the 1950s are sadly inadequate. Nevertheless, available data show the number of barristers doubling between the first and the last quarters of the nineteenth century, declining by a fourth following World War I, and remaining at that depressed level until well after World War II.

THE POSTWAR TRANSFORMATION

The period since World War II, and especially the last two decades, have witnessed a major transformation in both the means and the extent of control over the production of producers. The distinctive characteristics of barristers and solicitors continued to color their different responses, but the overwhelming changes that both branches confronted induced a significant convergence between them. Some ascriptive barriers to the Bar were lowered, and achievements were emphasized. The £100 deposit required before admission to an Inn was eliminated for most students, the £50 stamp duty on call to the Bar was abolished in 1947, and other fixed fees became less burdensome as a result of inflation. Although the Bar formally required a university degree in 1975, the growth of tertiary education and, more importantly, government grants to undergraduates made it easier to obtain this credential (which nearly 90 percent of entrants already held in any case). Nine years later the Bar added the requirement of at least a lower-second-class degree (although few students with an inferior degree had been passing the Bar examination and finding a pupillage and tenancy).

The Bar also began to relate entry barriers more closely to technical competence. Students without a law degree now must spend a year studying law in a polytechnic (often without further government support) and pass an additional examination. Not surprisingly, 84 percent of intending practitioners called to the Bar in 1983 were law graduates. Legal education thus has become the principal barrier to qualifying as a barrister, a point to which I return below. All entrants must take a year of vocational training prior to the final examination, and the number of places available at the Inns at Court School of Law has been limited in recent years (although students can study elsewhere). Final examination pass rates remain high, however: nearly 90 percent of intending practitioners succeeded on their first try in the early 1980s, although the proportion has fallen significantly in the last few years.

Yet, the Bar certainly has not relinquished all control to the academy. Three major entry barriers remain, which traditionally have been more ascriptive and less subject to external influence. First, the Bar mandated a one-year pupillage in 1959 (previously pupillage had been voluntary though very common); six years later, it prohibited pupils from taking briefs during their first six months. Although the pupillage fee declined in importance after World War II and was abolished in 1975, maintenance during this year remains a serious problem, since no government grants are available, Inn scholarships are few in number and inadequate in amount, and briefs are difficult to obtain even in the second six months. Furthermore, a bottleneck has developed as the number seeking pupillages has multiplied rapidly while the number of barristers willing to act as pupilmasters has remained constant. Although the Bar maintains that every intending practitioner is placed, competition has intensified, and personal contacts and ascriptive characteristics clearly weigh heavily.

Second, and more important, the Bar requires every private practitioner to obtain a tenancy (a place in chambers from which to practice). Like pupillage, this became a problem only recently. In the nineteenth century, fledgling barristers simply opened their own chambers; this would be prohibitively expensive today, and in any case a new barrister practicing alone would attract very little business. In the early twentieth century, natural attrition in a relatively static profession created space for all who wished to enter; however, the rapid growth in the number of Bar students and pupils in the last two decades has disrupted this accommodation. The problem of tenancies is unique to England as well as to the postwar period: advocates in Scotland and barristers in some Australian states practice individually, and office space and assistance by a pool of clerks are available to all new entrants. By contrast, the present shortage of tenancies in London is both severe and chronic. Until recently, all London chambers were located in one of the Inns; even now only five of the more than 200 London sets have moved outside, and several of those also are "outsiders" in terms of political orientation or racial composition. Chambers within the Inns are grossly overcrowded, however, partly because the Inns traditionally have leased much of their space to residential or other commercial tenants. In the six years between 1975 and 1981, when the Bar grew by 28 percent, available space in the Inns expanded only 8 percent. As a result, every year since 1965 there has been a shortfall in the tenancies available to barristers completing their pupillages, sometimes by as much as 50 percent. More than 100 qualified barristers (approximately a third of the number starting practice annually) have occupied the amorphous status of floaters ever since the Senate (the umbrella association of barristers) began keeping records in 1974. This physical shortage of space (which is largely the Bar's own doing) has greatly intensified competition for entry, increasing the weight that heads of chambers give to ascriptive qualities in accepting tenants and discouraging many students and pupils from entering private practice.

The third barrier confronting the qualified beginner also is peculiar to the Bar: because private practitioners cannot be employed, they must find business on their own. The difficulties of doing so remained acute in the early postwar period: most barristers lost money in their first year and made only a nominal amount in their second. Not surprisingly, almost a third of those who entered practice in 1950/51 had abandoned it five years later. And between 1955 and 1959, the number of barristers with less than ten years of experience who left practice ranged from half to three-quarters of the number entering practice that year. In this respect (and others), barristers resembled small-scale entrepreneurs, most of whose businesses fail, rather than professionals, who make a lifetime commitment to a career (although some barristers who leave private practice continue to use their legal skills as employees in the public or private sectors). Yet, the situation of the novice improved dramatically in the 1960s and 1970s as a result of the growth of legal aid, which ensured at least a minimum level of subsistence. Juniors (barristers who are not Queen's Counsel) with less than nine years of experience, practicing at the family, common law, or criminal Bars in London, or on circuit, obtained between 59 and 72 percent of their incomes from public sources (both legal aid and prosecution briefs) in 1974/75. Consequently, departures from practice of those with less than ten years of experience dropped dramatically after 1959; although absolute numbers have risen slightly since 1976, they still represent only a tenth to a quarter of those starting practice.

Solicitors responded differently to the postwar environment. The principal ascriptive barrier to becoming a solicitor—articles—underwent significant change. Out-of-pocket costs fell when Parliament abolished the stamp duty on articles in 1947 and premiums gradually disappeared about 1960. The length of articles was reduced by a year for both graduates and nongraduates; however, since the former now greatly outnumber the latter, the effective period of apprenticeship has been cut from five years to two. More importantly, clerks began to receive salaries: £200 in the 1950s, £500 in the 1960s, £1,600 in 1976, and £3,000 to £4,000 today, although this still is insufficient for maintenance. However, obtaining articles (like finding a tenancy for a pupil) has become a significant problem for the first time. Because the number of law graduates seeking articles increased rapidly, while the number of solicitors qualified and willing to take on clerks remained fairly constant, competition for articles intensified. Firms today receive dozens of applications for each position, students write even more letters in order to obtain a place, and those with contacts fare far better than do those who use more universalistic methods, such as the Law Society Register or a university appointments board. The scramble for articles serves both to distribute law graduates across the hierarchy of solicitors' firms and to discourage those with poorer degrees earned at less prestigious institutions from seeking to enter private practice.

Primarily for symbolic reasons, the Law Society has refrained from formalizing the academic barriers to entry. It still is posssible for mature students to become solicitors without obtaining A levels (examinations taken at the end of secondary school), although the proportion of entrants who do so is insignificant. Similarly, a university degree is not required, although more than 90 percent of new solicitors now are university graduates, and almost all of these are law graduates (compared with only a quarter in 1949). The two branches thus have converged in fact, if not in rule. All aspiring solicitors, like all barristers, must complete a vocational year; but almost three-quarters of the students at the Law Society's College of Law in 1980 had received local authority grants (although the proportions have dropped as the Thatcher Government has placed ceilings on local taxes and cut grants to local authorities). The rapid growth in the prevalence of legal education also has reduced the significance of professional examinations in controlling quality and numbers. The nine out of ten entrants with law degrees are exempt from the Common Professional Examination (CPE), which replaced the Intermediate Examination in 1980 and which, despite its name, is taken only by aspiring solicitors. More importantly, the high proportion of examinees with a legal education seems to be correlated with a rise in the pass rate on the Final Examination from an all-time low of 48 percent in 1952 to a high of 74 percent in 1977—a level approaching that of the Bar Final, which historically has been much easier. Yet solicitors still are more serious than barristers about ensuring technical competence. The Law Society has imposed a requirement of forty-eight hours of continuing education in the first three years of practice; the Senate, on the other hand, told the Royal Commission that postqualification education would not be "appropriate" to the circumstances of the Bar.

Both branches of the profession thus have lost to academic legal education much of their control over the production of producers. It would be difficult to overestimate the importance of this transformation. First, it is a transfer of the locus of control: from professionals and their associations to universities and polytechnics and the governmental bodies that determine their enrollments and funding. Second, because public education consistently has been more universalistic than private associations or individuals, this transfer largely eliminated the principal ascriptive barrier to the profession: the exclusion of half the population on the basis of gender (just as the growth of American law schools in the early twentieth century opened that profession to the sons of immigrants). Half a century before Parliament compelled the profession to admit women and long before the academy became the principal mode of professional qualification, University College, London, allowed women to read law. In 1967, when women constituted 5 percent of the Bar and 3 percent of solicitors, they were 17 percent of entering law students at university and 11 percent at polytechnics. They were 45 percent of all domestic undergraduate law students enrolled in universities in 1983/84 and 47 percent of full-time domestic law students admitted to polytechnics for the fall term in 1984. Women thus reached virtual parity with men inside the academy in about two decades.

The third element of this transformation in the institutional structure of control is the growing heterogeneity of the academy. Prior to World War II, academic legal education was concentrated at Oxford, Cambridge, and the three London colleges, which together enrolled three-quarters of all students; the remainder (mostly articled clerks preparing for Law Society examinations) were distributed among the seven older provincial universities. By 1980/81, Oxbridge had fallen to 12 percent, London (even with two more faculties) had 9 percent, the older provincial universities enrolled 24 percent, eleven other universities (both pre- and postwar) had launched law courses with 22 percent of the students, and the twenty-four new polytechnic law programs enrolled a third of all students. Not surprisingly, the convergence of three factors—a government eager to provide social services (of which education was a relatively inexpensive example), universities and polytechnics interested in expanding, and women determined to pursue careers—produced a dramatic increase in law enrollments, perhaps the most dramatic ever experienced in *any* country (see table 1). In 1938/39 there were 1,515 undergraduate law students; in 1980/81 there were 12,603 full-time students (and another 3,375 part-time, external, or mixed-degree students)—more than an eightfold increase. In the United States, law school enrollment expanded more slowly even during its period of most rapid growth (1890 to 1927) and has increased only threefold since World War II.

Although supply control had been transformed, it still was being exercised—if now by the academy. Law departments received between ten and twenty applications per place in the 1970s; although much of this imbalance is explained by multiple applications, little more than 40 percent of all applicants obtained a place anywhere. Furthermore, admission is not tantamount to graduation. Although at least nine out of ten university law students graduate (perhaps as many as nineteen out of twenty), only three-quarters of full-time and about a third of part-time polytechnic students complete their courses.

UNPRECEDENTED EXPANSION

Let me summarize these changes in control over the production of producers as a preface to examining their consequences. Out-of-pocket fees, which had been a significant barrier in the nineteenth century, diminished in importance in both branches. The formal educational requirements of the two branches converged in a law degree and a year of professional training, while local government grants became widely available to defray the cost of the former, if not always the latter. The solicitors Final Examination came to resemble the Bar Final as a hurdle that most law graduates could expect to overcome. In addition, the attrition of qualified barristers during the early years of practice because of insufficient business declined with the growth of legal aid. Nevertheless, significant differences still separated the two branches. If it was difficult to obtain apprenticeships in both, it was more difficult to find a pupillage. Articled clerks could expect to live on their salaries; pupils had to rely on other sources of income. More importantly, there were enough jobs for most who wanted to be assistant solicitors but not nearly enough tenancies for beginning barristers.

These changes in the structure of supply control had an extraordinary impact on the rates of entry into the two branches after World War II (see table 1). Although there was some catch-up in starts at the Bar for the first five years, the numbers began to decline by 1950. The efficacy of supply control is visible in the fact that the Bar actually *shrank* each year from 1955 to 1961, a total decline of 5 percent, and the 1950 rate of entry was not attained again until 1965. Then the transformation described above began to take effect as the number of first law degrees increased from 1,072 in 1965 to 3,564 in 1980, or 232 percent. Starts at the Bar, which averaged 104 a year between 1955 and 1964, rose to 150 between 1965 and 1969, 246 between 1970 and 1974, and 317 between 1975 and 1984—a threefold increase. The total number of barristers in private practice, which declined at an annualized rate of 0.7 percent between 1954 and 1961, increased at 3.5 percent a year between 1961 and 1969 and at a staggering 8.2 percent a year between 1969 and 1978, before slowing to 3.2 percent a year between 1978 and 1984. The number of private practitioners increased from 1,918 in 1961 to 5,203 in 1984, or 171 percent. Yet, the lower rate of growth in the last five years suggests that the Bar did not entirely lose control over supply, and the decline in the ratio of starts to calls (among barristers domiciled in the United Kingdom) after 1975/76 is consistent with my contention that the Bar's restriction on the number of tenancies remains a significant barrier.

Solicitors display a pattern of growth that is similar in gross but different in detail. The postwar catch-up, during which an average of 900 solicitors were admitted a year, ended in 1950. For the next fourteen years, average annual admissions fell to 701, as a result of which the profession grew at an annualized rate of only 1 percent during the 1950s. Thereafter admissions increased rapidly: an average of 1,120 a year between 1965 and 1969, 1,777 between 1970 and 1974, 2,391 between 1975 and 1979, and 3,380 for the first two years of this decade, before declining to 2,522 between 1982 and 1984. As a consequence, the profession grew at an annualized rate of 2.4 percent between 1959 and 1968 and 5.9 percent between 1968 and 1982, although growth has fallen off in the last two years. The total number of solicitors increased 139 percent between 1959 and 1984.

Although barristers and solicitors have shown similar periods of stasis and change in the last four decades, the differential impact of the postwar environment on their strategies of supply control also is apparent. Because the Bar relied so heavily on ascriptive criteria, it could offer less resistance to the increasing dominance of meritocratic ideology; and given its much smaller base, its rate of growth inevitably was much higher. However, control over the number of tenancies by the Inns and by heads of chambers was able to slow the growth of the Bar five years before the growth of solicitors began to decline. The same forces that produced the unparalleled rate of expansion in both branches during the 1960s and 1970s also explain why that expansion has levelled off. Law student enrollments, which have become the principal bottleneck, are relatively flat (see table 1). Whereas university enrollment increased at an annualized rate of 9.9 percent between 1961 and 1976, it increased at only 1.2 percent thereafter; polytechnic enrollment rose at an annualized rate of 65.9 percent between 1970 and 1976 but at only 7.0 percent between 1976 and 1980. Undergraduate enrollment in both university and polytechnic law departments declined slightly between 1982/83 and 1983/84. Furthermore, the entry of women into law departments, which explains much of the growth of these departments, has stabilized at just under half. We can expect both branches to continue to grow for several more decades because the rate of production will outweigh deaths and retirements in the much smaller cohort of older lawyers: over the last ten years an average of 2,540 solicitors have been admitted annually, but only 1,107 have left practice; 314 barristers have started but only 124 have left. The rate of growth will remain constant and gradually decline, however. In a sense, supply control has been reestablished through a new mechanism—formal education—and at a new level.

THE COMPOSITION OF THE PROFESSION

This new mechanism affects not only the size of the profession but also its composition. First, the radically different levels of recruitment before and after the 1960s have produced a small cohort of older lawyers and a much larger cohort of younger practitioners. Whereas only 34 percent of all barristers were within ten years of call in 1966, a decade later 57 percent fell in this category. Similarly, only 47 percent of solicitors were forty or younger in 1969, but a mere seven years later 58 percent had been in practice for less than sixteen years, almost all of whom would be under forty. It is noteworthy that this imbalance in age distribution is considerably more pronounced among barristers, a reflection of the fact that supply control, initially more stringent, was relaxed more profoundly, as well as of the smaller size of the Bar. Although I can only speculate, it seems plausible to suggest that the large cohorts of younger lawyers have been and will be increasingly dissatisfied with restrictive practices that favor older lawyers and with structures of governance that institutionalize gerontocracy.

When the academy displaced the profession as principal gatekeeper, explicit reliance on ascribed characteristics gave way to an ideology of meritocracy. The great achievement of the academy has been to admit women in numbers that now approach those of male entrants. As late as half a century after Parliament ended the profession's formal exclusion of women in 1919, they still were only 3 percent of solicitors and 5.4 percent of barristers. With the growth of law departments and the even more important changes in consciousness wrought by the feminist movement, the Bar began to change in the late 1950s. Although the proportion of women grew steadily, it also grew slowly and seems to have peaked in the mid-1970s at about 15 percent to 20 percent of starts, only half the proportion of women law students. The number of women solicitors, by contrast, did not begin to grow markedly until the 1970s; but by 1980, the proportion of new solicitors who were women equaled the proportion of law graduates who were women. These differences between the branches cannot be explained in terms of the Bar's claim to be more demanding, for women law graduates are, if anything, more capable than men law graduates. Incomplete statistics suggest that the proportion of women applicants admitted to law departments is less than half that of men (although women perform better in secondary school), and women law students do just as well as their male counterparts in obtaining honors degrees.

Two factors seem responsible for the difference and are difficult to separate. First, barristers still make more particularistic decisions about entrants. Women encounter greater problems than do men in securing pupillages and many more obstacles in obtaining both tenancies and business during the early years of practice. The first two decisions are controlled by heads of chambers, most of whom are elderly men likely to retain prejudices against women barristers. The third is influenced significantly by senior clerks, also mostly men, whose patriarchal views may be reinforced by the belief that women tenants will charge lower fees than men and thus earn the clerk less income. Where, as in Scotland, advocates practice individually rather than in chambers and are served by a common pool of clerks, women have come to represent half of all new advocates.

The second explanation for the low proportion of women barristers turns on structural factors rather than individual prejudices. It is extremely difficult to combine a career at the Bar with family responsibilities, either by working part time or by leaving practice and returning after child-rearing. By contrast, employment in a firm, a company, or a government office may open one or both possibilities to women solicitors. Whether individual or institutional biases are dominant, their effect is visible in the fact that women law students express a stronger preference than men for becoming solicitors and a weaker preference for the Bar.

The experience of black lawyers has been almost the opposite of that of women. Blacks from the colonies have been called to the Bar since at least the early nineteenth century, although few, if any, practiced in England. Indeed, in 1960, three-quarters of all Bar students were from overseas. With the growth of both law faculties and nationalism in the newly independent countries, however, this proportion rapidly declined. At the same time, as the black population of England increased, so did the number of black barristers, which now approximates 5 percent of the Bar. Blacks have responded to discrimination in the allocation of tenancies and briefs by forming all black chambers serving a largely black clientele. By contrast, there is no tradition of black solicitors; indeed, noncitizens were not admitted to this branch until 1974. For this reason, and also because of the greater difficulty of the solicitors' examinations and the larger size of the solicitors' branch, the approximately 200 black solicitors now in practice represent only 0.25 percent of the profession. The Bar, which relies more heavily on ascriptive criteria, paradoxically has been more open to racial minorities. The shift to qualification through the academy also has led to a second paradox. On one hand, the academy has admitted—indeed, actively recruited—an increasing number of overseas law students, whose tuition payments subsidize the cost of educating domestic students (just as the fees of overseas Bar students subsidized the Inns in the 1950s and 1960s, most of whose benefits were enjoyed by domestic white barristers). On the other hand, heightened competition for places in law departments has made legal education less accessible to domestic black applicants disadvantaged by inadequate primary and secondary schooling. The move from professional ascription to academic meritocracy thus has not greatly eased the path for racial minorities.

Nor has that transformation significantly affected the class composition of the profession. The traditional claim by barristers that they enjoy a superior social status was derived partly from the higher proportion of university graduates among them and the Bar's more exclusive ascriptive barriers. Yet the emergence of common qualifications for the two branches, and particularly the expectation that entrants to both will possess a law degree, seem to have erased these differences. Several independent studies in the late 1970s confirmed that Bar students and articled clerks had very similar class backgrounds. Convergence has been achieved by *narrowing* class composition, however, not broadening it. One reason is the centrality of the academy, which always has selected disproportionately from the upper social stata and continues to do so even after the creation of the polytechnics. This bias, ironically, was amplified by the elimination of another ascriptive barrier—gender. As the numbers seeking entry to law departments effectively doubled, competition for places intensified. Indeed, because women still must overcome substantial social and cultural barriers, those who succeed tend to come from even more privileged backgrounds than men law students.

The emergence of the academy as the principal gatekeeper to the legal profession thus made a major contribution to eliminating gender as an ascriptive barrier but, simultaneously, magnified the barrier of class and provided a new legitimation for the barrier of race. Furthermore, although we lack the data to test these hypotheses, it seems plausible to expect that class and race influence which academic institution a student attends and the quality of degree the student attains and that these, in turn, determine the nature of the apprenticeship and the first position the student obtains after qualifying. The academy thus not only is more selective but also performs the indispensable function of allocating graduates to positions within the professional hierarchy and justifying that allocation in meritocratic terms.

LIMITING COMPETITION

In order to control the market for its services, a profession must seek to regulate not only the production *of* producers but also production *by* producers. This occurs only at a later stage of the professional project: an occupational category that limited the competitive energies of its own members before they had demarcated themselves from other service providers quickly would succumb to outside competitors who were not similarly restrained. Control of production *by* producers also can enhance the status of the profession by disclaiming crass economic motives. We can distinguish two types of control over production by producers: the definition and defense of the professional monopoly against external competitors and the elaboration of restrictive practices limiting internal competition. These tend to occur sequentially.

MONOPOLY

The legal profession's attempt to define its monopoly was complicated by the existence of two branches concerned with patrolling the boundaries that divide them as well as those that exclude other occupations. During the course of the nineteenth century barristers and solicitors reached an accommodation (although not without considerable dissension): solicitors ceased to challenge the Bar's exclusive right of audience in the higher courts, and barristers relinquished any claim to perform conveyances (real estate transactions) or to serve clients without the intermediation of solicitors. The Bar has been very successful in defending its turf, perhaps because advocacy occupies the core of the legal profession's identity and is a highly visible activity, whose elaborate ritual and arcane language proclaim the esoteric qualities of law. Furthermore, solicitors share with barristers a common interest in excluding outsiders from the courts.

On the other hand, barristers and solicitors are opposed in their struggle over the right of audience in the higher courts, which traditionally also has conferred eligibility for appointment to the bench—not only a prize for those few who attain it but also an important foundation for the Bar's collective assertion of superior status. The greater difficulty of justifying a monopoly against fellow lawyers may help to explain the vigor with which the Bar opposed nineteenth-century proposals for common training with solicitors. Yet, the recent convergence of the two branches in terms of background, education, and qualifications may weaken the Bar's defenses. At the same time, the erosion of supply control among solicitors may stimulate the latter to press their claims more strongly. The historic compromise between the branches survived the Royal Commission inquiry of the late 1970s, in which the Law Society (unsuccessfully) sought only a modest expansion of solicitors' rights of audience. However, the recent threat of losing the conveyancing monopoly led to an immediate demand for equality with barristers. Although the Government summarily rejected this claim, its concern to cut costs, together with the fact that it presently pays for half of all barristers' services, renders the Bar's monopoly precarious. Even if it is not abolished, the monopoly still may be eroded through the progressive expansion of lower-court jurisdiction, increased use of employed lawyers (solicitors as well as barristers), and the grant to solicitors of specific, if not general, rights of audience. Nevertheless, barristers may preserve a good deal of the market for higher-court advocacy by means of informal conventions despite the demise of formal rules.

Solicitors always have had greater difficulty defining and defending their monopoly. Much of what they do is less visible and less obviously technical than higher-court advocacy. Unlike lawyers in the United States and some Canadian provinces, English solicitors never claimed a monopoly over legal advice. Furthermore, whereas solicitors have been quite restrained in challenging the Bar, lay competitors have been far more aggressive in invading the domain of solicitors. Banks and trust companies, accountants, real estate agents, companies, and trade unions all perform solicitors' work for their customers, employees, and members. The lay public also seems less tolerant of the solicitors' monopoly than they are of the barristers' exclusive right of audience, perhaps because consumers encounter the former more often and more directly. Public resentment was most visible, of course, in the long-standing critique of the conveyancing monopoly. Recent legislation has forced solicitors to share it with a new paraprofession of licensed conveyancers; however, there is continuing uncertainty about the role of banks and building societies (savings and loan associations). On first impression this incursion, which solicitors vigorously resisted, appears to be an awesome loss, without precedent in the annals of any other profession, for solicitors derive half of their incomes from conveyancing. Yet, the ultimate consequences are unpredictable. The change will be felt more heavily by smaller firms, which typically earn a higher proportion of their income from conveyancing. In order to remain competitive, they will have to expand their volume through advertising, routinize conveyancing through computerization, and transfer work to paraprofessionals, all of which will foster concentration and render solicitors more like their lay competitors—that is, less professional. At the same time, solicitors may find themselves challenged from another direction for the first time in a century. Barristers, pressed by their own loss of supply control, threatened by solicitors, and perhaps concerned with allaying criticism about the wastefulness of the divided profession, may renew their demands to deal directly with other professionals (such as accountants and employed barristers) and possibly even with lay clients.

The monopoly of each branch is threatened not only by the other branch and by outsiders but also from within: by employed barristers and solicitors, whose numbers are expanding because private practice is able to absorb a declining proportion of the influx of new entrants produced by the erosion of supply control (see table 2). The significance of these emergent categories is threefold. First, the demarcation between employed barristers and employed solicitors is far more tenuous than the line that separates the branches in private practice. Both categories not only share a common training but also may work for the same employer and perform similar tasks. Consistent with this, their monopolies have converged: employed barristers lack a right of audience in the higher courts. Second, employed lawyers are less protected from competition with other occupational categories, such as accountants, civil servants, and city managers. Third, the number of employed lawyers is augmented by reason of heightened demand as well as greater supply: clients (public and private) may prefer to employ lawyers rather than retain private practitioners because the former are less expensive and more easily controlled. Moreover, having put lawyers on their payroll, employers are likely to add their own voices to the call for expanding the rights of audience of employed lawyers and for allowing all employed barristers to perform conveyances and to brief barristers in private practice without the intervention of a solicitor.

INTRAPROFESSIONAL RESTRICTIONS

Private practitioners seek to control their market not only by regulating the production of services by outsiders (laypersons, the other branch, and employed lawyers) but also by limiting competition from fellow professionals. Just as barristers were first to control the production *of* producers, so they anticipated solicitors in elaborating a set of restrictive practices. Initially informal, these progressively were formalized during the nineteenth century as the Bar grew in size and subgroups declined in importance (such as the circuits—barristers who traveled with high court judges when they sat outside London). Formalization also publicized the rules, rendering them more vulnerable to external criticism. Consequently, the Bar recently has been forced to relax several of its more conspicuous restrictive practices: the two-counsel rule (a Queen's Counsel always must be assisted by a junior barrister), the two-thirds rule (a junior barrister who assists a Queen's Counsel must be paid two-thirds of the latter's fee), and barriers to practice on the circuits (extra fees that must be charged by a barrister who appears in a circuit but is not a member of that circuit).

This sequence illustrates the peculiar situation of the Bar: on one hand, the nature of its market makes the restriction of competition particularly urgent; on the other hand, its internal structure facilitates such restriction through informal means. The production and sale of barristers' services resembles the ideal of the free market more than do most such exchanges. The performance of barristers in court is highly visible to potential consumers (i.e., solicitors), and the measures of success or failure are superficially clear (if actually ambiguous). More importantly, the solicitor-consumers are themselves professionals and thus unusually well equipped to judge quality. Also, at least some of those consumers—the larger firms—possess considerable economic leverage by virtue of the amount of business they can offer. In the absence of restrictive practices (and without professional control over the production *of* producers), barristers would be driven to compete vigorously in terms of price and quality.

The Bar has minimized this danger in several ways. First, it has drastically curtailed competition between younger and older age cohorts by means of an artificial barrier between Queen's Counsel and juniors, which grants each a submonopoly (Queen's Counsel over advocacy in "heavier" cases, juniors over the preliminary stages of litigation). The production of Queen's Counsel, unlike the production of barristers, remains tightly controlled by the Lord Chancellor (who himself is a barrister). Second, the Bar has dampened horizontal competition among juniors. Although barristers still cannot form partnerships with each other (much less with solicitors or other professionals), the Bar is not simply an aggregation of 5,000 individual competitors. Rather, it is grouped into about 200 sets in London and another 100 in some two dozen provincial cities; there is little competition between barristers in different cities. London sets are prevented from proliferating by the formal requirement of a clerk, the informal but effective restriction to the Inns, and the limited accommodation available within each Inn. Third, the London market is differentiated further by subject-matter specialization. Fourth, the homogeneity of social background and function among barristers and their geographic concentration within the Inns (and within similar settings in most provincial cities) facilitate informal control. To the extent that the Bar has grown more hetereogeneous, the newer elements—especially black barristers—tend to form distinct markets. Finally, barristers are subject to hierarchic controls that reward conformity to restrictive practices: pupils are subordinate to pupilmasters and to those who allocate tenancies, younger barristers are subordinate to their heads of chambers and clerks, juniors who aspire to become Queen's Counsel are subordinate to judges who advise the Lord Chancellor, and even Queen's Counsel who seek appointment to the bench remain subordinate to the Lord Chancellor and the judges who advise him.

The very characteristics that allowed the Bar to establish control over the production *of* producers in the first place and to reassert it after the academy introduced more meritocratic entry criteria thus also allow it to preserve control over production *by* producers through informal means, even after the demise of formal rules. A Queen's Counsel still insists that a junior be briefed, and the junior still demands two-thirds of the leader's fee. Barrister's clerks establish ongoing relationships with solicitors' firms, which allow the clerk to refer work to other chambers (because no barrister is free or because the set does not handle that speciality) without fear of losing the firm as a future client. A barrister will decline to accept a client who already has briefed another barrister unless the latter consents. Barristers continue to charge and receive the full brief fee even if the case is settled (as most are) and to bill separate fees for multiple clients in a single matter even if their representation does not increase the complexity of the task. Perhaps most importantly, the small number of chambers, and thus of barrister's clerks, and the intimate relations among the latter allow them to reach informal understandings about the level of fees.

The restrictive practices of solicitors are different in several respects. First, the market for solicitors' services is less freely competitive. Although there are many more productive units (because solicitors outnumber barristers by almost ten to one and firms are smaller than chambers on average), the market for individual consumers is highly localized. Furthermore, unlike the solicitor who selects and evaluates barristers' services, the individual consumer of solicitors' services is a layperson who is likely to have little prior experience with law or lawyers. Such a client's relationships with solicitors generally are sporadic rather than continuous, and the lay consumer will encounter extreme difficulty in obtaining accurate information about price or quality. Consequently, not only does the solicitor-consumer have distinct advantages in purchasing barristers' services but the solicitor-producer also has distinct advantages in selling services to individual consumers (although not, of course, to companies or other institutions). It is striking that the relationship of each branch to its market is the obverse of the stereotype: solicitors paradoxically are *more* "independent" than barristers. Perhaps, then, one function of restrictive practices is to correct this disparity: to make barristers more "independent" of consumers and solicitors less so. Such an interpretation draws support from the fact that one of the most important restrictions on solicitors —the regulation of fees in contentious matters (litigation)—is imposed externally.

Because solicitors, when compared to barristers, are more numerous, geographically dispersed, and heterogeneous in background, organization, and function, restrictive practices also must be more formal. The Law Society promulgated ethical rules long before the Bar felt the need to formalize its own etiquette, therefore, and it regulated subjects, such as advertising and fees in noncontentious matters, that the Bar still leaves to informal controls. These rules and others—the limitation on the number of partners in a firm, the prohibitions on practicing another occupation, forming a partnership with other professions, or even sharing office space with other occupations, and the restriction on employed solicitors accepting private work from fellow employees—all served to dampen intra-professional competition. Several of these restrictive practices, like those of barristers, have succumbed to attack in recent years, however. The ceiling of twenty partners was lifted in 1967, with the result that forty-six firms now exceed that number; of these, two have at least sixty partners, three have fifty to fifty-nine, five have forty to forty-nine, and thirteen have thirty to thirty-nine. Scale fees (minima) were abolished five years later, although prices stayed level or even rose. And in 1984 the Law Society relaxed its ban on advertising, under pressure from external critics.

It seems unlikely that solicitors can continue to suppress competition by relying on the informal understandings that have worked so well for barristers. First, the same market characteristics that allow solicitors to dominate individual clients also encourage a firm that wishes to increase its market share to establish branch offices, merge with other firms, cut prices, and engage in aggressive advertising. Legal clinics successfully have pursued such strategies in the United States. Second, even if solicitors themselves are averse to such marketing strategies, they may be forced to adopt them by the threat of lay competition, especially now that the conveyancing monopoly has been diluted and perhaps broken. Whereas barristers may continue to control production by producers through informal understandings, solicitors thus seem likely to face increasingly unconstrained competition from outside the profession as well as within.

STIMULATING DEMAND

Historically, lawyers sought to control their market by limiting supply before they turned to the alternative strategy of creating demand. True, lawyers are at least partly responsible for the fact that substantive and procedural laws are so complex that laypersons must hire professionals both to litigate and to perform noncontentious transactions, such as conveyances and the distribution of estates. However, neither the institutional infrastructure nor the legitimating ideology for large-scale demand creation existed before the emergence of the welfare state after World War II. Furthermore, it is the recent erosion of professional control over the production *of* and *by* producers that motivated lawyers to seek to stimulate demand. But I do not want to overstate the argument that professions have shifted from supply to demand as the principal locus of market control: lawyers have done so slowly, reluctantly, and ineffectively. Once again, the two branches diverge in their strategies.

BARRISTERS AND THE PUBLIC SECTOR

In many ways, the Bar has encountered greater difficulty in influencing demand. Few people can be persuaded to engage in litigation voluntarily. Indeed, the principal sources of increased demand for barristers' services— criminal and matrimonial cases—are matters over which the profession has no control whatsoever. Barristers may, however, be the passive beneficiaries of solicitors' efforts to stimulate demand for their own services. All that barristers realistically can do to influence demand is seek to ensure that those who must litigate actually do retain counsel (a decision that often is made by the solicitor rather than the lay client). In pursuing this goal, barristers enjoy certain advantages: the state's obligation to provide legal assistance is less problematic in court than outside and less problematic in criminal proceedings than in civil; and there are no functional equivalents to barristers as advocates (as there are for solicitors as advisors, drafters, and negotiators).

The means of guaranteeing representation, of course, has been legal aid. Yet, the impetus for its creation cannot be attributed to the professional project of market control. First, the inspiration for civil legal aid originated with a Labour Government, not with the legal profession. Second, the institution emerged at a time when the supply of barristers actually was declining and traditional restrictive practices were firmly in place. Nevertheless, the growth of the Bar from the early 1960s clearly is inseparable from the expanding legal aid budget generated by rising crime and divorce rates, regardless of whether legal aid is seen as the cause of eroding supply control—encouraging law students to enter the Bar confident that they would be able to survive the early years of practice—or as a response to numbers that were augmented by other causes. Barristers derived more than a quarter of their incomes from legal aid in 1974/75—43 percent from all public funds (which also includes fees for prosecution). For all juniors, the proportions were almost a third and almost a half; indeed, juniors with a London criminal practice derived about two-thirds of their incomes from legal aid in 1976/77—more than 90 percent from all public funds.

The state thus paid for the doubling of the Bar. Furthermore, it did so without much effort on the part of barristers. Although the Bar has advocated greater client eligibility and more generous payments to barristers, much of the growth of the legal aid budget is attributable to the extrinsic social phenomena that generate demand for legal services, such as crime and divorce. Nor has the Bar had to worry about the impact of these new sources of demand on the distribution, and particularly the concentration, of business. Legal aid work is allocated to barristers in much the same fashion as are briefs from private clients: by solicitors dealing with barrister's clerks. Nevertheless, the dependence of the Bar on legal aid does pose new and significant problems. First, the state is both more powerful than many private clients and less willing to acquiesce in the Bar's restrictive practices: *it* sets the fees for criminal legally aided work, and legal aid committees decide whether a Queen's Counsel is required and whether the latter needs the assistance of a junior. These externally imposed conditions may become the conventions for private clients as well. Second, a Bar that derives half of its income from the state no longer can make as persuasive an argument for its independence and altruism—and thus for its claim to be a profession. Ironically, the very foundation of the Bar's strength—its monopoly of advocacy—has become a source of dependence.

SOLICITORS AND THE PRIVATE MARKET

In one respect, the situation of solicitors is similar. They also are unable to influence the single most important source of demand. Conveyancing, which has provided half of the income of solicitors for at least a century, rises and falls with the economy. Fortunately, the dramatic growth in the production of solicitors during the last two decades coincided with an equally pronounced (if considerably more erratic) increase in the value of housing, superimposed on a long-term rise in the prevalence of home ownership and the geographic mobility of the population. This may be part of the reason why solicitors have been so passive in the face of incursions by accountants and members of other occupations in the fields of tax advice, government regulation, and general business counseling. As real estate values stabilize or decline and solicitors lose some or all of their conveyancing monopoly, however, they will have to look elsewhere for new demand.

Unlike barristers, solicitors have not relied heavily on legal aid. One reason is that solicitors have earned only a quarter of their incomes from contentious work and only a small proportion of this from cases that are likely to be legally aided, such as criminal defense (4 percent), personal injuries (3 percent), and matrimonial matters (5 percent). Although solicitors render virtually all the legal advice defrayed by public funds, this generates a trivial proportion of their earnings. In 1975/76, legal aid accounted for only 6 percent of gross solicitor income. Solicitors remain less interested than barristers in legal aid because they find such work relatively unprofitable. Since solicitors have rights of audience only in the lower courts, the cases that they can handle are less serious and consequently command smaller fees; and the legal advice scheme also discourages lengthy or elaborate consultations. Legal aid matters can be processed profitably only when they are mass-produced. Consequently, whereas most barristers do a fair amount of legal aid work, at least in the early stages of their careers, and thus share a collective interest in the institution, only about a third of all solicitors' firms earn even a tenth of their incomes from this source.

Other forms of demand creation also pose serious problems for solicitors. It is not much easier to encourage individuals to use law facilitatively than it is to induce them to litigate. Moreover, whereas the intermediaries who select barristers are solicitors, the potential clients of solicitors are laypeople. Even if the latter may be more impressionable (a dubious assumption), they also are more difficult to reach because they are more numerous, more anonymous, and much less interested in legal services. Solicitors thus face a dilemma. They can engage in advertising directed at their mass market—indeed, the Law Society launched several institutional campaigns in the 1970s and recently allowed individual solicitors to advertise. Such efforts are likely to be expensive and relatively unprofitable, however, at least unless the investment is substantial and continuous over a long period. Alternatively, they can focus their informational activities on populations likely to need and want solicitors' services. This strategy also has substantial drawbacks. Even more than advertising, it smacks of commericalism and thus endangers the claim of solicitors to professional status. And it runs the risk of encouraging dependence on the favor of occupations that channel clients to solicitors—police, for instance, who advise criminal accused, or real estate agents who counsel home buyers. (Barristers, by contrast, fully control the subordinated occupational category that performs a similar function for them—the barrister's clerk.)

But the greatest problem is that successful efforts to create demand inevitably tend to affect its distribution. Cost-effective demand creation thus not only impairs the solicitors' image of noncommercialism but also intensifies intraprofessional competition. Advertising by an individual firm probably is a good deal more productive than the institutional campaigns of the Law Society, but it benefits only that firm. Direct solicitation of clients is even more efficient but has even fewer spill-over effects. The problem becomes more acute when public resources are used to create demand, for then all qualified producers seem to feel an entitlement to share equally in the additional business generated. Such a belief may underlie the Law Society's dissemination of lists of solicitors willing to handle legal aid matters, the rapid proliferation of Duty Solicitor schemes (which provide an initial solicitor contact to all those arrested), the rosters of solicitors who volunteer to work at or take referrals from Citizens Advice Bureaus, and the initial hostility of solicitors to law centers (legal aid offices) thought to concentrate publicly subsidized work among employed lawyers. Whereas the Bar runs the risk of losing its independence when it turns to publicly created demand, solicitors thus run the risk of intensifying intraprofessional competition when they seek to stimulate demand in the private market.

THE SOCIAL ORGANIZATION OF THE PROFESSION

Both the strategies and the successes of the professional project of market control influence, and are affected by, the social organization of the two branches. We can trace these linkages by examining differentiation within the legal profession, the nature of the productive unit, and the consequences of both for stratification.

INTERNAL DIFFERENTIATION

The nineteenth century was a period of professional consolidation, the end product of which was the present division into two main branches. The separate category of serjeants (from which judges had been drawn) was abolished in 1873. That same year the merger of law and equity reduced the distinctiveness of the Chancery Bar and formally eliminated the demarcation between solicitors and attorneys. Doctors of Law and proctors disappeared with the closure of ecclesiastical and admiralty courts. Special pleaders and conveyancers, who had emerged several hundred years earlier in response to the enormous complexities of pleading and of encumbering and transferring land, had vanished by the end of the nineteenth century. Therefore, the rationalization of courts and the decline in certain legal functions reduced professional differentiation.

The fundamental division of the profession into two branches persisted and even rigidified (although it did not fully survive transplantation to any of the colonial legal systems whose inspiration was English). For the relationship between barristers and solicitors, although often tense, ultimately is symbiotic. Solicitors, for their part, enjoy greater economic leverage. Larger firms wield considerable patronage through the distribution of briefs. Smaller firms derive economic power (if less legitimately) from their ability to delay payments to barristers, although the Bar recently has begun to retaliate. Barristers, however, can decline or return briefs and control the scheduling of work. Furthermore, the greater economic security of solicitors is counterbalanced by the superior social status of barristers—itself a composite of history, ascribed characteristics, functions, conventions of deference, the visibility of a few stars, and an exclusive relationship with the bench.

If the division into two branches seems relatively fixed, there have been significant changes in differentiation within each. The Bar always has been more centralized. Until recently, the higher courts in which barristers practice sat primarily in London and made only brief forays outside. The principal educational institutions—the Inns of Court (and later their School of Law)—also are located in London. Moreover, barristers' clients were either London solicitors or the London agents of provincial solicitors. Consequently, virtually all barristers practiced in London until the end of the nineteenth century. With the growth of provincial courts and the decline of circuits, however, provincial chambers expanded rapidly, containing a quarter of the Bar by the 1950s and nearly a third today. Solicitors, by contrast, serve clients who are scattered throughout the country (especially given the dominant role of residential conveyancing). They are excluded from the higher London courts. By the end of the nineteenth century they had established a number of provincial training centers for articled clerks, who naturally are found wherever there are solicitors. It is not surprising, therefore, that the distribution of solicitors for the last hundred years has been the inverse of the present distribution of barristers: two-thirds have practiced in the provinces and only a third in London. On this measure, as on others, the Bar enjoys greater social cohesiveness (although less than it had in the past), a fact that may help to explain the different role of professional associations in the two branches.

A second parameter along which differentiation has increased is employment (see table 2). Although we lack adequate data, it seems unlikely that any barristers were employed until the beginning of the twentieth century, at the earliest. Today, approximately half of those called to the Bar are employed by government or private enterprise. Some solicitors always have been employed in private practice; more recently, they have been employed by government (especially local government) and by commerce and industry. Consequently, employed solicitors rose from a quarter of those holding practicing certificates in 1939 to a third in 1957 and a half today. Furthermore, since many employed solicitors do not take out practicing certificates, the proportion must be even larger. Nevertheless, although a larger proportion of solicitors than barristers are employed, employment creates greates divisions within the Bar. Employed barristers need not complete a pupillage, they lack rights of audience, they do not observe Bar etiquette and are not subject to Bar discipline, and few ever enter private practice (although movement in the other direction is possible). Solicitors, by contrast, suffer no disabilities by virtue of employment. Moreover, although there is relatively little mobility between private practice and employment by public or private entities, *all* private practitioners spend at least three years as assistant solicitors employed by firms, and most spend the bulk of their professional lives as partners employing assistant solicitors. The growth of employment, like the geographic shifts described above, thus has had a greater effect on the social integration of the Bar than on that of solicitors.

The category of private practitioners is further differentiated in terms of clients served and subject matter handled. Here, again, the Bar has changed more profoundly. Not only is the Bar as a whole more dependent on public funds, but the degree of dependence varies greatly with the barrister's age and specialty, from 1.5 percent of the income of London Chancery and specialist Queen's Counsel to 91.7 percent for London juniors with a criminal practice. Even many "independent" practitioners thus are virtually employed by the state at the beginning of their careers. Most solicitors, by contrast, earn little or none of their incomes from legal aid; but the 5 percent who specialized in such matters earned a third of the £100 million in public funds paid to solicitors for contentious business in 1980/81. Both branches thus are witnessing the emergence of a dual market, one public and the other private, although the lines of division are very different.

Barristers and solicitors also differ in the nature and extent of subject-matter specialization. Barristers' chambers tend to specialize, rejecting briefs that fall outside their expertise. Most solicitors' firms are more generalist, although individual lawyers will specialize within the larger firms. Indeed, almost all smaller firms (which contain the vast majority of private practitioners) perform the same broad range of work, the core of which is conveyancing; in this they resemble the local greengrocer, chemist, or stationer, whose market niche depends on geographic convenience. This difference between the branches presumably reflects the fact that the clients of barristers are solicitors, who can channel work to specialist chambers, whereas the clients of solicitors are laypeople, who must be offered a full range of services in order to attract and retain their business. Therefore, a profession that had only three main divisions at the turn of the century—the bench, the Bar, and solicitors—now has many more— employed barristers and solicitors, private practitioners who rely largely on public funds, and specialist chambers. (In addition, academic lawyers have increased in numbers and prominence as a result of the new role of formal education.)

STRUCTURES OF PRODUCTION

When we turn from the social organization of the profession as a whole to the structure of the units within which private practitioners produce services, we find further changes in both size and composition, as well as significant differences between the branches. As a result of changes in the market for their services (in both supply and demand), solicitors' firms have grown, and their membership has altered. In 1802 the median solicitors' firm had 1.2 principals. A century and a half later the median firm had only 2.5 principals, three-quarters of all firms had fewer than four principals, and 93 percent had fewer than six. Even in 1979, 58 percent of all firms had only one or two principals, and 82 percent had fewer than five. Thus the bulk of solicitors' services still are produced within relatively small units. To the extent that this situation reflects the comfortable market niche secured by the conveyancing monopoly, it is likely to change as a result of incursions by licensed conveyancers and the competition that this fosters among solicitors (consequences that will be even more pronounced if banks and building societies are allowed to perform conveyances). As the erosion of market control makes it more difficult to extract the customary profits from clients, solicitors will be forced to intensify the extraction of surplus value from subordinates, a development that I discuss further below. Competition also fosters concentration. One likely trend is the expansion of firms through the creation of suburban branch offices; in 1978, for instance, a third of all firms already had at least two offices, and a tenth had three or more.

Furthermore, even if the median productive unit has remained small, a few large firms have emerged since World War II. I found none with more than ten principals prior to the war and only a dozen with as many as five. Yet, five firms had ten or more principals by 1950, twelve had reached this level by 1960, ten had at least twenty principals by 1970, and forty-six are this large today; the largest contains more than 200 solicitors. More than 3,000 solicitors, or 7 percent of those holding practicing certificates, belong to these forty-six large firms. Among the twenty-nine City firms with at least twenty principals, twenty had offices abroad—an average of 2.6 branch offices per firm.

The growth of these larger firms is partly a response to the size of their corporate clients and the need to specialize in order to handle more complex and more varied legal problems. But it also is related to changes in the use of subordinated labor, the explanation for which is both historical and economic. During the 1960s, managing clerks waged a partly successful campaign to professionalize. Legal executives, as they now were called, made somewhat awkward employees, for they were of the same age and gender as their employers and often from a similar social class, some were just as well trained, and they stayed long enough to expect advancement. The tensions within this relationship have been ameliorated in two ways. First, the role of legal executive has been significantly feminized: almost half of the "fellows" admitted by the Institute of Legal Executives (ILEX) in 1983/84 were women. The sexual division of labor and the patriarchal subordination of women both reinforce the male employer's authority. Second, some legal executives have been replaced by assistant solicitors; although 60 percent of the latter still are male, all are temporary employees, moving either up to partnerships or out to other positions. Their transitory subordination is more easily justified as training. The enormous increase in the production of solicitors, together with the rule requiring all new entrants to work as employees for three years before setting up on their own or in partnership with another, have provided a constant supply of eager recruits. There has been a concomitant decline in the number of new ILEX fellows since the 1960s and in the numbers of new ILEX students and associates since the 1970s. In the ten years during 1966 to 1976, the number of legal executives remained constant, while the number of articled clerks increased by a third, and the number of assistant solicitors grew almost 90 percent, with the result that the ratio of assistant solicitors to principals rose while the ratio of legal executives to principals fell.

These changes in the labor force may have been motivated by considerations of profitability as well as the fact that trainee solicitors were more available and perhaps more docile. The difference between the cost of labor to firms and its price to clients (i.e., the surplus value extracted) is greatest for assistant solicitors and least for legal executives, with articled clerks falling in between. The profitability of using the labor of assistant solicitors also increases with firm size; so does the ratio of assistant solicitors to principals. In 1976 the average firm with ten principals or more had twice as many assistants per principal as the smaller firms (although only a third again as many legal executives); in 1984/85, the average firm with sixty principals or more had two and a half times as many assistants per principal as did the firm with twenty to thirty principals. This more intensive and extensive exploitation of subordinated labor undoubtedly is part of the reason for the higher incomes enjoyed by principals in the larger firms. At the same time, only the larger firms can increase at a rate that holds out to assistants the possibility of a partnership whose rewards outweigh the sacrifices of a prolonged apprenticeship. If I am correct in attributing the growth of solicitors' firms to the relative availability, pliancy, and profitability of assistant solicitors as subordinates, we can expect further divergence between small and large firms in terms of the labor they employ. Solicitors may be fissioning into the two hemispheres whose polarization characterizes the American legal profession.

The structure of practice at the Bar has changed even more radically, but in different directions. Although most nineteenth century barristers (like most solicitors) practiced alone, by the late 1950s the average set contained more than seven barristers in London and five in the provinces. These figures have grown steadily to more than sixteen barristers per set in London today and twelve in the provinces. The emergence of large sets is a recent phenomenon: only 5 percent of London sets had more than fifteen barristers in 1965, whereas half did so by 1976. Today, nearly three-fourths of London sets contain at least fifteen barristers (excluding those in Lincoln's Inn, where Chancery practices tend to be smaller), and so do more than half of all provincial sets. Furthermore, unlike solicitors, few barristers still practice in small groups: a quarter of all London sets and half of all provincial sets contained fewer than six barristers in 1961, but now only 3 percent of London sets and 9 percent of provincial sets contain fewer than five barristers. Only 2 of the 336 sets have thirty barristers or more, however, and the largest, with forty-five barristers, does not begin to approach the size of the larger solicitors' firms.

Chambers have grown for some of the same reasons that impelled the expansion of solicitors' firms. Size confers its own prestige; together with internal diversity or "balance" among the members of a set (in terms of subject-matter specialization, length of experience, and reputation), it attracts and keeps business. Like firms (if to a lesser degree), chambers can benefit from economies of scale in the use of computerized billing and word processing. But the central dynamic of growth has been different because of the absence of subordinated labor: barristers in private practice cannot be employed (although young barristers may devil for older members of their chambers); and the barristers' clerk is an independent contractor, not an employee. Partners in solicitors' firms have a profound interest in the clerks they accept for articles and the assistant solicitors they hire: both will be performing work for which the partners are responsible and also are candidates for partnership. Barristers who accept pupils and heads of chambers who fill tenancies undoubtedly are concerned with the quality of those they select, but not for these reasons. Young barristers are acutely affected by the prominence of the older barristers in their chambers and the entrepreneurial skills of their clerk, however, for it is these that attract most of the work the new recruit is likely to obtain.

However, the greatest difference between chambers and firms is the role of the barristers' clerk. Whereas the work of legal executives closely resembles that of solicitors, the barristers' clerk performs *no* legal functions. Furthermore, whereas the legal executive is only minimally differentiated from the solicitor in terms of class and training and even may aspire to become a solicitor, the barristers' clerk generally comes from a working class background, has no education beyond secondary school, and never becomes a barrister. Despite these differences, the clerk is less subordinated than the legal executive or trainee solicitor and is a petty bourgeois rather than an employee. Barristers' clerks wield considerable power over the younger members of chambers: allocating briefs when solicitors have not specified a barrister or when the preferred barrister cannot accept the brief or has returned it; and influencing the selection of tenants, particularly from among pupils. Barristers' clerks also earn substantial incomes— more than most of the junior barristers in their chambers.

Most importantly, whereas solicitors' firms have grown, in part, because partners seek to enhance their profits through subordinated labor, the expansion of barristers' chambers redounds primarily to the economic benefit of senior clerks. Since most are paid a proportion of the brief fee and each set contains only one senior clerk (although the senior clerk may have to pay the salaries of the junior clerks), the senior clerk's income varies directly with the number of barristers in the set. Consequently, clerks certainly have not been unhappy about the lack of space in the Inns, which has inhibited the fission of sets. Given this space shortage, economies of scale, the self-interest of clerks, the prestige that attaches to growth and size, the commercial advantages of internal differentiation, and the relative absence of economic tensions within chambers because barristers do not share profits, we can expect further expansion. Although the unit of production has grown in both branches, this growth has very different meanings. For solicitors, it signifies the intensification of capitalist relations of production and a widening division between the larger firms that have followed this route and the smaller firms that have not. Although the prohibition of partnerships and employment at the Bar precludes this development, the growth of chambers does signify an intensification of hierarchy as greater power accrues to both the head of chambers (advised by other senior tenants) and the senior clerk.

STRATIFICATION

Inevitably, the forms of differentiation traced above also structure inequality within the profession. It is essential to distinguish stratification that is relatively permanent, and therefore threatens professional cohesion, from situations where assignment to a stratum is temporary, and mobility can strengthen professional integration. Geography affects the power, wealth, and status of practitioners in both branches, but these differences appear to generate more tension among solicitors, perhaps because the majority are located in the provinces while professional advantages are concentrated in London. The principal division among solicitors is firm size, however, which reflects clients served and functions performed and affects solicitor income and status. There appears to be little movement between large and small firms. Furthermore, recruitment to the larger firms seems to be influenced strongly by the academic institution attended and the degree attained, both of which correlate with background variables such as class.

This form of stratification is almost certain to intensify with the proliferation of large firms and their continued growth. Although barristers' chambers also differ by size and specialty, these variables do not appear to define as strongly the status of individual barristers within them, and there is increasing movement between sets. A very significant exception to both generalizations, however, are the so-called ghetto chambers occupied primarily by black barristers—a phenomenon that contradicts the universalistic pretensions of the Bar.

Other professional divisions are characterized by varying degrees of mobility. Although barristers still enjoy higher social status than do solicitors, the entry requirements of the two branches have converged, and transfer between them is far easier than it once was, if few avail themselves of the opportunity. Like all professions, those of the law hold out to their members the hope of attaining higher income, status, and power with age. But whereas most articled clerks become assistant solicitors and end as principals, and any solicitor who wishes can play a role in the local, if not the national, law society, the career ladder at the Bar is unusually long and steep, and progress up it far less certain. Not all pupils obtain tenancies; not all fledgling barristers earn their keep and remain in private practice; not all juniors become Queen's Counsel; not all Queen's Counsel become judges; and not all older barristers become heads of chambers or benchers. These status differences are reflected in income. Whereas the highest decile of solicitors earn only two-thirds more than the median and those forty years or older, only two-thirds more than those under thirty, the highest decile of barristers earn more than twice the median and those forty years or older, almost three times as much as those under thirty.

For solicitors, therefore, the problem posed by stratification is to explain the relatively permanent distribution that occurs at the beginning of legal careers: of law students among apprenticeships and of clerks who have completed their articles among law firms and other forms of employment. For the Bar, by contrast, the problem is to explain cumulative success and failure throughout a lifetime of testing. The early and irrevocable assignment of position within the system of stratification would seem to pose greater problems for the unity of solicitors than the later, more gradual, and apparently more reversible assignment of status to barristers. Stratification among solicitors has not been associated overtly with racism because there are so few blacks (although this is changing), and women have been hired by some of the larger firms in proportion to their representation among law graduates (if few have been given partnerships). At the Bar, however, it is clear that blacks, and to a lesser extent women, are severely disadvantaged. Although stratification at the Bar may be more fluid than it is among solicitors, the pretense that it simply reflects meritocratic principles—that success rewards ability and effort—thus is more thoroughly undermined by the visible correlation between the stratum attained and the race and gender of the aspirant.

PROFESSIONAL ASSOCIATIONS

In tracing the trajectory of the professional project among barristers and solicitors, I have not yet discussed the instrument through which they pursued their goals—the professional association. I will begin by describing the emergence and consolidation of structures for collective action during the nineteenth and early twentieth centuries before examining their responses to the challenges of the postwar period.

THE INSTITUTIONAL FRAMEWORK

Barristers entered the nineteenth century as a fully mature profession. They controlled entry and enjoyed an unchallenged monopoly over advocacy. Indeed, these privileges had been won so far in the past that they had acquired the unquestionable legitimacy of tradition. At the same time, the Bar's demographic and organizational characteristics facilitated informal social control. The Bar was small (less than a thousand actual practitioners), extremely homogeneous, and concentrated within a few square blocks of London. Because solicitors insulated barristers from direct client contact, the Bar was less subject to the centrifugal pressures of client loyalty. Barristers encountered fewer temptations to engage in financial misconduct, for they did not handle clients' money. Since most of their professional activities occurred in open court, they constantly were subject to the scrutiny of both judges and their fellow barristers.

Consequently, it is not surprising that formal structures for self-governance were relatively weak and highly decentralized. Each of the four Inns admitted its own students, called them to the Bar, and was responsible for discipline; however, there is no evidence that they exercised any real scrutiny over admissions or calls or took their disciplinary functions seriously. There was no official written code of conduct. The Inns had great difficulty in agreeing on common policies and generally acted independently. Each Inn was governed by its benchers—an elderly, self-perpetuating oligarchy. Content with the professional status of the Bar, they sought to contain change rather than foster it. Consequently, although the Inns cooperated in forming the Council of Legal Education in 1852, the Council had hardly any full-time staff until after World War II and attracted few students. And the Inns adopted a Bar examination in

1872 only as a reluctant concession to the example of solicitors and the threat of fusion.

During much of the nineteenth century, the circuits may have exercised more significant social control; however, their authority over entry and behavior was entirely informal and their actions even less coordinated than those of the Inns. Furthermore, their influence declined as the circuits grew in size and ultimately were supplanted by provincial bars. The only centralized professional association was the Bar Council, created at the end of the century at the initiative of younger barristers who feared that solicitors were threatening their market. More than either the Inns or the circuits, it actively sought to promote the economic interests of barristers and may have helped to formalize such restrictive practices as the two-counsel and two-thirds rules. The Bar Council derived all its financial support from the Inns, however, which were extremely parsimonious, and it enrolled only a small proportion of all barrristers. Until well after World War II, therefore, barristers were governed by a miscellany of uncoordinated institutions but actually relied on tradition and informal understandings to control their market and regulate professional behavior.

Solicitors present a marked contrast in almost every respect. At the beginning of the nineteenth century they were not a profession. It was not they, but the courts, that regulated entry, established restrictive practices, and exercised discipline. Informal controls were ineffective, for there were too many solicitors (approximately five times the number of barristers), and they were too dispersed (two-thirds were scattered across England) and heterogeneous (in both background and function). Nor did they have a viable institutional structure through which to act collectively. The eighteenth century Society of Gentlemen Practisers was moribund, and the only vital organizations were local law societies in a few provincial cities. It was precisely in order to professionalize that solicitors founded the Incorporated Law Society in the 1820s. Like all professional vanguards, the Society began as an elite organization, composed of a few London practitioners. It retained both characteristics throughout the nineteenth century: London solicitors dominated (although they were a minority of the profession); and fifty years after its inception only 25 percent of practitioners had joined. Provincial solicitors continued to invest primary loyalty in their local law societies, which formed federations that competed with the national organization until well into the twentieth century.The Law Society also was governed by elderly solicitors (the median age of council members in 1899 was sixty) who, once elected, generally served for life.

But even if the institutional structure was flawed, the Law Society energetically mobilized whatever resources it possessed to pursue the professional project. First, as we have seen, it erected the formal entry barrier of professional examinations. Although judges initially administered these, the Law Society soon took over. Solicitors were less successful in controlling production *by* producers, for the courts, rather than the Society, regulated fees and demonstrated their solicitude for the public interest by establishing maxima rather than minima. In response, the Law Society promulgated a practice rule prohibiting fee cutting and encouraged local law societies to set minimum fees at or near the judicial maxima.

Second, solicitors sought to persuade the courts to hand over disciplinary powers. The Society was authorized to present charges of misconduct to the Supreme Court in 1873, to conduct a preliminary hearing in 1888, and finally to constitute the disciplinary tribunal in 1919, although solicitors still could seek judicial review. Unlike barristers, solicitors did not rely on traditional conventions about proper behavior; ethical precepts were embodied in judicial decisions and, after the Law Society obtained statutory authority in 1933, in its practice rules.

Third, the Law Society responded to a problem that uniquely threatened the collective status of solicitors—financial misconduct. In 1901 alone, fifty-five solicitors declared bankruptcy, betraying the faith of clients whose money they held in trust accounts. In response, the Law Society successfully sought legislation making such conduct criminal; five years later it secured the right to suspend a practicing certificate on the same ground and required newly qualified solicitors to pass an examination in accounting. It also started to make ex gratia payments to clients who had suffered financial loss. In 1935, under legislative compulsion, it required solicitors to keep and report client accounts (although these rules were widely flouted and largely unenforced), and in 1942 it compelled solicitors to contribute to the compensation fund. Whereas barristers preserved their traditional decentralized institutions and relied heavily on informal control, solicitors thus created a new central institution that constantly sought to expand its formal control.

POSTWAR CHALLENGES

The changes the legal profession has experienced since World War II have induced some convergence in the structures and processes of governance in the two branches, but significant differences remain. The Bar, as we saw, has become more heterogeneous in terms of race and gender, more youthful, and more dispersed (more than a fourth of all barristers now practice primarily in provincial cities); however, governance of the Inns hardly has changed in response. There are no black benchers, although blacks constitute at least 5 percent of the Bar. Women constitute only 2 percent of the benchers, although they represent 12 percent of the Bar. In the mid-1970s, juniors constituted only 5 percent of the benchers, although they represented 90 percent of the practicing Bar. The doubling in the median size of chambers also has altered the structure of governance. On one hand, larger sets may shield their members from external influence, both formal and informal. On the other hand, the sets themselves may have become more important loci of control. Because the vast majority of heads are elderly white males, the hierarchy within chambers reinforces traditional authority. Extensive socializing among the small number of barristers' clerks strengthens this informal control. Yet a few may be able to retain some autonomy from informal influences because they have physically isolated themselves from the Inns or because their members, head, and clerk are predominately black, female, youthful, or politically dissident.

The greatest institutional transformation in the governance of barristers was the creation of the Senate of the Inns of Court and the Bar in 1966. Unlike the Bar Council (which it absorbed eight years later), the Senate enjoys both substantial resources and significant authority. Although membership is voluntary, more than 80 percent of private practitioners subscribe. In order to enhance its legitimacy, it has coopted laypersons onto certain committees, most notably those charged with discipline. Its governance still is not much more representative than that of the Inns (which continue to appoint twenty-four benchers to the Senate), however, for there are only three women and no blacks in the Senate. Furthermore, within that moiety of all barristers who are employed, probably no more than half belong to the Senate, and only 8 serve on its governing body of more than 100. In addition, although the Senate has centralized the disciplinary powers previously exercised by the four Inns, the new structure— like all forms of professional self-regulation—seems intended more to shield barristers from criticism than to change behavior or punish misconduct. Barristers, who are in the best position to observe their peers, file only 8 percent of all complaints. More than half of the complaints are dismissed without a hearing, and another quarter are either withdrawn or handled summarily. Only 3 percent of complaints between 1968 and 1982 led to disbarment, and only 1 percent led to suspension; the other 96 percent resulted in no significant penalty. In addition to these institutional changes in its structures of governance, the Senate formalized the substantive rules of ethics by promulgating the first Code of Conduct in 1980. Furthermore, dictum in a 1969 case exposing barristers to the threat of malpractice liability for noncontentious activities has led insurers to settle several claims and convinced the Senate to require barristers to carry professional indemnity insurance. Barristers today thus operate under a structure of formal, centralized self-regulation and the specter of increasing external regulation—a situation similar to that of prewar solicitors.

The Law Society also has had to cope with growing diversity in the background of solicitors, the functions that they perform, and the structures within which they practice. Although almost all private practitioners now belong to the Society, its governing council is not remotely representative of the general membership. Women presently hold more than 10 percent of practicing certificates and constitute more than 40 percent of newly admitted solicitors, but the first woman was appointed to the seventy-person council only in 1977. Most solicitors today are at the beginning of their careers, but most council members are at the end of theirs. London solicitors make up a minority of the profession, but they continue to dominate the council. Nearly one out of every ten solicitors is a sole practitioner, but there are none on the council; two-partner firms contain 16 percent of all principals, but such principals represent only 4 percent of council members. Employed solicitors are underrepresented within the Society and even more so on the council.

This disenfranchisement not only has caused tension and apathy within the Society but also has led to the emergence and growth of rival organizations. Local law societies continue to champion the parochial interests of their members. There are specialized associations representing London litigators, criminal solicitors, local government solicitors, employed solicitors, and now legal aid practitioners. The creation of the British Legal Association in the 1960s and its survival for two decades reflects the persistent dissatisfaction of younger solicitors, provincial solicitors, and solo and small firm practitioners. In addition, two other organizational structures threaten to compete with and perhaps even to supplant the professional association. Large firm principals, although still a minority, are likely to insist on governing their own domain, resisting interference by professional associations. At the other end of the status hierarchy, articled clerks, assistant solicitors, and junior employees in government or industry may prefer trade unionism to professionalism. That hallmark of a profession—the capacity to act collectively through a single organization—which solicitors struggled to attain during the nineteenth century, appears to be fragmenting as the interests of discrete and sometimes antagonistic segments are expressed through forms that may be antithetical to professionalism.

The institutions of self-regulation created by the Law Society in the early twentieth century have been strained by postwar changes. Although complaints per solicitor appear to have increased, many instances of misconduct still are overlooked. Solicitors, who are best situated to detect misconduct, file only 14 percent of the complaints. Clients also are reluctant to make accusations; only a third of those with grievances complained to anyone, and only 6 percent of complainants (or 2 percent of all aggrieved clients) addressed the Law Society. Even so, there are more than five times as many complaints per solicitor as there are for each barrister, probably because solicitors have so much more client contact. Yet Law

Society discipline, like that of the Senate, exculpates far more than it punishes. More than two-thirds of all complaints are found unjustified by the investigative body (the Professional Purposes Committee), and others are terminated with only a reprimand. In those cases sent to the Disciplinary Tribunal, less than half of the solicitors are struck from the roll or suspended. In summary, the Society punished less than 1 percent of all solicitors who were the object of complaints between 1973 and 1979. Public dissatisfaction with this record, together with periodic scandals, have led the Society to appoint lay members to the Disciplinary Tribunal, establish a Lay Observer to hear complaints about the disciplinary process, and, most recently, add laypersons to the Professional Purposes Committee (in response to the Glanville Davies affair); however, these reforms appear to have achieved neither a significant voice for the laity nor the restoration of public confidence.

Self-regulation has been threatened from other directions as well. First, although the Society hired a staff to investigate solicitor accounts in 1945 and has enlarged it steadily, the compensation fund has had to make increasingly greater payments to the clients of defaulting solicitors, rising from about £100,000 a year in the 1960s to nearly £2,000,000 in 1984 —an increase that far outstrips the combined effect of inflation and the growth of the profession. Given the sums involved, it is not clear how long the Law Society can preserve this as an ex gratia scheme rather than a legal liability. Second, more clients are charging solicitors with malpractice. In the 1960s, only about half of all solicitors carried malpractice insurance, and less than 10 percent were sued each year. The Law Society required insurance in 1976, and one index of the greater frequency, magnitude, and success of malpractice claims is the fact that premiums doubled in the next four years. Furthermore, the apportionment of the Law Society's master premium among solicitors recently became a point of bitter contention between the larger City firms and small firms and sole practitioners, leading to an upsurge in support for the position of the British Legal Association. Competence increasingly is evaluated by the courts rather than the Law Society, therefore, and there is a real danger that the latter also will lose some or all of its authority to punish ethical violations and to deal with financial misconduct.

THE TRAJECTORY OF PROFESSIONALISM

BARRISTERS AND SOLICITORS AS ALTERNATIVE MODELS

The history of barristers and solicitors during the last two centuries offers unparalleled insights into the trajectory of professionalism. These two branches must resolve similar problems because they perform overlapping functions within a common social, economic, and political environment. Yet, they entered the period with different endowments, have pursued different strategies, and confront different futures. At the beginning of the nineteenth century, barristers already were an established profession, legitimated by traditional warrants. Solicitors, by contrast, still had to carve out their place within the division of labor and weld disparate occupations into a unified whole, while trying to legitimate the new entity by reference to utility rather than history. The Bar was a small, homogeneous, geographically centralized collectivity performing a limited repertoire of functions. Solicitors (who lack any similar collective label) were a much larger aggregation of heterogeneous, geographically dispersed individuals performing a wide variety of functions.

These attributes and resources help to explain the divergent strategies adopted by the two branches in pursuing the professional project of market control and collective mobility. As long as possible, barristers sought to evoke an aristocratic ideal, employing ascribed characteristics— qualities of the whole person—as the principal, sometimes the sole, criterion for entry. Solicitors, by contrast, initiated their struggle for supply control by imposing measures of technical competence, which they gradually made more rigorous. Whereas the barriers to becoming a barrister were relatively informal and invisible—most notably pupillage (which was not required until after World War II), tenancy, and the difficulty of obtaining business—the professional examinations that the aspiring solicitor had to pass were highly formal and visible. The restrictive practices by which barristers limited intraprofessional competition—for instance, membership in a circuit, the role of chambers and clerks, or relations between seniors and juniors—were traditional and initially informal, although they were gradually formalized toward the end of the nineteenth century. By contrast, solicitors' scale fees were not only formal but imposed externally. The Bar saw no need to promulgate an ethical code and governed itself through a multiplicity of traditional institutions. Solicitors devoted considerable energy to refining ethical rules, created a single, formally representative, professional association, and publicly sanctioned the most egregious forms of misconduct.

At the beginning of the postwar period, therefore, the Bar had preserved largely intact a premodern profession that sought its warrant in gentility and tradition and controlled its market through relatively informal, invisible mechanisms, whereas solicitors had created a modern profession that derived its legitimacy from claims of meritocracy and utility and controlled its market through highly formal, visible mechanisms. Given these divergent histories, it was inevitable that the two branches would respond differently to the challenges of the last few decades. Both suffered an erosion in their control over supply, as a result of the growth of higher education and the decline of gender as an entry barrier. We might have expected solicitors to retain greater control through their reliance on more stringent, formal, visible, and meritocratic criteria; however, the reverse seems to be true. Although the increase in the number of barristers was earlier and proportionally greater, the Bar also has been able to reassert control first by continuing to apply its more traditional, informal, invisible, and ascriptive criteria in the selection of pupils, the grant of tenancies, and the allocation of business. Both branches also have responded to the erosion of supply control by diverting entrants away from private practice and into employment in government or industry and commerce, but once again this has done more to relieve the pressure of numbers within the private Bar. Half of all barristers now are employed; and because they lack a right of audience, they cannot compete with those in private practice (although both barristers and solicitors in employment can compete with private solicitors). Employed barristers are less well integrated within the profession, however, as shown by their lower rate of subscription to the Senate.

The erosion of supply control also undermines the professional project by increasing heterogeneity within the profession, thereby endangering both its unity and its collective status. The response of the Bar has been twofold. First, there has been some segregation of blacks, women, and political activists into separate chambers, as a result of both discrimination and self-selection. Although this may help to quarantine potential dissidents, it also publicly reveals internal disunity. Second, the Bar holds out to all entrants the promise of ascending a lengthy career ladder: earning more, handling weightier matters, representing more prestigious clients, taking silk, and becoming a head of chambers, a Senate member, a bencher, or a judge. This simultaneously controls and integrates recent entrants, who are both more diverse and less socialized than their predecessors; it also preserves the status of those at the top from taint by association with those at the bottom. But the legitimacy of this hierarchy depends on preserving an image of equal access to the apex: to the extent that strata become visibly associated with the race, gender, or class origins of their members, the hierarchy may become a source of internal tension and public opprobrium. Solicitors have had to confront the problem of integrating more women, but fewer blacks. Their solution has been an apprenticeship that is both longer—two years of articles and at least three as an assistant—and more intensively supervised. In the course of this, solicitors distribute new entrants fairly permanently to professional strata defined by firm size, specialty, and geographic location. Here, again, the legitimacy of the hierarchy will depend on whether partnerships and firms are perceived as equally open to all—especially to women.

Weakened control over the production *of* producers also endangers control over production *by* producers. Here, too, the Bar's restrictive practices have been more resilient. Although some rules had to be repealed when formalization exposed them to hostile public scrutiny, barristers still were able to dampen intraprofessional competition through informal understandings. Because advocacy constitutes the core function of the legal profession and contains a good balance of technicality and indetermination, the Bar's exclusive rights of audience have survived largely intact. But much of solicitors' work occupies the periphery of the lawyer's role; although tasks are technical, many also are determinate and thus can be performed by nonprofessionals. Just as solicitors constantly ceded ground to other occupations, so now they have lost their monopoly over conveyancing and with it their ability to set the fees for those conveyances they continue to perform. Barristers also have been more successful in creating demand because, as mediators between citizens and the most visible forms of state power, they perform a core function that the polity feels obligated to subsidize. Economic survival has been attained at considerable cost, however; when half the income of the Bar is derived from public funds, professional control over the market is problematic, indeed.

Both branches have had to respond to heightened competition and the consequent pressure to rationalize the market for their services. As barristers' chambers have grown in size, they have become increasingly significant as the unit of production, notwithstanding the prohibition against sharing fees. Especially in lesser matters, solicitors often send briefs to chambers rather than to specified barristers, and clerks enjoy considerable discretion in distributing them. By performing much of the dirty work of getting and allocating business, clerks relieve barristers of the need to engage in such patently commercial practices as advertising. Subject-matter specialization by chambers and informal understandings among the small number of senior clerks also suppress competition between chambers. Consequently, despite the increased size and importance of chambers and the growth of hierarchy within them, at least the more senior barristers remain independent professionals.

Solicitors have responded to competition differently. Previously, although most firms produced a similar range of services, they divided the market geographically. The rapid growth in the size of firms, the proliferation of branch offices, and now the possibility of advertising all foster concentration within markets that are becoming increasingly regional, if not yet national. Solicitors no longer can rely on conveyancing to assure themselves a comfortable living, and continuing incursions by lay competitors will compel solicitors to reach out toward new clients, subject matters, and functions, thereby increasing differentiation within the profession. However, the most significant development is likely to be the increasing employment of both solicitors and paraprofessionals. First as an employee and later as an employer, the solicitor is being transformed from an independent professional into a worker and then a capitalist; in both cases, the solicitor is inextricably enmeshed within capitalist relations of production.

The last problem confronting lawyers is their capacity to engage in the self-regulation that is both the privilege and the responsibility of all professions. Neither barristers nor solicitors satisfactorily have responded to the challenges of the postwar transformation. Their structures of governance remain unrepresentative, driving some lawyers to form alternative institutions while breeding apathy in others. In any case, the official associations have lost significant power over their members—to both the state and the ever-larger and more bureaucratic units of production, such as public and private employers, barristers' chambers, and solicitors' firms. Attempts to restore popular legitimacy by coopting laypersons onto governing bodies and disciplinary boards have produced no measurable increase in public respect. Self-regulation is being circumvented by malpractice claims. It is unclear whether either branch today can govern or discipline itself effectively.

THE FUTURE OF PROFESSIONALISM

In light of the experience of recent decades, what does the future hold for the English legal professions? The dilemma of prediction is that its stimulus typically is some unanticipated change but its technique remains the extrapolation of existing trends. At the risk of falling into just this error, I will refrain from trying to forecast further shifts as abrupt and unprecedented as the expansion of higher education and the entry of women, which initiated the present era of change, and content myself with speculating about the cumulative effect of recent tendencies. Barring a drastic contraction of academic legal education, which seems politically unfeasible even if it might be attractive to the present Government, both branches will continue to grow until the cohorts of older lawyers all have retired. Each branch will expand by about half before the end of the century and then grow at a lesser rate for another ten years. Women will constitute a fifth of the Bar and two-fifths of all solicitors. Because private practice cannot absorb these numbers, government and industry and commerce will employ the excess, with the result that legal education will become less a professional qualification and more a credential for membership in the administrative class (broadly conceived as including all those who exercise managerial functions in either the public or the private sector). Competition will intensify among those who persist in aspiring to be true professionals (as I have used that term)—that is, private practitioners.

Younger barristers will continue to be almost entirely dependent on public funds and, in that way, subject to state control. Younger solicitors will have little choice but to seek employment in increasingly hierarchical and bureaucratic firms, attracted by an ever-receding prospect of partnership. Moreover, all solicitors must resign themselves to losing more business to lay competitors; to the extent that firms respond by increasing their use of paraprofessionals, this will displace even more solicitors. If, as a result, the Law Society turns its attention in the other direction and renews its attack on barristers' exclusive rights of audience, the similarity of academic education and professional training in the two branches will make it increasingly difficult for the Bar to resist. The consequence may be fusion, although some lawyers will continue to specialize in advocacy in response to consumer choice rather than professional rules. Neither the Senate nor the Law Society will be able to represent or govern this increasingly heterogeneous collection of occupations. In any case, such professional associations will be largely irrelevant to employed lawyers (who will constitute a majority of both branches); and collective self-regulation will be supplanted by both direct state control and bureaucratic controls within the units of production.

Professionalism—in the sense in which both champions and critics have used that concept during the last two centuries—will not disappear. It will persist as both a nostalgic ideal and a source of legitimation for increasingly anachronistic practices, although it will lose considerable credibility. It will continue to reflect the experience of a dwindling elite—some profit-sharing partners in solicitors' firms and the handful of more successful barristers—who will remain largely impervious to state control and continue to dominate their markets and govern their professional associations. For the mass of lawyers, however, occupational life will mean either employment by a large bureaucracy, dependence on a public paymaster, or competition within an increasingly free market. Whichever they choose, these lawyers no longer will enjoy the distinctive privileges of professionals—control over the market for their services and high social status. The age of professionalism is ending.

Tables

2.1. Barristers, Solicitors, and Law Students

Year	Barristers				Solicitors			Education[c]	
	Census	Private practice	Starting practice	Calls to bar[a]	Census	Practicing certificates	Admitted to roll[b]	Law students	Law degrees
1985		5,367	335	945		46,490	2,687		
1984		5,203	325	902		44,837	2,728		
1983		5,032	323	1,052		42,984	2,596	14,362	3,816
1982		4,864	282	936		41,738	2,241		
1981		4,685	270	904		39,795	3,223		
1980		4,589	309	862		37,832	3,538	12,603	3,564
1979		4,412	302	896		34,090	2,552	12,105	3,411
1978		4,263	285	954		32,864	2,538	11,817	3,328
1977		4,076	326	843		32,812	2,480	11,430	3,102
1976		3,881	382	857		31,250	2,184	11,136	2,635
1975		3,646	364	902		29,850	2,203	10,273	2,374
1974		3,368	299	741		28,741	1,849	9,223	2,180
1973		3,137	321	913		27,379	1,764	8,259	2,004
1972		2,919	275	1,011		26,327	1,713	7,335	1,817
1971		2,714	222	979		25,366	1,682	6,574	1,709
1970		2,584	241	935		24,407	1,877	5,998	1,558
1969		2,448	137	688		23,574	1,365		1,558
1968		2,379	139	525		22,787	997		1,451

2.1. Continued

Year	Barristers				Solicitors			Education[c]	
	Census	Private practice	Starting practice	Calls to bar[a]	Census	Practicing certificates	Admitted to roll[b]	Law students	Law degrees
1967		2,333	206	559		22,223	1,107		1,306
1966		2,239	129	528		21,672	1,123		1,161
1965		2,164	138	751		21,255	1,009	4,204	1,072
1964		2,118	80	729		20,683	663	3,838	
1963		2,073	158	792		20,269	805	3,543	929
1962		1,964	110	737		19,790	766	3,401	
1961		1,918	108	687		19,438	685	3,169	
1960		1,919	85	682		19,069	711	3,070	876
1959		1,923	88	692		18,740	784	3,002	
1958		1,947	91	626		18,522	673	3,041	821
1957		1,968	97	546		18,344	734		
1956		1,973	111	523		18,165	745		
1955		2,008	114	601		18,143	695		
1954		2,010	136	513		17,831	603		
1953		1,907	155	536		17,687	649	2,640	
1952			165	597		17,628	588		
1951	3,084		174	501	19,689	17,396	717		
1950			156	551		17,035	926		
1949			196	514		16,318	895		
1948			177	481		15,567	877		576
1947			131	372		15,348	904		
1946				308			441		

Year						
1945		169		12,979	180	
1944		92		13,063	117	
1943		105		13,340	122	
1942		97		18,835	104	
1941		156		14,430	194	
1940		192		15,884	323	
1939		319		17,102	567	
1938		294		16,899	932	1,515
1937		290		16,478	831	
1936		312		16,299	751	
1935		293		16,132	630	
1934		332		15,941	655	
1933		319		15,783	595	1,804
1932		345		15,616	695	
1931	2,966	321	15,777	15,668	615	
1930		354		15,418	680	
1929		342		15,297	610	
1928		342		15,168	580	
1927		336		15,143	440	
1926		332		15,152	455	
1925		389		15,132	455	
1924		366		15,071	455	
1923		422		15,026	444	
1922		395		14,889	446	
1921	2,953	315	14,956	14,623	383	
1920		254		14,767	606	
1919		298		14,380	335	

2.1. Continued

	Barristers					Solicitors		Education[c]	
Year	Census	Private practice	Starting practice	Calls to bar[a]	Census	Practicing certificates	Admitted to roll[b]	Law students	Law degrees
1918				149		14,040	81		
1917				136		13,846	95		
1916				176		14,362	111		
1915				203		14,988	158		
1914				344		15,887	351		
1913				503		16,788	485		
1912				414		16,759	494		
1911	4,121[d]			357		16,739	489		
1910				356		16,841	501		
1909				337		16,797	561		
1908				304		16,725	512		
1907				322		16,741	590		
1906				298		16,624	591		
1905				322		16,508	593		
1904				276		16,455	637		
1903				260		16,362	558		
1902				290		16,265	557		
1901	4,733[d]			245		16,136	584		
1900				210		16,006	593		
1899				291		15,950	633		
1898				260		15,810	581		
1897				241		15,629	698[e]		

Year				
1896		264	15,518	698[e]
1895		270	15,424	698[e]
1894		299	15,402	698[e]
1893		303	15,281	698[e]
1892		270	15,165	698[e]
1891	4,823[d]	275	15,167	662
1890		271	15,090	716
1889		230	14,896	842
1888		259	14,788	829
1887		266	14,311	882
1886		257	13,893	
1885		256	13,592	
1884		246	13,390	
1883		233	13,066	
1882		268	12,961	808
1881	4,792[d]	256	12,565	
1880		272	12,688	
1879		262	12,263	
1878		187		
1877		252		
1876		204		
1875		259		
1874		270		
1873		280		
1872		259		
1871		244	10,576	
1870		227		

2.1. *Continued*

Year	Barristers				Solicitors			Education[c]	
	Census	Private practice	Starting practice	Calls to bar[a]	Census	Practicing certificates	Admitted to roll[b]	Law students	Law degrees
1869				228					
1868				203					
1867				182					
1866				211					
1865				189		10,200			
1864				178					
1863				165		10,418			
1862				179					
1861	3,071			121	11,386	10,029			
1860				120					
1859				137		10,047			
1858				132					
1857				113					
1856				113					
1855				119			347		
1854				140					
1853				157		10,200			
1852									
1851	2,816				11,350	9,957			
1850						10,087			
1849						9,943			
1848									

Year				
1847				
1846				
1845			10,188	
1844			9,042	
1843			9,939	391
1842				
1841	2,088	11,684[f]		
1840				
1839				
1838				
1837				
1836				
1835			10,436	
1834				
1833				
1832		8,702	8,061	
1831			9,083	

[a]Between 1948 and 1974 overseas students gradually increased from a third of all calls to three-fourths before falling back to a fourth. Almost none of these entered practice in England. Prior to 1948 the proportion of calls represented by overseas students is not available but must have been considerable. No calls to Gray's Inn were recorded before 1890.

[b]Figures for 1924–1934 inclusive are estimates.

[c]First degree full time; excludes mixed degree, part-time, external, and postgraduate students.

[d]Census combines solicitors and barristers; this figure is difference between census and solicitors with practicing certificates. It overstates number of barristers because many solicitors do not take out practicing certificates.

[e]Average for the years 1892–1897 inclusive.

[f]Includes law writers and law students.

2.2. Distribution of Solicitors Holding Practicing Certificates Among Practice Categories, 1939, 1955, and 1957–1985

Year (ends 10/31)	Partnership	Assistant solicitor	Sole practitioner	Sole practitioner and other employment	Sole practitioner and assistant solicitor	Sole practitioner and partnership	Partnership and assistant solicitor	Partnership and other employment	Commissioner for oaths	Consultant	H.M. Forces	Not in active practice, retired, unemployed	Commerce, industry, and nationalized enterprises	Central government[a]	Local government	Other full-time employment	Practicing abroad
1985	22,053	11,793	4,031	121	80	58	—[b]	—[b]	—[b]	2,057	—[b]	114	1,989	163	2,896	1,037	98
1984	19,875	12,610	3,840	269	24	60	—[b]	—[b]	—[b]	2,034	—[b]	22	1,829	100	3,000	1,175	12
1983	19,467	10,591	3,908	338	32	52	—[b]	—[b]	—[b]	1,906	—[b]	46	1,931	106	2,869	1,679	19
1982	19,065	10,860	3,398	337	46	117	18	166	2	1,773	1	44	1,799	66	2,899	1,005	102
1981	18,377	10,701	3,060	239	41	100	18	42	4	1,673	2	28	1,715	68	2,746	873	108
1980	17,922	9,580	2,815	305	16	96	16	92	6	1,590	3	15	1,636	166	2,627	869	78
1979	17,419	8,537	2,634	343	27	89	15	98	5	1,464	2	33	1,513	215	2,594	761	21
1978	17,061	7,645	2,478	184	16	89	14	66	4	1,382	2	32	1,238	258	2,520	771	104
1977	16,808	6,989	2,691	135	56	109	29	48	4	1,280	3	86	1,092	296	2,465	702	82
1976	16,400	6,223	2,895	131	65	153	22	39	2	1,031	1	33	952	336	2,370	561	36
1975	15,956	5,775	2,894	123	48	64	30	39	6	1,001	1	68	985	353	1,710	746	51
1974	15,387	5,226	2,778	163	66	89	24	69	9	965	2	49	1,143	428	1,965	344	34
1973	14,670	5,712	2,773	108	56	73	8	15	9	392	2	50	983	48	1,883	574	23
1972	13,657	5,860	2,719	143	131	139	11	11	7	381	1	42	851	48	1,804	484	38
1971	13,585	5,015	2,725	139	131	142	12	10	11	385	1	47	822	48	1,785	475	33
1970	13,401	4,252	2,738	127	128	133	12	10	8	391	1	52	795	49	1,776	501	33
1969	13,077	3,825	2,754	127	112	129	12	10	6	398	1	50	773	49	1,748	472	31
1968	12,784	3,474	2,769	112	95	119	12	9	6	380	1	50	745	47	1,721	430	33
1967	12,184	3,428	2,874	149	105	113	12	7	8	342	1	63	732	49	1,667	408	28
1966	11,686	3,367	2,987	181	122	120	17	28	7	296	1	71	677	47	1,672	363	30
1965	11,377	3,274	3,006	196	131	147	18	35	13	274	1	66	657	47	1,635	344	33
1964	11,099	3,142	3,014	161	135	141	15	43	8	230	2	62	632	48	1,592	327	31
1963	10,851	3,017	3,045	138	151	156	20	52	12	201	2	65	581	55	1,566	320	37
1962	10,539	2,943	3,057	124	139	167	12	53	8	198	7	47	523	54	1,544	336	39
1961	10,192	3,044	3,138	155	98	149	15	45	3	147	19	54	470	57	1,507	310	25
1960	9,897	2,887	3,289	163	104	122	17	43	7	122	28	57	458	46	1,464	351	14
1959	9,760	2,785	3,277	140	115	128	18	45	10	86	12	46	452	34	1,446	361	19
1958	9,717	2,704	3,245	138	113	117	18	43	5	68	40	48	407	35	1,413	347	18
1957	9,661	2,520	3,207	143	149	125	19	42	10	39	31	67	430	26	1,409	328	14
1955	9,500	2,500	3,500										404	37	1,375	309	
1939	6,937	2,256	3,986										512		1991		

[a] The central government obviously made two abrupt changes in its policies concerning whether solicitor employees had to take out practicing certificates, in 1974 and in 1981.

[b] No longer separately identified.

NOTE

An earlier version of this chapter was presented as the Chorley Lecture in June 1985 and published in 49 *Modern Law Review* 1 (1986). The data on English lawyers that ground my argument are presented and documented thoroughly in my book *The Legal Profession in England and Wales* (Basil Blackwell, 1987). Consequently, I have omitted all references here. I have used the adjective "English" throughout as a shorthand reference to England and Wales; my comments do not apply to Northern Ireland or Scotland.

I have been assisted in this research by so many people and institutions that I cannot thank them all individually. The Law Department of the London School of Economics kindly offered me hospitality during the fall of 1982. The Academic Senate, the Law School Dean's Fund, and the Committee on International and Comparative Studies of the University of California, Los Angeles and the Law and Social Science Program of the National Science Foundation (Grant Numbers SES 81-10380, 83-10162, and 84-20295) all provided generous financial support. Aubrey Diamond helpfully arranged for me to present some of these ideas at a seminar at the Institute of Advanced Legal Studies, the participants at which offered invaluable comments and criticism. The Chorley Lecture provided a stimulus and opportunity to develop them more fully. Stuart Anderson, Philip Lewis, Simon Roberts, David Sugarman, and Michael Zander have read drafts and furnished essential information, and Geoffrey Bindman has patiently answered endless questions. My intellectual debt to the sociological writings of Eliot Freidson and Magali Sarfatti Larson will be obvious throughout.

3

The Legal Profession in Scotland

An Endangered Species or a
Problem Case for Market Theory?

ALAN A. PATERSON

Readers of professional legal journals in the United Kingdom could well be forgiven for believing that the profession now is facing a period of unprecedented crisis. A numbers explosion in the Scottish legal profession has prompted talk of unemployment and of the need to impose quotas on entry. The threat to the solicitors' conveyancing monopoly and the erosion of the restrictive practices of both branches of the profession under government pressure has increased lawyers' awareness of competition and market forces. Not content with its successes in stimulating government action, a burgeoning consumer movement is further undermining the profession's powers of self-regulation by campaigning for higher standards of competence and ethics and a more independent complaints procedure. Finally, the spiraling cost of legal aid on both sides of the border raises the specter of government cuts in legal aid expenditure and hence in the fee income of lawyers with a substantial legal aid practice.[1] Richard Abel (see chapters 2 and 5) views these developments as symptoms of the decline of professionalism, which he defines as the ability of an occupation to control the market for its services. Each problem outlined above, he claims, has eroded the profession's control of the supply of lawyers and legal services. In this chapter I shall argue that (at least in the Scottish context and possibly elsewhere) Abel's account of professions is misleading and that he has misinterpreted the signs; cycles of growth and competition have played an integral part in the profession's history.

It is clear from the recent burst of writing on the sociology of the professions (for bibliographies, see Dingwall and Lewis [1983] and Freidson [1986]) that we are no nearer to consensus on the definition of a profession. Freidson (1983: 19), however, surely is right in arguing that writers must continue to define what they understand by the concept and that such definitions will consist of sets of attributes. In my view, occupations in Scotland that have evolved into professions over the last few centuries have been marked, inter alia, by a service ethic, high social status, possession of a corpus of expert knowledge (not shared with other occupations), and autonomy—that is, the ability to regulate admission, promulgate ethical standards, and discipline their members.[2] Abel argues (chapter 2) that a profession also must possess the ability to act collectively through a single organization. I also agree that, particularly in times of crisis, occupations we recognize as professions are likely to seek to develop, influence, or even control the market for their services. Nevertheless, this in no way distinguishes professions from guilds, trade unions, or many occupations today. It is not clear, therefore, why the pursuit of market control should be chosen as a defining characteristic, let alone *the* defining characteristic, of a profession.

HISTORICAL BACKGROUND

To see the weakness of a market control approach, particularly in the Scottish context, one must know the historical background of the profession. The Scottish profession (like the English) is a divided one. By far the larger sector consists of solicitors (formerly known also as "writers" or "law agents"). Most practicing solicitors work in private practice (either on their own or in partnerships), but in recent years an increasing proportion have been attracted into industry and local or central government. Traditionally, solicitors in private practice have been perceived, and have seen themselves, as general "people of business." As such, they have offered professional services in a wide variety of areas ranging from the purchase, sale, and lease of land and other property to the making of wills and the administration of trusts and estates and from advice on commercial, company, tax, and family matters to advice and (in the lower courts) advocacy in civil and criminal litigation.

The smaller sector of the profession consists of the Scottish Bar or Faculty of Advocates. Most advocates who practice do so in the private sector, although a minority are employed or instructed on a regular basis by central government. Advocates have a monopoly of audience in the higher courts; with some minor exceptions, they can receive instructions only through practicing solicitors, not directly from clients. Judges in Scotland and England normally are not treated as members of the legal profession (although judges appointed from the Bar—i.e., all superior court judges and some in the inferior courts—continue to be members of the Faculty of Advocates). In fact, it can be argued that judges are not members of any profession (Paterson, 1983).

Before the sixteenth century "men of law" (as lawyers were known) usually were drawn from the ranks of the clergy. Because there were no

Scottish universities prior to the fifteenth century, legal education (which was confined to the art of the notary and canon law) was acquired either by apprenticeship or in monasteries, cathedrals, and such continental universities as Paris, Orleans, Avignon, Bologna, or Cologne.[3] The split profession can be traced to this era, for by the fifteenth century a division of labor was evolving between the notaries (appointed by the pope or local bishops), who tended to specialize in the drafting of writs and deeds, and pleaders, who concentrated on court appearances.

The founding in the fifteenth and sixteenth centuries of the first Scottish universities with courses in civil (i.e., Roman) and canon law had little impact on the training of Scottish lawyers. The great majority continued either to study at continental universities or to acquire their skills through apprenticeships. By the early sixteenth century civil law had ceased to be taught in the Scottish universities, and canon law was taught there only sporadically until the Scottish Reformation in 1560. Thereafter, legal studies suffered an almost terminal decline from which they did not recover until the beginning of the eighteenth century.

Perhaps of greater significance was the substantial increase in the number of notaries (particularly lay notaries) during this period, in part because a 1469 statute enabled the king to appoint notaries. The expansion brought with it a loss of homogeneity and a lowering of ethical standards, felt all the more keenly because of the role of the notary in land transactions. Indeed, the problem of "false nottars (notaries)" looms large in sixteenth century legislation: a 1563 act introduced a Register of Admission; another in 1587 regulated apprenticeships and qualifications. The efficacy of these reforms was undermined, however, by the lack of an organization to lead the occupation.

If notaries were the precursors of contemporary solicitors, the origins of the Bar could be traced to the procurators and prelocutors who undertook court appearances during the sixteenth century. In 1532 the College of Justice was founded in Edinburgh. This body included Scotland's highest court (the Court of Session), the clerks to the Signet (who were responsible for affixing the Signet Seal of the King's secretary of state to legal documents), and a group of up to ten procurators with exclusive rights to practice before the court. During the next hundred years the Faculty of Advocates (the Scottish Bar) evolved from this group of procurators. The Faculty had (and still has) no written constitution, but in its origins, traditions, and structure it was (and in some respects still is) nearer to continental bars than to that of England and Wales. Its members, like English barristers of the same period, were recruited largely from the higher social strata: between 1532 and 1688 half of the Faculty came from noble families (Donaldson, 1976: 162). Of the sixty advocates admitted between 1575 and 1608, two-thirds claimed to have an academic qualification (Hannay, 1933: 145). Throughout the seventeenth and early eighteenth centuries, many aspiring advocates in pursuit of an academic qualification made their way to the Protestant universities of Holland to be instructed in civil law—often by Scottish teachers.[4]

During the seventeenth century the Faculty began to elect its own leader (the dean). This office was modeled closely on the batonnier of the Paris Bar, and its remit included disciplining members of the Bar. Yet the Faculty of Advocates arguably did not achieve the status of a profession until the very end of the century, for control over admissions remained with the Court of Session judges. In 1664 the Faculty obtained the right to set up its own admissions procedure, which was modeled closely on the examinations and laureation procedures of European universities (Cairns, 1986: 260). Candidates first had to pass a written examination in civil law. Next, they were required to compose and defend (in Latin) before the entire Faculty a thesis on a specified topic in civil law. If the Faculty voted to admit them, candidates had to present a "public lesson" (again in Latin) to the Court of Session on the same civil law topic (Cairns, 1986: 255; Hannay, 1933: 160). The court also retained the right to admit candidates who had not taken the civil law examinations provided they had long attended the court and knew Scottish law. Candidates for this "extraordinary entrance" procedure frequently had received much more by way of practical training than either their far more numerous counterparts who took the examination in civil law or contemporaneous entrants to the English Bar. Because advocates were concerned about the competition engendered by the great number of entrants and also because of the social stigma attached to entrants who had not undergone a costly continental education, the Faculty tried another ploy. In 1678 they more than doubled the fee for candidates seeking to enter by civil law examination, raising it to the substantial sum of £30. Candidates for admission by the less prestigious route of dispensation of the court (trial in Scottish law) were required to pay twice this amount. The increases were a blatant attempt to control the supply of advocates but were justified by the Faculty as needed to establish the now celebrated library of the Faculty. At first the court refused to authorize the increases, but in the face of evidence that all entrants since 1678 voluntarily had paid the new fees,[5] the court gave way in 1683. Finally, in 1692 the Faculty gained the right to examine even candidates who entered by trial in Scottish law, in which cases it agreed that the Lords of Session (the court) should be "well informed of the person's integrity, good-breeding, honest deportment and fitness for exercising the office of an advocate."[6]

Ironically, just as the Bar's attempts to establish its autonomy and hence its identity as a profession were bearing fruit, it was losing control over part of its market. The general procurators with exclusive rights to practice before the court in 1532 fulfilled the dual role of agent and advocate. As business expanded, the procurators delegated work other than advocacy to their clerks or first clerks. This appears to have encouraged some of the clerks to the Signet (who had formed themselves into the Society of Writers to the Signet by 1594) to attempt to serve as both conveyancers (in competition with notaries) and agents before the court. Eight statutory instruments and one act of the Scottish Parliament were passed during the sixteenth and seventeenth centuries in an attempt to curtail the activities of self-styled agents or "opportune sollisteirs"—but to no avail. By the start of the eighteenth century, Writers to the Signet and others frequently were acting as agents before the court, although it did not license the office of agent or solicitor until 1754. The Faculty of Advocates clearly had lost its long battle to retain its monopoly rights as agents. (History does not record whether the loss was perceived as presaging the demise of the profession.) Further confirmation of the emergence of solicitors as a separate occupational group came in 1772, when a statutory instrument gave them responsibility for maintaining high entry standards. Candidates were required to demonstrate a satisfactory knowledge of the business of agent and to be of good moral character (Barclay, 1984: 6).

Apart from the growth of business (particularly bankruptcy litigation) at the end of the seventeenth century, another reason for the failure of the Faculty of Advocates to defend its monopoly over the role of agent may have been that its members had other concerns. Twice in the 1670s the advocates boycotted the Bar—once over a government attempt to limit fees and once over the Crown's attempts to prevent appeals from the Court of Session from going to the Scottish Parliament. With the departure of the Scottish king to London in 1603 and the demise of the Scottish Parliament following the constitutional union between England and Scotland in 1707, the Faculty became a national forum of considerable significance. From the midseventeenth to the mideighteenth centuries the lesser gentry, who constituted about half of the Faculty, were led by a vigorous and substantial elite drawn from the nobility and families of political consequence. Moreover, in contrast to the English Bar and continental bars of the time (Ranieri, 1985), few members of the Faculty appear to have joined the Bar merely for the social status attached to the role of advocate. Of the 200 advocates in 1714, 170 were in daily practice. Such was the poverty of Scotland that even those from the substantial landed classes needed a career to supplement their incomes. "Membership of the Faculty of Advocates afforded entry to a profession, a way of earning a living and a prestigious one" (Shaw, 1983: 31). Nevertheless, by the end of the eighteenth century, the social elite had begun to turn their backs on the Bar, as they did in England. During the next century less than one entrant in eight was the son of a man of rank. As the Bar lost its homogeneity, its corporate identity and self-esteem began to suffer. With political power centered in London and little control over industrial or mercantile wealth, the Faculty's claims to civic leadership looked increasingly threadbare (Phillipson, 1976: 193).

The influx of sons of professionals or nonlanded families to the Faculty in the latter part of the eighteenth century owed much to the partial erosion of the financial and social barriers to entry to the bar. The emergence of private colleges of Scots law for Writers to the Signet and advocates and the establishment of Chairs in Law at Edinburgh[7] and Glasgow Universities in the first part of the century afforded a cheaper, if less prestigious, alternative to an expensive continental education. Perhaps even more important was the transformation in the Faculty's attitude to its admissions procedures. In the past the trials in civil law had been seen less as a test of knowledge useful for practice than as a guarantee that entrants had received a broad liberal education (preferably at a European university). The trials flowed from the Faculty's vision of itself as a learned body of honorable gentlemen participating in a "pan-European legal culture" (Cairns, 1986). Cairns argues that the eighteenth-century Scottish Enlightenment led the Faculty to see the trials as a means of assessing ability to practice. Achievement began to replace ascription. The new rationalist conception of the admissions test led inevitably to a demand that entrants should have a knowledge of Scottish as well as civil law, and the Faculty's rules were amended accordingly in 1750.

The Society of Writers to the Signet, on the other hand, required only a lengthy apprenticeship and an oral examination that, prior to the eighteenth century, "was none too strict" (Hannay, 1936: xii). Until the nineteenth century the Society generally drew its members from less exalted ranks than the Faculty. The status of being a "WS" (as Writers to the Signet colloquially were known) carried some social prestige and the potential for substantial financial rewards, but it lacked the cachet of being an advocate. Yet the Society was not without its social pretensions. Apprentice Writers to the Signet seem to have had a choice between wearing a wig or their own hair, but dancing and fencing lessons were "absolutely necessary" (Shaw, 1983: 26). In towns where busy inferior courts (sheriff courts) were situated (e.g., Aberdeen, Glasgow, Edinburgh, Dumfries, and Paisley), admission to the local Faculties of Procurators was in the hands of the courts, which usually required an apprenticeship followed by an oral examination and payment of a modest fee. Although entrants were required to treat their examiners to dinner in a local tavern, expertise in the social graces was not a prerequisite (Muirhead, 1948).

Law agents competed fiercely for work during much of the eighteenth and nineteenth centuries, and advertising was not uncommon. By the end of the eighteenth century, all the members of the Faculty of Advocates were acting exclusively as advocates. The Writers to the Signet, having successfully invaded the preserves of the Faculty, found themselves hard pressed by the competition within their own ranks. Earlier attempts to limit their numbers to less than forty "for the benefit of the public" had failed. By 1731 their numbers had grown to 110, "to the great loss of the whole body, for half the members could not possibly live upon their incomes" (Haldane, 1979: xiii). The Writers were facing competition from other agents also. In response they strove hard to prevent the latter from organizing and becoming members of the College of Justice. Although the Society of Solicitors in the Supreme Courts (the SSC Society) eventually was established in 1784, the Royal Charter granted in 1797 expressly preserved the rights and privileges of the Writers' and the advocates' first clerks as agents. Despite the imposition of an annual tax on all licensed solicitors in 1785, the number of Writers to the Signet continued to increase: 200 in 1803 and an astonishing 685 by 1836. Perhaps in response, new regulations promulgated in 1851 required entrants to pay fees of more than £500, complete a five-year apprenticeship, and attend university or receive "a liberal education." It is not clear, however, that this was intended to control supply. Although there was a drop in the number of entrants during the following decade, this caused great consternation within the Society, since its library and staff were dependant on entrance fees. By 1890 there were only 440 Writers to the Signet. At the outbreak of World War I, numbers had risen to 626, but it was not until the 1970s that the total exceeded 700.

Throughout much of the nineteenth century the Writers to the Signet sought to assert monopolies or privileges against other practitioners of law, eliciting quick responses from the younger and less prestigious SSC Society.[8] Competition (and the imposition of an £85 stamp duty on admissions) also brought about the demise of the Society of Advocates' First Clerks, who amalgamated with the SSC Society in 1850. By 1859 there were 220 SSCs, who claimed to have more than half of the agency business in the supreme courts. They were not satisfied, however. Although they unsuccessfully challenged the exclusive rights of audience that the local Faculties of Procurators asserted in "their" sheriff courts; however, they successfully asserted against the procurators their exclusive rights (together with the Writers to the Signet) to act as agents in the supreme courts. In 1873, following a Royal Commission report, the Law Agents Act was passed, abolishing the exclusive privileges of all solicitors' societies.

The Faculty of Advocates, as we have seen, also was troubled by competition both within its own ranks and from law agents in the late seventeenth century. The raising of entrance fees in 1678 did little to control numbers. In fact, admissions continued to rise until the early eighteenth century, when a severe shortage of business seems to have discouraged candidates. By the middle of the century, however, with the erosion of financial barriers to entry, numbers were increasing again.[9] Between 1660 and 1800 an average of sixty advocates were admitted per decade. In the early part of the nineteenth century, however, admissions to the Faculty rose dramatically (paralleling a similar rise in admissions of Writers to the Signet and English solicitors), reaching a peak of 180 per decade—an unprecedented rate of increase never matched even in modern times. Work for the Scottish Bar does not appear to have expanded as rapidly, and many entrants soon left practice. Although admissions had declined to 100 per decade in 1860, an anonymous advocate complained that five-sixths of those called since 1850 still were practicing, despite a great shortage of litigation. This "singular exception to the natural law of supply and demand" he attributed to the ignorance of entrants about the prospects of professional success (Anon., 1860: 446). We can see, therefore, that the recent numbers explosion in the Scottish legal profession and the high level of competition among its members are not unprecedented. They do not herald the end of the profession, nor are they necessarily the result of a failure in market control mechanisms.

EDUCATION AND RECRUITMENT IN MODERN TIMES

In the nineteenth century many Scottish lawyers began to attend Scottish university law courses. An 1825 statute laid down that all procurators, writers, and law agents should serve an apprenticeship of at least three years and satisfy the examination requirements of their Society or Faculty. Many apprentices (particularly in Edinburgh and Glasgow) prepared for these examinations at university classes.[10] Attendance at university classes was strongly recommended for advocates and compulsory for Writers to the Signet and SSCs, but attendance meant no more than that. The professional bodies still conducted examinations. An 1830 report indicated that, although the Scottish law class at Edinburgh University contained 250 students, there never had been "any examination whatever" in the class (Barclay, 1984: 154). This revealed the influence professional bodies had exercised on legal education in Scottish universities since its revival in the early eighteenth century. The chairs in law established in Edinburgh, Glasgow, and Aberdeen Universities during the eighteenth and early nineteenth centuries were the direct result of pressure from the Faculty of Advocates, the Society of Writers to the Signet, and the SSC. Because the professional bodies retained a strong say in appointments to the chairs, incumbents invariably were practitioners (many of whom continued to practice). It is not surprising, therefore, that university law classes were geared toward the professional examinations.[11]

The educational standards for admission to the practice of law gradually became more stringent throughout the nineteenth century. The Faculty of Advocates added conflict of laws to its professional examinations and made attendance at university law classes compulsory. For aspiring law agents the more prestigious societies and faculties introduced written examinations. Attempts to raise the quality of university legal education were less successful. Few of those who attended the classes graduated from the universities, perhaps because the first Scottish law degree by examination, the LL.B., was not introduced until 1862. This part-time degree took three years and was available only to students who already held an Arts degree. Soon thereafter an 1865 statute sought to standardize the legal curriculum and the examination regulations for practitioners before the sheriff courts; it also excused LL.B. graduates from the professional examinations. This concession was withdrawn almost immediately, for the Law Agents Act of 1873 introduced new requirements for the admission of all law agents (procurators, writers, and solicitors). They had to be twenty-one years old, serve an apprenticeship of five years (three if they held a degree from a British university), and satisfy the examiners appointed by the Court of Session as to their legal knowledge.[12] Possession of the LL.B. degree no longer conferred exemption from the professional examinations set by the court's examiners. The Court of Session insisted that all applicants attend classes and pass examinations in Scottish law and conveyancing in a Scottish university. In 1886, however, the court concluded that it had exceeded its powers under the 1873 act, and this requirement was not reintroduced until 1931. A further part-time degree, the B.L., was introduced in 1874, which did not require possession of an Arts degree but still qualified its holders for the shorter apprenticeship period of three years. Since it did not confer exemption from professional examinations, however, most students attending law classes failed to obtain a law degree until the twentieth century.

In contrast to the increasingly rigorous requirements demanded of aspiring law agents, the once proud calling of the notary, with its moral attributes, education, Latiny, penmanship, and knowledge of the law (Durkan, 1983), had declined in stature. An apprenticeship no longer was necessary, there were no compulsory law classes, and the examination was largely perfunctory. In 1823 one Craig satisfied the examiners and was admitted as a notary public although he was "ignorant of law, of Latin and of grammar" and "was the father of two natural children."[13] By the latter part of the nineteenth century the office had become a back door into legal practice. To prevent further abuses, an 1891 statute declared that no one could become a notary without first qualifying as a law agent.

The Law Agents Act of 1873 had other effects. The abolition of the monopolies of the individual societies and faculties meant that any Scottish law agent could practice in any court in Scotland, although the Faculty of Advocates retained their exclusive right of audience before the supreme courts. A more curious side effect of the act was that it eliminated the one national organization of solicitors—the General Council of Procurators—but put nothing in its place. In the next forty years several proposals to establish a national society of law agents attracted support from most of the ancient societies and faculties but foundered on the opposition of the Writers to the Signet and the SSC Society, who wished to retain such prestige and privileges (including the power to examine their own apprentices and discipline their own members) as they still possessed. The leading elements in the occupational group thus rejected the creation of a national profession for fear of losing prestige and status. While particular societies and faculties appeared to pursue the professional project, their support for the Law Agents Act of 1873 was aimed at preserving monopolies within the occupational grouping rather than establishing monopoly rights against other occupations.

A Joint Committee of Legal Societies in Scotland was created in 1922 "for discussion of matters of common interest," but it was not until the Solicitors (Scotland) Act of 1933 that one body—the General Council of Solicitors in Scotland—was set up with powers to control the admission and conduct of all members of the profession. Curiously, therefore, while "England's national professional organisation came into being at the formative stage of the profession and came from within the profession ... Scotland's was placed at the head of an occupational body which was very much developed" (Hadfield, 1977: 148). In fact, under both the definition of "profession" offered at the opening of this chapter and that used by Abel (chapter 2), Scottish solicitors did not constitute a national profession until the creation of the General Council.[14] At any rate, within sixteen years this body also had been superseded by another, the Law Society of Scotland, in which membership was (and still is) compulsory for all Scottish solicitors.

Entry to the solicitors' branch changed significantly in the first half of the twentieth century. Once entrants were required to pass university law examinations and law graduates who had taken the appropriate subjects again were exempted from the General Council's examinations, the law degree became (by the 1930s) the most common route. (For much of the century, graduate entry was more common among Scottish solicitors than English, perhaps because an English law degree did not confer exemption from all the professional examinations.) Three-quarters of the entrants took law degrees by 1950, a trend that was reinforced by the abolition of part-time law degrees and the introduction of the full-time LL.B. as a first degree in 1961. By 1979, 96 percent of entrants to the solicitor's profession held a Scottish law degree. A very similar situation prevails in the

Faculty of Advocates, where a law degree containing the appropriate subjects has guaranteed exemption from most of the professional examinations since 1919.

Abel (1982) argues that, since a university law degree now is almost the only route of entry to the legal profession in England, the profession has lost control over the supply of producers of legal services. To assess the applicability of this argument to Scotland it is necessary to look in greater detail at both legal education and the admissions procedures for advocates and solicitors. There are five university law schools in Scotland (see table 1). There are no private law schools, part-time schools, or nonuniversity (e.g., polytechnic) schools. Although the schools vary in size and antiquity, their intakes differ by place of origin rather than social class. Each school tends to draw at least half of its enrollment locally. In its own opinion, at least, the largest and oldest law school (Edinburgh) also is the most prestigious. However, the similarity of admissions criteria and the absence of a consensus as to the relative merits of the schools among either solicitors' firms recruiting trainees or the Faculty of Advocates has meant that school attended has less impact on career than it does in England or the United States.

Scottish law schools receive many more applications than they have places, and demand has increased steadily over the past fifteen years. In 1972, 2,301 applications competed for 463 places (a ratio of 4.9 : 1), but in 1983, following government cuts, there were only 500 places for 3,410 applications (a ratio of 6.8 : 1). This is about half the level in England and Wales; however, given multiple applications, the real level of demand in both countries probably is nearer to 2.2 applicants for each law school place. Because the law schools have responded to the excess of demand over supply by requiring a high level of academic attainment at school, however, many who would like to become lawyers never even apply. Selection is based almost solely on secondary school performance; there is no equivalent of the United States Law School Admissions Test, and few applicants are interviewed. During 1975 to 1981, graduates and mature students accounted for 23 percent of admissions to Edinburgh University Law Faculty; the figures in the other law schools probably were lower.

This apparently meritocratic admissions procedure has undoubted but unintended effects on the social composition of the law student population. There is a strong correlation in Scotland between social class background and academic achievement. Not surprisingly, therefore, Scottish law students are relatively homogeneous and vary little between law schools. Social classes I and II (professionals, employers, and managers in the Registrar General's categorization) accounted for 77 percent of law students admitted to Glasgow between 1971 and 1979 and 68 percent of those admitted to Edinburgh from 1976 to 1980. A survey of students carried out in 1978/79 on behalf of the Royal Commission on Legal Services in Scotland (Hughes Commission, 1980) revealed that 15 percent of law students had close relatives who were or had been lawyers in Scotland. Surveys of entrants carried out by the Law Society of Scotland (the latest in 1980) produced similar results (as did a recent survey in England; see Podmore [1980: 31]); however, there is some evidence that these figures have declined. Preliminary research suggests that the largest single parental occupational group from which Scottish law students now are drawn is the teaching profession.

Unquestionably, the most striking feature of the current law student population is the proportion of women. In 1970 less than 20 percent of law students in Scotland were women. By 1980 the figure had risen to between 35 and 40 percent. Now it is very close to parity; in 1983, following three years in which the majority of the incoming students were women, Edinburgh University Law Faculty became the first Scottish law school in which they were a majority. As the number of women has risen the social origins of students have become more elitist. The availability since 1961 of a government grant to all full-time first-degree law students (covering all fees and a means-tested contribution to maintenance) might have been expected to enlarge the number of low-income students, but the correlation of social background and academic achievement has worked against them. Instead, middle-class women students have squeezed out working-class men. There also are fewer students with a prior degree; they do not qualify for a grant, and bursaries are few. As university fees rise, it is becoming increasingly difficult for these students to support themselves (even though they are permitted to complete their studies in two as opposed to three years).

The number of law students increased 80 percent between the early 1960s and 1977 (see tables 1 and 2), as a direct result of the growth in higher education and government funding. Since 1976 (following government cuts in higher education) admissions to law school have been reduced. With the expansion of the law schools a substantial academic legal profession emerged. Practitioners who taught part time gradually were replaced by full-time academics, many of whom never had qualified as practitioners. This development had a major impact on both the quality of the teaching and the range and content of the courses. Since undergraduates wanted to take the core professional subjects to gain exemption from the professional examinations, however, few took advantage of this wide range of courses. Academic teachers became aware of the problems caused by attempts to squeeze the required and core courses into the curriculum, just as solicitors and graduates began to feel that there were problems with apprenticeships, caused partly by the unprecedented increase in numbers during the 1970s (see table 3).[15] By the late 1960s law graduates expected a higher standard of training than the profession was providing. A report by the Law Apprentices Association in 1973/74 commented on the rudimentary arrangements for practical training in many firms, the lack of a training syllabus, and the absence of assessment during or after training. A survey of apprentices revealed widespread variations in the quality of the training and the use of apprentices for trivial or menial tasks. The increased pace and volume of work in modern offices was making practitioners less willing to devote time to instructing apprentices, and the growing complexity of the law, coupled with greater specialization, was making a thorough, all-around training unattainable.

Following lengthy discussions between the universities and the Law Society, a one-year, full-time, postgraduate Diploma in Legal Practice was introduced in 1980. It consists of several professional subjects formerly contained in the undergraduate curriculum (procedure, accounts, conveyancing, and taxation) and a number of practical subjects (e.g., advocacy and pleading, finance and investment, company management, and legal aid) to compensate for the perceived deficiencies in apprenticeships. All aspiring solicitors and almost all who wish to join the Faculty of Advocates must obtain the Diploma in Legal Practice. This development parallels the vocational courses established by the professional bodies in England and Ireland and the innovations in clinical legal education in the United States, Canada, and Australia, but in other respects these responses to the problem of practical training had little in common. The diploma contains no clinical component. It is not case oriented and relies on simulation when cases are discussed. It was not particularly influenced by the English Ormrod Committee on Legal Education (1971), although the government decision to fund diploma students may well have been. Rather, the diploma was very much a product of the Scottish situation. Although it is taught within the universities, the tutors all are practitioners who teach part time (a curious reversal of the trend toward full-time academics, which began in the 1960s). This suits the universities, since practitioners are less expensive than full-time academics, and it also suits the profession, which retains greater control over education. Like their counterparts in Northern Ireland (but unlike those in England), all students taking this postgraduate vocational course have been entitled to a full government grant; however, government cuts in spending for higher education reduced the number of grants to 410 in 1985/86. Although the universities could admit students without grants, it is likely that institutional jealousies engendered by the cuts will discourage this. The government thus is exercising indirect control over the supply of legal practitioners; yet, this seems to be merely an unintended consequence of financial policies.

Following the introduction of the Diploma in Legal Practice, apprenticeships have been abolished, except for nonlaw graduates (who still can undertake a three-year apprenticeship before embarking on the diploma).[16] Law graduates who successfully have completed the diploma become "trainees," under a two-year "contract of training" with a solicitor. There is no expectation that trainees will receive instruction in all of the three main areas of work handled by most Scottish solicitors: conveyancing, trusts, and litigation. After one year the trainee receives a limited practicing certificate. Following a decline in apprenticeships during the early 1960s, the demand for apprenticeships (fueled by the ever-increasing stream of LL.B. graduates) grew steadily from 1964 to 1979 (see tables 2 and 3). The figures suggest that approximately 80 percent of law graduates in the late 1970s were entering the profession. One unexpected consequence of the introduction of the diploma and traineeships has been that the perennial student desire "to keep one's options open" has led 90 percent of graduates since 1980 to seek to take the diploma. This is why the number seeking to enter the profession has only now begun to drop, even though the number of law graduates peaked in 1979.

ADMISSION TO THE PROFESSION

Entry to the Faculty of Advocates is regulated by the Faculty, not by legislation. Candidates must pass (or gain exemption from) the relevant professional examinations, pass a special examination in evidence and procedure, complete the diploma and traineeship, and serve nine months of pupillage or "deviling" with a practicing member of the Faculty. The public defense (in Latin) of a civil law thesis was abolished only in 1966, but long before then it had become a formality. So, too, had the vote by the Faculty on admissions, although this is retained. The real barrier to entry remains what it has always been—money. As in England, "devils" receive no remuneration during pupillage and do not begin to earn for at least another nine months (even in these days of legal aid). In addition to finding living expenses for two years, entrants must pay entry fees; together with the cost of wig, gown, and formal attire, these exceed £1,000. During the last decade admissions have been running at an average of thirteen a year (see table 4). This is high but not as high as in the early eighteenth and nineteenth centuries. However, the number of women admitted (nineteen in the decade) is unprecedented.

Under the latest statutory provisions (Solicitors [Scotland] Act of 1980, s. 6), Scottish solicitors must be at least twenty-one years old, complete a course of training approved by the Law Society Council, pass the necessary professional examinations (or gain exemption from them), obtain the Diploma in Legal Practice, satisfy the Law Society Council that they are fit and proper persons, and pay the admission dues (approximately £70 at present). Admissions of solicitors always have varied cyclically (see tables 3 and 5). During the late 1950s and early 1960s, entry to the profession was declining rapidly.[17] After 1970, however, the number of entrants rose steadily, and between 1970 and 1984 the annual rate of admissions increased from 112 to 427, a rise of 280 percent. The increase in total numbers probably has reached its peak, but a third trend—the rapid growth in the number of women entering the profession—assuredly has not ended. In 1985, 44 percent of those admitted to practice as solicitors were women, compared to 11 percent in 1975 (see table 12).

SUPPLY CONTROL

It is questionable whether the foregoing trends in legal education and recruitment to the profession can be described fairly as a profession struggling to attain and ultimately losing control over the supply of legal services (Abel, 1982; Larson, 1977). The profession never has been organized so that it easily could determine its own size. The ascriptive barriers to entering the English Bar (see chapter 2) long have applied in Scotland as well (although the lack of a chambers system has eased pupillage and entry to the Faculty of Advocates). The need to be self-supporting for two years (or to have wealthy parents, a working spouse, or an understanding bank manager) has not changed with the recent increase in law graduates. The Faculty's choice not to offer loans or bursaries or pay those in pupillage from the proceeds of a levy shows that it has not lost whatever measure of supply control it previously possessed.

The ascriptive barriers facing aspiring solicitors also have been similar on both sides of the border. Even if there was a Scottish solicitors' profession prior to 1933, it did not exercise substantial control over these barriers. The stamp duty payable on entry (abolished in 1947) and the importance of contacts for securing an apprenticeship were not subject to professional control. Even the supply of apprenticeships never has been controlled directly by the Law Society Council or its predecessors, although the prestigious societies sometimes influenced it: after 1850 the Society of Writers to the Signet required apprentices to pay £500 to the Society, and some local Faculties of Procurators restricted apprenticeships to relatives of members. The supply of apprenticeships generally has been determined by the decisions of individual firms. Today only a third of all firms accept apprentices or trainees. Whereas apprentices and trainees now are paid about £5,000 a year, before 1960 it was not uncommon for apprentices to pay a premium for the privilege of working for little or nothing. While this state of affairs may have been the outcome of market forces, it is not clear that "the profession" ever controlled these matters. It cannot have lost what it never possessed.

Although the profession was concerned by the decline in admissions in the early 1960s and the substantial increase in the 1970s and 1980s, its only response has been to issue exhortations to the law schools. The Law Society Council has not endeavored to reduce the number of entrants by raising the standard of the professional examinations (which currently are easier than their university counterparts) or that of the Diploma in Legal Practice (which is taught and marked by members of the profession). It has not sought reductions in the number of diploma places, and it is very unusual for anyone to be excluded on the grounds of "moral unfitness." While the leaders of the profession did try in 1984 and 1985 to emulate their English counterparts by requiring three years of experience before solicitors could practice on their own (ostensibly to control quality), this was rejected by the profession because of its supply control implications.

The advent of almost universal graduate entry also does not represent a loss of supply control by the profession, for the latter still can stipulate the university courses (and their content) that confer exemption from the professional examinations, as well as the contents of the diploma course. One can argue instead that the profession has retained control of legal education in these crucial respects but successfully passed most of the burden of training entrants to the universities (as occurred in the United States), the state (which foots the bill), and the small minority of the profession who teach the diploma for very meager financial rewards. Abel claims that graduate entry caused the major increase in women entering the profession, which significantly eroded supply control. Even if the prejudice against women in the professions can be viewed largely as a supply control issue, this argument is difficult to sustain. Women have been able to graduate from law school and enter the profession since 1920, yet it was only in the 1970s that their numbers began to rise. Perhaps the fairest conclusion to draw is that the profession's powers to regulate its size have not changed greatly in the past century and that the profession never has tried to exercise such powers as it does possess (Slater, 1982).

COMPOSITION OF THE PROFESSION

The education and recruitment patterns outlined above inevitably exercised a strong influence on the size and composition of the profession. Between 1860 and 1967 the size of the practicing Scottish Bar varied about 15 percent above and below 115 advocates (see table 6), but since 1962 the number has risen steadily from 116 to 195 (84 percent), increasing 52 percent in the decade from 1975 to 1984. This correlates very closely with the increase in Scottish law graduates over the same period. In modern times only about half of the Faculty of Advocates has been in active practice (see table 6) because an advocate, once admitted, remains a member of the faculty even after ceasing to practice or after accepting an appointment incompatible with practice at the Bar. In 1982 the Faculty included 93 judges, 14 academic lawyers, 6 Members of Parliament, 18 advocates working in central government or in industry, another 15 working abroad, and 173 practicing privately. Because most entrants begin in private practice, however, the size of the practicing Bar and competition at the lower end have increased substantially in the last decade.

Reliable statistics about solicitors are in shorter supply. Apart from the records of the prestigious societies, Scottish legal historians have failed to produce even estimates of the size and composition of the solicitors' branch before 1850.[18] Between 1861 and 1911 the number of qualified solicitors (those "enrolled") rose from 1,973 to 3,900 (98 percent) (see table 7). Following World War I and the Great Depression, the number fell to about 3,300 and remained static until after World War II. The number appears to have grown steadily from 3,479 in 1951 to 6,951 in 1984 (99 percent). In fact, the postwar figures are misleading since, as we saw earlier, they conceal a cyclical major downturn in admissions (260 percent) between 1949 and 1965 (see table 5). The figures for private practitioners give us a clearer picture of the supply of legal services. There were 3,555 solicitors in private practice in Scotland in 1911, a peak not reached again until 1978. There were 5,045 in 1985, an increase of 71 percent in a decade. From 1976 to 1985 the number of solicitors holding practicing certificates rose from 3,745 to 6,175 (64.9 percent) (see table 8), closely paralleling the rise in admissions to the profession during this period (in Scotland and elsewhere in the common law world). Nevertheless, it is not possible to ascertain whether the absolute number of individuals doing legal work has reached unprecedented levels because for much of the nineteenth century and the first quarter of the twentieth century a substantial proportion of the work now performed by qualified solicitors was done by unqualified law clerks, who also carried out the clerical tasks since transferred to women secretaries (see table 7).

The changes in the principal sectors within the solicitor's profession since 1954 are shown in table 9. In 1954, 13 percent of the practicing profession worked outside the private sector; the figure rose to 20 percent by 1975 and dropped to 18 percent in 1985 (it was 13 percent in England in 1982). Clearly the central government sector (which rose 334 percent in 30 years) has been the major growth area, and local government also showed a steady increase, but most growth occurred before 1975 in both cases. In-house lawyers, while still comparatively few, also have been increasing, but all the increase occurred in the last decade. During the last decade the private sector has grown faster than the public (71 percent vs. 53 percent), but the private profession has absorbed these increases by greatly expanding the number of qualified assistants rather than the number of partners or sole practitioners. It seems, therefore, that the substantial corps of subordinate employees found in nineteenth and early twentieth century legal offices (see table 7) has been recreated.[19]

Because most of the large number of recent entrants have been in their early twenties, the age profile of the profession has altered dramatically. Between 1962 and 1966 the number of enrolled solicitors under forty years old declined by 20 percent, and those over fifty increased by a similar proportion. Thereafter, the growing number of young recruits led to a rapid fall in the average age. In the mid-1960s only 33 percent of the profession was under forty; in 1972 the proportion still was only 35 percent; however, by 1985, 60 percent was under forty and 27 percent, under thirty. As Abel suggests (chapter 2), this substantial shift in age profile may lead to dissatisfaction with "restrictive practices" and "structures of governance that institutionalize gerontocracy," but it is too early to judge.

The major effect of the changing patterns of education and recruitment has been the increase in the number of women practitioners. Abel (chapter 2) attributes this to the law schools but seems to acknowledge later that this explanation is too facile. After a long battle in the courts and Parliament, women won the right to graduate from Scottish universities in 1889. The first woman did not enroll in a Scottish law school until 1907, and it was only after the Sex Disqualification (Removal) Act of 1919 that women were permitted to enter the profession. Yet, despite the subsequent increase in graduate entry, there was no sign of any substantial growth in the number of women entering the profession for many years. The first woman advocate was admitted in 1923 and the second, in 1949—twenty-six years later. By 1985 a mere 31 women ever had been admitted to the Faculty of Advocates (most of them after 1975), and in 1984 only 16 of the 195 practicing advocates (8 percent) were women (see tables 4, 5, and 11). Women advocates now encounter little prejudice from their colleagues, and prejudice among instructing solicitors (once a considerable problem) has declined markedly (Paxton, 1984). Moreover, the flexibility of work at the Bar makes the profession eminently suited for those with family obligations. Nevertheless (and contrary to the English position), women always have formed a smaller proportion of the Bar than of the solicitors' profession.

In 1972 only 4 percent of practicing solicitors were women. The substantial rise in the admission of women solicitors began in the early 1970s, a few years before the increase in women advocates but long after graduate entry had become the norm and ten years after the introduction of the full-time LL.B. degree with government grants for all students. The rise in the proportion of women solicitors (from 9 percent to 21 percent of enrolled solicitors in the last decade) seems attributable less to graduate entry than to changes in intellectual climate during the 1960s (particularly the rise of the feminist movement).

Nevertheless, the fact that 44 percent of new solicitors now are women does not necessarily mean that discrimination against women in the profession has been eliminated. A 1984 survey of women solicitors (Millar, 1985) revealed that many report encountering discrimination in their careers and feel that male attitudes in the profession have not changed to meet modern conditions. They strongly supported changes in working practices, including the introduction of part-time partnerships, home-based legal practice, and leaves of absence.

There is some empirical support for these attitudes. Women have yet to become principals in any significant numbers. In 1961 there were only 5 women among the 1,209 principals (partners or sole practitioners) in Edinburgh and Glasgow (Scotland's two main cities). By 1985 only 86 (6 percent) of the 1,530 principals in Edinburgh and Glasgow were women, despite the fact that 19 percent of all practicing solicitors in those cities were women. This low figure can be attributed partly to the fact that most women solicitors are young. Yet it is an ominous sign that only 2 of the 148 principals in Scotland's six largest firms in 1984 were women, and it is not clear whether female assistant solicitors are being offered profit-sharing, as opposed to salaried, partnerships as often as are their male counterparts. Whatever difficulties women have experienced, they have not turned away from private practice (as some of their American sisters seem to have done).

This recent influx of women is unlikely to alter the class composition of the profession. In the first sixty years of the twentieth century the absence of university grants and the dearth of scholarships or bursaries, the premiums required of law apprentices, the meager salaries of apprentices and assistants, the stamp duty, the "goodwill" payments required of many new partners, the importance of family connections, and the class consciousness of certain firms ensured that practicing solicitors were predominately middle class in origin (as they were in England and the United States). As we have seen already, the introduction of university grants and the increase in salaries—which might have broadened the social base of the profession— have been offset by the greater number of middle-class women entering the profession, making it more difficult for lower-class men to enter.

ORGANIZATION AND DISTRIBUTION OF SCOTTISH LAWYERS

The recent pattern of recruitment to the profession has had a profound impact not only on its composition but also on its organization and distribution. Because members of the Scottish Bar have exclusive rights of audience in the highest civil and criminal courts (the Court of Session and the High Court of Justiciary), both of which are in Edinburgh, all advocates have chambers there, and attempts to establish chambers in Glasgow have failed, despite the substantial amount of criminal work there. In fact, the Hughes Commission (1980: vol. 2, appendix 10) estimated that at least 10 percent of the Bar's work involves appearances before the sheriff courts (the local courts), tribunals, and inquiries (the Faculty of Advocates estimated the proportion to be 30 percent). In this respect the Scottish advocate differs from many continental advocates, whose work is confined to the higher courts and resembles an English barrister. However, the lack of "provincial bars" in Scotland ensures that the Scottish advocate is much more a "supreme court advocate" than many in England or Ireland.

Despite the substantial flow of entrants to the Scottish Bar, which has heightened competition among junior advocates, even they have not sought changes in work practices, such as the creation of a provincial Bar, the right to form partnerships, or fusion of the two branches. This conservatism may be attributable partly to the fact that litigation (particularly criminal work) has risen as the practicing Bar has grown.[20] Another factor may be the lack of an English chambers system, which has prevented the formation of minority or radical chambers. Moreover, there are considerably fewer employed advocates and private practitioners in proportion to the population than in England. As a result of all these factors, a far smaller proportion of the Scottish than the English Bar specializes. This is true despite the fact that Scottish advocates responded to competition from English barristers in the House of Lords by introducing a formal distinction between seniors (Queen's Counsel) and juniors in 1897. Scottish Queen's Counsel (a larger proportion of the Bar than in England) spend less time on written pleadings than juniors, but otherwise their work is similar.

Nevertheless, recent changes in the recruitment of advocates may increase the division of labor at the Scottish Bar. Many solicitors still instruct women advocates mainly in family matters (Paxton, 1984). Because advocates lost considerable work to solicitors when the sheriff courts were permitted to handle divorce cases in 1984, some advocates will either have to secure more of the divorce work that continues to come to the Court of Session or persuade solicitors to instruct them more frequently in other fields. Another sizeable group of young advocates specializes in criminal defense. Given that annual legal aid payments to the Bar now exceed £2 million, both of these sectors within the Faculty of Advocates could be vulnerable to the cuts in Scottish legal aid presently being considered by the Government. In 1975/76 only 9 percent of Queen's Counsel's fees and 39 percent of juniors' fees were derived from legal aid (see table 13). Since advocates' earnings from legal aid have increased 700 percent in the past decade, however, well over half of the incomes of very junior members of the Bar probably now comes from legal aid. A decade ago the Scottish Bar as a whole undoubtedly was less dependent on legal aid than its English counterpart (see chapter 2). Although contemporary data on the earnings of the Scottish Bar are unavailable, it does seem less differentiated (and thus less stratified) than the English.

For most of the last hundred years about half of all Scottish solicitors (both practicing and nonpracticing) have been based in the four main cities (Aberdeen, Dundee, Edinburgh, and Glasgow). Although the population per solicitor ignores the market significance of corporate clients, it is noteworthy that the population per solicitor in private practice in this century consistently has been lower in Scotland than in England, although the reverse has been true at the Bar (see table 14; also Podmore [1980: 14]). One reason may be that twentieth century English firms have tended to rely more on unqualified staff. Moreover, Scottish solicitors have continued to be general "people of business" to a greater extent than their English counterparts. The steady rise in practicing solicitors since the early 1960s has not been paralleled by growth in the general population (see table 14). Edinburgh (the business and governmental capital) and recently Aberdeen (the center of the North Sea oil boom) have had a higher density of private practitioners than would be warranted by their populations (see table 15).

Table 16 shows the geographic distribution of firms (by size) in 1984. By combining it with the 1984 population estimates for the predominantly rural regions of Scotland we get the ratio of firms to population (see table 17). This supports the finding in England and Wales that rural areas are not underserved by solicitors (Watkins et al., 1986). In rural southern Scotland the ratio of firms to the population is considerably below the national average, but in the far northern regions of Grampian, Highland, and Islands, the ratio is well above the national average. This statistic, however, takes no account of problems created by distance and deficiencies in the public transport system. Until the mid-1970s all but 9 of the 141 firms in Edinburgh, all but 11 of the 198 firms in Glasgow, and all but 3 of the firms in Dundee were located in the city centers. Less than 10 percent of firms had branch offices, and even fewer had branch offices in the suburbs. However, a recent pilot study (Keatinge, 1980) revealed that solicitors' firms have been moving into industrial areas and particularly into new and developing towns, and between 1975 and 1980, ninety branch offices were opened in Scotland. Although the majority were located in the central belt, only three of the twenty-nine opened between 1974 and 1976 were in Glasgow or Edinburgh, as compared to twenty-two of the sixty-five opened between 1977 and 1980. Two trends seem to have been at work. First, there has been a growth of linked offices across the country. Ten firms now have offices in both Glasgow and Edinburgh; in addition, seventy-seven firms in the two cities also have offices elsewhere in Scotland. Second, there has been a considerable increase in suburban branch offices.[21] In 1970 there were only seven branch offices in Glasgow and Edinburgh; in 1980 there were over forty; and by 1985 Glasgow alone had seventy-seven and Edinburgh, forty-two—a seventeenfold increase in fifteen years. (The corresponding figures in Aberdeen were six and eighteen.) Approximately half of the new offices in Edinburgh were located in major district shopping centers, as they were in Birmingham (Bridges et al., 1975); these often also contain branch offices for Building Societies. The other half have been situated in or near local authority housing areas, usually by litigation firms seeking to attract legal aid work. Litigation firms have been even more active in Glasgow. By the end of 1985 there were over 155 head and branch offices in the suburbs of Glasgow and Edinburgh, in marked contrast to the picture in the early 1970s. Abel (chapter 2) atttributes the growth of branch offices to the greater availability—and exploitability—of subordinate labor (qualified assistant solicitors) during this period. Whether this is correct, or whether branch offices proliferated because of other market forces (such as heightened competition), they certainly have helped the profession to absorb the influx of entrants since the early 1960s.

The distribution of solicitors' firms by size is very similar in Scotland and England (see table 18). Before 1950 there were no Scottish firms with ten or more partners. There were two by 1960, seven by 1971, twenty-seven by 1977, and more than fifty today. The first twenty-partner firm did not emerge until the mid-1970s, but there are now eight (one of which has thirty-two partners). It is clear, therefore, that in Scotland (as in England and the United States) large firms have increased in both number and size. In Scotland this often occurs through the amalgamation of practices, but the cause is the requirements of corporate clients. Growth permits lawyers to specialize and firms to offer a wide range of services. As early as 1970, nearly half of the private practitioners in Scotland and three-fourths of those in large firms considered themselves to be specialists (Campbell, 1971). At the other end of the spectrum, the ratio of sole practitioners to firm partners is declining in England. In 1936, 36 percent of English solicitors were sole practitioners; by 1978 the proportion was only 12 percent. In 1971, 13 percent of Scottish solicitors were in sole practice; six years later the figure had dropped to 10 percent (Campbell, 1971; Hughes Commission, 1980: vol. 1, p. 317). In the United States, however, the trend to larger units has not had such an impact on solo practice. In 1985 almost half (47 percent) of those in private practice were solo practitioners—a drop of only 3 percent since 1970. This probably is a product of the density of lawyers and the high level of competition among them. Interestingly, the decline in solo practice has been halted, if not reversed, in both Scotland (see table 18) and England, perhaps as a result of the increased numbers entering the profession or the growing dissatisfaction of assistant solicitors with their subordinate role in larger firms.

The stereotype of solo practice, which has emerged from American research, is a graduate from a less prestigious law school performing routine work for "one-shot" clients in the areas of criminal, family, and personal injury law. Consequently, sole practitioners earn much less than partners in the larger firms. Remuneration surveys in England and Wales reach similar conclusions. However, the Hughes Commission (1980) discovered relatively little variation in earnings by firm size in Scotland (see table 19). Sole practitioners earn the same proportion of their income from conveyancing work as do other private practitioners, rather less from company work, and rather more from litigation than do those in large firms.[22] A pilot study (Miller, 1981) suggests that sole practitioners in Scotland form neither a homogeneous nor a stable population:

> Taking into account how long the practice has existed and how many employees it has, one may tentatively and rather impressionistically sketch in a typology of sole practitioners. First, there are those who have been in sole practice for a long period, perhaps fifteen years or more. They tend to have two or three employees. Their practice has stabilised at a level of moderate success. They work in only a few fields of law.... Secondly, there are those who have been in sole practice for a period of eight to fifteen years or so. They may be subclassed into those whose practice is still gradually expanding towards a point where further expansion is necessary (a group which largely consists of practitioners who concentrate on conveyancing and wills, trusts and executries); those whose practice has already stabilised and those who are hanging on in very small practices against both the odds and the balance sheet. Thirdly, there are those who have only been in sole practice for six or seven years or less. Amongst these are many who will sooner or later move out of sole practice. Some practices expand rapidly, and quickly cease to be "sole." These solicitors perhaps receive their greatest reward from ambition-fulfilment rather than remuneration or pleasure at giving a good service. Of the rest of this group, a large number will be general practitioners who do a fair amount of legally-aided work. They have the greatest personal satisfaction from their work, but seem rarely to survive beyond five or six years as sole practitioners: either because the lure of mammon becomes too enticing, or because they, too, expand beyond sole practice.

Sole practitioners in Scotland seem to be unusual in other respects. They are proportionately represented on the Council of the Law Society. Few newly qualified solicitors embark on solo practice, despite the absence of a

"three-year" rule, until they have completed a number of years as a qualified assistant in a larger firm. In summary, while solicitors in Scotland
undoubtedly are differentiated in their spheres of work,[23] stratification
more closely resembles the sectoring described by Bucher and Strauss
(1961) than the bipolar model of Heinz and Laumann (1982).

MONOPOLIES, RESTRICTIVE PRACTICES, AND DEMAND CREATION

For market control theorists, supply is limited not only by restricting the
production of producers but also by regulating production by producers.
The latter includes the pursuit and defense of professional monopolies and
the proliferation of restrictive practices. We have seen that Abel's argument that the legal profession has lost control over the production of
producers is less than convincing when applied to Scotland. At first sight,
professional control over production by producers might appear less problematic. The Faculty of Advocates gained exclusive rights of audience in
the higher courts in the sixteenth century and has not been challenged
seriously since. Nevertheless, elite groups of solicitors early wrested law
agency work away from the Faculty. Solicitors also successfully campaigned for the transfer of some matters (such as divorce cases) to the
lower courts, where they share rights of audience. The Scottish Bar's
monopoly of judicial appointments in the sheriff courts has been substantially eroded by solicitors in the last twenty years. Even the Bar's
exclusive rights of audience in the higher courts recently have come
under direct attack from a solicitors' profession that still is smarting from
government-inspired attempts to breach its conveyancing "monopoly."
Certainly competition between the two branches is growing once again
after two centuries of symbiosis.

Solicitors (in both England and Scotland) pose more problems for market control theorists. If they did seek legally protected monopolies, they
were singularly ineffectual. The de jure monopoly of solicitors in Scotland
is very small. Unlike lawyers in North America and some parts of the
Continent, U.K. solicitors never have enjoyed a legal monopoly over the
provision of legal advice. Their rights of audience before the courts are
shared with advocates and pro se litigants. Their monopoly over applications to confirm the appointment of executors (administrators) for decedents' estates excludes only those acting for gain. Even their conveyancing
monopoly (over the preparation of writs for land transactions) is, strictly
speaking, a misnomer since no statute prevents one from conveying property on one's own behalf or for another person without pay (Solicitors

[Scotland] Act 1980, s. 32). The monopoly does not cover negotiation of the purchase or sale of property, exchange of contracts, searching of the Register of Sasines (the Land Register), or the various other steps involved in property transactions. Having said this, we should note that the Hughes Commission (1980: vol. 1, p. 130) concluded:

> It appears that solicitors have a virtual monopoly in all conveyancing work after the completion of the missives. The Keeper of the Registers has told us that it is very rare indeed for a writ to be presented for recording by anyone other than a solicitor. The difficulties and complexities of the legal procedures ... and the requirement for personal undertakings to be given in letters of obligation, have all helped to maintain a monopoly for solicitors in conveyancing work which is in practice more extensive than that conferred by statute.[24]

Nevertheless, de facto monopolies are more vulnerable than de jure ones. Until the 1930s many country solicitors enjoyed a de facto monopoly of tax advice, banking, and estate agency work in their localities. Within the next twenty years the competition from accountants (whose numbers increased by over 150 percent between 1931 and 1951) and bankers had destroyed the first two monopolies, and in recent years estate agents have begun to destroy the third; however, the legal protection of the conveyancing monopoly has enabled solicitors to defeat encroachments by unqualified entrepreneurs in this field. Moreover, the fact that legislation is required to remove this monopoly has given the profession time to mount an effective lobby in Parliament, which may well be sufficient to defeat the present Government's waning enthusiasm for freer markets.

While it would be fruitless to deny the existence of restrictive practices at the Bar and among solicitors, it is far from clear that they have operated as the market control theorists argue. The division between Queen's Counsel and juniors certainly does not. The "two-counsel" rule or the rule that a junior should receive two-thirds the fee of the Q.C. were not designed to limit competition but to boost the income of the junior Bar. The regulation of solicitors' fees in Scotland, whether by the courts or the profession, has been concerned with setting maxima as much as minima. The restriction on partnership sizes introduced in 1948 applied to all kinds of partnerships. It was not an anticompetitive device but a measure to protect the public and no longer applies to professional partnerships.

Even the rules against sharing fees with unqualified persons, touting, and advertising were not primarily anticompetitive. They did not emerge until as late as the 1930s. Their purpose was to bolster the dignity and status of the profession. Appealing though the suggestion may be to our cynical instincts, the elite lawyers who passed these rules were afraid that unseemly methods of advertising would harm not their business—corporate clients do not normally respond to such advances—as much as the image of the profession.

Abel (1982) argues that when a profession loses substantial control over the production of and by producers of legal services, it must turn to another strategy to absorb the consequent overproduction, namely, demand creation. In his earlier writings on the English legal profession, Abel (1982), like Bankowski and Mungham (1976), attributed the growth of legal aid and the emergence of neighborhood law centers to demand creation by the profession. As Paterson and Nelken (1984) have argued, this is to mistake cause for effect. It overlooks the fact that the impetus for both of these developments did not come from the profession. In fact, the profession in the United Kingdom resisted the introduction and development of legal aid as it resisted the growth of law centers. Only when it was failing did the profession resort to its more successful tactic of cooptation. Abel (chapter 2) now seems to accept the validity of this argument. The profession, he concludes, has only turned to demand creation "slowly, reluctantly, and ineffectually." The original impetus for legal aid, he concedes, cannot be attributed to the professional project of market control. Outside the sphere of publicly funded legal services, evidence of concerted efforts by the profession to create demand is even more difficult to find. The few institutional advertising campaigns in the United Kingdom appear to have been designed more to retain the profession's hold on its traditional areas of work than to create demand in new areas of law. Ironically, the one clear example of demand creation by the profession as a whole, the introduction in 1982 of a Legal Expenses Insurance scheme run by the Law Society, has been an almost total failure.

The problem for market theorists is that there is more demand creation by individual lawyers than by the profession acting collectively. The increase in solicitors' branch offices has been achieved by the entrepreneurial activities of individual firms—sometimes in the face of restraint from the profession's governing body. Individual advertising also is confined to a small minority of the profession, and its introduction in 1985—seen by some as professional demand creation—was quite the reverse in the United Kingdom. It was forced on an unwilling profession by government threats. Individual demand creation, far from being a response to competition, more often intensifies competition.

PROFESSIONAL ASSOCIATIONS

Whether one believes in market control theory or merely that occupations pursuing professional status must be able to act collectively, professional associations clearly are of major significance for the sociology of the professions. In this respect, as we have seen, the Scottish Bar resembles its continental cousins more closely than its English neighbor. Its association is the Faculty of Advocates, an independent corporation with five officers elected annually. The dean of the Faculty is responsible for asserting the rights of the Bar, maintaining high standards on the part of its members, and advising about and adjudicating questions of discipline. In carrying out these duties, the dean is assisted by a council of fellow advocates, the membership and size of which is left to the dean's discretion. Deans normally seek a reasonable cross section of the Bar in terms of experience and areas of practice. The dean also nominates the Faculty's Board of Examiners and suggests candidates to fill vacancies on the Faculty's ad hoc or standing committees, both of which the Faculty almost always accepts. Reposing so much power in the hands of one office bearer can lead to dissension, especially if sectors of the Bar (such as young juniors or the criminal Bar) feel that they are being ignored.

The present national association of solicitors (the Law Society of Scotland) was established by statute in 1949. Its objects include the promotion of the interests of solicitors and of the public in relation to that profession (Solicitors [Scotland] Act of 1980, s. 1[2]). Critics (including a sizable minority of the profession) have not been slow to observe the potential for conflict between these objects. Nevertheless, all practicing solicitors must join the society, obtain an annual practicing certificate, and pay an annual subscription.[25]

The Law Society operates through its council and a large number of standing, ad hoc, and statutory committees, although the day-to-day work is performed by full-time staff. The council consists of forty elected solicitors representing local constituencies and eight coopted members representing salaried solicitors employed in public services, commerce, and industry. Moreover, there is a small but significant number of younger solicitors and sole practitioners on the council. In these respects the Scottish Law Society Council is more representative of the profession than its English counterpart, although there still are few women. Since this latter deficiency has not yet been seriously challenged, the everyday complaints among the profession about the council's alleged misdeeds have not led to the proliferation of alternative professional bodies, which Abel claims are emerging in England.

Like the Amercian Bar Association, the Law Society performs a legitimation function, concerning itself with law reform and judicial nominations (for the lower courts) and promoting the public image of the profession. Perhaps more importantly, the Society sets the educational, training and admission requirements for entrants and sets fees for noncontentious work. It also is responsible for establishing standards of professional behavior, investigating complaints, and disciplining misconduct.

ETHICS, COMPLAINTS, AND THE CONSUMER MOVEMENT

Because the ability to set and enforce its own ethical standards is one of the defining characteristics of a profession, how the tasks are performed is of considerable importance. The Faculty of Advocates has no written code of conduct, and the scope of the unwritten understandings is unsettled. This poses problems for new entrants, who now must pass an examination in professional ethics. The normative vacuum is defended by the Faculty on the somewhat curious rationale that "everyone knows what the rules are"—which is patently untrue—and that to spell out the rules would invite "maverick" members of the Bar to sail close to the wind—a strange argument for lawyers to make. The Faculty copes with the resulting uncertainty by treating the dean as the repository of wisdom and knowledge on all ethical questions. Even though deans may differ from their predecessors, it is the incumbent who determines whether an advocate has been guilty of professional misconduct. Sanctions normally are restricted to private or public censure by the dean, although one late eighteenth century advocate was expelled from the Faculty for cheating at cards at a party. If an advocate seriously transgresses the unwritten rules, the dean may suggest cessation of practice for an indefinite period. There is little published information concerning the operation of these disciplinary procedures, but there have been allegations that they have been applied more severely to junior advocates with substantial criminal practices.

The Law Society has issued a number of practice rules under its statutory powers to regulate professional practice and discipline solicitors (Solicitors [Scotland] Act of 1980, s. 34). Nevertheless, as the Hughes Commission observed (1980: vol. 1, p. 287), "the general standards of conduct and ethical requirements which apply to solicitors are largely unwritten. There is no official code or guide to professional conduct for solicitors in Scotland." Until recently the Law Society has been reluctant to reduce to writing the general understanding that exists among solicitors for fear of producing either vague generalities or rigid and inflexible rules. In 1982 the Law Society agreed that there should be a short code of conduct, partly for the benefit of lawyers from other member states of the European Community, but this has yet to emerge. It seems certain, however, that a compulsory course in professional ethics will shortly be introduced in the diploma.

There is no independent body charged with investigating complaints against solicitors. Those that reach the Law Society are processed by professional staff, who ask the solicitor to respond. If the complaint relates to professional negligence, the client will either be told that the Society can take no action or be referred to one of a panel of forty solicitors (colloquially known as "troubleshooters"), who are willing to act (at the normal fee) for members of the public in such matters. Although professional indemnity insurance is mandatory (a Master Policy was introduced by the Law Society in 1977, when several insurance companies withdrew from the market), many individuals who have had one bad experience with the legal profession find it difficult to accept the fact that their only recourse is to retain another lawyer and commence litigation.

Those complaints thought to merit detailed examination are referred to the Law Society's Complaints Committees, which can send the case to the Scottish Solicitors' Discipline Tribunal. In addition, a client who has "suffered pecuniary loss by reason of dishonesty on the part of any solicitor" can seek reimbursement from the Guarantee Fund voluntarily maintained by the profession.[26]

The Scottish Solicitors' Discipline Tribunal consists of ten to fourteen solicitors recommended by the Council of the Law Society and appointed by the Lord President (the chief judge of the Court of Session) and four lay members appointed by the Lord President. Although members of the public may take complaints to the tribunal, almost all the cases it hears are prosecuted by the Law Society. If the tribunal finds the case proved it may order the solicitor struck off the Roll, suspended from practice, fined up to £4,000, or censured (Solicitors [Scotland] Act of 1980, s. 53). Appeal lies with the Court of Session. The tribunal has found itself hampered by the lack of a clearly defined code of professional conduct. On two recent occasions it has ruled that a solicitor's behavior constituted unprofessional conduct (something just short of professional misconduct) and would not be punished. The tribunal added, however, that any solicitor who repeated these offenses might well be found guilty of professional misconduct. Prospective "legislation" of this sort is necessary only when the profession is ignorant of the ethical rules that should regulate its behavior. In 1985 alone the tribunal had struck five solicitors off the Roll, suspended three others from practice for a period of five years, and fined nine more in amounts ranging from £250 to £2,500.

Nevertheless, as in England, the disciplinary procedure is invoked very sparingly. Aggrieved clients lodge about 1,000 complaints a year with the Law Society.[27] The Scottish Secretariat rejects between two-thirds and three-quarters of these as "not justified." Of the minority that go to a Complaints Committee, no action is taken in about half; between twenty and thirty cases a year go to the Scottish Solicitors' Discipline Tribunal (see table 20). Since 1976 Scotland has had a Lay Observer (an ombudsman without teeth) who examines allegations by the public that the Law Society has not investigated their complaints properly. If this is substantiated, the Lay Observer can only return the matter to the Law Society.

It is not surprising that the consumer movement recently turned its attention to the competence, ethical standards, and complaints procedures of the legal profession. Quite apart from the concern that the profession is acting as the judge in its own cause, consumers are profoundly dissatisfied by the distinction drawn by the Law Society (and its English counterpart) between misconduct and negligence. This presupposes a clear dividing line, when these categories actually are ill defined and overlap, and it deprives the client, whose solicitor has been incompetent but inflicted no quantifiable loss, of any remedy at all. Nevertheless, the public seems to be overcoming its reluctance to assert claims of professional negligence. Insurance premiums under the Master Policy have risen by 150 percent in two years, and further increases are in the pipeline.

Despite the Guarantee Fund, the troubleshooters' panel, and compulsory indemnity insurance, the Hughes Commission (1980) criticized both the procedures for investigating and the remedies for redressing misconduct, negligence, and incompetence. It called on the Law Society to discipline its members for incompetent work and suggested that the Scottish Solicitors' Discipline Tribunal should be given the power to award compensation to claimants rather than requiring them to initiate a separate action based on professional negligence. The Scottish Lay Observer has called for similar reforms, as well as a code of conduct. The English Lay Observer proposed that informal arbitration handle minor complaints of clients, and such a scheme is now being implemented. In both countries the consumer movement is calling for an independent complaints procedure. The Scottish Law Society continues to procrastinate about a code of conduct; although it now accepts the Hughes Commission proposals concerning compensation, it is firmly opposed to an independent complaints procedure. Nevertheless, it has accepted the need for changes in the complaints procedures and has created a working group on legal competence. These measures are not likely to satisfy critics inside and outside the profession. Those on the inside already are arguing that the Law Society should preserve its freedom of action by relinquishing its dual role and becoming a trade union, leaving others to safeguard the public interest. Even were this to occur and an ethical code and independent complaints procedure be introduced, this would not presage the end of the profession but merely a change in the character of the professional association.

CONCLUSION

This review of the history and current status of the Scottish legal profession has shown that it has not lost control over the supply of producers, its control over production by producers (through monopolies and restrictive practices) is largely unimpaired, and it has not turned to demand creation. Although under pressure from an organized consumer movement for the first time, the profession is displaying its customary resilience and shows little sign of fragmentation or decline. Why should Scotland be so different from the picture of the English legal profession contained in chapter 2? Perhaps, because of its historical affinity with civilian legal systems, Scotland is an exception that supports market control theory? I think not. The major developments affecting the Scottish legal profession in recent years—the numbers explosion (partly a result of the postwar "baby boom"), the increase in women entrants, the growth of litigation, and the evolution of the consumer movement—have occurred in many other Western countries.

The essence of Abel's argument is that the substantial growth in the number of law graduates in common law countries (particularly women) constitutes an erosion in the control over supply enjoyed by the legal profession. This presupposes that the legal profession previously had exercised substantial control when entrants did not attend university. The evidence for this is slim. The Scottish and Canadian chapters (here and chapter 4) expressly argue that collectively the profession (as opposed to market forces) exercised little control over either the number of articles or apprenticeships or the quality of the training provided through them. Such restrictions as existed were ascriptive barriers largely outside the control of the profession as a whole. The evidence from the other common law countries does not contradict this picture. The growth of graduate entry to the profession does not necessarily indicate an erosion of supply control since the profession determines which courses exempt graduates from later examinations and the content of these courses. Rather, the profession in both the United States and the United Kingdom has succeeded in transferring responsibility for training lawyers to the universities without greatly affecting the power of the profession to control the supply of producers. In most common law countries professional examinations continue to be a potential barrier to entry. The example of Japan shows that a state examination can be made a substantial barrier if the political will is present. The evidence from the chapters in this book is that although the pass rate on professional examinations fluctuates, these examinations do not constitute a substantial obstacle to those who persist in repeating. Most common law countries also have a "moral fitness" test for admission to the profession, which could have been used to restrict numbers. Rhode (1985) found that it had excluded relatively few in the United States, and replication of her study elsewhere undoubtedly would produce the same conclusion. Further, although leading members of the profession in the United States, Canada, and the United Kingdom publicly have expressed concern about the large number of entrants, no common law profession seriously has attempted to impose a ceiling on admissions.

With respect to control of production by producers, Abel argues that the profession's monopoly and restrictive practices have been considerably weakened. Again, the supporting evidence from the common law countries is far from convincing. Despite the rise of competition and consumer movements, there is little sign of a genuine erosion of professional monopolies. In the United Kingdom the much vaunted attack by the state on the conveyancing monopoly has proved to be largely symbolic. In some respects the monopoly has been widened. As Abel himself demonstrates in regard to England, restrictive practices frequently have reappeared in an informal guise after being formally repealed. Even the relaxation of the rules against individual advertising in a number of common law jurisdictions during the last decade has made a significant impact on the market only in the United States.

As for demand creation, Abel himself appears to be less than convinced of the profession's ability and willingness to act collectively to create demand. The evidence from the United States, the United Kingdom, and New Zealand confirms that the initiative for legal services programs has not come from the organized profession, which initially opposed and only later coopted them.

While it is easy to agree with Abel that the profession in many common law countries is facing troubled times as a result of growing numbers, heightened competition, active consumer movements, and real or threatened cuts in the legal services budgets, it is necessary to view such developments in a historical context. Substantial increases in admissions to the profession and high levels of competition within it are not new but cyclical phenomena. Market forces and the profession's efforts to control them always have fluctuated. Even the heterogeneity and segmentation of the profession today may not be unprecedented. The challenge of the consumer movement is important, but it is unlikely to herald a new era of patronage control over the profession. At most, it is an indicator that today's society is more "streetwise" than its recent predecessors were. Public trust in the legal profession has been eroded. As a consequence, there has been closer scrutiny of the unwritten agreement granting the profession autonomy, monopoly rights, and high status in exchange for high standards, a service ethic, and self-discipline. Yet society is not tearing up the agreement. Rather, having seen that the profession failed to deliver its promises, society merely is renegotiating the bargain. In short, it is premature to argue that the legal professions in the common law world are now in decline.

Tables

3.1. Undergraduate Law Students in Scotland

	1965/66	1970/71	1975/76	1977/78	1980/81
Aberdeen	124	212	352	414	380
Dundee	123	192	243	274	287
Edinburgh	430	443	508	511	512
Glasgow	357	299	391	435	447
Strathclyde	—	114	206	230	224
Total	1,034	1,260	1,700	1,864	1,850

Source: Hughes Commission (1980).

3.2. University Law Graduates

Year	Number	Year	Number
1970	312	1978	503
1971	352	1979	545
1972	329	1980	529
1973	350	1981	542
1974	371	1982	483
1975	406	1983	486
1976	443	1984	529
1977	487		

Source: Law Society.

3.3. Apprenticeships, 1935–1979; Traineeships, 1982–1985

Year	Apprentices and trainees	Year	Apprentices and trainees
1935	170	1964	113
1950	174	1969	215
1951	173	1970	248
1952	155	1971	245
1953	145	1972	278
1954	108	1973	315
1955	83	1974	314
1956	85	1975	328
1957	83	1976	354
1958	93	1977	385
1959	105	1978	390
1960	78	1979	430
1961	75	1982	392
1962	35	1983	399
1963	47	1984	393
		1985	420

Source: Law Society.

3.4. Admissions to the Faculty of Advocates, 1975–1985

Year	Men	Women	Total
1975	15	2	17
1976	11	2	15
1977	8	3	11
1978	15	—	15
1979	17	—	17
1980	13	2	15
1981	9	4	13
1982	10	2	12
1983	9	4	13
1984	9	—	9
1985	14	1	15

Source: Journal of the Law Society.

Alan A. Paterson

3.5. Admission of Solicitors, 1949–1985

Year	Men	Women	Total
1949	182	9	191
1950	160	10	170
1951	137	12	149
1952	113	12	125
1954	93	16	109
1955	118	16	134
1956	97	12	109
1957	80	7	87
1958	74	7	81
1959	73	9	82
1960	77	6	83
1961	86	8	94
1962	82	11	93
1963	63	13	76
1964	65	4	69
1965	46	7	53
1966	73	16	89
1967	117	24	141
1968	97	13	110
1969	126	22	148
1970	102	10	112
1971	183	29	212
1972	189	35	224
1973	206	35	241
1974	202	41	243
1975	230	67	297
1976	224	59	283
1977	225	82	307
1978	239	69	308
1979	244	106	350
1980	265	132	397
1981	261	135	396
1982	242	139	381
1983	264	154	418
1984	256	171	427
1985	233	182	415

Source: Law Society.

3.6. Size of the Faculty of Advocates

Year	Nominal	Practicing	Queen's Counsel
1710	250	170	
1832	442	?	
1860	300	115	
1876	337	130	
1962	281	106	
1967	285	114	
1975	322	128	32
1979	361	148	36
1982	387	173	44
1984	407	195	50
1985	417	202	50

Source: Legal directories.

3.7. Number of Enrolled Solicitors and Law Clerks and Size of Population

Year	Population	Enrolled solicitors	Law clerks
1861	3,062,294	1,973	2,882
1871	3,360,018	1,946	3,013
1881	3,735,573	2,284	3,912
1891	4,025,647	2,815	4,624
1901	4,472,103	3,600	5,628
1911	4,759,445	3,900	5,423
1921	4,882,497	3,347	NA
1931	4,842,980	3,304	NA
1938	5,006,689	3,128	NA
1951	5,096,415	3,479	NA
1961	5,179,344	3,780	NA
1971	5,228,563	4,083	NA
1981	5,130,735	5,830	NA

Note: Enrolled solicitors and law clerks in this table include those in retirement or those who for other reasons were not practicing their trade or profession.
Source: Official census reports.

3.8. Practicing Solicitors

Year	Numbers	Year	Numbers
1954	3,306	1980	4,810
1975	3,666	1981	5,065
1976	3,745	1982	5,329
1977	4,162	1983	5,620
1978	4,400	1984	5,884
1979	4,574	1985	6,175

Source: Law Society.

3.9. Distribution of Practicing Solicitors by Type of Practice

	1954	1975	Percent change since 1954	1977	1985	Percent change since 1954
Private practice principals	2,420	2,608	8	2,732	3,427	42
Qualified assistants	445	336	− 25	624	1,618	264
Local government	253	400	70	406	530	109
Central government and public bodies	106	283	167	357	461	334
Industry/commerce	48	36	− 25	42	111	131
Miscellaneous	34	3		1	28	
Total	3,306	3,666	11	4,162	6,175	87

Source: Law Society.

3.10. Age Distribution of Enrolled Solicitors

Age groups	1968 Number	%	1972	1976	1980	1984 Number	%
Under 30	398	10.3	683	1,104	1,472	1,891	27.2
30–40	833	21.5	780	982	1,555	2,240	32.2
40–50	769	19.9	861	871	860	911	13.1
50–60	1,002	25.9	849	730	780	826	11.9
60–70	577	14.9	746	849	742	623	9.0
70–80	197	5.1	207	272	383	403	5.8
Over 80	85	2.2	78	58	61	45	0.6
Unknown	7	0.2	10	11	14	12	0.2
Total	3,868					6,951	

Source: Law Society.

3.11. Women Advocates in Practice

Year	Total	Year	Total
1974	3	1980	8
1975	4	1981	13
1976	5	1982	13
1977	6	1983	16
1978	8	1984	16
1979	8	1985	17

Source: Paxton (1984).

3.12. Enrolled Women Solicitors

Year	Women admitted to profession	Percent of all admissions	Women on the roll	Percent of all solicitors on the roll
1975	31	22	—	9
1976	59	21	514	10.5
1977	82	27	583	11
1978	69	22	654	12
1979	106	30	749	13
1980	132	33	864	15
1981	135	34	980	16
1982	139	36	1,102	17
1983	154	37	1,212	18
1984	171	40	1,370	20
1985	182	44	1,520	21

Source: Law Society.

3.13. Sources of Advocates' Fees, 1975/76

	Percent Queen's Counsel	Percent juniors
Criminal legal aid	3	10
Other criminal	1	3
Civil legal aid	6	29
Other civil	65	47
Miscellaneous	3	1
Total	78	90
Advocates depute or part-time procurators fiscal	6	4
Other fees	16	6

Source: Hughes Commission (1980: vol. 1, p. 330).

3.14. Ratio of Solicitors in Private Practice to Population

Year	Population	Solicitors	Population per solicitor
1911	4,759,445	3,555	1,339
1938	5,006,689	3,129	1,600
1954	5,127,738	2,865	1,790
1962	5,179,344	2,603	1,990
1971	5,228,563	2,663	1,963
1976	5,179,649	3,175	1,631
1982	5,130,735	4,329	1,185
1985	5,146,000	5,045	1,020

Sources: Census returns, almanacs, and directories.

3.15. Private Practitioners and Ratio to Population in the Principal Cities

Year	City	Percent total population	Solicitors	Percent total solicitors	Population per solicitor
1911	Aberdeen	3.4	181	5	950
	Dundee	3.5	122	3.4	1,352
	Edinburgh	9	952	27	445
	Glasgow	16	733	21	1,070
1938	Aberdeen	3.5	170	5	1,017
	Dundee	3.6	110	3.5	1,650
	Edinburgh	9	757	24	599
	Glasgow	22	691	22	1,628
1976	Aberdeen	3.7	224	7	861
	Dundee	3.7	106	3.3	1,825
	Edinburgh	9	763	24	595
	Glasgow	16	811	25.5	1,028
1984	Aberdeen	3.7	303	6.3	628
	Dundee	3.4	135	2.8	1,294
	Edinburgh	8.1	874	18.8	480
	Glasgow	15	1,032	21	739

Sources: Census returns, almanacs, and directories.

3.16. Geographic Distribution of Firms, by Size, November 1984

Local government region	Total	Number of partners			
		1	2–4	5–9	≥ 10
Lothians					
Edinburgh	148	54	40	37	17
Other places	39	20	16	3	—
Strathclyde					
Glasgow	255	99	101	44	11
Other places	227	92	106	27	2
Tayside	88	27	47	12	2
Central	32	8	20	4	—
Fife	42	12	23	6	1
Borders	25	2	17	6	—
Dumfries and Galloway	36	6	29	1	—
Grampian	91	25	39	24	3
Highland and Islands	47	19	21	7	—
Total 1984	1,030	364	459	171	36
Total 1977	908	292	443	146	27

Source: Law Society.

3.17. Ratio of Population to Firms in Rural Areas, 1985

Region	Firms	Population	Population per firm
Scotland	1,030	5,146,000	4,996
Borders	25	101,000	4,040
Dumfries and Galloway	36	150,000	4,167
Grampian (excluding Aberdeen)	40	269,000	6,725
Highland (excluding Inverness)	22	156,000	7,090
Islands	9	74,000	8,222

Sources: Law Society, population estimates.

3.18. Distribution (in Percent) of Firms by Size

| | Scotland | | England | |
	1977	1984	1979	1985
Sole practice firms	32	35	34	33
2–4 partners	48	45	48	48
5–9 partners	17	17	14	14
10 partners or more	3	3	4	5

Source: Law Societies.

3.19. Sources of Solicitors' Income, 1976/77

	All firms		Sole practitioner		2–4 partners		5 or more partners	
	£	%	£	%	£	%	£	%
Domestic conveyancing	29,154	34.0	8,303	34.4	22,551	34.9	71,078	33.1
Executry and trust	18,180	21.2	5,183	21.5	15,244	23.7	41,059	19.1
Court	13,544	15.8	4,734	19.6	9,768	15.1	33,982	15.8
Company (including commercial conveyancing)	10,025	11.6	1,382	5.7	5,055	7.8	33,569	15.7
Commission on sale of heritable property	5,150	6.0	1,810	7.5	5,045	7.8	9,235	4.3
Other (including all other commissions)	9,789	11.4	2,720	11.3	6,941	10.7	25,688	12.0
	£85,842	100.0	£24,132	100.0	£64,604	100.0	£214,611	100.0
Number of firms	431		100		243		88	
Income per fee earner	£12,624		£10,969		£12,667		£12,125	

Source: Hughes Commission (1980: vol. 1, p. 318).

3.20. Disposition of Complaints

Year	Number of complaints	Percent justified in Law Society's opinion	Number to Discipline Tribunal	Number to troubleshooters	Number to Lay Observer
1974	759	66	13	—	—
1975	908	63	13	38	—
1976	956	47	12	15	15
1977	1,016	25	18	22	21
1978	1,005	30	11	38	14
1979	962	46	18	28	9
1980	839	30	32	37	17
1981	717	27	25	39	26
1982	633	30	21	26	33
1984	1,045	23	19	26	107
1985	888	28	35	33	86

Sources: Law Society annual reports, *Journal of the Law Society*, annual reports of the Scottish Lay Observer.

NOTES

1. Legal aid reviews have been conducted in Scotland and England by the relevant government departments with an eye to cutting or curbing spiraling expenditures. Both reviews recommended that independent boards (rather than the Law Societies) should administer legal aid. The Scottish proposals have been implemented in the Legal Aid (Scotland) Act of 1986.

2. This list is not exhaustive, nor would I argue that every occupation considered a profession in Scotland today necessarily possesses all these attributes; however, the great majority are likely to possess most of them.

3. Strained relations with England meant that few Scottish students attended Oxford or Cambridge Universities during this period.

4. During this period more than 800 Scottish students matriculated at the Universities of Leiden, Utrecht, and Groningen alone (Phillipson, 1976: 194).

5. The Faculty of Advocates recorded that the fees were "cheerfully met by all honnest and ingenious spirits" (Hannay, 1933: 156).

6. The success of the Faculty of Advocates in controlling supply can be judged by the fact that between 1707 and 1750, 260 of the 295 entrants took the trial in civil law. The Faculty sought to control not just numbers but also social background.

7. The Chairs of Civil and Scottish Law in Edinburgh were funded by the novel expedient of a tax of 2 pence (Scottish) on every pint of ale or beer sold in the city of Edinburgh (Black, 1982: 33).

8. The SSC Society was not above a little pettiness of its own, as its minutes books attest. It was objections from the SSC Society that helped to prevent the Society of Writers to the Signet from obtaining a Royal Charter in the nineteenth century.

9. Relatively rapid fluctuations in the rate of admissions were possible because advocates were not (and are not) permitted to form partnerships, neither did they have to find a place in chambers since all advocates had individual chambers, frequently located in their own homes.

10. In some sheriff courts the examinations were no more rigorous than before, although now it was the examiners who entertained the candidates to a substantial dinner before the oral examination (Barty, 1934).

11. For an excellent account of legal education in Scotland in the nineteenth century, see Bates (1980).

12. The prestigious societies retained control over admission to their own ranks. At the turn of the century they were complaining that the Law Agents Act of 1873 had harmed the public "since young men whose general education is inadequate for any profession and whose knowledge is but rudimentary, eked out with a brief spell of cram, find too easy access to the position of agents" (Barclay, 1984: 175).

13. 2 Shaw 249.

14. For an interesting contemporary speech by a leader of the profession confirming this, see 1934 *Scots Law Times* (*News*), p. 54.

15. Between 1960 and 1980 law graduates desiring to enter either branch of the profession had to undergo an apprenticeship in a solicitor's office (two or three years for a solicitor and at least one year for an advocate).

16. There were nineteen such apprentices in 1982.

17. Between 1949 and 1956 the annual rate of admissions fell from 191 to 53—a decline sufficient to alarm even the Law Society (Law Society, 1956).

18. Even the figures for the period 1850 to 1950 must be treated with caution since their source—the census returns—usually fails to distinguish between solicitors in private practice and those who have chosen to work elsewhere or have retired.

19. In addition to those listed in table 9, in 1984 there were a further 648 enrolled solicitors who were not in practice, including academics (about 50 of the 150 or so academics in Scottish university law faculties have qualified as solicitors), judges in the sheriff courts (about twenty), and business executives.

20. Between 1975 and 1984 the granting of legal aid certificates increased from 10,932 to 18,353 a year in civil cases and from 12,586 to 61,288 in criminal cases. Total payments from the Legal Aid Fund to advocates during the same period increased from £300,000 to £2.2 million.

21. Bridges et al. (1975) discovered a similar, although earlier, growth in Birmingham, England, from 13 percent of all offices in 1951 to 23 percent in 1971.

22. The Hughes Commission (1980: vol 2, p. 371) also found that sole practi-

tioners earn 18 percent of their gross fees from legal aid—twice as much as other firms.

23. Aitkenhead et al. (1985) found that conveyancing accounted for 32 percent of Scottish solicitors' cases but 48 percent of trainee solicitors' cases.

24. Entry into the European Economic Community (EEC) has not altered matters since the European Communities (Services of Lawyers) Order of 1978, enabling lawyers qualified in other EEC countries to draw or prepare property writs for gain in Scotland, applies only to movable property.

25. In 1985/86 the subscription was £200. Approximately 43 percent is allocated to the salaries of Law Society staff, and the remainder is spent on handling complaints, institutional advertising, and courses in continuing legal education.

26. Unlike the client security funds throughout most of the United States and Canada, there is no financial limit to the claims that can be made against this fund (the highest recorded claim in Scotland exceeded £200,000). In 1984 the Law Society of Scotland paid out £130,734. Whether the profession will be able to sustain such an open-ended commitment in the future is doubtful.

27. It is interesting that 16 percent of complaints are filed by other lawyers, in contrast to their silence in the United States (Abel, 1982: 43).

REFERENCES

Abel, Richard L. 1982. "The Politics of the Market for Legal Services," in Philip A. Thomas, ed., *Law in the Balance*. Oxford: Martin Robertson.

Aitkenhead, M., Noreen Burrows, R. Jagtenberg, and E. Orucu. 1985. "European Law and the Practitioner," 30 *Journal of the Law Society of Scotland* 270.

Anon. 1860. "Prospects of the Legal Profession," 4 *Journal of Jurisprudence* 445.

Bankowski, Zenon, and Geoff Mungham. 1976. *Images of Law*. London: Routledge & Kegan Paul.

Barclay, J. B. 1984. *The S.S.C. Story 1784–1984*. Edinburgh: The Edina Press.

Barty, A. 1934. "The Early Days of the Incorporated Society of Law Agents in Scotland," 2 *Scottish Law Gazette* 35.

Bates, T. St. J. N. 1980. "Mr. M'Connachie's Notes and Mr. Fraser's Confessional," 25 *Juridical Review* 166.

Black, Robert. 1982. "Practice and Precept in Scots Law," 27 *Juridical Review* 31.

Bridges, Lee, Brenda Suffrin, Jim Whetton, and Richard White. 1975. *Legal Services in Birmingham*. Birmingham: Birmingham University.

Bucher, Rue, and Anselm Strauss. 1961. "Professions in Process," 66 *American Journal of Sociology* 325.

Cairns, John W. 1986. "The Formation of the Scottish Legal Mind in the Eighteenth Century," in Neil MacCormick and Peter Birks, eds., *The Legal Mind*. Oxford: Clarendon Press.

Campbell, Colin M. 1971. *Public Attitudes to the Legal Profession in Scotland.* Edinburgh: The Law Society of Scotland.

Dingwall, Robert, and Philip Lewis. 1983. *The Sociology of the Professions.* London: Macmillan.

Donaldson, G. 1976. "The Legal Profession in Scottish Society in the Sixteenth and Seventeenth Centuries," in D. N. MacCormick, ed., *Lawyers in Their Social Setting.* Edinburgh: W. Green & Son.

Durkan, J. 1983. "The Early Scottish Notary," in Ian B. Cowan and Duncan Shaw, eds., *The Renaissance and Reformation in Scotland.* Edinburgh: Scottish Academic Press.

Freidson, Eliot. 1986. *Professional Powers.* Chicago: University of Chicago Press.

Hadfield, Brigid V.A.M.M. 1977. "The Legal Profession in Scotland." LL.M. thesis, Queens University, Belfast.

Haldane, A. R. B. 1979. "The Society of Writers to Her Majesty's Signet," introduction to G. H. Ballantyne, *The Signet Library, Edinburgh and Its Librarians 1722–1972.* Edinburgh: Scottish Library Association.

Hannay, R. K. 1933. *The College of Justice.* Edinburgh: T. & A. Constable.

———. 1936. "The Early History of the Scottish Signet," in *The Society of Writers to the Signet.* Edinburgh: T. & A. Constable.

Heinz, John P., and Edward O. Laumann. 1982. *Chicago Lawyers.* Chicago: American Bar Foundation; New York: Russell Sage.

Hughes Commission. 1980. *The Royal Commission on Legal Services in Scotland, Report* (2 vols.) (Cmnd. 7846/1). Edinburgh: HMSO.

Keatinge, Alistair. 1980. "The Distribution of Solicitors in Scotland." Unpublished undergraduate project report, University of Edinburgh.

Larson, Magali Sarfatti. 1977. *The Rise of Professionalism.* Berkeley, Los Angeles, London: University of California Press.

Law Society. 1956. "Editorial," 1 *Journal of the Law Society of Scotland* 12.

———. 1977. *Evidence of the Law Society to the Hughes Commission,* vol. 1. Edinburgh: The Law Society.

Millar, William M. 1985. "The Role of Women in the Profession," 30 *Journal of the Law Society of Scotland* 86.

Miller, Alan. 1981. "Sole Practice in Scotland." Unpublished undergraduate project report, University of Edinburgh.

Muirhead, J. S. 1948. *The Old Minute Book of the Faculty of Procurators in Glasgow.* Glasgow: The Faculty of Procurators.

Paterson, Alan A. 1983. "Becoming a Judge," in Robert Dingwall and Philip Lewis, eds., *The Sociology of the Professions.* London: Macmillan.

Paterson, Alan, and David Nelken. 1984. "The Evolution of Legal Services in Britain: Pragmatic Welfarism or Demand Creation?" 4 *Windsor Yearbook of Access to Justice* 98.

Paxton, Adele. 1984. "Getting Even?" *Scots Law Times (News)* 53.

Phillipson, Nicholas T. 1976. "Lawyers, Landowners and the Civic Leadership of Post-Union Scotland," in D. N. MacCormick, ed., *Lawyers in Their Social Setting*. Edinburgh: W. Green & Son.

Podmore, David. 1980. *Solicitors and the Wider Community*. London: Heinemann.

Ranieri, Filippo. 1985. "Vom Stand zum Beruf: Die Professionalisierung des Juristenstandes als Forschungsaufgabe der Europäischen Rectsgeschichte der Neuzeit," 13 *Ius Commune* 83.

Rhode, Deborah. 1985. "Moral Character as a Professional Credential," 94 *Yale Law Journal* 494.

Shaw, John Stuart. 1983. *The Management of Scottish Society, 1707–1764*. Edinburgh: John Donald Publishers.

Slater, Caroline. 1982. "Manpower Planning," 27 *Journal of the Law Society of Scotland* 51.

Watkins, Charles, Mark Blacksell, and Kim Economides. 1986. "The Distribution of Solicitors in England and Wales." Exeter: University of Exeter (Access to Justice in Rural Britain Project, Working Paper 8).

4

Canadian Lawyers

A Peculiar Professionalism

HARRY W. ARTHURS, RICHARD WEISMAN,
AND FREDERICK H. ZEMANS

Canada is a federal state, embracing two official languages and legal cultures and ten provincial jurisdictions. Its lawyers are dispersed across 3,000 miles in diverse social settings and economic circumstances, but their functions are not formally defined or faithfully recorded. Our attempt to capture a complex reality is made especially difficult because of the extreme paucity of secondary writing on the Canadian legal profession. These caveats notwithstanding, we believe that Canadian materials may, indeed, contribute to current theorizing about the professions.

Students of the sociology of law (e.g., Abel, 1981; Heinz & Laumann, 1983) recently have begun to develop an historical and comparative approach to the legal profession, complementing the valuable work of Freidson (1970), Johnson (1972), and Larson (1977) on the more general problem of the professions. Central to this approach is the assumption that "all occupations under capitalism are compelled to seek market control, the attainment of which is the defining characteristic of a profession" (Abel, 1981: 1120).

Freidson, in his seminal work on the sociology of medicine (1970), distinguished professions from other occupations by virtue of their position of hegemonic privilege in the division of labor. Larson (1977) saw two elements as crucial to the professional project: the creation of a systematic body of knowledge on which to ground claims to exclusive competence and the achievement of control over the production of producers of this knowledge. Because the university emphasized formal training, espoused meritocratic standards, and enjoyed high public credibility, it became the primary vehicle by which professional organizations could attain these objectives.

Several ambitious recent attempts to track the professional project point to a decline in professional dominance. Abel suggests that both in England (see chapter 2) and the United States (see chapter 5) the profession has lost significant control over the supply of legal services and that the defensive strategies, by which it has sought to regain control, have been markedly ineffective. Heinz and Laumann (1983) also offer evidence of professional transformation and decline by describing the increasingly sharp division of the metropolitan bar into mutually exclusive subgroups based on function, income, ethnicity, and education. The rapid shift from private practice to employment in both the public and private sectors may be further evidence of departure from the professional ideal, in which members exercise control over the terms and conditions of their work (Abel, 1981: 1159–1160). Similar trends toward a loss of both market control and autonomy have been observed in medicine, although the causes of deprofessionalization differ (Coburn et al., 1983; McKinlay & Arches, 1985).

If the theories of Freidson, Larson, and Abel are to have general explanatory value, they must be able to accommodate contexts other than the American experience from which they were primarily drawn. Can a theory of the political economy of the professions transcend national boundaries? Local political forms, culture, economic circumstance, and social organization, and especially the notorious parochialism of formal law, all would seem to argue against this. Canada's transformation from an agrarian colony to a modern industrial nation during the formative period of professionalism especially might be expected to yield a distinctive pattern, unlike that of the two countries that most influenced its professional history—England and the United States. Given these considerations, the wonder is not that the Canadian experience seems to invite modification of the "professional project" thesis but rather that it seems generally to confirm it.

TERMINOLOGY

In general parlance, legal practitioners everywhere in Canada are called "lawyers" ("avocats" in Quebec). The historical distinction between barristers and solicitors no longer has any functional significance (see, e.g., Law Society Act, Rev. Stat. Ontario 1980, c. 233, s. 28; Barristers and Solicitors Act, Rev. Stat. Nova Scotia 1967, c. 18 ss. 3–5; Barristers and Solicitors Act, Rev. Stat. British Columbia 1979, c. 26, s. 42). In Quebec "notaires" are concerned with the formalization, authentication, and preservation of title documents, wills, and other legal instruments.[1] Lawyers who perform adjudicative or regulatory functions may suspend or terminate their formal professional membership and will be referred to thereafter as judges, members of a board or commission, and so on.[2] A purely honorific title, "Queen's Counsel," has been awarded to a rather large number of lawyers in some provinces, (such as Ontario), and fewer in others. It does not signal preeminence in advocacy (as it does in England) but merely some degree of seniority and professional or public repute—if anything.[3]

Lawyers perform a variety of tasks, many of which require little or no specialized training but are functionally related to others that do (Colvin, 1979; Macfarlane, 1980; Colvin et al., 1978). The two historic functions of lawyers, conveyancing and litigation, have acquired an extended meaning. For Canadian lawyers, the modern analogue to "conveyancing" is the practice of commerical law, which includes the negotiation, drafting, and interpretation of commercial documents; advising and planning for commercial transactions; corporate and tax planning; and general business and political advice. Lawyers also advise individual, nonbusiness clients about family relationships, financial affairs, dealings with government over pensions, and other benefits and employment contracts.

"Litigation" in the strict sense includes representation of parties in a dispute that will be adjudicated by a court. It now also encompasses representation before government regulatory regimes, interpretation of existing legislation, attempts to change legislation, and contacts with the media.

A small but growing group of lawyers is concerned with the "scientific jobs" in law. These include not only legal academics but also employees of government departments, law reform commissions, research staffs of corporations and community groups and specialist researchers in large law firms. Finally, some lawyers are deeply involved in political and administrative functions that seldom engage the skills employed by those in private practice. Corporate and governmental administrators, lobbyists, journalists, and elected officials are found along the broad spectrum of these "nonlegal" occupations.

The more attenuated the connection with the original knowledge base of lawyer functions, the more likely it is that nonlawyers will be important actors in the same field (Colvin, 1979; Quinn, 1978; Evans & Trebilcock, 1982); thus, business advice often involves accountants. Lay persons are advocates in many tribunals not mandated to administer conventional legal rules. The development of "legal science" increasingly attracts the participation of economists, sociologists, scientists, and philosophers. Lawyers are not even dominant in public policy development and administration (Marmour & White, 1978; Ronson, 1978; Altman & Weil, Inc., 1980).

In matters more closely related to conveyancing and litigation, however, lawyers tend to assume an exclusive or dominant role. "Law clerks" or "legal assistants" typically work under the supervision of qualified lawyers (Taman, 1978; Zemans, 1982). Sometimes they are given considerable latitude in preparing routine documents and prosecuting legal proceedings, especially in minor matters (see table 1). "Community legal workers," "lay advocates," or "paralegals" perform analogous functions in legal aid offices (Gold, 1978; Thomasset, 1981; Taylor, 1981; Zemans,

1982).[4] Typically, however, the latter enjoy rather greater autonomy, particularly in areas such as community mobilization and legal education. Neither "law clerks" nor "community legal workers" need have any particular training or formal credentials, although courses and training programs are available (Marmor & White, 1978; Ronson, 1978).[5]

Accountants, trade union representatives, and others do have limited rights of audience in certain forums,[6] and they may negotiate, draft, and interpret certain legal documents as long as they do not engage in the "practice of law." Their activities typically involve immigration, labor relations, social welfare, and landlord–tenant problems, but they also extend to taxation, estate planning, and the financial and corporate transactions of middle-class and corporate clients. In some jurisdictions, patent attorneys or patent agents may practice industrial property law (Patent Act, Rev. Stat. Canada, 1970, c. 203, s. 15), "conveyancers" perform title searches and related functions (Trebilcock & Reiter, 1982: 101), notaries public and *notaires* authenticate documents, and commissioners swear affidavits (Schloesser, 1979).

SOCIOGRAPHIC DATA AND SOCIAL POSITION

NUMBERS

The following data describe lawyers who are licensed to practice, but an increasing proportion of those who obtain a professional qualification do not enter private practice. In Ontario, the most populous province, the proportion of graduates entering private practice declined from 86 percent to 70 percent over a period of about ten years, while the number of qualified lawyers doubled (Law Society of Upper Canada, 1983b).

In 1982 there were about 39,000 lawyers in Canada (including Quebec notaires) (Canadian Law List, 1983). This represents significant growth since the mid-1960s as well as a significant decline in the ratio of population to lawyers. In Ontario, the ratio fell from 1,142 in 1960 to 574 in 1981 (Law Society of Upper Canada, 1983b: 227). Between 1931 and 1981 the number of lawyers expanded much more rapidly (278 percent) than that of physicians (183 percent) or dentists (123 percent), although slightly less rapidly than that of architects (309 percent).

These changes seem to have resulted in part from a demographic anomaly. The low numbers entering the profession in the 1940s and 1950s produced equally low numbers of retirements and deaths in the 1970s and 1980s. The birth rate peaked at 27.6 live births per 1,000 population between 1956 and 1960 and then declined to a low of 15.5 in 1977. The combination of these two factors amplified the drop in the ratio of population to lawyers. There was little change in the popularity of law studies among university students, however: They attracted 2.2 percent of total enrollment in 1962 and 2.9 percent from 1973 to 1983 (Consultative Group on Research and Education in Law, 1983). Nonetheless, because the changes occurred after a protracted period of stability (Stager, 1982), they have come to be perceived (especially in professional circles) as unprecedented. In fact, they seem to be part of a long-term trend in which episodes of rapid expansion alternate with lengthy periods when the supply remains constant or contracts (Nelligan, 1950; 1951).

REGIONAL DISTRIBUTION

Two provinces contain nearly two-thirds of all Canadian lawyers; three contain nearly four-fifths (see table 2). Lawyers are clustered in the most economically advanced and densely populated parts of the country and in government centers (Berger, 1979). Winnipeg contains almost 80 percent of Manitoba lawyers, and Edmonton and Calgary combined contain more than 80 percent of Alberta's lawyers, although only half of the population (Statistics Canada, 1981). Toronto, a provincial capital and the commercial center of the country, located in the midst of the industrial heartland, contains about 10 percent of the population but about 25 percent of all lawyers. Conversely, small towns in remote areas often have few lawyers and almost certainly a much higher ratio of population to lawyers than is found in the major metropolises.

DEPLOYMENT WITHIN THE PROFESSION

There also are considerable differences between metropolitan and non-metropolitan practice and even between the city core and suburbs (Berger, 1979; Mullagh, 1977; Snider, 1981; Colvin et al., 1978). General practitioners predominate outside metropolitan centers (Berger, 1979; Ribordy, 1982a: 83). This is partly because there are too few people to support specialization and partly because specialists tend to perform services on behalf of governments, corporations, and other institutional clients, whose head offices often are located in the larger cities. Almost all medium-sized and large law firms are located in the central business and financial districts of the larger cities. Lawyers catering to a "household clientele" tend to be found increasingly in suburban shopping precincts and in storefronts in working-class and ethnic districts (Colvin et al., 1978: 25–220). Outside the central business districts, small firms and solo practitioners predominate (Arthurs et al., 1971; Berger, 1979).

Identifiable subgroups of lawyers outside private practice have emerged recently. While there were only some 40 law teachers in all of Canada as recently as 1950, the number now has grown to over 650 (Consultative Group on Research and Education in Law, 1983: 30). Government lawyers working at the municipal, provincial, and federal levels have experienced a similarly dramatic increase in numbers. The Province of Ontario employed approximately 6 lawyers in the Ministry of the Attorney General in 1945; by 1981 the ministry's head office employed 150 and local Crown attorneys' (prosecutors') offices another 500 (Leal, 1982). In the later year, 1,098 out of 15,011 Ontario lawyers were employed by various levels of government (Stager, 1981). Community clinic lawyers in Ontario increased from 18 in 1976 to 60 in 1983 (Zemans, 1980). Across the country legal aid services employed 534 lawyers in 1979/80 (National Legal Aid Research Centre, 1980/81). Corporate staff lawyers (sometimes called "house counsel") have expanded their numbers greatly, especially in the past ten years (Feltham & Campin, 1981). Finally, several hundred lawyers work for community groups, trade unions, legal aid or legal services schemes, and advocacy organizations such as the Environmental Law Association or the Civil Liberties Association—forms of practice that were almost nonexistent fifteen years ago.

THE NUMBERS DEBATE

The relatively rapid increase in the number of lawyers admitted to practice, especially during the past five to ten years, has produced a widespread conviction among members of the bar (and some members of the public) that there are "too many lawyers."[7] In the absence of any other standard for measuring the appropriate number of lawyers, this belief typically is supported by reference to the alleged stagnation or decline in lawyer incomes in recent years. It is by no means clear how incomes have been affected by rising numbers, however. In fact, with considerable variation by type of practice, seniority, clientele, and location, Canadian lawyers have managed to maintain their relatively advantaged position (Altman & Weil, Inc., 1982; Financial Post 20 [20 November, 1982]). And to the extent they have not done so, the cause appears to be recent reversals in Canada's economic fortunes (Stager, 1982: 116–118; Ribordy, 1982b; 1983). During a period in the early 1980s when the economy was running considerably under capacity, unemployment in many industries was high, real estate and other commercial markets were depressed, and business expansion was negligible, it was not surprising that lawyer incomes would suffer.

Fluctuation in lawyer incomes is difficult to measure. Average annual incomes may, indeed, have remained relatively stable, which would signify an actual decline after adjusting for inflation; however, this may be attributable to the large influx of relatively low earning recent graduates. There is no evidence that the real earnings of senior "elite" lawyers have suffered. On the contrary: for reasons that will be discussed below, the present economic situation may well have amplified existing disparities, to the prejudice of new entrants, solo practitioners and small firms, lawyers serving a "household clientele" or legally-aided clients, and salaried lawyers (see table 3).

A second ingredient in the "numbers debate" is the allegation that incompetence has increased (Yachetti, 1983). Because lawyers must cut prices to compete, it is argued, they also will trim the quality of service provided. Moreover, lawyers whose traditional sources of business (e.g., real estate transactions) have diminished will be tempted to try types of legal practice (e.g., criminal law) in which they are not experienced. These allegations remain unsubstantiated. While the latter suggestion seems plausible, the former is at odds with the fact that the recent significant increases in claims for incompetence result from the activities of experienced lawyers and from errors committed by them during a period of considerable prosperity (Law Society of Upper Canada, 1983b). Indeed, one commentator has argued that too few lawyers trying to satisfy too much demand also may produce incompetent performances (Stager, 1982: 33–34).

Regardless of the facts, it is undeniable that many lawyers favor limiting entry (Yachetti, 1983: 105). However, it is by no means clear that the profession possesses the power to give effect to this view. While the applicability of antitrust legislation to the legal profession is uncertain (Hunter, 1983), any attempt by the bar to restrict numbers probably would result in considerable public outcry (Law Society of Upper Canada, 1983b: 234, 238). Governments facing financial constraint might be willing to trim the number of graduating law students in order to save both the cost of legal education and claims on legal aid funds, however, since younger lawyers rely more heavily on such work (Berger, 1979: 49–50).

Finally, the impact of market forces has been felt most severely by recent graduates, who have suffered periods of unemployment or been displaced into nonlegal careers in business, government, or elsewhere (Stager, 1982; Zemans, 1986; Consultative Group on Research and Education in Law, 1983). At present, however, law schools continue to enjoy a vast surplus of highly qualified applicants for the limited number of places.

CONNECTIONS WITH OTHER INSTITUTIONS

Legal Connections

Lawyers generally identify closely with, and tend to support, legal institutions such as the courts and organizations such as the Bar Association; however, judges may inspire deference or criticism (or both) rather than close collegiality. Law professors may consider themselves as either critics of "the system" or deferential to authority (Laskin, 1972). In addition, government officials, legal aid and clinic lawyers, tribunal members, and other lawyers employed by nonlegal employers are exposed to centrifugal influences by virtue of their identification with the institutions or organizations where they work.

Nonlegal Connections

Some specialist practitioners maintain close connections with other professions with which they collaborate. For example, physicians and lawyers comprise the membership of the Medical-Legal Society (MacEachern, 1976), and lawyers and accountants belong to the Canadian Tax Foundation. Much more common, however, are the involvements of lawyers with their business clients because of annual retainers (sometimes reflecting decades of close association), the acceptance of directorships, participation in active management, and partnerships or coventure arrangements. Lawyers also often serve as lobbyists, informal intermediaries, and a responsive audience for their business clients (Clement, 1975b; Gall, 1977; Pike, 1980; Adam & Lahey, 1981).

Lawyers maintain connections with political parties, religious and ethnic groups, and special-interest groups such as consumers' associations, credit unions, and conservation and civil rights organizations. While this sometimes may be motivated by a desire to attract business, it often reflects a genuine and intense involvement in the cause espoused by the organization. Lawyers constitute important links among the widest variety of institutions, social sectors, and political perspectives. Indeed, this "linkage" function may be seen as divided loyalty, which may help to explain why lawyers so often are viewed with suspicion by the nonlawyers with whom they are associated.

LAWYERS AND POLITICS

Lawyers are extensively involved in politics (Pasis, 1970; Jackson & Atkinson, 1980; Goodman, 1971; Porter, 1965). Between 1930 and 1985, six of the nine prime ministers were lawyers (including one, Pierre E. Trudeau, who was a law professor). Together they held office for thirty-five of the fifty-five years. Significant numbers of federal cabinet ministers, provincial premiers and cabinet ministers, and legislators have been lawyers. While the proportion of elected officials who are entrepreneurs, teachers, and members of other occupations is increasing, lawyers remain vastly over-represented in all Canadian political contexts. For example, 25 percent of the members of the federal House of Commons were lawyers in 1983, a higher proportion than in the British Parliament (17 percent in 1974) or the German Bundestag (5 percent in 1972) (Canadian Parliamentary Guide, 1983; Jackson & Atkinson, 1980: 156). Survey evidence indicates that a majority of the public prefer legislators who are lawyers (Samac, 1985). Moreover, politics is more easily combined with law than with other careers (Porter, 1965: 393).

Lawyers also are deeply involved in party politics as campaign managers, policy advisers, and strategists. They have not dominated senior policy positions and administrative positions in government, however, with two exceptions: (1) administrators performing adjudicative functions frequently are lawyers; and (2) Royal Commissions, often used in developing major policy initiatives, tend to be chaired by serving or retired judges.

PUBLIC ATTITUDES TOWARD THE LEGAL PROFESSION

The public is ambivalent toward lawyers. On one hand, it views them as untrustworthy; on the other hand, it respects Supreme Court judges; and those who have used lawyers' services are very satisfied; (Yale, 1982; More, 1982; but see Moore, 1980). There is ample literary evidence that Canadians dislike legalism, the aggressive and obfuscatory style of lawyers, and their apparent influence (Robins, 1971; Farris, 1972). Canadians also view themselves as law-abiding; they recently adopted a constitutional Charter of Rights and Freedoms (Russell, 1982; Arthurs, 1984), and they are quick to assume that "there ought to be a law" to deal with perceived social, economic, and even cultural problems.

In one important respect, however, Canadian lawyers have at least avoided attracting public censure, if they have not won public approbation. The introduction of legal aid in Canada proceeded without significant professional opposition, even with professional acquiescence and occasional support. In some provinces, the profession advocated the establishment of legal aid in order to win the right to administer the plan. By contrast, the medical profession resolutely opposed the introduction of medical insurance and has continued to criticize it, seek ways of working outside it, and encourage public opposition to the notion of "state medicine." Ironically, none of these maneuvers appears to have damaged public admiration for, and trust in, physicians.

THE DEMOGRAPHIC BACKGROUND OF LAWYERS

SIGNIFICANCE

Canada is a country of considerable ethnic diversity, especially since World War II (Richmond, 1967). Whereas members of ethnic minorities and disadvantaged groups in the United States gained entry to the profession through unaccredited, low-status, part-time law schools, no such route existed in Canada. In most provinces, there was—and is—only a single law school (two at most) rather closely identified with the provincial professional body. Full-time legal education became universal in Canada after World War II, largely as a result of pressure from within the academic community striving to improve standards, rather than (as has been suggested in the United States) (Auerbach, 1976) as a result of professional attempts to preclude entry by unwanted minorities (Bucknall et al., 1968; Laskin, 1983). There is no obvious national hierarchy of schools, however, although some are favored by geographic location or historical circumstance (Adam & Lahey, 1981:685). Most students attend law school in their home province or in the nearest province with a law school and, once called to the bar, rarely move to another province to practice law (see table 4). There is, therefore, no Canadian counterpart to the American elite law schools, whose graduates may clearly be identified by their social backgrounds or professional careers.

AGE

Because various Canadian provinces offer eleven, twelve, or thirteen years of primary and secondary education and because various jurisdictions require from two to four years of prelaw university education, the age for beginning law studies varies considerably. Every province requires a three-year law degree, however, together with some period of service under articles (apprenticeship). In addition, most provinces require systematic practical instruction in law, either contemporaneous with, before, or after articling. The minimum age for entry to practice thus is between twenty-four and twenty-seven. Indeed, since most law students have at least a first degree in some other field, many have pursued graduate studies in other disciplines or other careers, and some undertake graduate studies in law before entering practice, the actual age of entry is much higher than the minimum (McKennirey, 1983:124; Levy, 1972:12, 23—25; Huxter, 1981). Still, the rapid growth of the profession recently has rendered it much more youthful (see table 5).

GENDER

Although Canada was the first country in the British Empire to admit women to legal practice (in 1896) (Harvey, 1970), the number of women in law school remained minuscule until about 1970. Women now constitute 35 percent of new entrants in most jurisdictions (Berger, 1979; Zemans, 1986: 20—21; McKennirey, 1983:3) and 15 percent of all lawyers (see table 6).

As a result of conscious effort, women have been appointed in increasing numbers to law faculties, boards, commissions, and courts (including the Supreme Court of Canada, which now has its first female puisne judge). They rose from 4.4 percent of full-time law teachers in 1971/72 to 14.2 percent in 1982/83; however, they still are not well represented in the elite of the legal profession (Guppy & Siltanen, 1977; Huxter, 1981; Adam, 1981). Male judges and magistrates outnumbered female by more than eight to one in 1981—more than nineteen to one on the federal bench. Nor are women found in proportionate numbers in all types of practices.

ETHNICITY

There is a clear preponderance in the legal profession of members of the well-established charter groups: French Catholics in Quebec and English Protestants in the rest of Canada (Adam & Lahey, 1971; Arthurs et al., 1971: 500 ff.; Cadres Professionels, Inc., 1968). Some of the more established immigrant groups have managed to achieve significant representation within the profession on a local or regional basis, however, sometimes far in excess of their numbers within the general population— English Protestants in Montreal and Jews in several metropolitan centers. Children of newer immigrant groups, such as Italians and Ukrainians, also are beginning to appear in discernible numbers. Some of the most recent arrivals, such as West Indians and Asians, Portuguese and Greeks, still are significantly underrepresented, and despite conscious efforts to recruit and support native law students, their numbers remain very small (University of Saskatchewan Native Law Centre, 1981). Students from non-metropolitan areas doubtless end up practicing law in the largest cities, while relatively few seem to migrate in the opposite direction.

CLASS

Historically, law has claimed to be an "open profession." Indeed, one of its functions (reflected in the early requirements) may have been the recruitment, socialization, and certification of members of an incipient "new upper class" of considerable importance in colonial society (Baker, 1983; Smith & Tepperman, 1974).

For at least the past generation, however, entry into the legal profession, and especially access to its most prestigious positions, has been enjoyed disproportionately by individuals from professional families and other privileged socioeconomic groups (Arthurs et al., 1971; Levy, 1972; Lajoie and Parizeau, 1976; Adam & Lahey, 1981). Indeed, entry into the professions generally, and into other elites, has not been significantly democratized, largely because recent immigrant groups, the poor, and other disadvantaged minorities have been unable to overcome educational and financial barriers (Clement, 1975b; Porter, 1965; Newman, 1975). These barriers have been raised by increasing competition to enter law school since the 1960s and by the more recent downturn in the Canadian economy. Individuals from disadvantaged circumstances are found in diminishing numbers as one ascends the educational ladder (Porter, 1979; Cuneo & Curtis, 1975). Costs have risen as well: law school fees ranged from Can$340 to Can$625 in 1966/67 but were between Can$808 and Can$1,615 in 1984/85.

Many law schools have sought to admit mature students who have not attended university, native peoples, and other qualified individuals whose credentials may have been adversely affected by social or economic circumstances (McKennirey, 1983). Within the profession, meritocratic criteria have enabled some highly qualified individuals to attain legal positions from which they previously would have been excluded.

STRATIFICATION WITHIN THE PROFESSION

White Anglo-Saxon Protestant males are overrepresented in large corporate law firms, not only in English Canada but also in the predominately French city of Montreal, and Jews, Catholics, members of ethnic minorities, and women are underrepresented (Adam & Lahey, 1981; Arthurs et al., 1971:516–518). There is a tendency toward ghettoization, however, especially within the "household sector" of legal practice. "Ethnics," particularly Jews, have tended disproportionately to practice in such areas as criminal law, real estate, service to small businesses, and domestic relations (Colvin et al., 1978; Arthurs et al., 1971:512–513, 517).

STRUCTURE OF THE LEGAL PROFESSION

HISTORY

The history of the legal profession differs considerably from province to province; the civil law jurisdiction of Quebec is the most obvious special case (Lortie, 1975; Sinclair, 1975; Lachance, 1966; Buchanan, 1925). During the early period most of the very few lawyers were foreign trained. Some came directly from the United Kingdom, some were loyalist emigrés from postrevolutionary America, and others (especially judges and law officers) served in Canada before or after other colonial postings (Parker, 1982; MacAlister, 1928; Riddell, 1928).

In the older colonies such as Nova Scotia and Upper Canada (Ontario), local professional bodies soon assumed regulatory functions in imitation of the English Inns of Court, acting sometimes under statutory mandate and sometimes under executive control and direction (Johnston, 1972; Smith, 1948; Riddell, 1928; MacAlister, 1928). When there were few trained lawyers available, a considerable amount of legal business was conducted by nonqualified functionaries such as conveyancers and notaries (Gibson & Gibson, 1972). Throughout the nineteenth century, however, the profession gradually asserted its monopoly (Newman, 1974; Orkin, 1971; Hawkins, 1978; Cole, 1983). Yet as late as the midtwentieth century, lay magistrates were being appointed in Ontario, the most heavily urbanized and legally most advanced of the common law jurisdictions.

The professional body in each province, often called the "Law Society," exercised licensing functions, set standards of admission and professional conduct, and disciplined misconduct. It also retained active control of legal education until the late nineteenth century and dominated it thereafter by the joint or sole proprietorship of law schools, specification of formal educational requirements, and informal articulation of what lawyers "ought to know" (Bucknall et al., 1968; Laskin, 1983; Baker, 1983: 68).

The "numbers problem" first surfaced in the 1830s and 1840s, when lawyers and others complained about overproduction in Upper Canada. Until the midnineteenth century, law was a relatively "open" profession, in which lax standards of entry (several years of apprenticeship) posed no serious obstacles. Thereafter, more rigorous educational requirements alternated with periods of relative (even total) laxity, reflecting divergent views about whether the Law Society should pursue its project of professional socialization through formal or informal, centralized or decentralized, training schemes.

From the end of the nineteenth century, Law Societies (outside Ontario) exhibited declining interest in legal education. In many jurisdictions they gradually ceded to the universities responsibility for formal instruction in law, but everywhere they retained control over entry through a required period of apprenticeship. These changing educational requirements had, and sometimes were perceived to have had, an adverse impact on access to the profession by poor students, those from outlying areas, and foreign lawyers who had emigrated to Canada (Baker, 1983; Bucknall et al., 1968). During the Great Depression this impact was considerable, especially since it coincided with the general impoverishment of universities.

In the years following World War II, however, provincial law societies have been involved only marginally in providing basic legal education (Laskin, 1983: 153; Arnup, 1982; Bucknall et al., 1968). Today, professional associations focus on three matters: (1) "practical" professional education immediately prior to admission and on a continuing basis thereafter; (2) regulatory functions, especially those connected with the protection of client funds and other aspects of lawyer honesty and, to a lesser extent, those directed toward maintaining intraprofessional relations; and (3) public functions, including the management of legal aid schemes, dissemination of public information about law, protection of the professional monopoly, and lobbying on behalf of the legal profession.

THE SCOPE OF PRACTICE

The right to define the scope of practice is no less valuable a prerogative in protecting the professional monopoly than is the regulation of entry. The Canadian legal profession uses the same device as its counterpart in the United States, namely, statutory provisions against unauthorized practice. Until recently, the clear trend has been to extend the jurisdictional claims of lawyers across a wide spectrum of practice situations—from advocacy to the preparation of documents intended to have legal effect and ultimately to legal advice (Davies, 1952: 25; Orkin, 1957: 248–253; see, e.g., Law Society Act, Rev. Stat. Manitoba 1970, c. L100.5.48 [2] [7]. The fact that most statutes permit people to act on their own behalf or as unremunerated agents does little to dispel the suspicion that restrictions on practice have less to do with protecting consumers than with protecting markets.

Certain exemptions or limited rights to "practice" have been granted, explicitly or by acquiescence, to occupations that could not function if the statutory provisions were enforced literally. Some provinces exempt insurance claims adjusters and real estate agents as long as they function within narrowly defined limits; others allow public officials to draft legal documents (e.g., Legal Profession Act, Rev. Stat. Alberta 1980, c. L-9, s. 93 [2] [a]; Barristers and Solicitors Act, Rev. Stat. British Columbia 1979, c. 26, s. 1; see Colvin et al., 1978). Provincial statutes authorize the appearance of "agents" before small claims courts and administrative agencies (e.g., Statutory Powers Procedures Act, Rev. Stat. Ontario 1980, c. 484; Rules of the Provincial Court, Ontario Leg. 797/84). And federal legislation allows lay representation in minor criminal matters (Criminal Code, Rev. Stat. Can. 1970, c. C-34 s. 735). Rights of audience are widely exercised by trade union officials before labor boards, accountants before taxation tribunals, and more generally by law clerks and articled students (apprentices) employed by law firms.

In "gray areas" that the monopoly does not clearly reach, explicit jurisdictional understandings ensure due regard for professional interests. Trust companies thus are allowed to draw wills, provided they are "reviewed" by private practitioners, and community clinics may dispense legal advice and service in less important matters through law students and lay advocates, if significant remunerative work is forwarded to qualified private practitioners.

Judicial interpretation of jurisdictional statutes also has tended to enlarge the protected scope of professional practice. The preparation of papers for probate, the drawing of wills, the drafting of legal documents by a collection agency, applications for incorporation, and the processing of uncontested divorces all have been designated "unauthorized practice" when performed for gain by a nonlawyer, even in the absence of compelling statutory language (e.g., *R. v. Engel and Seaway Divorcing Service* [1974], 11 O.R. [2d] 343). A recent ruling appears to set some limits on the legal monopoly, however, by requiring that activities be reserved to lawyers only if it can be demonstrated that the public otherwise would be placed at risk (*R. v. Nicholson* [1979], 96 D.L.R. [3d] 693 [Alta. C.A.]).

Legal action against "unauthorized practice" typically is initiated by law societies, which usually intervene at the request of a member. There is some indication that the adverse market conditions of the late 1970s and early 1980s are reflected in an increasing number of complaints received by the unauthorized practice committees of professional bodies. In Ontario, for example, ten to sixteen complaints were received annually between 1968 and 1973; during the next eight years this increased to thirty-five to ninety per year (Professional Orgnaizations Committee, 1980: 242). It should be noted that most complaints are either diverted or negotiated. Very few lead to actual prosecution. Because of the transparent element of professional self-interest, an Ontario commission recently recommended that no prosecution for unauthorized practice be commenced except with the written consent of the attorney general of the province (ibid.).

PROFESSIONAL AUTONOMY AND PUBLIC ACCOUNTABILITY

Despite the success of provincial Law Societies in dominating the market for legal services, the professional hegemony of Canadian lawyers has not gone entirely unchallenged. Both the demand from professional groups that provincial legislatures mediate jurisdictional disputes and attempts by several occupational associations to secure certification or licensure regimes have caused governments to reevaluate their policies toward the professions in general. Moreover, governments have been increasingly responsive to appeals from consumer groups for greater accountability by the professions. Although public debate has focused on the organization and financing of the health occupations, the position of the bar in the division of labor also has been examined by several governmental commissions and inquiries over the past fifteen years (Royal Commission Inquiry into Civil Rights, 1968; Commission of Inquiry on Health and Social Welfare, 1970; Economic Council of Canada, 1969; Professional Organizations Committee, 1980).

No province has gone further than Quebec in modifying the relationship between the state and the professions. In 1973, several years after a provincial Royal Commission spoke extensively to the issues, Quebec enacted a Professional Code, which formally expanded public control over all professional groups, including the bar, far beyond the controls prevailing in other provinces (Stat. Quebec 1973, c. 43). The central innovation is the organization of all professions into corporations with parallel mandates and the subordination of these corporations to an overarching provincial Professions Board, all of whose members belong to some profession but are appointed by the provincial cabinet. The board ensures that each profession fulfills its statutory obligations, approves regulations proposed by the professions, including fee schedules, and publishes decisions in disciplinary cases. A provincial Professions Tribunal hears appeals from the disciplinary tribunal of each body. Although other provinces have rejected these changes on the ground that they threaten the independence of the bar, there is little to justify this fear (Issalys, 1978; Pepin, 1979; Arthurs, 1982).

A much more typical response to demands for professional accountability has been to leave the bar's historic governing structures essentially intact while engrafting additional elements designed to provide the public symbolic reassurance but no real control (Arthurs, 1982). The experience of Ontario is instructive (Arthurs, 1971). Responding to the recommendations of a Royal Commission of Inquiry, the Ontario legislature in 1970 created a "Law Society Council," composed of representatives of the profession's governing body and other legal "estates" as well as some public members and charged with reporting to the legislature annually about how the profession discharged its public responsibilities. Lacking a fixed agenda, its own secretariat, and public members with identifiable constituencies, the council soon ceased to function. In its place, the legislature mandated the direct appointment of four lay members to the governing body (about 10 percent of its membership). Hostages to fortune, and no more influential than their individual exertions and talents dictate, these lay members have largely deflected public demand for further state control of the profession without actually providing any effective means of enforcing public accountability. Similarly, a statutory admonition that the provincial attorney general (an ex officio member of the governing body) should serve as guardian of the public interest has had little practical result.

Lay membership of local and provincial legal aid committees does seem to give some support and direction to attempts to provide legal services to the poor. Public accountability seems to depend on episodic pressure from a variety of external sources, however: a Royal Commission or legislative committee investigating some aspect of professional practice or governance; newspaper editorials or legislative debates signaling concern with the bar's policies; occasional threats of investigation or prosecution by the combines (antitrust) authorities; or adverse comments on the behavior of lawyers or law societies by judges, in the course of litigation or extrajudicially.

Given the relatively nonintrusive and sporadic nature of these criticisms and demands for accountability, it is difficult to see much connection between the profession's virtual obsession with "independence of the bar" and any real threat. Rather, the shibboleth of independence is a central premise of professional ideology, pronounced for internal consumption more than to persuade an external audience.

REGULATION OF ENTRY

Except for a few local idiosyncracies concerning subject requirements, everyone with a basic credential (LL.B.) from any Canadian Law school may complete the professional requirements for admission in any Canadian jurisdiction (other than Quebec, which has a civil law system). For at least twenty years, emphasis has been placed on the "portability" of law degrees among Canadian jurisdictions (Murray, 1979; Berger, 1979: 41), although this is subject to several practical restraints.

First, "portability" applies only at the moment of graduation from law school. The interprovincial mobility of practitioners has been inhibited by various measures designed to discourage either transfers or simultaneous practice in several jurisdictions (Murray, 1979). The recent enactment of a constitutional guarantee of "occupational mobility" (Canadian Charter of Rights and Freedoms, s. 6[2]), however, coupled with the first appearance of "interprovincial" law firms, may alter this position (Clarry, 1982).

Second, even though LL.B. degrees are "portable" in principle, attempts have been made to encourage employers to fill articling positions with graduates from inside the province. These have been only partially successful because firms wish to hire the best available candidates.

Third, those without Canadian credentials obviously do not benefit from this arrangement. Holders of foreign degrees find it very difficult to requalify in Canada and almost always must complete further formal education, as well as professional training. The requirement that all entrants possess Canadian citizenship recently was challenged unsuccessfully on constitutional grounds (Re Skapinker [1984], 9 D.L.R. [4th] 161; see Lenoir, 1981).

It might seem possible to control entry by regulating the number of articling positions, and such restrictive practices may, indeed, exist in small communities; however, most Law Societies have undertaken to secure articles for all local graduates. Likewise, except for a few well-publicized and atypical instances, Law Societies have not attempted to restrict entry by ensuring artificially high failure rates on bar admission examinations (Bowlby, 1982). The pass rate for the Law Society of Upper Canada's Bar Admission Course was 98 percent in 1973 and 99 percent in both 1979 and 1985.

In general, then, entry into the profession is effectively determined by the award of an LL.B. degree. Indeed, because Canadian law schools have a very low failure rate (due to the high entry standards) (Browning, 1976), acceptance to an LL.B. program virtually ensures ultimate admission to practice.

Although professional bodies may exert influence on governments that financially support university law programs, or even on the policies of law faculties themselves, they do not ultimately control law school admissions. Canadian law schools experienced very considerable growth from the mid-1960s through the mid-1970s (see table 7; also Consultative Group on Research and Education in Law, 1983: 25). Existing faculties expanded greatly, and new schools were opened. Nevertheless, law students constituted about the same proportion of postsecondary students at the end of the period as at the beginning.

Factors inhibiting the further growth of law faculties lay largely outside professional control. Law schools were reluctant to grow because of the difficulties of recruiting and retaining teachers, unfavorable student-faculty ratios, and inadequate financial support. Despite the fact that declining birth rates might have been expected to reduce the number of applicants for admission to law school by the early 1980s, fierce competition persists, with the ratio of applications to available places running between 5 : 1 and 10 : 1 (see table 8).

The unanswered question, however, is the extent to which law schools have internalized professional assumptions and values, unconsciously responding to the widespread desire of lawyers to limit growth during a period of economic contraction (Consultative Group in Research and Education in Law, 1983: 42). In Ontario, this desire was manifest in the response to a 1981 survey conducted by the Law Society, in the creation in 1983 of an Ontario Lawyers' Association overtly committed to limiting numbers, and in the prolimitation rhetoric of most candidates seeking election to the profession's governing body in the 1983 quadrennial election.

This pressure was resisted at several points, however. Professional governing bodies disclaimed authority to restrict numbers and, fearing legal and political repercussions, were reluctant to seek necessary statutory changes. These governing bodies, moreover, generally are dominated by established practitioners who are less exposed to fluctuations in the economy and thus can afford the luxury of taking a principled stand in favor of the play of market forces. Since the level of government support for legal education is indirectly linked to enrollment, law faculties understandably are reluctant to consider entry controls.

In any event, restriction of entry is unlikely significantly to alleviate economic problems within the profession in the absence of a strategy to redeploy existing or future practitioners to areas of potential demand (Stager, 1982: 134). The effect of market forces already is being felt. The number of lawyers in private practice is growing more slowly, and many new graduates (and some established practitioners) have been diverted into new areas of activity, such as legal aid (Berger, 1979: 18, 49, 50), and especially into nonpractice roles in business, government, and elsewhere. Between 1971 and 1982 the proportion of Ontario lawyers in private practice declined from 86 percent to 71 percent (Law Society of Upper Canada, 1983b: 227).

PROFESSIONAL ASSOCIATIONS

Voluntary Organizations

Canadian Bar Association.   This is the only national body of Canadian lawyers. It is organized into provincial branches whose membership ranges from the entire practicing bar in some provinces (as a result of compulsion) to a rather lower level in Quebec (because notaries are excluded). The Canadian Bar Association (CBA) performs many of its functions through special sections organized around areas of professional practice such as labor relations, estate planning, and taxation or around special interests such as legal education. The function of these sections is largely educational but also includes participation in law reform and the expression of views on matters of public concern or professional interest. The CBA thus expended considerable effort and funds in recent national debates over constitutional changes (CBA, 1978). It also has adopted relatively liberal resolutions on such matters as capital punishment, abortion, search and seizure, and the rights of prisoners and the disabled; however, the CBA regularly endorses modestly conservative positions on taxation and government regulation of the economy. Understandably, the organizational behavior of the CBA and its ideology and formal public positions all seek to advance professional interests and values, although pronouncements often are couched in terms of public contribution and responsibility (Mackimmie, 1963).

In addition to these functions, the CBA traditionally has provided important social links, although these probably are diminishing as the profession expands, diversifies in functions, and stratifies in terms of social background and economic rewards. More important, in recent years, have been services to members, including insurance and pension schemes and advice on law office management.

Local Lawyers' Clubs. Most communities in which lawyers practice have at least one organization whose membership is open to all local practitioners. Almost all are devoted to parochial interests, such as social activities, seminars, and the provision of a local law library.

At least before recent amendments arguably made antitrust legislation applicable to legal services (*A.G. Canada* v. *Law Society of British Columbia* [1982], 137 D.L.R. [3d] 1 [Sup. Ct. Can.]), it was quite common for local law associations to adopt minimum fee tariffs for standard transactions and services. In Ontario, 1 percent or 1.25 percent commonly was charged the purchaser or the vendor for conveying a house. Such tariff arrangements apparently still are enforced in small communities by social pressures. Local organizations also may engage in restrictive practices, such as agreeing not to employ articling students in order to limit competition.

As the legality of these arrangements has been challenged (Henderson, 1977; Posluns, 1980), local law associations have turned from direct attempts to control prices to efforts to persuade provincial governing bodies to restrict entry and to adopt legally binding fee tariffs, breach of which would lead to disciplinary sanctions.

Professional Specialist Organizations. Organizations have been formed of criminal lawyers, corporate counsel, Crown attorneys, advocates, and other specialists. A few are national, such as the Canadian Association of Law Teachers. One or two embrace a broad spectrum of lawyers, such as the "Osgoode Society" (for legal history). Other groups set ambitious goals, such as the Continuing Legal Education Society of British Columbia, which pursues its mandate on behalf of the provincial branch of the Bar Association, the Law Society, and the law faculties.

Special Constituencies within the Profession. There are a number of relatively small organizations uniting lawyers on the basis of characteristics other than common professional interests. The Women's Law Association is an older organization; Women and Law is a younger grouping of feminists (lawyers and laypersons) concerned about both the role of women within the profession and the impact of law on women. The Thomas More Lawyers' Guild contains Catholic lawyers, and there are organizations of Jewish lawyers and of members of other religious or ethnic groups, such as native peoples. The Law Union contains progressive lawyers and other legal workers (Martin, 1985). At the other end of the spectrum is the recently founded Ontario Lawyers' Association, which might be described as a right-wing grass-roots organization.

Quasipublic Professional Bodies

A number of bodies operate under the joint auspices of the legal profession and the government. Three examples illustrate their range of interests. The Canadian Law Information Council (CLIC) promotes computerized data retrieval, assesses the knowledge needed by the profession, and educates the public about law. The Canadian Institute for the Administration of Justice (CIAJ) organizes conferences and stimulates research on the cost of justice and the organization of the judiciary.

Since 1970, legislation in almost all Canadian provinces has required that interest on lawyers' trust accounts (see table 9) be paid to a "law foundation" for public purposes (which obviously benefit the profession as well), such as law libraries, legal research and education, public legal education, and legal aid.

Compulsory Organizations

Everyone practicing law must belong to the provincial law society. Termination or suspension of membership terminates or suspends the right to practice. Practicing law without membership is an offense.

The governing body is controlled by an elected executive, whose members generally are called "benchers." Older lawyers, those practicing in cities, members of large, prestigious firms, and leading civil and criminal advocates are overrepresented in these bodies, whereas rank-and-file practitioners; women; and lawyers employed by government, universities, or corporations tend to be underrepresented (Orkin, 1971: 116–124; see tables 10, 11, this chapter). Except in Ontario, however, where elections are at large, the governing body is elected from defined geographic constituencies and, therefore, may be relatively close to the views of most practitioners; minority and dissident viewpoints seldom are represented.

The clublike character of governing bodies is reflected in their relatively restrained behavior. There is some virtue in their passivity. For example, with one notable exception (*Re Legal Profession Act, Re Martin* [1949], D.L.R. 106 [B.C. Law Soc.], aff'd [1950], 3 D.L.R. 173 [B.C.C.A.]), the Canadian legal profession avoided attempts to enforce ideological conformity, even during the most intense period of the cold war. Indeed, leaders of the bar defended those accused during the notorious "spy trials" in the late 1940s. An air of "noblesse oblige" still often characterizes the official positions of law societies on public policy issues (Chadwick, 1981); however, members have little opportunity to influence the policies of the governing body. The annual meeting usually is pro forma, and members can express their views on the decisions taken by their representatives only through elections.

Governing bodies still do respond to pressure from voluntary organizations. For example, provincial law societies and provincial CBA branches compete or cooperate in the area of continuing legal education. Organizations of defense counsel may affect the rules of professional conduct. In addition, local law associations may shape decisions relating to the establishment of legal clinics.

Because the provincial law societies exercise delegated statutory powers and collaborate with government in legal aid and law reform, leaders of the profession seek to avoid political controversy (Giffen, 1961; Orkin, 1971). While considerable attention recently was devoted to fending off an inquiry by the Province of Ontario into professional governance (Professional Organizations Committee, 1980), the Law Society simultaneously responded to well-founded concerns about its disciplinary system.

In general, the governing bodies of the Canadian legal profession have been fairly astute politically. They have perceived that there is more to be gained by cooperating with government than by opposing it. For example, the profession's governing body supported the establishment of a Legal Aid Plan in Ontario, despite some rank-and-file skepticism, with the result that the Law Society was given responsibility for administering the scheme. Similarly, the professionally-administered plan accommodated criticism of the fee-for-service aspects by funding community-based clinics.

Law societies have hewed rather carefully to the line that their primary functions are to regulate admissions, standards of conduct, and (recently) competence (Thom, 1974). Admissions committees in most Canadian provinces have been relatively lax in scrutinizing the nonacademic credentials of applicants, refusing to deny entry for minor drug convictions and other offenses connected with adolescent crises or student culture. In one recent unusual case, a lawyer convicted of a criminal offense involving egregious sexual misconduct with minors was disbarred (ibid.); a similar fate befell a lawyer implicated in the theft of valuable securities (*Novak v. Law Society of British Columbia* [1972], 31 D.L.R. [3d] 89 [B.C.S.C.]). It is relatively rare that anyone is disbarred except for dishonesty or other misconduct directly connected with professional functions, however. Of those disbarred in Ontario between 1945 and 1965, 83 percent improperly used client funds, 6 percent committed other fraud or forgery, and 8 percent neglected client affairs (Arthurs, 1970).

SYSTEMS OF PROFESSIONAL CONTROL: CODES OF ETHICS

Provincial governing bodies have statutory power to discipline their members for "conduct unbecoming a barrister or solicitor" or "unprofessional conduct" (e.g., Law Society Act, Rev. Stat. Ont. 1980, c. 233, s. 34). In some jurisdictions, these vague standards are made more precise by additional statutory language (e.g., Barristers and Solicitors Act, Rev. Stat. British Columbia 1979, c. 26, s. 50) or, more frequently, by regulations (subordinate legislation) adopted subject to the approval of the provincial cabinet (and, in Quebec, of the Professional Council) (Professions Code, Rev. Stat. Quebec 1977, c. c-26, ss. 12, 13, 94, 95). Ontario, for example, regulates the handling of trust funds very extensively (Law Society Act, Rev. Stat. Ontario 1980, c. 233, s. 63; Rev. Reg. Ont. 1980, Reg. 573).

Most provinces have also adopted professional conduct rules (Law Society of Upper Canada, 1983c), which are treated as guidelines rather than binding codes by bodies responsible for discipline. These codes generally were inspired by those adopted by the CBA (1920; 1974). The 1920 CBA Code was extremely vague (having been modeled on a contemporary American Bar Association document) and did not respond to the changing nature of legal practice for the next half century. Never amended and seldom referred to in disciplinary proceedings or even hortatory discussions of professional ethics, it remained a well-kept secret.

By contrast, the 1974 code was well publicized, formally adopted in most provinces, and more influential in both disciplinary proceedings and discussions of appropriate standards of professional conduct. Yet it, too, is overly vague and insufficiently rooted in reality. The code appears to adopt the perspective of the client and the public. For example, restrictions on advertising—for clearly anticompetitive purposes—are contained in a rule entitled "Making Legal Services Available" and couched in terms of the desire to avoid either burdening the public with the cost of advertising or misleading the public.

Disciplinary enforcement is preoccupied with ensuring the honesty of lawyers (Arthurs, 1970). Regulations prescribe methods of accounting for client funds; all law societies conduct regular audits, and some engage in "spot audits"—there were 864 in Ontario in 1984. Noncompliance with these rules, even when one is negligent rather than dishonest, generally leads to discipline. Dishonesty is almost certain to result in disbarment, except when there are unusual mitigating circumstances, such as mental problems or personal tragedies. Victims of lawyer dishonesty receive payments (generally within high but fixed limits) from a compensation fund to which all lawyers must contribute. Payments in Ontario rose from Can$737,000 for 88 claims in 1981 to Can$1,182,000 for 216 claims in 1984 (Law Society of Upper Canada, Annual Reports).

Lawyers almost never are disciplined except when the public is injured by fraud, perjury, or some other criminal act (Arthurs, 1970; see also table 12, this chapter). Between 1966 and 1979 the number of complaints rose in Ontario, but the number of disbarments remained constant at approximately four a year; since then it has risen to twelve in 1980, nineteen in 1981, twenty-five in 1982, and twenty-one in 1984 (Law Society of Upper Canada, Annual Reports). Otherwise, the disciplinary process is used to enforce professional interests only in a few high-profile cases when the authority of the Law Society is challenged. For example, a recent well-publicized and extensive advertising campaign by a lawyer evoked the threat of disciplinary sanctions and stimulated extensive litigation before leading to relaxation of the rules (*Jabour* v. *Law Society of British Columbia* [1982], 137 D.L.R. [3d] 1 [Sup. Ct. Can.]).

Informal enforcement processes may influence professional behavior, however; these processes include investigations by the law society and threats to investigate, informal admonitions or formal warnings by the governing body, and social and economic sanctions by formal and informal local lawyer groups. Such informal processes generally are directed toward either matters of intraprofessional concern or minor infractions relating to public behavior or service to clients.

Self-regulation is least satisfactory in ensuring competence (Hurlburt, 1979). While there is a great deal of exhortation and a certain amount of education, there has been very little enforcement of quality standards by means of systematic or random testing. Indeed, until the adoption of the new CBA Code of Professional Conduct (rule 2) in 1974, incompetence was not explicitly declared to be unacceptable. As a consequence, the few lawyers who have been disbarred for incompetence are those who have suffered a virtually total collapse of personality and become unable to carry on their practice; in such cases, removal from practice is viewed as nondisciplinary.

Recently, however, the provincial bars have sought to reassure the public by requiring lawyers to carry "errors and omissions" insurance.

Within a few years after its introduction, claims—and hence premiums—
began to mount (see table 13), especially in real estate practices (see table
14). This engendered considerable concern and led to the development of
three strategies designed to enhance competence, thereby reducing both
claims and premiums (Swan, 1982; Hurlburt, 1979): (1) programs of continuing legal education and "claims control" have been instituted (Gold,
1972: 23), (2) rehabilitative programs assist lawyers whose practices appear
to be falling below an acceptable standard (Marshall, 1980), and (3) proper
standards of practice are encouraged by experience rating of insurance
premiums (in Ontario, rates varied between Can$825 and Can$3,300 in
1983/84).

Victims of incompetence also may sue lawyers for damages (Belobaba,
1978; Pritchard, 1978), and judgments appear to be increasing in number
and size. Finally, a judge may intervene when an advocate performs incom-
petently, although this remains exceptional (*Re Solicitor* [1971], 1 Ont. Rep.
138).

Specialization has been increasing, at least in larger urban centers (Arthurs et al., 1971; Esau, 1979; Colvin et al., 1978; Colvin, 1979). Nevertheless, clients still encounter difficulty finding lawyers who can provide
competent service even in such prosaic household "specialties" as criminal
law, family law, or civil litigation (Trebilcock & Reiter, 1982). Proposals to
certify specialists, thereby ensuring their competence and enhancing their
visibility to clients, were adopted in principle by the CBA in 1983; however, the law societies remain adamantly opposed to both formal certification and systems of self-designation. Instead, the profession has attacked
those who "advertise" their specialty and thereby seek competitive advantage (Professional Organizations Committee, 1980).

SYSTEMS OF PROFESSIONAL CONTROL: PROCEDURES AND
INSTITUTIONS

If a complaint against a lawyer progresses beyond the stage of informal
discussion, the disciplinary committee conducts a formal hearing, prosecuted by the Law Society staff or special counsel. The committee's decision often is subject to approval by, or appeal to, the full governing body
(e.g., Law Society Act, Rev. Stat. Ontario 1980, c. 233, ss. 33, 34, 39). The
committee can reprimand, limit the right to practice, suspend, or disbar.
Some law societies also have the power to impose financial penalties (e.g.,
Barristers and Solicitors Act, Rev. Stat. British Columbia 1979, c. 26,
s. 51[1]) and to suspend those suffering from physical or mental illness,
while managing their practices to protect client assets and interests. The
sanctioned lawyer (but not the complainant) can seek judicial review of

legal or procedural errors; however, judges are reluctant to retry facts or review penalties absent egregious injustice (*Prescott* v. *Law Society of British Columbia* [1971], 19 D.L.R. [3d] 446 [B.C.C.A]).

The profession thus controls both the prosecution and adjudication of misconduct. There is no provision for a "lay observer" or any other lay participation in the disciplinary process, except for the involvement of lay benchers, if any. Moreover, since most dishonest lawyers are bankrupt, clients can only seek ex gratia payments from the profession's compensation fund.

EDUCATION, SOCIALIZATION, AND ALLOCATION

HISTORICAL DEVELOPMENT

For most of the nineteenth century, and through the first half of the twentieth in some provinces (including Ontario, the largest common law jurisdiction), apprenticeship was the primary means by which Canadian lawyers were educated. Full-time law schools began to appear about 1880, but both the University of Montreal (1878) and Dalhousie University law faculties (1883) had minuscule professorial complements until after 1945, depending largely on part-time lecturers from the bench and the bar. A similar situation prevailed at the Universities of Saskatchewan and Alberta. Elsewhere, provincial law societies opened their own law schools—alone or in collaboration with universities—again primarily using practitioners as teachers (Bucknall et al., 1968; Baker, 1983; see also table 15, this chapter). When A. Z. Reed completed his classic study of legal education in Canada and the United States in 1928, therefore, it was clear that the Canadian legal profession enjoyed even more control over the production of lawyers than did its U.S. counterpart (Reed, 1928: 530).

By 1925, seven out of nine provinces required at least two years of college before entry to law school, and the others required some post-secondary study. All provinces required at least three years of legal studies, and four required attendance at local law schools. All required a period of office work and a final examination (Reed, 1925: 3; see also table 16, this chapter).

Although some law schools (including the largest common law school, Osgoode Hall in Ontario) were operated by the legal profession itself, some by a university, and some jointly by a university and the local bar, these alternatives were neither conflictual nor competitive; they merely coexisted, each reigning supreme in a particular province. Moreover, all schools had agreed on a common curriculum proposed by the CBA in the early 1920s (Reed, 1928: 203). Finally, the development of academic education was inhibited by the sheer lack of full-time instructors: there were no more than sixteen full-time law teachers in all of Canada in 1928 (Reed, 1928: 373; Bucknall et al., 1968; Baker, 1983). It is no wonder, then, that the same assumptions that led Reed to propose a dual system of legal education in the United States persuaded him to recommend a uniform system of legal education in Canada.

The bar's monopoly over all phases of the production of lawyers lasted until the 1950s, when the university law faculties gradually claimed increasing authority over legal education. In 1957, under pressure from the academic community, Canada's largest legal professional body, the Law Society of Upper Canada (Ontario), negotiated a new arrangement with the universities giving the professoriat ultimate responsibility for the LL.B. curriculum (Arnup, 1982; Bucknall et al., 1968). In 1968 the Law Society transferred its own law school to York University (Arthurs, 1967). Similar developments in other provinces during the 1950s and 1960s, coupled with the rapid proliferation and expansion of law faculties, assured the universities their present dominance of legal education, but they seemed unprepared to assume the responsibility. As late as 1950, there were only about 40 full-time law teachers in all of Canada; fewer than 100 were added in the next decade. By 1970, however, numbers had tripled to about 450, and by 1980 they stood at 650. Between 1960 and 1980 there was considerable innovation in curriculum, teaching methods, and modes of research, sometimes engendering expressions of professional concern (MacDonald, 1979; Veitch, 1979; MacLaren, 1974). At no time, however, did law schools challenge the profession's ideology or intellectual capital (McKennirey, 1983: 118; Consultative Group on Education and Research in Law, 1983). In addition, the provincial law societies continued to control the professional training phase, which generally includes a period of apprenticeship and formal instruction in various adjectival and practical matters, as well as skills training.

LEGAL EDUCATION AS A STRATEGY OF SOCIALIZATION AND ALLOCATION

There is no scholarly tradition in Canadian law to challenge professional priorities. The strategy of the law schools has been to stand at a distance from the profession, sometimes through a scholastic concern with doctrinal analysis and sometimes through a robust critique of professional knowledge and ideology. At the same time, academics seek to be perceived as highly "professional" without being involved in, or even considering, all the activities of practicing lawyers. Legal education projects an artificial and misshapen representation of legal reality, rather like Durer's rhinoceros.

Law schools try to socialize students to an academic model of legal practice and social reality. Although the attempt largely fails, the profession lavishes considerable energy on resocializing students to professional attitudes and values through articling and the bar admission courses and also through indoctrination of new graduates. Moreover, the bar has a valuable ally: the majority of law students, who tend to identify with what they imagine to be the professional project.

There are few exceptions to these generalizations. The University of Quebec at Montreal deliberately embarked on an alternative vision of legal education, emphasizing its social dimension and expressing overt antagonism toward professional elitism (Mackay, 1979). Recently founded law schools in Calgary and Victoria made important pedagogic innovations. McGill, Ottawa, and Moncton all have responded to the bilingual and bisystemic nature of Canadian law. Several schools are committed to clinical legal education. Interdisciplinary studies, even joint degrees in law and some other field (typically business), have become available in most law schools. Students seize these varied opportunities relatively rarely, however, and the innovations affect the margins rather than the "professional" mainstream of LL.B. studies.

Professional control of entry to practice, coupled with professional administration of articling and bar admission courses, discouraged the emergence of private, entrepreneurial "cram" schools. Nothing ensured that the profession's own educational programs would maintain high standards (Law Society of Upper Canada, 1972). For example, articling is regarded as essentially a matter between student and principal. Law societies do exhort both to pursue the objectives of articling, but there is virtually no quality control. Teaching is a sideline for the articling principal, who is primarily (and sometimes totally) preoccupied with the service of clients. Students are likely either to be passive observers or to perform delegated tasks—at best of legal research and drafting, at worst of mere logistical support. The functions of an articling student seldom relate directly to the practical business of interviewing, advocacy, or negotiation. This may explain why articling is regarded as paid employment (although salaries are well below market rates for newly admitted lawyers).

Articling has acquired a secondary importance as an entree to future jobs, however. Large law firms use articling as a screening device to identify junior lawyers who may be hired on their call to the bar. Small law firms may use articling students to cope with their work loads, selecting occasional recruits when additional business warrants expansion. This is not automatic: a 1980 study revealed that 66 percent of students did not return to work at the firm where they articled, and more than 40 percent had not found any job by the end of the six-month bar admission course that follows the articling year in Ontario (Huxter, 1981: 18). Nevertheless, students compete energetically for articling jobs (ibid.). The prestige, income, and work quality offered by large law firms makes them the first choice of many (see table 17). While these firms historically tended to recruit primarily on the basis of the "old school tie," now they emphasize academic credentials. This reflects the need for able students and juniors to handle sophisticated legal work, the diminishing acceptability of discrimination, and the growing economic power of various minority groups who are more likely to take their legal business to law firms that hire their best young members.

Large firms have little tolerance for idiosyncratic personal behavior, political views, or lifestyles. As a result, a few "ethnic" law firms have emerged, which sometimes deliberately dilute their parochial character by adding members of other groups. More recently, too, some "political" left-wing lawyers have formed firms or adopted space-sharing arrangements.

Lawyers tend to remain in the practice setting that they enter during articles or on their first jobs, although large law firms weed out some recruits after a probationary period, some small firms amalgamate with each other or with large firms, and a few individual practitioners change their practices because of either unusual success or failure (Adam & Lahey, 1981; Huxter, 1981; Berger, 1979; Colvin et al., 1978: 101).

DIVISION AND STRATIFICATION WITHIN THE LEGAL PROFESSION

THE MYTH OF A SINGLE LEGAL PROFESSION

The Canadian legal profession clings strongly to the notion that all its members engage in a common activity, share common attitudes, pursue common interests, and participate equally in the common enterprise of delivering legal services to the public. There is merely a single professional credential earned in a single fashion in each jurisdiction (except Quebec, with its *Chambre des Notaires*), a single provincial professional organization, no formal recognition of specialties or distinctive ethical codes for those who pursue them, and only loose, voluntary organizations of lawyers distinguished by special roles or interests.

The myth is patently at odds with the facts, however. Within the profession, there is a clear division of labor, clientele, and rewards (see table 18). Moreover, both the profession and the public accord differential respect and recognition to individuals and practice roles.

Why, then, does the profession insist so vigorously on its unity and homogeneity? We propose three possible explanations: (1) there is a dearth of "hard" facts about Canadian lawyers and very little self-scrutiny by the profession, (2) the myth of professional unity helps to reinforce existing hierarchies by making them less visible, and (3) a unified profession can better protect its autonomy and influence public and governmental opinion than one that speaks with many voices.

"ELITE" LAW FIRMS

Elite law firms in Canada tend to resemble those in the United States (albeit on a somewhat reduced scale and with some distinctive Canadian touches) as a result of commonalities in their work, clientele, recruitment, and organization. Indeed, they share some multinational clients, are involved in transactions stretching across national boundaries, belong to international legal organizations, derive their legal knowledge from common sources, and occasionally are linked by international partnerships or networks of law firms.

Elite firms contain between 25 and 200 lawyers. In 1971, 10 percent of all firms earned almost half of all fees, while half of all firms earned only 14 percent (Statistics Canada, 1971). In 1985, 10 firms had more than 100 lawyers, and another 15 had between 50 and 100 (Canadian Law List, 1985). Although most operate from a single office found in the business or financial district of a large city (see table 19), a few now have branches abroad, while others are expanding on a multicity or interprovincial basis, despite local protectionism (Black v. Law Society of Alta. [1985], 5 West Wkly Rep. 284).

Elite law firms tend to be organized hierarchically. They employ a number of articling students, from whom they often choose associates. At the end of a probationary period associates either become partners or leave (see table 20). Admission to partnership occasionally occurs as a result of merger with, or absorption of, another law firm or through lateral movement.

Elite firms also depend heavily on office managers, accountants, and librarians, as well as large numbers of law clerks. Indeed, the number of specialists and law clerks sometimes equals or exceeds the number of professionally qualified lawyers (Taman, 1978; Colvin et al., 1978), and, of course, every elite law firm will employ large numbers of highly skilled secretaries and clerical personnel and invest heavily in office equipment (CBA, 1985). A managing partner or management committee is responsible for making and administering personnel policy, overseeing the financial affairs of the firm, and defining its relationship to its clients and the community at large.

Elite firms generally have significant corporate, tax, litigation, and conveyancing departments and sometimes specialize in industrial property, labor, transportation, and communications or estate planning as well (Colvin et al., 1978: 145). Certain lawyers may be identified as having a special aptitude for legal research and tend to perform it for other members of the firm. Senior partners may become preoccupied with the affairs of major clients, whom they cultivate and advise on business strategies, governmental and community relations, and other matters that may not involve the application of legal knowledge (Clement, 1975a; Gall, 1977; Porter, 1965; Newman, 1975). While many of these senior partners remain interested in "lawyers' law" and counsel their junior colleagues, some have "graduated" from the practice of law. Often it is partners in their forties and fifties who perform the most sophisticated legal work, but some may be drawn increasingly into the affairs of their corporate clients and occasionally leave the firm permanently or temporarily to serve as senior executives of major business organizations (Batten, 1980).

The financial lifeblood of the firm is the performance of legal services for its ongoing clients—major business, financial, or governmental institutions (Batten, 1980; Clement, 1975a; Gall, 1977; Colvin, 1979). The relationship of the elite firm to its clientele is further cemented by recruiting important individuals who have left politics or the public service and seconding firm members to various governmental bodies. Specialist departments also attract clients, often referred by other lawyers. Fearing to lose future referrals, firms take pains to ensure that the client is returned to the referring lawyer upon completion of the task at hand. Elite firms also may maintain a modest "household" practice, reflecting commitments that antedate the firm's rise to eminence, catering to the legal needs of individuals employed by their corporate clients, and responding to partners' beliefs about their professional and community responsibilities.

Because their clients are mainly wealthy institutions, elite law firms are able to charge very high fees and to compensate associates—and especially partners—accordingly (see table 21; Altman & Weil, Inc., 1980). Close association with a corporate clientele also affords these lawyers unusual opportunities to develop their own investments and business activities (subject to professional conduct and "insider trading" rules) (Adam & Lahey, 1981; Smith & Tepperman, 1974). Elite firm lawyers also enjoy the opportunity to become involved in extremely sophisticated legal work that demands, and generally elicits, a very high level of competence (Batten, 1980). Also, because elite firms are large and hierarchically structured, they can allow members to become active in professional bodies, community organizations, part-time law teaching, postgraduate study, or political activity.

The very conditions that generate these rewards also exact a considerable price. Members may be particularly concerned to avoid conduct that might alienate clients. This produces an extreme commitment to meeting deadlines, covering all eventualities, and avoiding technical errors. The pace and intensity of professional work may well constrain the personal lives of the lawyers. Moreover, because of the close relationship that often develops between elite firm lawyers and their corporate clients, the former—if not self-selected prior to joining the firm—subsequently may be socialized in matters ranging from personal dress and deportment to political perspectives.

METROPOLITAN MEDIUM-SIZED FIRMS

Medium-sized firms of ten to thirty lawyers often share many character-istics with the elite firms. Indeed, they often are either the remaining elite firms of an earlier period, which have opted against significant growth, or incipient elite firms, perhaps based on the merger of several small partner-ships. Some, however, are organized around a small number of specialties and do not purport to offer a complete line of legal services. The latter may provide incomes that, while very generous, are considerably lower than the extravagant professional and business incomes available in the elite firms.

Medium-sized metropolitan firms often aggressively pursue both new recruits and clients. Some have hired very able women and members of minority groups, whereas others, for essentially the same reason, appar-ently have opted for impeccable social credentials in their recruitment.

SOLO PRACTITIONERS AND SMALL FIRMS IN METROPOLITAN AREAS

The general practitioner is a central figure in the mythology of the legal profession. Solo practice and small partnerships were the most common form of legal practice until after World War II. The trend toward larger firms was evident by the 1950s (Nelligan, 1950, 1951), however, and it accelerated thereafter. Solo practitioners declined from 43 percent of all Ontario lawyers in 1950 to 21 percent in 1966 (Arthurs et al., 1971: 522–523). By the 1970s, far fewer lawyers were practicing on their own or in partnerships of two to five lawyers; however, the tendency toward consolidation was halted, and possibly reversed, by recent economic con-ditions and the rapid growth of the profession. Established firms are ex-panding at a slower rate, and small and medium-sized firms are wary of adding to their overheads by hiring new lawyers. For the first time in many years, a significant number of able young graduates find themselves in solo practice by default rather than by choice (Huxter, 1981: 177).

Solo and small firm practitioners fall into three quite different groups. First, there are the specialists (Arthurs et al., 1971: 507 ff.; Colvin et al., 1978: 158), including some of the most highly regarded practitioners of criminal and family law. Operating largely for noncorporate clients, these specialists do not require the elaborate staffs and facilities characteristic of the elite firms. Criminal defense counsel, especially, tend to reject the paraphernalia of modern practice (Schumiatcher, 1979). Although an extensive (if imperfect) legal aid system exists, it is not unusual for leading defense counsel to refuse to accept legally-aided clients, preferring to act without charge in order to underline the traditional independence of the bar and its service ethic. A few lawyers (many of them solo or small firm practitioners) are heavily dependent on legal aid, however (see table 22).

A second category of small firm practitioners are lawyer-entrepreneurs. A number of lawyers devote their energies to land assembly and mortgage financing, especially during several protracted periods of real estate speculation. Despite their considerable economic success, entrepreneurial lawyers seldom enjoy high repute within the profession. A disproportionately high number of disbarments occurred within their ranks, perhaps because they too readily accepted marketplace assumptions about relationships with investors and partners, rather than the much more circumscribed fiduciary role prescribed by codes of professional ethics (Arthurs, 1970).

In the shadow of economic difficulties, a number of young lawyers have begun to try unconventional ways of providing legal services through "law shops," charging lower fees in standardized matters, in franchised offices in store fronts, department stores, or other unconventional settings. Established lawyers have responded with hostility, invoking restrictions on advertising in order to inhibit expansion (*Re Klein and Law Society of Upper Canada; Re Dvorak and Law Society of Upper Canada* [1985], 16 D.L.R. [4th] 489). Young lawyers also have become involved in producing law reports, manuals, and practitioner-oriented texts and providing research services for law firms.

By far the greatest concentration of solo practitioners and small partnerships is in the "household sector": house transfers, uncontested divorces, debt collection, other minor civil litigation, and dealings with various levels of government (Arthurs et al., 1971: 522 ff.; Yale, 1982: 38). Because house transfers probably generate the most income, lawyers serving the household sector are particularly vulnerable to economic fluctuations, especially in the residential real estate market. Since the profit on any individual transaction is small, only volume can produce high earnings. Lay assistants, especially stenographers and title searchers, can handle most of this work, leaving the lawyer free to supervise employees and deal with clients (Colvin et al., 1978).

Because most individuals require legal services only occasionally, the solo practitioner or small partnership constantly must attract clients. This is especially difficult in large cities, where social contact is attenuated and competition for legal business is relatively fierce because of the impossibility of creating and enforcing informal understandings about price maintenance and other restrictive practices. Disproportionate numbers of Jews and Catholics and members of other minority groups are located in this sector of practice (Arthurs et al., 1971: 523). Because the household sector offers only limited opportunity for sophisticated legal work, and because of their own personal characteristics, these practitioners enjoy limited job mobility. They will seldom be able to offer prospective employers highly developed skills and reputations.

Ideological commitments formed or reinforced during service in a law school or other community clinic setting lead some young graduates to choose practice in the household sector or in criminal or family law. Others enter loose associations or partnerships that focus on such issues as women's rights, employment law, immigration, and prisoners' rights.

LAWYERS IN SMALLER CENTERS

Practice in smaller centers seems to be concentrated within a narrower spectrum of settings. For several reasons, the largest firms are much smaller, and solo practice is potentially more rewarding and prestigious than it might be in Toronto, Montreal, or Vancouver. On one hand, large industrial or commercial concerns with plants or offices in small communities tend to rely for their important legal needs on the elite metropolitan firms, whose contacts are with their bankers, directors, and head office managers rather than with local operational personnel. On the other hand, when household clients in small centers encounter atypical or complex legal problems, such as a patent, a murder charge, or a regulatory issue, they may seek the aid of an outside expert.

Offsetting the more limited opportunities for professional advancement is the much greater scope for community recognition and collegial support. Lawyers frequently join local elites, finding their way into politics, civic works, and charities. Moreover, lawyers in small communities make formal and informal arrangements concerning fees, assist each other with personal problems in the event of disability (or even professional misconduct), and share knowledge and techniques.

LAWYERS EMPLOYED IN BUSINESS, GOVERNMENT, AND EDUCATION

Lawyers working as legal professionals in settings other than private practice share certain common characteristics: (1) their identification with

their employer's organizational aims and style produces a distinctive sub-
culture setting them apart from private practitioners; (2) they are specialists with a highly developed sense of the particular political, social, and
economic context of law; and (3) because their earnings are not related
to the number of transactions processed or "billable hours" worked, employed lawyers are spared both the insecurity of solo practice and the intense pressure within elite firms. In a society characterized by increasing
bureaucratization, institutional growth, legal complexity, and a more re-
fined division of labor, therefore, the number of employed lawyers has
increased over the past two decades, their status has improved, and their
rewards have been enhanced.

PUBLIC INTEREST

Because legal aid offices, community clinics, and advocacy organizations
are chronically short of funds, lawyers in these roles often are poorly paid
and carry heavy caseloads. Since these lawyers develop special skills and
insights into particular areas of law and campaign to reform them, however, their contribution and influence are out of all proportion to their
numbers and rewards. Their close and ongoing identification with a single
"client" and cause tends to differentiate them from other lawyers in terms
of ideology, lifestyle, and perception of the legal system.

STRATIFICATION: PUBLIC AND PROFESSIONAL RANKING

Lawyers derive their prestige from at least three sources: professional
skills, public activities, and association with other prestigious persons and
institutions. It is not uncommon for a lawyer to be highly regarded by
colleagues as a careful conveyancer, tax planner, or procedural specialist
yet be virtually unknown to the general public. Conversely, lawyers who
are extremely active in business, community affairs, politics, or journalism
may be extremely well known to the public yet lack standing within the
profession. This often is the fate of lawyers employed in business, government, and the universities. Public and private reputations tend to coalesce
for lawyers in elite firms, which are involved in major transactions or
litigation and deliver specialized legal services of high quality.

These rankings may be reflected in the bestowal of government honors
—appointments to the bench and to boards and commissions of enquiry
and ad hoc special assignments. In some provinces, moreover, political
patronage may strongly influence the appointment of Queen's Counsel

and somewhat influence the appointment of lower court judges (Fowler, 1978; Robins, 1974; Angus, 1967; Ratushny, 1976). Rankings also are evidenced by election to governing bodies of law societies and voluntary organizations (Trebilcock et al., 1979). Here, too, political influences tend to dominate peer judgments about reputation.

THE MATERIAL CIRCUMSTANCES OF PRACTICE

There is a fairly direct correlation between the location, size, and attractiveness of law offices and their infrastructure (office machinery, libraries, and support staff) and the affluence of their clientele. Even solo lawyers have sought to lower costs by adopting labor-saving devices, employing paraprofessional staff (Altman & Weil, Inc., 1980: 13), locating offices in older buildings or outside the central city or sharing premises with common library facilities, reception, and telephone service.

However, cost-cutting has its limits. Law society regulations require the submission of annually audited accounts. All practitioners must pay an annual fee to the provincial professional body, contribute to a compensation fund, and pay premiums for "errors and omissions" insurance—a total of about Can$1,500 per annum in Ontario in 1984. Lawyers may bill whatever they wish, subject to subsequent arbitration by a court official (an "assessment officer" in Ontario) and the theoretical (but actually negligible) risk of professional sanctions for overcharging (Reiter, 1978: 66).

Lawyers and clients, especially large institutional clients, also may reach general understandings or explicit contractual arrangements concerning fees. Litigants in most Canadian provinces may arrange to pay a fee contingent on the outcome of the lawsuit (Arlidge, 1974; Halpern & Turnbull, 1982), although some lawyers refuse to accept them. Moreover, even in jurisdictions that do not formally permit contingent fees, lawyers often (and properly) take into account the "results achieved" in setting their fees, charging less to impecunious and unsuccessful litigants (Law Society of Upper Canada, Professional Conduct Handbook, rule 10, ss. 1 [e], 2).

Statutory tariffs cover some matters, such as the probate of wills, while court schedules of "party-and-party" costs regulate how much a losing litigant must pay for the winner's legal fees (Orkin 1968). These official indices influence what lawyers charge their own clients, adjusted for the importance of the matter, the results achieved, and the time expended (*Re A Solicitor* [1972], 3 Ont. Rep. 433). Many local lawyers groups also have adopted minimum or suggested fee tariffs for standard nonlitigious services.

Governments intervene to affect the price of legal services as well. They have enacted legislation defining the scope of the professional monopoly, thereby restricting competition by lay persons or other occupational groups (such as accountants) and increasing lawyer income (Trebilcock & Reiter, 1982: 84 ff.); however, government affects professional incomes most strongly through legal aid schemes. Although legal aid fee structures do not govern private legal services, they may set a standard that paying clients will use. Legal clinics, legal aid staff lawyers, and publicly reimbursed private practitioners may undercut existing market prices.

This undercutting may reflect government-imposed budget limitations as well as economies of scale. In some provinces many lawyers earn a significant portion of their incomes from legal aid. When the government cuts the budget, lawyers who depend on legal aid funds may find themselves pressed to the wall. Professional criticism of cutbacks in legal aid thus expresses both a concern for access to justice and a desire to preserve professional incomes (Bowlby, 1983: 145–147).

These factors differently affect the various professional strata. Elite law firms and certain specialists generally disregard suggested fee tariffs. Solo lawyers who practice family or criminal law may be highly sensitive to the level of legal aid expenditures but largely indifferent to attempts to establish minimum conveyancing charges. Those specializing in real estate may cooperate in price-fixing, especially if they work in small communities.

THE REGULATION OF NONPRICE COMPETITION

The rules of professional conduct regulate nonprice competition primarily through limitations on the form and content of advertising (Hudec & Trebilcock, 1982; Evans & Wolfson, 1982). While the controls generally are more restrictive than those in the United States, there nevertheless are important differences among the provinces. Manitoba, the most liberal jurisdiction, permits lawyers to advertise price and nonprice information in any medium as long as they do not mislead the public, avoid "puffery," accurately describe the services offered, and adhere to the fees quoted (Mitchell, 1982: 129). Ontario not only forbids all advertising of fees (except for the cost of an initial consultation) but also limits nonfee advertising to publication of the lawyer's professional card in newspapers and other printed matter (Law Society of Upper Canada, Professional Conduct Handbook, rules 13, 14). However, the same law society also introduced a lawyer referral system that informs clients of practitioner specialties and entitles clients to an initial consultation at relatively low cost; and it established a "Law Line" telephone service providing basic information on typical legal problems and directing callers to the referral service (Bowlby, 1982: 158 ff.).

In Ontario, the Professional Organizations Committee (1980: 192) noted that individuals and small businesses in large urban settings are most likely to lack information about legal services because they are less frequent consumers than large corporate clients and because informal referral networks are less effective in large metropolitan areas. The CBA and many provincial bodies have adopted a rule whose commentary notes that "when considering whether or not limited advertising in a particular area meets the public need, consideration must be given to the clientele to be served" (Code of Professional Conduct, c. xiii, s. 6).

There is some evidence that urban solo practitioners and those in firms with less than four lawyers most strongly support the liberalization of advertising rules (Sharpe, 1981: 279). Their colleagues in rural areas and small cities oppose any easing of these restrictions by an even greater margin, however. The Supreme Court of Canada recently held that neither federal combines (antitrust) legislation nor quasiconstitutional guarantees of freedom of expression prohibit such restrictions (*Jabour* v. *Law Society of British Columbia* [1982], 137 D.L.R. [3d] 1 [Sup. Ct. Can.]).

Codes of conduct also prohibit lawyers from "touting" by approaching potential clients directly, claiming "specialist" status, attracting publicity in the media, or encouraging real estate agents, clubs, or other intermediaries to "steer" business to them (Law Society of Upper Canada, Professional Conduct Handbook, rule 13, ss. 7–8). Lawyers may not practice in multiprofessional firms, which could make internal referrals (Quinn, 1978); in some provinces, they may not practice another profession or occupation that could attract legal clients.

These measures limit the profession's urban "proletariat"—solo and small firm practitioners—at the behest of its intermediate orders, practitioners in smaller centers. Although metropolitan solo practitioners do not "poach" the clients of country lawyers, the latter seem to fear that greater competition in their own locales will disturb existing patterns of practice. Anticompetitive rules also provide a legitimate device for harrassing nonconformists in country towns and small cities. In larger centers, where enforcement is more difficult, some competition persists within the household sector despite the rules.

Elite firms and specialists attract business by joining clubs, serving as corporate directors, becoming involved in politics, providing community service, teaching part-time, and writing books. They seek to suppress competition in order to strengthen the profession's image as a superior social class rather than a "mere" trade or business. Since such restraints also invite public disapproval without conferring economic benefits, however, elite lawyers and leading specialists have no interest in actually enforcing anticompetitive rules.

EFFECT ON THE PROFESSION OF RECENT
DEVELOPMENTS IN LEGAL SERVICES DELIVERY

Legal aid programs not only have encouraged more lawyers to practice criminal and family law; they also have created jobs for salaried professionals in community-based clinics in Ontario, Nova Scotia, and Saskatchewan and in government legal aid bureaus in Quebec. Indeed, legal aid may have a greater impact on lawyers and their professional careers than on low-income Canadians. Ontario established the first provincially funded judicare scheme in 1967. The number of accused represented increased from 1,587 persons in 1963 (Friedland, 1964) to nearly 41,000 in 1983, at a cost of Can$21 million, or Can$523.86 per case (Law Society of Upper Canada, 1983a: 49). National expenditures on legal aid rose from Can$62 million in 1975/76 to Can$90 million in 1978/79, and per capita expenditures from Can$2.71 to Can$3.81, although the latter figures vary greatly among provinces. Between 1978/79 and 1984/85, the total expenditures increased from Can$31 to Can$60 million in Quebec and from Can$34 to Can$70 million in Ontario.

Because the provinces are responsible for administering justice, their legal aid programs differ significantly (Zemans, 1979; 1983: 373–435). Federal cost-sharing agreements require the provinces to administer a flexible means test that considers income, disposable assets, indebtedness, maintenance obligations, and other expenses (National Legal Aid Research Centre, 1981: 2; Statistics Canada, 1981: 20). In addition to providing legal services for representation in court, many Canadian legal aid schemes have adopted the Scottish duty counsel system, which provides a salaried lawyer to anyone making a first court appearance after having been taken into custody. In some remote areas of the country, including the Yukon and the Northwest Territories, duty counsel travel with the court. Most are private lawyers paid a per diem, but Ontario recently hired full-time duty counsel on two-year contracts to appear on bail applications and guilty pleas in the criminal courts of metropolitan Toronto. Part-time duty counsel also serve in the family courts.

In order to ensure that legal aid remains independent of government, seven provinces have created autonomous corporations. In both Ontario and New Brunswick, a committee of the provincial law society administers the program. Within judicare jurisdictions, most regions have Area Committees composed primarily of volunteers, most of whom are lawyers, who set policy and deal with appeals from refusals of service.

New Brunswick and Alberta reimburse private practitioners for providing legal aid. Nova Scotia and Prince Edward Island deliver almost all legal aid through salaried lawyers. Although Ontario provides most legal services through private lawyers, community clinics and the duty counsel program do employ salaried lawyers. Most other provinces deliver legal services through a mixed system, which has become known as "the Canadian compromise" between the English judicare and American salaried models. In response to the inception of community clinics, the Ontario profession commissioned its own "independent" study in 1972, which reviewed the arguments for and against salaried legal services and, not surprisingly, concluded:

> Except for limited special purposes which may suggest the full engagement of a solicitor for Legal Aid purposes, we remain of the view that the public is better served by a profession forced to compete for public patronage (rich or poor) in circumstances most likely to offer the public a meaningful choice and where the lawyer is only paid for the work done. (Law Society of Upper Canada, 1972: 42)

Nevertheless, the profession gradually accepted community clinics, partly because two judicial inquiries strongly supported them and encouraged government to increase their funding (Task Force on Legal Aid, 1974; Commission on Clinical Funding, 1978). About half of the more than fifty clinics now operating provide specialized services (such as environmental law or worker health and safety) or target particular constituencies (native Canadians, the handicapped, and Spanish-speaking clients). Community-elected boards of directors can establish standards for financial eligibility and criteria for selecting cases. Some clinics form part of multiservice centers, which offer clients not only legal assistance but also other social and medical services. Canadian clinics employ a larger ratio of paraprofessionals to lawyers than do American legal services programs, although the ratio has declined in recent years. Most Ontario clinics have developed a strategic approach to legal services, involving community education, community development, and law reform litigation.

Yet most Canadian legal aid remains concerned with the discrete claims and readily categorized legal problems of individual clients. Avrum Lazar (n.d.), a federal evaluator of legal aid programs, recently observed: "When money was more readily available, discussions about legal aid concentrated on meeting needs. Now discussions focus on controlling cost."

A British Columbia study concluded that there was little difference in the unit cost of criminal defense provided by salaried and private lawyers (Brantingham & Burns, 1981). A 1981 study of Quebec's mixed delivery system confirmed the cost-effectiveness of the salaried model, however, which had been demonstrated in an earlier Quebec study (Gervais & Cloutier, 1982: 134 and appendices; Maheur, Noiseux Roy et Compagnie, 1979). The British Columbia and Quebec studies, as well as one in Ontario, suggest that some private practitioners are specializing in legal aid, at least in criminal matters. Even so, they may remain less expert than salaried lawyers.

Judicare systems generally pay lawyers only 75 percent of market fees. This involuntary charitable contribution was intended to express the profession's concern for the plight of the poor, but it also assumed that all lawyers would participate in legal aid, sharing their collective responsibility equally. Data indicate, however, that less than half of all lawyers have remained on the legal aid panels, and the vast majority of those handle very few cases (Ribordy, 1982c: 28; Brantingham & Burns, 1981: 59–60). Ontario recently assessed all lawyers an annual legal aid levy of Can$175 to assist in funding increased payments and to legitimate the profession's contribution to legal aid.

Despite the fact that many private practitioners derive virtually all their income from judicare, the organized profession barely tolerates the salaried legal aid lawyer (Morris & Stern, 1976). Clinic lawyers tend to associate primarily with other clinic employees, and employees in thirteen out of the forty-seven Ontario clinics have taken the unusual step of seeking collective bargaining rights through a union. Private lawyers also perceive their colleagues who specialize in legal aid as being on the fringes of the profession. The latter tend to practice in collectives and to locate their offices in one area or even one building. Many have been the prime movers in the development of "left-wing" law groups, such as the Ontario Law Union and Lawyers for Social Responsibility (Martin, 1985).

CONCLUSION

The cherished notion of a unified profession must give way to the more accurate portrait of lawyers divided by function, clientele, and practice setting, ranked in terms of prestige and income, differing in their concern for anticompetitive restraints, and often disagreeing about professional policies and public positions.

The ideology of professional solidarity does mediate the differences of interest and identity, however, enabling the bar to close ranks in the face of internal or external threats. This helps to explain the severe sanctions imposed for trust violations and other acts of dishonesty, which undermine the fiduciary relationship between lawyer and client. Devotion to the notion of unity also may reinforce the profession's extreme sensitivity to any challenge to its independence.

The Canadian bar continues to manifest the indicia of classic professionalism. Perhaps because of the strength of the "professional project," subgroups have been slow to assert their distinctive interests and have submitted to professional governing bodies dominated by private practitioners overwhelmingly concerned with market control at the expense of innovation and development. The profession's desire to govern legal aid programs also reflects its hegemonic tendencies. Its preoccupation with preventing the "socialization" of legal services (following the example of medicine) retards the emergence of new areas of practice.

Despite eroding market control, the governing bodies of the Canadian bar enjoy greater formal and effective autonomy than do their American counterparts. Canadian lawyers have greater immunity from antitrust and other regulatory legislation than do those in England. These differences do not falsify general theories of the profession, but they do suggest that each society has the capacity to mold its own legal profession. Comparative examination must be sensitive to these particularities.

Tables

4.1. Percentage of Firms Employing Law Clerks Which Use Them in Particular Activities

Function	Substantive area								
	Family	Wills	Estates and probate	Title searching and conveyancing	Corporate law and securities	Collections (debtor-creditor)	Taxation	Civil litigation	Criminal litigation
Interviewing clients	30	16	21	34	5	19	0	32	35
Fact gathering	50	16	22	42	18	18	0	43	41
Preparing pleadings or legal documents	20	0	11	22	23	19	0	32	18
Letter writing	30	5	20	28	18	16	0	37	35
Filing documents	30	10	27	50	38	24	0	63	53
Negotiations	0	0	0	8	0	5	0	18	18
Advocacy	0	0	0	1	0	2	0	6	6
Dealing with lawyers	20	5	16	45	12	13	0	33	29
Legal research and analysis	0	0	0	16	10	9	0	25	18
Search of public records	50	21	37	64	48	20	0	60	47
Preparing clients' fees and disbursements	30	11	20	24	12	14	0	23	24
	(N = 10)	(N = 19)	(N = 19)	(N = 246)	(N = 40)	(N = 44)	(N = 2)	(N = 45)	(N = 17)

Sources: Colvin et al. (1978: 249); Zemans (1982).

4.2. Geographic Distribution of Canadian Lawyers, 1981

Province	Percent
Newfoundland	0.8
Prince Edward Island	0.3
Nova Scotia	2.7
New Brunswick	2.0
Quebec	25.3
Ontario	39.3
Manitoba	3.5
Saskatchewan	3.0
Alberta	9.8
British Columbia	13.1
Yukon and Territories	0.2

Source: Statistics Canada (1981).

4.3. Median Income of Lawyers and Staff by Firm Size, 1979 and 1981 (Can$)

Status	Number of lawyers in firm											
	1		2–6		7–11		12–19		20–29		30+	
	1979	1981	1979	1981	1979	1981	1979	1981	1979	1981	1979	1981
Partners and proprietors	30,000	30,000	40,000	49,077	59,500	68,284	69,742	90,600	82,525	99,876	93,500	129,021
Associates	—	—	20,000	24,000	24,325	30,000	23,868	27,500	26,113	32,440	27,750	40,000
Administrators	—	—	16,681	21,750	22,000	24,300	21,710	28,250	—	33,300	—	39,000
Paralegals	15,000	15,923	13,000	18,100	17,998	16,120	18,365	17,000	17,400	20,500	17,689	—

Source: Altman and Weil, Inc. (1982: 14).

4.4. Interprovincial Mobility of Lawyers

Percentage of lawyers practicing in province in 1978 who were	Alb	BC	Man	NB	NWT	NS	Ont	Que	Sask	Yukon
In same community in 1973	83	85	95	86	0	94	94	95	87	67
In different community but same province in 1973	7	10	3	8	0	4	5	3	8	11
In different province in 1973	10	5	2	6	100	2	1	2	5	22

Abbreviations: Alb—Alberta; BC—British Columbia; Man—Manitoba; NB—New Brunswick; NS—Nova Scotia; Ont—Ontario; Que—Quebec; Sask—Saskatchewan.
Source: Berger (1979: 14).

4.5. Age Distribution of Canadian Lawyers (in Percent), 1931–1981

Year	Age 25–34	35–44	45–54	55–64	65 +
1931	27	31	20	13	8
1941	23	25	26	15	10
1951	27	25	20	17	10
1961	34	27	17	11	9
1971	36	28	17	9	7
1981	48	26	14	7	3

Source: Statistics Canada (1931–1981).

4.6. Lawyers and Notaries in Canada, by Sex, 1931–1981

Year	Male	Female	Total	Female as percent of total	Decennial percentage increase		
					Male	Female	Total
1931	8,004	54	8,058	1	—	—	—
1941	7,791	129	7,920	2	−3	139	−2
1951	8,841	197	9,038	2	13	53	14
1961	11,759	309	12,068	3	33	57	34
1971	15,535	780	16,315	5	35	152	35
1981	29,030	5,175	34,205	15	87	563	110

Source: Statistics Canada (1931–1981).

4.7. Undergraduate Law Students, 1956/57–1979/80

Year	Total number	Annual increase, %
1956/57	2,651	0.7
1958/59	2,714	1.2
1959/60	2,710	0.0
1966/67	4,464	9.2
1967/68	5,071	13.6
1968/69	5,735	13.1
1969/70	6,443	12.3
1976/77	9,204	6.1
1977/78	9,402	2.2
1978/79	9,456	0.6
1979/80	9,590	1.4

Source: Statistics Canada (1981).

4.8. Competition to Enter Law School

	1978/79	1980/81
First-year applications received	26,066	24,423
Offers made	6,890 (26.4%)	7,412 (30.3%)
First-year enrollment	3,317 (12.7%)	3,270 (13.4%)
Total enrollment	9,480	9,410

Source: McKennirey (1983: 72–73).

4.9. Annual Revenues of Law Foundations From Interest on Trust Accounts, Can$

Year	Ontario	Saskatchewan	British Columbia
1974	—	171,196	—
1975	4,056,684	383,995	—
1976	4,333,973	526,854	—
1977	4,545,742	468,495	—
1978	4,795,610	500,700	—
1979	5,200,767	580,575	—
1980	8,142,784	627,098	4,132,751
1981	16,001,874[a]	1,278,834[a]	—
1982	12,591,707[a]	1,538,824[a]	6,600,959[a]
1983	8,515,688	950,409	—
1984	9,869,816	871,743	4,454,563
1985	—	1,051,820	—

[a] The increase is attributable to high interest rates.
Source: Law Foundation, Annual Reports.

4.10. Distribution (in Percent) of Members and Elected Benchers of Law Society of
Upper Canada, by Firm Size, 1978

Firm size	Metropolitan		Nonmetropolitan		Total	
	Benchers	Members	Benchers	Members	Benchers	Members
1	9.3	11.0	8.0	13.0	17.3	24.0
2–4	4.0	16.0	18.7	29.0	22.7	45.0
5–9	6.7	6.0	21.3	9.0	28.0	15.0
10+	28.0	13.0	4.0	3.0	32.0	17.0
Total	48.0	46.0	52.0	54.0	100.0	100.0

Source: Trebilcock et al. (1979).

4.11. Distribution (in Percent) of Members and Elected Benchers of Law Society of
Upper Canada, by Employment Context

Employment context	Benchers elected in 1971 and 1975	Membership in February 1977
Law firm	93.75	78.4
Academic	6.25	1.2
Other	0.0	14.4
Retired or out of province	0.0	5.9

Source: Trebilcock et al. (1979: 209).

4.12. Complaints Heard by Convocation of Law Society of Upper Canada, by Nature of Misconduct, 1972–1984

Reason	Number of cases	
Financial		233
Books, records, accounts	78	
Misappropriation (misapplication of clients' money)	59	
False and misleading statements, documents, records	32	
Borrowing from clients	28	
Failure to account to clients	14	
Conflict of Interest	12	
Conduct unbecoming		16
Failure to carry out clients' instructions		13
Failure to report to client or serve diligently		12
Failure to respond to LSUC communications		26
Admissions and agreed statements		36
Total		336

Source: Law Society of Upper Canada, Annual Reports.

4.13. Premium for Ontario Errors and Omission Insurance and Claims Experience

	Premium, Can$	Claims per 1,000 lawyers
1971	100	
1972	110	29.2
1973	110	37.0
1974	135	46.3
1975	135	48.5
1976	200	70.0[a]
1977	375	49.3
1978	375	74.3
1979	450	83.6
1980	665	96.4
1981	820	
1982	1,068	

[a] Distortion attributable to change in insurer.

Source: Law Society of Upper Canada, Annual Reports; Law Society of Upper Canada (1983b).

4.14. Causes of Loss for Payments by Ontario Errors and Omissions Insurance, 1977–1982

Cause	Percent losses	Percent claims
Missed limitation	13	16
Defective search	20	16
Ignorance of law	8	7
Failure to follow client's instruction	14	15
Undertakings	8	3
Poor communication with clients	2	2
Conflict—working for two or more parties	2	2
Other	33	39
Total	100	100
Real estate matters	62	53

Source: Law Society of Upper Canada, Annual Report (1982: 155).

4.15. Law Faculties and Enrollments, 1925

School	Teachers		Students
	Full-time	Part-time	
Dalhousie	3	20	50
McGill	3	12	64
Osgoode Hall	3	3	353
Saskatchewan	3	2	42
Manitoba	3	7	55
Montreal	0	17	149
Alberta	3	4	56
Laval	0	22	89
New Brunswick	0	17	20
Vancouver	0	—	31

Source: Law Society of Upper Canada (1927).

4.16. Costs, Prerequisites, and Length of Legal Training, 1927/28

School	Tuition, Can$	College prerequisite (years)	Course length (years)	Academic year (weeks)	Concurrent with clerkship
Alberta	115	2	3	24	No
Vancouver	15	1	3	24	Yes
Manitoba	108–118	2	4	28	Yes (2 of 4)
New Brunswick	102	2	3	24	Yes
Nova Scotia	162	2	3	29	No
Ontario	100	2	3	29	Yes
McGill	162–122	2	3	30	No
Montreal	160	Degree	3	32.5	Yes
Laval	125	Degree	3	32.5	Yes
Saskatchewan	71	2	3	27	No

Source: Reed (1928).

4.17. Mean Number of Lawyers and Articling Students by Firm Size, Ontario, 1977

Firm size (lawyers)	Toronto		Rest of Ontario		Total	
	Lawyers	Articling students	Lawyers	Articling students	Lawyers	Articling students
1	1	0.1	1	0.1	1	0.1
2–4	2.5	0.3	2.6	0.3	2.5	0.3
5–9	6.6	1.1	6.1	1.2	6.3	1.1
10+	23.4	4.2	12.0	1.6	19.8	3.4

Source: Colvin et al. (1978: 103).

4.18. Clientele (in Percent) by Firm Size, Ontario, 1976

Number of lawyers in firm	Public corporations	Nonpublic corporations and unincorporated businesses	Legal aid recipients	Other funding	Government and nonprofit	Other
1	3	17	14	61	3	1
2–4	4	21	11	60	3	1
5–9	8	30	8	48	5	1
10+	16	42	4	33	5	0

Source: Colvin et al. (1978: 87).

4.19. Distribution (in Percent) of Firms by Size of Firm and City, Ontario, 1977

City size	Firm size (lawyers)			
	1	2–4	5–9	10+
Under 30,000	16.6	20.4	13.7	0
30,000–100,000	14.3	17.7	18.0	8.3
100,000–500,000	23.6	24.8	30.2	19.4
500,000+	45.6	37.1	38.1	72.2

Source: Colvin et al. (1978: 160).

4.20. Length of Time (in Percent) to Partnership, by Firm Size

Years to partnership	Number of lawyers in firm				
	1	2–5	6–10	10+	Total
Under 5	54.5	59.8	34.3	14.3	44.2
5	36.4	26.8	40.0	51.4	36.4
Over 5	9.1	13.4	25.7	34.3	19.0

Source: Canadian Bar Association (1985).

4.21. Income of Lawyers by Experience and Firm Size, 1985, Can$

Year of admission	1 Partner		2–5 Partners		6–10 Partners		11 Partners or more	
	Partners	Associates	Partners	Associates	Partners	Associates	Partners	Associates
1984				25,200		21,000		26,200
1983			50,300	29,100		28,400		32,600
1982			57,400	35,000		27,700		37,400
1981			50,300	33,300		37,200		41,000
1980								49,200
1979			65,900					
1978					72,400		86,300	
1977								
1974–1976	47,500		73,800	45,400[a]	85,000	39,800[a]	107,300	
1970–1973			73,700		91,700		120,900	
1964–1969			90,400		90,300		136,200	
Before 1964			98,900		94,300		145,000	

[a] Prior to 1978

Source: Canadian Bar Association (1985).

4.22. Distribution of Legal Aid Payments by Lawyer, Ontario, 1985

Amount paid (Can$)	Number of lawyers	Percent of lawyers paid
1–1,000	1,329	27.3
1,000–5,000	1,671	34.3
5,000–10,000	730	15.0
10,000–20,000	589	12.1
20,000–30,000	241	4.9
30,000–40,000	119	2.4
Over 40,000	191	4.0

Source: Law Society of Upper Canada (1985: 17).

NOTES

We wish to thank David Stager of the University of Toronto Department of Economics for his guidance regarding statistical data and Richard Abel, Philip Lewis, and Terrence Halliday for their encouragement, stimulation, and frank criticism. An earlier version of this chapter appeared in 1986 *American Bar Foundation Research Journal* 447.

1. Notaries Act, Rev. Stat. Quebec 1977, c. N-2. The Quebec notary "becomes the confidential advisor in family affairs; he is entrusted with the winding up and management of estates; makes reports on titles, secures charters for joint stock companies; receives oaths and statutory declarations; acts as legal advisor for his clients; negotiates loans and acts as agent for the sale of real estate" (Canadian Law List, 1985: 1158–1159). In all other Canadian provinces, except British Columbia, notaries are limited to taking affidavits; "notarizing" documents (i.e., attesting them to be true); and drawing, passing, or issuing deeds and contracts (see, e.g., Ontario's Notaries Act, Rev. Stat. Ontario 1980, c. 319, s. 34). All lawyers in private practice and most lawyers employed by governments or corporations also hold an appointment as a notary. Nonlawyer notaries usually are corporate officers or in businesses such as travel agencies, where notarization of documents frequently is required. The Professional Organizations Committee estimated that there were 552 nonlawyer notaries in Ontario.

2. Provincial law societies provide for readmission (see, e.g., Law Society Regulations, Law Society of Upper Canada [1975], ss. 30[2], 31). However, they limit the return of judges or government administrators to avoid conflicts of interest (see, e.g., *Manitoba Professional Conduct Handbook*, 1982: 64; Barreau de Quebec, 1976: s. 99 [a]).

3. See Laskin (1969) and Fowler (1978). In Ontario, any lawyer in good standing with at least twelve years' experience and peer recommendations can

apply. There has been no limit on the number of appointments and no require-ment to canvass the views of the profession or the judiciary. Roberts (1984) estimated that 3,000 of the province's 16,000 lawyers were Queen's Counsel. In 1986 the provincial government generated considerable controversy by announc-ing that it would cease to recommend further appointments and was abolishing existing titles retroactively.

4. Zemans (1986: 9–10) found that the ratio of community legal workers to lawyers in Ontario legal aid clinics was slightly greater than 2 : 1 in 1980, but by 1984 it had dropped to 1.6 : 1.

5. Altman and Weil, Inc. (1980: 14) found that there were 0.23 paralegals per lawyer in Canada compared to 0.17 in the United States. The highest ratio is in Ontario (0.25) and the lowest, in Quebec (0.10). Small firms and sole practitioners have a higher ratio than do large firms.

6. See, for example, Statutory Powers Procedures Act, Rev. Stat. Ontario 1980, c. 484, s. 10; Rules of the Provincial Court (Civil Division), Ontario Reg. 797/84; Criminal Code, Rev. Stat. Canada 1970, c. 34, s. 735. There are no rules permitting Canadian law students to appear in superior courts. A study of Toronto labor arbitration between 1971 and 1973 revealed that trade unions use lawyers in approximately one-third of cases—42 percent where an employee has been discharged. In all other cases, a union representative appeared for the member (Goldblatt, 1974: 30–42).

7. In determining the "real market" for legal services it is necessary to consider the effect on aggregate demand of corporate as well as individual clients, of changing intensities of legal regulation, and of overall fluctuations in economic activity.

REFERENCES

Abel, Richard L. 1981. "Toward a Political Economy of Lawyers," 1981 *Wisconsin Law Review* 1117.

Adam, Barry. 1981. "Stigma and Employability: Discrimination by Sex and Sexual Orientation in the Ontario Legal Profession," 18 *Canadian Review of Sociology and Anthropology* 216.

Adam, Barry, and Kathleen Lahey. 1981. "Professional Opportunities: A Survey of the Ontario Legal Profession," 59 *Canadian Bar Review* 674.

Altman and Weil, Inc. 1980. *Economic Survey of Canadian Law Firms*. Ottawa: Canadian Bar Association.

———. 1982. *Economic Survey of Canadian Law Firms*. Ottawa: Canadian Bar Association.

Angus, W. 1967. "Judicial Selection in Canada—the Historical Perspective," 1 *Canadian Legal Studies* 220.

Arlidge, Bruce. 1974. "Contingent Fees," 11 *Ottawa Law Review* 374.

Arnup, John. 1982. "The 1957 Breakthrough," 16 *Law Society of Upper Canada Gazette* 180.

Arthurs, Harry W. 1967. "The Affiliation of Osgoode Hall Law School with York University," 18 *University of Toronto Law Journal* 197.

———. 1970. "Discipline in the Legal Profession in Ontario," 7 *Osgoode Hall Law Journal* 235.

———. 1971. "Authority, Accountability and Democracy in the Ontario Legal Profession," 49 *Canadian Bar Review* 1.

———. 1982. "Public Accountability of the Legal Profession," in Philip Thomas, ed., *Law in the Balance.* Oxford: Martin Robertson.

———. 1984. "The Law Giveth, the Law Taketh Away: Notes from an Agnostic on the Rule of Law in Canada." Conference, York University.

Arthurs, Harry W., Larry Taman, and J. Williams. 1971. "The Toronto Legal Profession: An Exploratory Survey," 21 *University of Toronto Law Journal* 498.

Auerbach, Jerold. 1976. *Unequal Justice: Lawyers and Social Change in Modern America.* New York: Oxford University Press.

Baker, G. B. 1983. "Legal Education in Upper Canada 1785–1889: The Law Society as an Educator," in David Flaherty, ed., *Essays in the History of Canadian Law,* vol. II. Toronto: Osgoode Society.

Barreau du Quebec. 1976. *Documentation Professionelle.* Montreal: Editions Y Blais.

Batten, Jack. 1980. "Tory, Tory," in *Lawyers,* chap. 5. Toronto: Macmillan.

Belobaba, Edward. 1978. "Civil Liability as a Professional Competence Incentive." Ontario: Professional Organization Committee.

Berger, E., Ltd. 1979. *Demographic Survey of the Canadian Bar.* Ottawa: Canadian Bar Association.

Bowlby, John. 1982. "Annual Report of the Treasurer," 16 *Law Society of Upper Canada Gazette* 133.

———. 1983. "Annual Report: 1982," 17 *Law Society of Upper Canada Gazette* 126.

Boyd, M. 1981. "Status Attainment in Canada," 18 *Canadian Review of Sociology and Anthropology* 657.

Brantingham, P., and Peter Burns. 1981. "The Burnaby, British Columbia Experimental Public Defender Project: An Evaluation." Ottawa: Department of Justice and Vancouver: British Columbian Legal Services Society.

Browning, B. G. 1976. *Admissions Criteria Research Project.* Winnipeg: University of Manitoba (unpublished).

Buchanan, Anselan. 1925. *The Bench and Bar of Lower Canada Down to 1850.* Montreal: Burtons.

Bucknall, B., T. Baldwin, and J. Lakin. 1968. "Pedants, Practitioners, and Prophets: Legal Education at Osgoode Hall to 1957," 6 *Osgoode Hall Law Journal* 137.

Cadres Professionels, Inc. 1968. "Les Avocats du Quebec: Etude Socio-economique." Montreal: Cadres Professionels.

Canadian Bar Association (CBA). 1920. *Canons of Legal Ethics.* Ottawa: Canadian Bar Association.

————. 1978. *Towards a New Constitution.* Ottawa: Canadian Bar Association.

————. 1985. "National Law Firm Survey." Ottawa: Canadian Bar Association.

Canadian Law List. 1983. Aurora, Ontario: Canada Law Book, Inc.

————. 1985. Aurora, Ontario: Canada Law Book, Inc.

Canadian Parliamentary Guide. 1983. Ottawa: Government Publications Office.

Clarry, John. 1982. "Interprovincial Law Firms," 16 *Law Society of Upper Canada Gazette* 266.

Clement, William. 1975a. *The Canadian Corporate Elite: An Analysis of Economic Power.* Toronto: McLelland and Stewart.

————. 1975b. "Inequality of Access: Characteristics of the Canadian Corporate Elite," 12 *Canadian Review of Sociology and Anthropology* 33.

Coburn, D., G. M. Terrance, and J. Kaufert. 1983. "Medical Dominance in Canada in Historical Perspective," 13 *International Journal of Health Services* 407.

Cole, Curtis. 1983. "A Developmental Market: Competition and Professional Standards in the Ontario Legal Profession, 1881–1936," 6 *Canada–U.S. Law Journal* 125.

Colvin, Eric. 1979. "The Division of Legal Labour," 17 *Osgoode Hall Law Journal* 595.

Colvin, Selma, David Stager, Larry Taman, Janet Yale, and Frederick H. Zemans. 1978. *The Market for Legal Services: Paraprofessionals and Specialists.* Toronto: Professional Organizations Committee (Working Paper No. 10).

Commission of Inquiry on Health and Social Welfare (Castonguay-Nipreau Commission). 1970. *Report.* Quebec: Government of Quebec.

Commission of Clinical Funding. 1978. *Report.* Toronto: The Commission.

Consultative Group on Research and Education in Law. 1983. *Law and Learning.* Ottawa: Social Sciences and Humanities Research Council.

Cuneo, C., and J. Curtis. 1975. "Social Ascription in the Educational and Occupational Status Attainment of Urban Canadians," 12 *Canadian Review of Sociology and Anthropology* 6.

Davies, A. L. 1952. "Unauthorized Practice of Law," 10 *University of Toronto Faculty of Law Review* 17.

Economic Council of Canada. 1969. "Interim Report on Competition." Ottawa: Economic Council of Canada.

Esau, Alvin. 1979. "Specialization and the Legal Profession," 8 *Manitoba Law Journal* 255.

————. 1981. "Recent Developments in Specialized Regulation of the Legal Profession," 11 *Manitoba Law Journal* 133.

Evans, Robert G., and Michael J. Trebilcock, eds. 1982. *Lawyers and the Consumer Interest.* Toronto: Butterworths.

Evans, Robert, and Alan D. Wolfson. 1982. "Cui Bono—Who Benefits from Improved Access to Legal Services?" in Robert G. Evans and Michael J. Trebilcock, eds., *Lawyers and the Consumer Interest.* Toronto: Butterworths.

Farris, John. 1972. "Let's Kill all the Lawyers,"3(2) *Canadian Bar Journal* 4.

Feltham, I. R., and E. A. Campin. 1981. "The Emerging Role of Corperate Counsel." Banff, Alberta: National Conference of Corporate Counsel (unpublished).

Fowler, Kathryn. 1978. "Queen's Counsel: Honour Without Meaning?" 2(3) *Canadian Lawyer* 30.

Freidson, Eliot. 1970. *Profession of Medicine: A Study in the Sociology of Applied Knowledge.* New York: Dodd, Mead and Company.

Friedland, Martin. 1964. *Legal Aid Working Papers.* Toronto: Joint Committee on Legal Aid.

Gall, Gerald. 1977. "The Lawyer as Lobbyist," 15 *Alberta Law Review* 400.

Gervais, Pierre P., and Robert Cloutier. 1982. *Evaluation de l'Aide Juridique.* Ste-Foy, Quebec: Ministère de la Justice.

Gibson, D., and L. Gibson. 1972. *Substantial Justice: Law and Lawyers in Manitoba 1670–1970.* Winnipeg: Peguis.

Giffen, P. T. 1961. "Social Control and Professional Self-Government: A Study of the Legal Profession in Canada," in S. D. Clarke, ed., *Urbanism and the Changing Canadian Society.* Toronto: University of Toronto Press.

Gold, N. 1972. "Competence and Continuing Legal Education," in N. Gold, ed., *Essays on Legal Education.* Toronto: Butterworths.

————. 1978. "The Interface between the Paraprofessional and the Professional: Some Reflections on the Lawyer and the Community Legal Services Paralegal Worker," in National Workshop on Paralegalism, ed., *Public Sector Paralegalism in Canada Today.* Vancouver: National Legal Aid Research Centre.

Goldblatt, M. 1974. *Justice Delayed ...* Toronto: Labour Council of Metropolitan Toronto.

Goodman, E. 1971. "The Lawyer in Public Life," in Law Society of Manitoba, ed., *Isaac Pitblado Lectures on Continuing Legal Education.* Winnipeg: Law Society of Manitoba.

Guppy, L., and J. Siltanen. 1977. "A Comparison of the Allocation of Male and Female Occupational Prestige," 14 *Canadian Review of Sociology and Anthropology* 320.

Halpern, P., and S. Turnbull. 1982. "An Economic Analysis of Legal Fees Contracts," in R. G. Evans and M. J. Trebilcock, eds., *Lawyers and the Consumer Interest.* Toronto: Butterworths.

Harvey, Cameron. 1970. "Women in Law in Canada," 4 *Manitoba Law Journal* 9.

Hawkins, Robert. 1978. "A State of Siege: The Legal Profession in Ontario at the Turn of the Century" (unpublished).

Heinz, John P., and Edward O. Laumann. 1983. *Chicago Lawyers: The Social Structure of the Bar.* New York: Russell Sage and Chicago: American Bar Foundation.

Henderson, G. 1977. "Advertising and Professional Fees under the Combines Investigation Act," in Law Society of Upper Canada, ed., *The Professions.* Toronto: DeBoo.

Hudec, Albert, and Michael Trebilcock. 1982. "Lawyer Advertising and the Supply of Information in the Market for Legal Services," 20 *University of Western Ontario Law Review* 53.

Hunter, Lawson 1983. "Are There Too Many Lawyers? The Government's View," 6 *Canada–U.S. Law Journal* 199.

Hurlburt, W., ed. 1979. *The Legal Profession and Quality of Service*. Ottawa: Canadian Institute for the Administration of Justice.

Huxter, Marie. 1981. "Survey of Employment Opportunites for Articling Students and Graduates of the Bar Admission Course in Ontario," 15 *Law Society of Upper Canada Gazette* 169.

Issalys, Pierre. 1978. "The Professions Tribunal and the Control of Ethical Conduct among Professionals," 24 *McGill Law Journal* 588.

Jackson, R. J., and M. M. Atkinson. 1980. *The Canadian Legislative System*. Toronto: Gage.

Johnson, Terence J. 1972. *Professions and Power*. London: Macmillan.

Johnston, George. 1972. "The Law Society of Upper Canada 1797–1972," 6 *Law Society of Upper Canada Gazette* 1.

Lachance, A. 1966. *Le barreau au Canada sous le regime Français*. Quebec: Société Historique de Québec.

Lajoie, Andrea, and Claude Parizeau. 1976. *La Place de Juriste dans la Société Québecoise*. Montreal: Themis.

Larson, Magali Sarfatti. 1977. *The Rise of Professionalism: A Sociological Analyisis*. Berkeley: University of California Press.

Laskin, Bora. 1969. *The British Tradition in Canadian Law*. London: Stevens.

———. 1972. "The Common Tie between Judges and Law Teachers," 6 *Law Society of Upper Canada Gazette* 147.

———. 1983. "Cecil A. Wright: A Personal Memoir," 33 *University of Toronto Law Journal* 148.

Law Society of Upper Canada. 1927. *Proceedings in Convocation*. Toronto: Law Society of Upper Canada.

———. 1972. *Report of the Special Committee on Legal Education* (MacKinnon Committee). Toronto: Law Society of Upper Canada.

———. 1982. *Community Legal Services Report*. Toronto: Law Society of Upper Canada.

———. 1983a. *Ontario Legal Aid Plan Annual Report*. Toronto: Law Society of Upper Canada.

———. 1983b. "The Report of the Special Committee on Numbers of Lawyers," 17 *Law Society of Upper Canada Gazette* 222.

———. 1983c. *Professional Conduct Handbook*. Toronto: Law Society of Upper Canada.

———. 1985. *Ontario Legal Aid Plan Annual Report*. Toronto: Law Society of Upper Canada.

Lazar, A. n.d. *Legal Aid in the Age of Restraint*, quoted in M. J. Mossman, *Legal Aid in Canada* (1983; unpublished).

Leal, H. Allan. 1982. "Are There Too Many Lawyers?" 6 *Canada—U.S. Law Journal* 166.

Lenoir, Robert. 1981. "Citizenship as a Requirement for the Practice of Law in Ontario," 13 *Ottawa Law Review* 527.

Levy, M. 1972. "Attitudes of the Most Likely to Succeed: A Survey of the First Year Class, Osgoode Hall Law School, 1971–72." Toronto: York University (unpublished).

Lortie, Leon. 1975. "The Early Teaching of Law in French Canada," 2 *Dalhousie Law Journal* 521.

MacAlister, A. 1928. *The Bench and Bar of the Provinces of Quebec, Nova Scotia and New Brunswick*. Montreal: John Lovell.

MacDonald, Rod. 1979. "Legal Education on the Threshold of the 1980's," 44 *Saskatchewan Law Review* 39.

MacEachern, W. 1976. "Medicine, Law, and Politics," 24 *Chitty's Law Journal* 109.

MacFarlane, P. D. 1980. "The Legal Profession in Canada: A Research Perspective and Prospectus," 28 *Chitty's Law Journal* 50.

Mackay, Pierre. 1979. "L'Enseignement du droit dans une perspective de changement social," 44 *Saskatchewan Law Review* 73.

McKennirey, J. 1983. *Canadian Law Faculties*. Ottawa: Social Science and Humanities Research Council.

Mackimmie, K. A. 1963. "The Presidential Address," 6 *Canadian Bar Journal* 347.

McKinlay, J., and J. Arches. 1985. "Towards the Proletarianization of Physicians," 15 *International Journal of Health Services* 161.

MacLaren, J. 1974. "Legal Education: Common Law Canada," 11 *Université de Ottawa Colloque International du Droit Comparé* 54.

Maheur, Noiseux Roy et Compagnie. 1979. "Etudes des coutes d'execution des classiers juridiques," in *Commission des Services Juridiques*, Seventh Annual Report of the Commission des Services Juridiques. Montreal: Commission des Services Juridiques.

Marmor, T., and W. D. White. 1978. *Paraprofessionals and Issues of Public Regulation* Toronto: Professional Organizations Committee (Working Paper No. 16).

Martin, Robert 1985. "The Law Union of Ontario," 7 *Law & Policy* 51.

Marshall, Allan. 1980. "Practice Advisory Services," 14 *Law Society of Upper Canada Gazette* 357.

Mitchell, Chester W. 1982. "The Impact, Regulation and Efficacy of Lawyer Advertising," 20 *Osgoode Hall Law Journal* 119.

Moore, J. 1980. *The Attitudes of Canadians Toward the Law and the Legal System* (unpublished).

More, R. 1982. "Perception of the Law and the Legal System: A Preliminary Report of the Findings," in Dale Gibson and Janet Baldwin, eds., *Law and a Cynical Society? An International Conference on Law and Public Opinion*. Calgary: Carswell Legal Publications.

Morris, Pauline, and Ronald N. Stern. 1976. *Cui Bono? A Study of Community Law*

Offices and Legal Aid Society Offices in British Columbia. Vancouver: Ministry of the Attorney General.

Mullagh, M. E. 1977. "The Law Firm in British Columbia: Economics, Organization, Size and Composition," 11 *Law Society of Upper Canada Gazette* 270.

Murray, E. 1979. *Transfer of Professionals from Other Jurisdictions to Ontario.* Toronto: Professional Organizations Committee.

National Legal Aid Research Centre. 1981. *Legal Aid Services in Canada 1979/80.* Ottawa: National Legal Aid Research Centre.

Nelligan, John. 1950. "Lawyers in Canada: A Half-Century Count," 28 *Canadian Bar Review* 727.

——. 1951. "Income of Lawyers," 29 *Canadian Bar Review* 34.

Newman, James. 1974. "Reaction and Change: A Study of the Ontario Bar, 1880–1920," 32 *University of Toronto Faculty Law Review* 51.

Newman, Peter. 1975. *The Canadian Establishment,* vol. 1. Toronto: Seal Book.

Orkin, Mark. 1957. *Legal Ethics.* Toronto: Cartwright.

——. 1968. *The Law of Costs.* Toronto: Canada Law Book.

——. 1971. "Professional Autonomy and the Public Interest: A Study of the Law Society of Upper Canada." D. Jur. thesis, York University, Osgoode Hall Law School.

Parker, Graham. 1982. "The Pedigrees of the Nova Scotia Judiciary," 2(2) *Now and Then* 36.

Pasis, H. E. 1970. "Lawyers and Political Participation." M.A. thesis, McMaster University.

Pepin, Giles. 1979. "L'Avenir du Professionalisme au Quebec," 39 *Revue du Barreau* 820.

Pike, R. 1980. "Education, Class, and Power in Canada," in R. J. Ossenberg, ed., *Power and Change in Canada.* Toronto: MeLelland and Stewart.

Porter, J. 1965. *The Vertical Mosaic.* Toronto: University of Toronto Press.

——. 1979. *The Measure of Canadian Society: Education, Equality, and Opportunity.* Agincourt, Ont.: Gage.

Posluns, Donald. 1980. "Professional Advertising Policies under the Amended Combines Investigation Act," 4 *Canadian Business Law Journal* 235.

Prichard, Robert. 1978. "Professional Civil Liability and Continuing Competence," in L. Klar, ed., *Studies in Canadian Tort Law.* Toronto: Butterworths.

Professional Organizations Committee. 1980. *Report.* Toronto: Professional Organizations Committee.

Quinn, John. 1978. *Multidisciplinary Services: Organizational Innovation in Professional Service Markets.* Toronto: Professional Organizations Committee (Working Paper No. 7).

Ratushny, Ed. 1976. "Judicial Appointments: The Lang Legacy," in A. Linden, ed., *The Canadian Judiciary.* Toronto: Osgoode Hall Law School.

Reed, Alfred Z. 1925. "Advance Extract," in Carnegie Foundation, Twentieth Annual Report. New York: Carnegie Foundation.

————. 1928. *Present-Day Law Schools in the United States and Canada.* New York: Carnegie Foundation.

Reiter, Barry J. 1978. *Discipline as a Means of Assuring Continuing Competence in the Professions.* Toronto: Professional Organizations Committee (Working Paper No. 11).

Ribordy, Francois. 1982a. "Les avocats de Sudbury 1891–1981." Sudbury, Ont.: Université Laurentienne (unpublished).

————. 1982b. "Sudbury's Lawyers 1891–1981." Paper presented to Tenth World Congress of Sociology, Mexico City (unpublished).

————. 1982c. "Les Services d'Aide Juridique à Sudbury," 5(4) *Canadian Legal Aid Bulletin* 18.

————. 1983. "Cent ans de présence des avocats à Sudbury," 17 *Law Society of Upper Canada Gazette* 51.

Richmond, A. 1967. *Post-War Immigrants in Canada.* Toronto: University of Toronto Press.

Riddell, W. 1928. *The Bar and Courts of the Province of Upper Canada or Ontario.* Toronto: Macmillian.

Roberts, Alasdair. 1984. "The Ubiquitous Q.C.," 18 *The Advocate* 39.

Robins, Sidney. 1971. "Our Profession on Trial," 7 *Law Society of Upper Canada Gazette* 1.

————. 1974. "The Appointment of Queen's Counsel," 8 *Law Society of Upper Canada Gazette* 157.

Ronson, J. 1978. "The Training of Paralegals in Ontario," 12 *Law Society of Upper Canada Gazette* 192.

Royal Commission Inquiry into Civil Rights (McRuer Commission). 1968, Ontario.

Russell, P. 1982. "The Effect of a Charter of Rights on the Policy-Making Role of Canadian Courts," 25 *Canadian Public Administration* 1.

Samac, Z. 1985. "The Lawyer as a Politician: Results of a Survey" (unpublished).

Schloesser, N. 1979. *History and Organization of Notaries in Ontario.* Toronto: Professional Organizations Committee.

Schumiatcher, M. 1979. *Man of Law: A Model.* Saskatoon: Western Producer.

Shupe, William. 1981. "Legal Advertising in Saskatchewan: Tune-up or Overhaul," 45 *Saskatchewan Law Review* 259.

Sinclair, A. 1975. "L'avocat au Québec: 209 ans d'histoire," 16 *Cahiers du Droit* 689.

Smith, D., and L. Tepperman. 1974. "Changes in the Canadian Business and Legal Elites 1870–1970," 11 *Canadian Review of Sociology and Anthropology* 97.

Smith, W. Earl. 1948. "The Law Society of Upper Canada," 26 *Canadian Bar Review* 437.

Snider, L. 1981. *Legal Services in Rural Areas: An Evaluation Report.* Ottawa: Department of Justice.

Stager, David. 1981. "Report to the Special Committee on Numbers." Toronto: Law Society of Upper Canada (unpublished).

————. 1982. "The Market for Lawyers in Ontario: 1931 to 1981 and Beyond," 6

Canada—U.S. Law Journal 113.

Statistics Canada (1931–1981). *Census of Canada*. Ottawa: Minister of Supply and Services.

———. 1981. *Legal Aid, 1981*. Ottawa: Minister of Supply and Services.

Swan, John. 1982. "Regulating Continuing Competence," in Robert G. Evans and Michael J. Trebilcock, eds., *Lawyers and the Consumer Interest*. Toronto: Butterworths.

Taman, Larry. 1978. "The Emerging Paraprofessionals," in P. Slayton and Michael J. Trebilcock, eds., *The Professions and Public Policy*. Toronto: University of Toronto Press.

Task Force on Legal Aid. 1974. *The Report of the Task Force on Legal Aid*. Ontario: Ministry of the Attorney General.

Taylor, Thom H. 1981. "Paralegals in Saskatchewan Community Legal Services Clinics," 4 *Canadian Legal Aid Bulletin* 89.

Thom, Stuart. 1974. "The Nature and Function of the Law Society of Upper Canada," 8 *Law Society of Upper Canada Gazette* 173.

Thomasset, Claude. 1981. "Les juristes non avocats au Québec," 4 *Canadian Legal Aid Bulletin* 89.

Trebilcock, Michael, and Barry Reiter. 1982. "Licensure in Law" in Robert G. Evans and Michael J. Trebilcock, eds., *Lawyers and the Consumer Interest*. Toronto: Butterworths.

Trebilcock, Michael, C. Tuohy, and A. Wolfson. 1979. *Professional Regulation: A Staff Study of Accountancy, Architecture, Engineering and Law in Ontario*. Toronto: Professional Organizations Committee (Working Paper No. 17).

University of Saskatchewan Native Law Centre. 1981. *Programme of Legal Studies for Native People*. Saskatoon: University of Saskatchewan Native Law Centre.

Veitch, Edward. 1979. "The Vocation of our Era for Legal Education," 44 *Saskatchewan Law Review* 21.

Yachetti, Roger D. 1983. "The Views of the Practicing Bar," 6 *Canadian—U.S. Law Journal* 103.

Yale, Janet. 1982. "Public Attitudes Towards Lawyers: An Information Perspective," in Robert G. Evans and Michael J. Trebilcock, eds., *Lawyers and the Consumer Interest*. Toronto: Butterworths.

Zemans, Frederick. 1979. "Canada," in Frederick H. Zemans, ed., *Perspectives on Legal Aid: A Comparative Survey*. London: Frances Pinter.

———. 1982. "The Non-Lawyer as a Means of Providing Legal Services," in Robert G. Evans and Michael J. Trebilcock, eds., *Lawyers and the Consumer Interest*. Toronto: Butterworths.

———. 1983. "Recent Trends in the Organization of Legal Services," in W. J. Habscheid, ed., *Effectiveness of Judicial Protection and Constitutional Order*. Bielefeld: Gieseking.

———. 1986. "The Changed Legal Profession." *Osgoode Hall Law Journal* (forthcoming).

5

United States

The Contradictions of Professionalism

RICHARD L. ABEL

The trajectory of professionalism among American lawyers is unusual in several respects. They began to professionalize later than lawyers in almost any other nation—not until the end of the nineteenth century. They embarked on this project with fewer resources, because the political rupture with England a century earlier and the later Jacksonian attack on privilege disrupted traditional procedures for qualifying as a solicitor or barrister. The United States differed in this from those common law countries that preserved their ties to England much longer—Canada, Australia, New Zealand, and India, whose barristers often were called to the English Bar and whose solicitors followed an apprenticeship quite similar to that of their English counterparts. Indeed, the United States displays a surprising parallel to continental European legal systems (which some late nineteenth century educational reformers consciously sought to emulate) in that the rise of professionalism coincided with the expansion of the university.

If the legal profession rose from humble beginnings, however, it achieved everything promised by the paradigmatic American fables of Abraham Lincoln and Horatio Alger—greater wealth and political influence than are enjoyed by any other national legal profession, although, like other parvenus, an uncertain social status. This qualified success also was typically American in that it was coveted by many but achieved by few; most American lawyers proudly claim the hollow title of "professional" but share few of its perquisites. As a result, the internal differentiation of the profession has reproduced—indeed, magnified—the heterogeneous backgrounds of American lawyers, which are an inevitable reflection of the national experience.

These unique features in the history of American lawyers serve to reveal—indeed, highlight—the many contradictions within the professional project. An occupation becomes a profession by controlling the

186

supply of those who produce its services while justifying such control in terms of the public interest. Whereas the object of American physicians was to eliminate competing schools of healers, the problem for American lawyers was to establish *any* controls over production, which were virtually nonexistent until the last quarter of the nineteenth century. Yet, although bar associations eventually succeeded in controlling both the numbers who qualified as lawyers and the background characteristics of those who did so, this very success had long-term consequences that threatened to undermine the professional project. Limits on entry never achieved anything like total homogeneity, and the ascriptive differences that emerged, when superimposed on professional stratification, belied professional claims of community and meritocracy. The virtual exclusion of women and minorities until the late 1960s temporarily may have enhanced the status and income of white male lawyers but at a considerable cost in legitimacy. Moreover, the experience of the last two decades dramatically demonstrates that efforts to control supply cannot prevail indefinitely against the economic forces of a market economy and the political attack on ascriptive barriers under the banner of the dominant liberal ideology.

Having controlled entry into the profession, lawyers sought to suppress competition among qualified producers by promulgating restrictive practices in the guise of ethical codes. But whereas the struggle to erect entry barriers tended to unify the profession (if lawyers from different strata disagreed about the urgency of the campaign and the tactics to be used), the attempt to dampen competition aggravated internal tensions— economic differences between those who wished to compete and those who did not—and ideological disagreements between those seeking to elevate the status of the profession by giving it a noncommercial tone and others relatively unconcerned about status. Furthermore, restrictive practices become increasingly difficult to justify in a society that at least pays lip service to laissez-faire ideology and extols consumer sovereignty.

With the erosion of professional control over the production *of* producers of legal services and *by* those producers, lawyers have turned increasingly to market strategies that seek to augment demand; but these are even more problematic. First, whereas control over supply seeks to reduce intraprofessional competition (if with only limited success), efforts to stimulate demand inevitably intensify such competition. Second, to the extent that the profession successfully persuades the state to subsidize demand or constructs private schemes for third-party payment, it inescapably sacrifices some control to those new paymasters. Third, demand creation undermines the profession's legitimacy insofar as it belies professional pretensions to altruism, noncommercialism, and independence. Fourth, by proclaiming and documenting the "unmet need" for legal services, lawyers open themselves to the reasonable request that they satisfy such need, with pay or without. Finally, it is very doubtful that the demand for legal services, particularly among individual consumers, can be expanded significantly.

American lawyers pursued the project of market control through their professional organizations, and they justified those institutions by the axiomatic identification of professionalism with self-regulation. But the actual experience of self-regulation has tended to undermine the profession's claim to privileged immunity from external oversight. Controls over misconduct were established quite late. They were ineffective in detecting, investigating, and punishing misconduct, and the public was fully aware of these failings. Both the substantive rules and the disciplinary process have been unresponsive to consumer grievances, especially since neither does anything to ensure continuing technical competence among lawyers. Discipline also has aggravated tensions within the profession, because ethical rules stigmatize the behavior of low-status lawyers while tolerating the functional equivalent among the elite. As external dissatisfaction with professional self-regulation has accumulated, courts, legislatures, administrative agencies, and consumers have asserted increasing control over lawyers.

Professions emerge out of the functional division of labor among occupations and persist only as long as they reflect some coherent, unitary category within that functional differentiation. I argued above that the unity of the American legal profession always has been qualified by the diverse backgrounds of its members, a heterogeneity that has increased in the last two decades with the entry of women and racial minorities. These ascriptive differences are unequally distributed across a set of roles that have undergone progressive differentiation, both functional and structural. Until after World War II, a single role dominated the profession—the private practitioner, working independently or with a partner or associate. Since then, however, several changes have threatened this clear professional identity. First, the number of employed lawyers has increased to the point where it approaches the number of independent practitioners. Second, as law firms have expanded, many independent practitioners have become employers of numerous subordinates and members of large bureaucratic organizations. Third, several distinct subgroups have grown in both size and coherence: judges, government employees, lawyers employed in business enterprises, and law professors. These changes have profound implications for the profession. Increasing differentiation and stratification undermine the sense of professional community and threaten the capacity of lawyers to engage in self-governance. They also enhance the importance of those institutions (primarily formal education) that allocate lawyers to professional roles.

With the erosion of control over supply, heightened competition, loss of independence to public and private third-party paymasters, growth of external regulation, the flight into employment, and the dissolution of community, the professional project of the first half of the twentieth century is in serious disarray.

CONTROLLING THE PRODUCTION OF LAWYERS

Although the newly independent United States had more than its share of lawyers, many of whom played a major role in establishing and staffing the nascent state and federal governments, they were not a profession. The entry barriers, which distinguish a profession from an occupation, remained poorly defined for the first hundred years of independence. Although colonial American lawyers had qualified in much the same way as their English counterparts, those paths were closed. After the Revolution there was no point in being called to the Bar at one of the Inns of Court in London, and America possessed no comparable institutions. Like English solicitors, some American lawyers did continue to serve an apprenticeship of up to five years, but even in England this was enforced only loosely at the end of the eighteenth century.

When the Jacksonians attacked privilege and monopoly in the 1840s, therefore, they encountered little resistance. Professional associations of lawyers had been weakened by the flight of the Tory elite following the Revolution. In any case, they were organized by city or county, whereas only state governments could control entry to the profession. The frontier functioned as a safety valve for the overproduction of lawyers, offering the alternative of migration to those who could not find sufficient work on the eastern seaboard. Consequently, whereas fourteen out of nineteen American jurisdictions required lawyers to complete an apprenticeship in 1800, only nine out of thirty-nine did so in 1860. Formal education, liberal or professional, was neither demanded of lawyers nor acquired by most of them until the end of the nineteenth century. For there were few postsecondary institutions, and the new nation lacked a highly rationalized body of legal doctrine that either called for, or rewarded, extensive study. As late as the eve of the Civil War, there were fewer than 1,000 law students throughout the country, most of them enrolled in small schools, of indifferent quality, offering short courses of a year or two. No jurisdiction insisted on law school training, and only a few even allowed academic study to substitute for whatever period of apprenticeship they required. In 1891 it was estimated that 80 percent of all practicing lawyers never had attended law school.

Yet, formal legal education began to expand about 1890 and rapidly displaced apprenticeship as the mode of qualification. This was not the result of state coercion. Although the number of jurisdictions requiring apprenticeship rose from nine out of thirty-nine in 1860 to sixteen out of thirty-nine in 1881, only six of these even granted law students any reduction of the mandatory apprenticeship, and as late as 1923, not a single jurisdiction insisted on any academic legal education. Nevertheless, the number of law schools doubled between 1890 and 1910, and the number of law students increased fourfold. By the end of the next decade virtually no one was entering the profession by means of apprenticeship. The significance of this transformation cannot be overestimated, although the reasons for it remain obscure. First, as the profession began to grow more rapidly under the impact of immigration and economic expansion, the number of lawyers willing to take apprentices was insufficient to satisfy the pressures for entry. Second, immigrants and their sons encountered particular difficulty in finding apprenticeships. Third, lawyers began hiring women secretaries with typewriting and stenographic skills to replace law clerks. Fourth, as states required written bar examinations, formal legal education offered better preparation for it—and even exemption in jurisdictions that conferred the "diploma privilege" on law school graduates. Furthermore, the formal training that replaced apprenticeship was extremely undemanding: schools imposed few educational prerequisites, if any; courses were brief, standards were low, and schedules accommodated part-time or even full-time work.

In the years following the Civil War, American lawyers possessed even fewer of the characteristics of a profession than they had exhibited a hundred years earlier. Starting in the 1870s, however, elite lawyers began to seek professional status by forming bar associations, first in the major cities—New York and Chicago—and then nationwide, with the founding of the American Bar Association (ABA) in 1878. The ABA established a Section on Legal Education and Admissions to the Bar in 1893, and the elite law schools united to form the Association of American Law Schools in 1900. Despite considerable rivalry, both groups shared the avowed purpose of "raising standards" and, not incidentally, reducing the number of entrants. Progress toward this goal was slow, however. States, not local or national governments, controlled entry to the profession. Voluntary statewide professional associations emerged late, and they remained weak because they enrolled only a fraction of all practitioners. In response, lawyers turned to governmental compulsion, in the form of "unified" or "integrated" bar associations to which all practitioners had to belong; six were created in the 1920s, fifteen in the 1930s, four in the 1940s, three in the 1960s, and three in the 1970s—eventually representing three-fifths of all jurisdictions. The conjunction of several factors gradually increased the determination of the organized profession to control entry: the expansion of legal education (the number of law students doubled again in the

1920s), resulting in the growth of the legal profession by a third during this decade; prejudice against eastern and southern European immigrants and their sons, who increasingly were seeking admission; the advent of the Great Depression at the end of the decade, which drastically reduced the demand for lawyers services; and envy of physicians, who dramatically had curtailed the number of entrants.

The first step in this project was to require some formal education of lawyers before they commenced their professional training. Here, as everywhere, the profession started from scratch. In 1896, less than 10 percent of American law schools (7 out of 76) required entrants to possess even a high school diploma; seven years later nearly half did so (51 out of 104). A few elite law schools competed for students by raising entrance requirements; but most law schools competed by lowering them, correctly fearing that they would lose enrollment if they increased their demands too rapidly. Although all 65 full-time law schools required two years of college by 1925, therefore, 66 of the 106 part-time or mixed schools still accepted students with less than two years of college in 1927. The latter schools could be persuaded to change their requirements only by state compulsion; but as late as 1927, thirty-two out of forty-nine jurisdictions had no prelegal requirement, and eleven of the other seventeen required only high school. Under pressure from voluntary and integrated bars, however, the states rapidly adopted prelegal requirements: thirty-eight had done so by 1935 and forty-four by 1942. Today, only California admits lawyers who have not graduated from college.

We can see the impact of these higher requirements on the educational background of lawyers. In the last quarter of the nineteenth century, only about a fourth of all law students had college degrees (although the proportion varied greatly with the prestige of the law school attended— strong evidence that, even a hundred years ago, the American legal profession was stratified by background and education). Of course, the level of prelegal education was much lower among the vast majority of lawyers who still qualified through apprenticeship. Furthermore, the level actually may have declined with the emergence of part-time law schools, many of which were proprietary enterprises that sought to expand enrollment by lowering standards. From this minimal starting point, change occurred very slowly. Among those who took the California Bar Examination in 1932, 35 percent had no college education and only 40 percent had college degrees. By 1948, however, a study of entrants to 107 of the 122 ABA-approved law schools revealed that two-thirds had completed at least two years of college. By 1970, 90 percent of all practicing lawyers had some college education, and 73 percent had college degrees.

The real hole in the dike was not prelegal education, however, but professional training itself, and this hole widened before it was plugged. At

first, elite lawyers saw academic legal education as a means of professionalizing, especially since most of them had studied law at university. Bar
associations consequently urged states to require formal study. In 1891,
only three jurisdictions demanded three years of professional training,
which could be satisfied either in the academy or through apprenticeship.
By 1904, nineteen jurisdictions had such a requirement, and the number
rose to forty-one out of forty-nine by 1928. We saw above that the
academy rapidly displaced apprenticeship around the turn of the century.
Two other alternatives—correspondence schools and private law study—
gradually were eliminated, so that 76 percent of all practicing lawyers had
attended law school by 1948 and 97 percent by 1970. There is an irony in
this evolution from apprenticeship to the academy. Apprenticeship is a
highly particularistic institution, in which entrants are selected on the basis
of personal contacts and ascribed characteristics; however, it is less effective as a sorting device that justifies the ultimate location of the lawyer
within the professional hierarchy. Formal education is far more universalistic, either admitting all applicants or selecting among them on the basis
of more or less objective measures of performance, but its imprint is more
permanent. The hierarchy of educational institutions has a profound impact on the allocation of graduates to positions within the stratified profession. The displacement of apprenticeship by the academy thus admitted
a more heterogeneous group of entrants but also did more to legitimate
inequality among them.

Having ensured the monopoly of law schools, professional associations
turned their attention to the length of the course. In 1870, 17 law schools
offered a two-year course, and another 14 taught students for only a year.
As late as 1927, eighteen jurisdictions still did not require three years of
law study, and 10 of the 176 law schools across the country were less than
three years long. Making three years of academic legal education the
prerequisite to entry actually increased rather than reduced the number of
entrants, however, because it stimulated the expansion of part-time law
schools. In 1889/90, only 12 percent of American law students attended
part time; by 1915/16, nearly half (48 percent) did so. Two-thirds of those
taking the Illinois bar examination in Chicago that year had studied at
part-time or mixed schools. The ABA responded by establishing standards
for law schools that part-time institutions found it difficult or impossible to
meet and then by seeking to persuade states to deny entry to graduates of
unapproved schools. Although this was justified publicly as essential to
raise the level of technical competence in order to protect consumers, there
was no evidence that graduates of full-time schools were better lawyers.
And the organized profession made no secret of its desire to control both
the total number of new lawyers and the proportion from immigrant
backgrounds.

The first list of ABA-approved schools, published in 1921/22, included only 31 of the 148 law schools. Six years later, there still were twice as many unapproved schools as approved, and the former contained twice as many students. One reason why the campaign had achieved so little was that only nine jurisdictions demanded graduation from an approved school as late as 1935. During the next three years, however, the ABA and state bar associations persuaded another fourteen jurisdictions to impose that requirement, with the result that the proportions of students attending approved and unapproved schools had reversed by 1939. Forty years later, forty-six of the fifty-one jurisdictions required graduation from an approved school. Today, only about 5 percent of all law students attend unapproved schools, almost all of which are located in California. Students in California must pass an additional bar examination at the end of their first year, and very few ultimately succeed in entering the profession. The ABA monopoly thus is complete.

If one goal of the ABA campaign against unapproved schools was to curtail part-time legal education, it was extraordinarily successful. In 1928 fully two-thirds of all American law students were enrolled in part-time institutions. But the combined effects of ABA standards, the Great Depression (which curtailed both the demand for lawyers and the financial ability of students to attend law school), and the radical drop in law school enrollments during World War II reduced part-time enrollments to a low of 13 percent of all students at ABA-approved schools in 1979; and since then the proportion has risen to only 18 percent. Monopoly power also entails the responsibility to exercise it even-handedly and not appear too self-interested. Law schools have continued to seek and to obtain ABA approval, particularly in the last two decades, with the result that the number of approved schools doubled in the fifty years after the ABA attained hegemony. This unanticipated outcome reveals the ephemeral quality of the professional project, as we will see below.

Control over the production of lawyers not only limits their numbers but also defines their characteristics. Cost is a central mechanism. The decline of part-time education made the legal profession much less accessible to those who needed to work in order to support themselves and pay for their education. Full-time institutions also entailed greater living expenses (because students could not live at home) and demanded much higher tuition. Furthermore, the tuition charged by full-time institutions has increased tenfold in the last fifty years—thirtyfold at some schools— and most rapidly since the 1960s. The total annual cost of attending a private law school now approaches $20,000, and even the minority of public institutions cost almost half as much. True, this rise has been accompanied by the growth of financial assistance, from both the schools themselves and the federal government; however, most of that assistance has taken the form of loans. As a result, lawyers begin practice with tens of thousands of dollars of debt accumulated during seven years of post-secondary education, which strongly influences the range of career alternatives they are willing to consider.

The cutthroat competition to enter law school today seems an inescapable fact of life. Until the mid-1920s, however, *all* law schools accepted every applicant who possessed the minimum qualifications of prelegal education. Yale was the first school to adopt a selective admissions policy, in 1926, but as late as the 1950s even Harvard still was admitting half of its applicants. Competition became severe only in the 1960s, when elite schools began to receive five to ten applications per place. In 1976, 3.4 times as many people took the Law School Admission Test as were accepted by law schools the following year. As a result, the scores necessary to gain entry rose rapidly. The top 90 ABA-approved schools were as selective in 1975 as the top 8 had been in 1961; all 163 ABA-approved schools were as selective in 1975 as the top 27 had been 14 years earlier. In 1975/76, 40 percent of applicants failed to gain admission to any ABA-approved school. Whereas first-year law students in 1969 had college grades similar to those of all college graduates and much lower than those of beginning graduate students, entering law students in 1981 had much better grades than did those graduating from college the previous year or entering graduate school. Because parental occupation, education, income, and wealth were strongly correlated with the applicant's performance in college and on the Law School Admission Test, family background influenced admission to law school, just as parental income was increasingly necessary to pay for legal education.

Until recently, completing law school was a greater obstacle than gaining admission. Well after World War II fewer than half of all entering students graduated from many law schools. In recent decades, attrition has declined to less than 10 percent of matriculates, although it is higher among the relatively small number of part-time students. Clearly, the decline in attrition is related to the heightened competition for admission. I would argue that this shift in the point of selection has rendered the winnowing process less meritocratic rather than more, however: background variables arguably have a greater impact on admission to law school than they do on performance within it. Whereas the shift from apprenticeship to the academy rendered the profession more diverse but also more stratified, the shift from easy entry and high attrition to competitive entry and low attrition narrowed the background characteristics of those to be allocated among strata.

We strongly associate professions with a licensing examination required by the state, which serves as both the fundamental guarantee of quality and the principal mechanism for controlling numbers. Yet the bar examination has performed those functions for American lawyers only at certain times and with respect to particular categories of entrants. For a long time attending law school and passing the bar examination were alternatives rather than sequential hurdles. During the last quarter of the nineteenth century many jurisdictions automatically admitted graduates of law schools situated within their own borders and even those from out-of-state schools. Naturally, this so-called diploma privilege was favored by the schools themselves, which enjoyed higher enrollments as a result, and was opposed by the organized profession, which wanted to control entry. The profession gradually prevailed, and the number of jurisdictions granting the diploma privilege dwindled to fifteen in 1949 and five in 1973, with the result that the proportion of entrants admitted in this fashion dropped from 10 percent in the 1930s to 2 percent today.

Even after the bar examination was required, it was not always a significant obstacle. Written examinations first were introduced only in 1870 and did not become widespread until the end of the century. They were administered locally, allowing applicants to shop around for the most lenient within their own states. Only four out of forty-nine jurisdictions had central examination boards in 1890, but the number rose to thirty-seven by 1917. Even then, examiners were poorly paid and few in number. Although there was a slight decline in the pass rates during the first two decades of the twentieth century, the rates fluctuated widely. Only toward the end of this period did a distinction emerge between the industrialized states on one hand, characterized by major cities, substantial immigration, large and growing populations, sizable legal professions, a high proportion of part-time law students, and considerable pressure to enter the profession—which had lower and declining pass rates—and the more rural states on the other hand, either agricultural or frontier, with relatively homogeneous native populations, little immigration or population growth, a small legal profession, and little pressure for entry—which had constant and high pass rates.

The Great Depression affected both categories. Between 1929 and 1930, pass rates fell in fourteen states and rose in only six (out of the thirty-six for which figures are available). Three-quarters of all jurisdictions had lower pass rates in 1933 than in 1927, although the number taking the examination actually had decreased. In many jurisdictions the decline was precipitous—a fall of up to 40 percentage points. It was widely recognized, and just as widely accepted, that bar examiners were imposing a quota in light of the reduced demand for lawyers' services. Pass rates reached a low point in 1935, which also was the bottom of the Great Depression, and then began to climb as the number of examinees dropped.

Even when rates were lowest, the examination may not have been a barrier to the persistent; several studies estimated that 90 percent of repeaters ultimately passed.

With the end of the Great Depression and the reduction in the number of applicants as a result of both World War II and the organized profession's greater control over legal education, pass rates rose steadily from a national average of 45 percent in 1935 to 76 percent in 1974, before declining to 64 percent in 1984. These averages concealed differences similar to but even greater than those that had emerged at the beginning of the century, however. In a few predominately rural states, of which North Dakota was the examplar, virtually everyone passed the bar, although the intimate nature of rural society undoubtedly made it difficult for an outsider to obtain business. In states where the examination had been difficult before the Great Depression and became more so during it, pass rates rose in the late 1930s and 1940s as a result of the decline in applications caused by both the Depression and the war. Rates fell after the war, as the profession reasserted supply control in the face of the large number of returning veterans seeking entry. They rose again during the 1960s and especially the 1970s, as competition to enter law school greatly intensified. They fell during the 1980s, however—thirty-two out of fifty-two jurisdictions experienced a decline between 1983 and 1984—in response to the increase in both the number of law students and the proportion of minority students, a subject I return to below. Limitations on entry to law school thus seem to diminish the importance of both law school examinations and professional examinations as mechanisms of supply control, although law school grades still influence the allocation of graduates to roles in the professional hierarchy.

The aspirant who has completed prelegal education, gained admission to law school, graduated, and passed the bar examination still has three other hurdles to overcome. In 1909 the ABA applauded the decision by some state bars to exclude noncitizens from practice and urged the other jurisdictions to follow suit. By 1946, all forty-eight states had done so. Yet, patently ascriptive criteria are very difficult to defend within a liberal polity, and this one was struck down by the U.S. Supreme Court in 1973. Each state bar also erected protectionist barriers against out-of-state lawyers, limiting their appearances in particular matters and insisting that they become residents before taking the bar examination or being admitted to practice. These rules were strengthened between 1930 and 1960, as part of the project of supply control. States began to relax them in the 1970s, however, and the U.S. Supreme Court struck them down in 1985, although some jurisdictions responded by eliminating the reciprocity they previously had extended to others. Finally, most state bars introduced or elaborated character examinations in the 1920s and 1930s in order to discourage or exclude immigrants from entering the profession. However, these also were difficult to justify, had little impact, were attacked in court in the 1960s and 1970s, and have minimal significance today.

Each mechanism of supply control discussed above displays the same general pattern: increasing stringency until the 1960s and relaxation thereafter. More prelegal education was required, but the growth of public universities made it more widely available. Law school became obligatory, and most part-time programs were eliminated, but the number of ABA-approved law schools expanded, and their enrollments increased. Attrition among law students, once quite high, fell sharply. The bar examination was introduced to limit numbers, but increasing proportions of law students passed it. In addition, the requirements of citizenship, residence, and "character" have been eliminated or relaxed. Perhaps the central irony of this narrative is the fact that, in constructing its project of supply control on the foundation of the university, the profession ultimately lost control over supply to the university, whose interests diverge significantly from those of lawyers.

THE CONSEQUENCES OF SUPPLY CONTROL

NUMBERS

We can trace the fortunes of supply control through the fluctuations in the numbers who sought to qualify, succeeded in entering the profession, and actually practiced as lawyers (see table 1). Law school enrollments increased fourfold between 1890 and 1930, in response to the shift from apprenticeship to academic education and the desire of immigrants and their sons to become professionals. Enrollments then declined steadily from 1927 through World War II. The brief postwar surge failed to compensate for wartime losses in the production of lawyers, resulting in what appears to be an underproduction of some 30,000 law students in that generation. The attainment of supply control is visible in the fact that the rate of production of lawyers was only 11 percent higher in the 1950s than it had been in the 1930s, although the profession it was reproducing was 50 percent larger and the economy—and hence the demand for lawyers' services—was booming. The period of stasis ended abruptly in the 1960s. Law school enrollments nearly tripled between 1961 and 1976, remained steady until 1982, and declined slightly since then. Most of the recent growth has occurred at the bottom of the educational hierarchy, not the top.

The expansion of legal education was reflected in the rate of admissions to the profession, which increased almost fourfold between 1900 and

1928. It then declined every year but one until 1945—a steadier and stronger trend than that exhibited by law school enrollments, confirming that the bar examination became an even more significant barrier during this period. Bar admissions also showed a much smaller shortfall as a result of World War II—only about 1,500 attorneys—suggesting that many entrants attended law school for less than the full three years. Between 1954 and 1963, the rate of admissions was only 1 percent higher than it had been in the 1930s. Once again we find a threefold increase in bar admissions between 1963 and 1979, a plateau until 1982, and a decline in the last few years.

It is not possible to extrapolate the practicing strength of the profession from entry levels unless we know something about departures. Although national statistics are not readily available, we do know that law is a lifetime career for most entrants, so that departures are largely a function of the size of the cohort who entered approximately forty years earlier. It thus seems plausible to expect that the retirement in the early 1960s of the large cohort who qualified in the 1920s further dampened the growth of the profession; conversely, the retirement in the 1970s through the 1990s of the much smaller cohorts who qualified in the 1930s through the 1950s should amplify the rate of growth.

Fragmentary and approximate data on the size of the profession are consistent with the preceding account. The number of lawyers increased rapidly between 1870 and 1900, responding to economic growth and unconstrained by any effective supply control. The first two decades of the twentieth century witnessed slower expansion, partly as a result of World War I, which sharply curtailed law school enrollments. Increase was high in the 1920s and low in the 1930s and 1940s. The success of supply control is strongly supported by the fact that the ratio of lawyers to population in 1950 was identical to what it had been in 1900, despite the fact that the economy was many times larger. Growth began again in the 1950s and reached an extraordinary 53 percent in the 1970s, the highest rate of any decade, but it has fallen slightly during the 1980s.

Of course, fluctuations in the growth and size of the legal profession cannot be attributed entirely to its own machinations. Many other factors exert an influence. I already mentioned the impact of wars. The Civil War drastically reduced enrollment in southern law schools. World War I caused a 75 percent decline in national enrollment in two years and World War II an 80 percent decline. The Korean and Vietnam Wars also compelled men to postpone their careers. To the extent that such events increase the scarcity of professional labor, they tend to produce an age cohort that is unusually privileged and, I believe, unusually conservative. For similar reasons, fluctuations in the birth rate approximately twenty-five years earlier can affect the size of the cohort contemplating a career in law.

Even if that cohort remains constant, the interest of its members in

becoming lawyers may vary. Immigration from eastern and southern
Europe at the turn of the century produced a second generation of
immigrants' sons eager to become lawyers in the 1920s and 1930s, as
evidenced by the disproportionate growth of the legal profession in cities
with major immigrant populations and the rapid expansion of part-time
law schools. Similarly, the civil rights and feminist movements of the
1960s and 1970s, together with the growth of public higher education and
affirmative action programs, greatly increased both the desire and the
ability of women and minorities to enter the legal profession (a topic that I
discuss further below).

The attraction of law relative to other occupations also fluctuates, for
reasons that are both materialistic and idealistic. The economic rewards of
law practice are partly a function of the efficacy of supply control. The
generation that reached professional maturity during the 1950s and 1960s
thus benefited from the constriction of supply attained during the 1930s
and 1940s, as well as from the postwar economic boom. But in a society in
which career choices are at least partly free, such an imbalance cannot long
be maintained, and the high incomes enjoyed by lawyers doubtless contributed to the rise in law school enrollments starting in the late 1960s.
Coincidentally, law also exerted an unusual attraction for that idealistic
generation of college students because of its association with the many
movements for social change. Yet both stimuli to growth recently have
lost some of their vigor. With the increase in the production of lawyers, a
law degree no longer offers the best return on an investment in education.
Moreover, there is widespread disillusionment with law as an instrument
of change at the same time that idealism generally has declined. The
conjunction of these factors helps to explain the recent fall in law school
applications and enrollments.

Thus far I have focused primarily on supply variables; fluctuation in
demand obviously also is significant, if more difficult to measure. Because
lawyers devote far more energy to business clients than to individuals,
changes in the economy are more important than changes in the population. The drastic fall in economic activity during the Great Depression
was accompanied by a widespread decline in lawyer income and the
inability of new entrants to earn a living. The starting salaries paid to
employed lawyers increased slowly in the 1950s and 1960s and then very
rapidly during the 1970s, although this increase has decelerated in the last
few years. Cross-sectional comparisons confirm that the level of economic
activity is reflected in demand for lawyer services and that economic sectors
differ in the amount of demand they generate. If the service sector con-
sumes more legal services per unit cost than the older smokestack industries did, as seems to be the case, the long-term expansion of the former at
the expense of the latter may signal a continuing expansion of the demand
for lawyers. Census data tend to confirm this: total receipts of all law firms

, with payrolls rose from $5.2 billion in 1967 to $9.7 billion in 1972, $17.1 billion in 1977, and $34.3 billion in 1982—an increase of 560 percent during a fifteen-year period in which the consumer price index rose only 287 percent and the index for services, 332 percent.

THE CHARACTERISTICS OF LAWYERS

Age

Although there have been slight variations in the age at which lawyers entered and left practice over the last 100 years, most of the changes in the age profile of the profession are a function of increases or decreases in the size of the entering cohorts. The large cohort who began practicing in the 1920s and 1930s suffered from the combined effects of an excess of supply and a decline in demand following the onset of the Great Depression. Their success in increasing the profession's control over supply, together with the effects of the Great Depression and World War II, produced a postwar profession with a large senior generation and a small junior generation. Both benefited from the postwar economic boom. The result was the intense conservatism of the 1950s, a national phenomenon that took the form among lawyers of preoccupation with economic self-interest, little resistance to McCarthyism, and even less support for the nascent civil rights movement.

Since the mid-1960s, the age pyramid has been inverted, like the cones of an hourglass. Those who entered during the 1970s displayed a pronounced preference for government employment and public-interest practice, if they also gravitated toward large firms. This may explain the profession's brief flirtation with liberal social movements: civil rights, protests against the Vietnam War, legal aid, and public interest law. These inversions of the age profile are constant—the consequence of alternating larger and smaller cohorts produced by the impermanence of supply control in a market economy together with the lagged response of career choices caused by imperfect information about the relative rewards of various alternatives. One byproduct is significant intergenerational tension resulting in struggles to control professional associations and the formation of competing groups.

Ethnicity

Changes in age composition are an unintended consequence of decisions motivated by other considerations. But the professional project is just as

concerned to control *who* become lawyers as it is to limit their numbers;
indeed, each form of control influences the other. Until very recently,
ethnicity, religion, and generation of immigration were central criteria of
social status (in some environments they still are). As late as 1910, the
American legal profession was overwhelmingly Protestant and native
born: 74 percent were the children of parents born in America, and another
20 percent were born in America themselves. There is ample evidence that
professional associations energetically sought to exclude the sons of recent
Jewish and Catholic immigrants from southern and eastern Europe by
raising the requirements of formal prelegal and legal education, imposing
character tests, and even resorting to quotas. However, the efforts failed: in
New York City, the proportion of new entrants who were Jewish rose
from 26 percent in the first decade of the twentieth century to 80 percent
between 1930 and 1934, before declining to 65 percent in the 1950s. Law
remains disproportionately attractive to members of minority religions,
perhaps because it promises upward mobility to the children of small
businessmen, for whom other routes remain less accessible. The attempt to
limit numbers by controlling background thus could not withstand demands framed in terms of the dominant egalitarian ethos.

Although Jews and Catholics have entered the profession in large numbers, they continue to be concentrated within its lower strata: as solo
practitioners, in small firms, and in government. If explicit prejudice has
declined, recent studies confirm that ethnoreligious background still influences the law school that a student attends, which affects the graduate's
first job and subsequent career (although the strength of this influence may
vary geographically). The differentiation of legal roles is reproduced at the
level of social status and income and in the governance of professional
associations. In a society where religion and ethnicity still count, the legal
profession maintains its standing by keeping minority religions and ethnicities in the background.

Class

Liberalism proscribes state action (and now also the more visible forms of
private action) that discriminates on the basis of ascriptive characteristics.
But liberalism tolerates—indeed, requires—distinctions in terms of characteristics that ostensibly are achieved, such as class. Until World War II,
the lack of formal prelegal educational requirements and the availability of
part-time legal education rendered the legal profession quite accessible to
those from working-class backgrounds. Since the war, however, class recruitment has narrowed as a result of heightened competition for places in
university law schools. Intergenerational inheritance of professional status

is high: a very large proportion of lawyers have parents or close relatives in the profession. Among lawyers in practice today, those in the younger cohort are more likely to come from a privileged background.

The entry of women has intensified class bias. First, it nearly doubled the number of those seeking to become lawyers, thereby increasing competition for places. Every study has confirmed that the indices used by law schools in admissions decisions—undergraduate grades and Law School Admission Test scores—are strongly correlated with socioeconomic status. Second, because women still must overcome substantial social, psychological, and cultural barriers, both to enter the legal profession and to succeed within it, those who do so tend to come from more privileged backgrounds than their male counterparts. Therefore, whereas the new entrants from minority religions and ethnicities in the 1920s and 1930s also tended to be from lower class origins, this is not true of the women who entered in the 1970s and 1980s, and it is only partly true for members of racial minorities.

Gender

The recent success of women in entering the legal profession should not allow us to forget that they were the object of explicit discrimination until well into the twentieth century. No women were admitted to practice until the 1870s, and about a dozen of the forty-five jurisdictions continued to exclude them as late as 1900. Some professional associations barred women until 1937, and some law schools continued to do so until 1972. As a result of both formal and informal barriers, women remained an insignificant proportion of the profession until the 1970s—between 1 and 3 percent—except when men were unavailable (during World War II) or where they were uninterested (in the unapproved, low-prestige, part-time law schools).

In light of this history, the change in the last two decades is nothing short of revolutionary. Between 1967 and 1983, the enrollment of women in ABA-approved law schools increased 1650 percent, from 4.5 percent of the total to 37.7 percent. Indeed, after 1973 *all* the increase in law school enrollment is attributable to the growth in the number of women. Even so, the proportion of women has risen more slowly within the legal profession than it has within many other professions and service occupations, and it appears to be peaking at about 40 percent. Furthermore, a smaller proportion of women law graduates enter practice, and a higher proportion of those who enter leave during the first few years.

Within the profession, women occupy roles different from those of men.

They are overrepresented in government and teaching and particularly in legal aid and public defender offices, and they are underrepresented within private practice and the judiciary. As teachers, they tend to occupy positions of lower status. Within private practice they are more likely than men to be either solo practitioners or associates in large firms and less likely to found in small firms or to be partners. In New York City between 1928 and 1932, they earned only 61 percent as much as men lawyers, and this disparity persists today.

A number of factors explain these differences, but ability is not one of them: women perform as well as men, and often better, in college, in law school, and on the bar examination (a superiority that may be related to their more privileged class backgrounds). True, women lawyers are younger than men lawyers; but the income and status differences between the sexes remain when we control for age, although they diminish. Rather, men and women both expect the latter to shoulder the burdens of child-rearing, and women thus choose legal careers that allow them to work part-time, to take leaves of absence, and to control their working hours, sacrificing income and status in the process. Alternatively, women lawyers must postpone marriage much longer than men, which often means foregoing both marriage and children. In addition, women display a principled preference for work in the public sector. Finally, women continue both to experience and to anticipate discrimination, choosing more meritocratic settings where bias is less likely to be expressed: the public sector rather than the private and large firms rather than small. The role of women within the profession is in flux, and only time will tell whether men and women come to share the burdens of childrearing more equally, whether women's preferences for public interest work persist, and whether men grant women positions of power, such as partnerships, as women gain greater experience.

Race

Like women, racial minorities suffered explicit discrimination until well into the twentieth century; unlike women, they continue to experience enormous disadvantages in entering and succeeding within the profession. Most law schools excluded blacks or admitted only a small quota until after World War I; in the South, where most blacks lived, no white law school admitted them until 1935, and many schools continued to exclude them as late as the 1950s. Bar examiners identified applicants by race and often failed all black examinees. The ABA excluded blacks until 1943. Therefore, it is hardly surprising that blacks constituted only 0.5 percent of the profession in 1900, less than 1 percent in 1910, and still only 1.3 percent in 1970, although they were almost ten times as large a proportion of the population (11.1 percent).

In 1965, when affirmative action programs were initiated to correct these injustices, there were only 800 minority law students out of a total enrollment of 65,000, or just over 1 percent. In 1983/84 there were 12,444 minority law students at ABA-approved schools, or 9.9 percent of enrollment. However, it is essential to keep this increase in perspective. First, although affirmative action programs often are criticized as "reverse discrimination," all they did was reopen to racial minorities the doors that had been open to *ethnic* minorities in the 1920s and 1930s but then were closed as the profession attained supply control during the 1940s and 1950s, often with the encouragement of those same ethnic minorities, who now were inside. Second, racial minorities still encounter substantial obstacles in entering the profession. A much lower proportion of minorities than whites complete high school and acquire a bachelor's degree, both of which now are universal prerequisites. A smaller proportion of minority college graduates than whites attend law school. There are few part-time schools whose schedules allow them to earn tuition and living expenses, both of which cost much more today than they did fifty years ago. The economic, social, and educational disadvantages of minority applicants severely handicap them in the intense competition for entry into law school. Furthermore, unlike members of ethnic minorities seeking admission in the 1920s through 1950s, racial minorities today also must compete with women applicants.

It thus is not surprising that the number of black and Mexican-American law students peaked in 1976, even *before* the U.S. Supreme Court limited affirmative action programs. If we extrapolate present enrollments to the year 2000, a generation after the beginning of affirmative action, minority lawyers still will make up only half the proportion of the profession that minorities are of the population, whereas women will be underrepresented by only a fifth; however, even these figures are overly optimistic. Minority law students suffer a significantly higher rate of attrition than do their white counterparts, both because of prior educational disadvantage and because they experience greater economic hardship and more insistent family responsibilities while they are law students. Also, the proportion of minority law graduates who pass the bar examination is only about half that of whites. Unless there are radical efforts to achieve true racial equality in the larger society, "meritocratic" entry barriers will continue to reproduce the historical underrepresentation of racial minorities within the legal profession.

The careers of minority lawyers who succeed in entering the profession diverge from those of their white counterparts even more than the careers of women lawyers diverge from those of men. Again, minority lawyers are greatly overrepresented in government and legal aid and underrepresented in private practice. They are underrepresented among law teachers (a mere 0.5 percent) but have made greater gains in the judiciary, where they benefit from the power of minority voters and the attempt by white politicians to enhance their political legitimacy by appointing minority judges. Within private practice, older lawyers are disproportionately solo practitioners, both because white firms would not hire them and because there are too few minority businesses to sustain minority law firms. In recent years, large firms (although not smaller ones) have begun to hire minority law graduates; although blacks now represent about 2.5 percent of associates at the larger firms, they are only 0.5 percent of partners, however, and many firms still have no black partners. Only some of this disparity can be attributed to the relative youthfulness of minority lawyers.

Just as racial minorities encountered greater difficulties than did women in becoming lawyers, even after explicit discrimination disappeared, so they have found it more difficult to attain positions of power and status within the profession, although there is some evidence that black lawyers enjoy higher incomes than women lawyers. Given the different significance of race and gender in American society, it is not surprising that a higher proportion of women lawyers than men lawyers at large law firms are black. The relative assimilation of women and minority lawyers also is reflected in the strength of their professional associations. Although the National Association of Women Lawyers has been in existence for decades, it enrolled only 2 percent of women lawyers in 1980. By contrast, the National Bar Association enrolls two-thirds of black lawyers today. Just as ethnic minorities found themselves at the bottom of the professional hierarchy during the first half of this century—in government or solo practice—so racial minorities may remain concentrated in those sectors for the foreseeable future.

RESTRICTIVE PRACTICES: CONTROLLING PRODUCTION BY PRODUCERS

DEFINING THE MONOPOLY

Controlling the production *of* producers necessarily is the first stage of the professional project. Only when this has been achieved and a professional association created can the latter seek to restrict competition. The initial target of such protective measures is outsiders who offer professional services. Around the turn of the century, bar associations focused on court clerks who helped parties to litigate without retaining a lawyer. In the 1920s and 1930s professional associations turned their attention to other occupations that advised laypersons and helped them draft legal documents. By 1948, more than 400 bar associations had formed committees to fight what they characterized as the "unauthorized practice of law." These bodies sought legislative and judicial action defining the professional monopoly as broadly as possible—indeed, American lawyers are unusually imperial in their exclusive claim to the entire field of legal advice. Bar associations obtained civil injunctions and criminal prosecutions against those who intruded. They also entered into agreements with representatives of other occupations, dividing the market between them. Although lawyers did not always succeed in asserting their territorial claims, they continued to expand their jurisdiction until the 1960s.

But monopolies are inherently unstable in any relatively free economy. Although lawyers defended them in terms of client interest, clients never complained about external competitors; however, clients were insufficiently organized to attack the professional monopoly. This role was played by competing occupations, who had a higher stake and greater resources. In 1962 Arizona realtors successfully used the initiative process to challenge the monopoly of lawyers in land transactions. In 1977 Virginia title insurers won a similar decision in federal court. The monopoly was becoming a liability for lawyers. The ABA ended publication of its journal, *Unauthorized Practice News*, in 1977. The California State Bar Association rescinded twenty-eight market division agreements under pressure from the U.S. Justice Department, and the ABA soon followed suit. Although some state and local bar associations continue to pursue lay competitors, the publicity attracted by such obviously self-serving behavior could be highly embarrassing. When the Florida State Bar Association successfully sought the prosecution and imprisonment of a former legal secretary for assisting laypersons in filling out forms for pro se wills, divorces, and applications for unemployment compensation, the governor felt compelled to pardon her.

DEFENDING THE TURF AGAINST OTHER LAWYERS

Lawyers also seek to protect themselves from competition by other lawyers. Here, again, restrictions are fairly recent, coinciding with the attainment of control over the production of producers. As late as 1930/31, forty-four out of forty-nine jurisdictions admitted out-of-state lawyers without an examination if the applicant's jurisdiction granted reciprocity to lawyers from the admitting state. As states limited new admissions, however, so they curtailed the migration of lawyers from other jurisdictions. This development began in states that were particularly attractive to migrants. In California, 30 percent of the lawyers admitted between 1920 and 1930 had migrated from other states. In 1931 California imposed an examination, a character test, and a $100 fee, which together reduced the number of lawyer immigrants from an average of 169 a year during the 1920s to an annual average of 43 between 1932 and 1935 (only 8.5 percent of all admittees). Even though all the examinees already were qualified practitioners, the pass rate on the California lawyers' examination was only 45 percent between 1943 and 1948 and fell as the number of applicants rose; pass rates in other jurisdictions also were low.

The National Conference of Bar Examiners, founded in 1931, immediately began providing states with information on the character of out-of-state lawyer applicants. By 1947, thirty-five jurisdictions were using its services, and it conducted 1,354 investigations the following year, leading to the exclusion or withdrawal of 10 percent of the out-of-state attorneys who sought admission, a proportion that increased with time. Many jurisdictions also lengthened the period of time an out-of-state lawyer had to practice before being admitted on motion. By 1982, twenty-three out of fifty-four jurisdictions required all applicants to the bar to pass an examination, despite the fact that by then almost all out-of-state applicants already would have passed part of the same test when they took the multistate portion of the bar examination in the state where they were practicing. As a result of these restrictions, the proportion of bar admissions represented by migrating attorneys has remained relatively constant for the last thirty years despite the significant increase in interstate commerce, practice, and mobility.

Jurisdictions also discouraged the entry of out-of-state attorneys by requiring them to establish residence within the state (sometimes for as long as twelve months) before beginning to practice and often even before taking the bar examination—a significant economic sacrifice for a lawyer with an established practice. In 1954, thirty-nine states had such a requirement; in 1985, forty-one still retained it, although seven states had been forced to drop it as a result of judicial challenges. That year the U.S. Supreme Court abrogated all residence requirements. Nevertheless, some states already have responded by eliminating reciprocity (requiring all applicants to take an examination, even if admitted in another jurisdiction) and by requiring out-of-state entrants to declare their intent to practice full time in the admitting state.

PRICE FIXING

Although fixing prices has been illegal in the United States since the passage of the Sherman Act in 1890, professions long were considered to be exempt. Bar associations began promulgating minimum fee schedules during the Great Depression, when an excess in the supply of lawyers forced some to cut prices. A 1964 ABA survey collected and published 26 state and more than 700 local fee schedules, urging other associations to follow suit and those with lower floors to raise them. A 1971 study disclosed that 90 percent of lawyers in jurisdictions with fee schedules used them in setting prices. Conformity was greatest at the base of the profession, where competition was most severe. Schedules had the desired effect of increasing both fees and income—hardly surprising, since professional associations punished those who engaged in obvious price cutting. When the legality of this practice finally was challenged in 1975, the U.S. Supreme Court held that it violated the Sherman Act. One longitudinal study revealed that prices dispersed and dropped as a result. There is little evidence of aggressive price competition among lawyers today; it is only the threat of competition from other occupations that drives down prices.

ADVERTISING

Like so many other restrictions on self-promotion, the ban on advertising emerged fairly late in the professional project. Advertising by lawyers was widespread and apparently unobjectionable until the ABA promulgated its first ethical code in 1908. The new prohibition had a radically different impact on practitioners at the top and the bottom of the professional hierarchy. Large firms do not need to go looking for business every day because they have ongoing relationships with clients who constantly demand legal services. These ties are strengthened by social interaction, kinship, hiring "rainmakers" (partners whose primary function is to generate business), and placing partners on the boards of clients (although this is diminishing). Solo and small firm practitioners, however, serve individual clients who have sporadic needs for legal services. The most comprehensive American study revealed that more than a third of all adults never have consulted with a lawyer, and even those who have done so consulted lawyers an average of little more than twice in a lifetime. Convincing laypeople that they could benefit from seeing a lawyer and that they should see a particular lawyer requires aggressive salesmanship. Those few lawyers who were willing to run the (minimal) risk of disciplinary action and violate the rules against solicitation and advertising gained a significant competitive advantage. Despite this patent hypocrisy, however, the rules survived and were invoked in periodic crackdowns on ambulance chasing.

In 1977, however, the combination of heightened competition resulting from the rapid increase in the number of young lawyers, the rise of the consumer movement, and ideological critiques of state "interference" in the economy led to a successful challenge to these anticompetitive practices. The U.S. Supreme Court held some (although not all) restraints on lawyer advertising to be an unconstitutional violation of free speech. Even though the ABA interpreted this decision broadly, many states continued to impose substantial limitations on advertising, however, leading to an ongoing series of U.S. Supreme Court decisions refining the distinctions between direct mail advertising and solicitation, commercial and noncommercial solicitation, and the permissible use of graphics and misleading partial truths.

Lawyers have been reluctant to take advantage of their new economic freedom, just as they have been unenthusiastic about engaging in price competition. They oppose collective advertising as inefficient and individual advertising as divisive, although some younger lawyers in smaller firms do not share this view. (Clients, not surprisingly, are much more favorable to advertising.) Two years after the U.S. Supreme Court's decision, only 3 percent of lawyers were advertising; four years later less than 15 percent were doing so. One reason was continued professional restrictions: the amount of advertising varied directly with the liberality of the rules. Nevertheless, there was evidence that the price of legal services decreased as advertising became more widespread.

SPECIALIZATION: RECAPTURING CONTROL BY REDEFINING THE MARKET

At late as the 1940s, 78 percent of a sample of Pennsylvania practitioners characterized themselves as generalists. This self-image has changed dramatically since then: the proportion dropped to 41 percent among California lawyers in 1960 and to 30 percent among Chicago practitioners in the late 1970s. The growth of specialization was not evenly distributed across fields: prosecutors, patent lawyers, and those who did corporate tax work were highly specialized, whereas there was little specialization among those in the fields of general corporations, family or commercial law, or personal real estate transactions. Not surprisingly, the attitudes of lawyers toward formal specialization (like their attitudes toward advertising) depended strongly on the extent to which they specialized themselves. The first formal specialization scheme was launched in 1973, and by 1985 such programs existed in twelve states. Nevertheless, continuing opposition from generalists has ensured that all such plans are based on self-designation or experience rather than requiring additional formal education and examination. Greater pressure for specialization has come from judges critical of what they see as the incompetence of many litigators. Consequently, a number of federal district courts have required a quasi-apprenticeship before a lawyer can appear. If specialization continues to intensify and rigidify, functional differentiation may replace geographic dispersion as a significant mechanism of market control.

THE FUTURE OF RESTRICTIVE PRACTICES

The project of controlling the production *of* producers tends to unite all those within the charmed circle of qualified professionals: elite lawyers want to enhance the collective status of the profession, and lawyers at the base want to protect their economic interests. At the same time, it inevitably increases the pressure by those outside to get in and thus, in any relatively free economy, leads to an erosion of supply control. By contrast, the project of controlling production *by* producers not only engenders opposition from outsiders—lay competitors and consumers—but also divides qualified professionals along strata, pitting those who are doing well and wish to dampen competition against those who want to engage in it in order to do better. In the United States the arbiters of this conflict generally are judges, who are at least somewhat disinterested and autonomous; consequently, the outcome does not simply reflect the relative power of the two groups. It thus should not be surprising that the restrictive practices erected by the American legal profession during the first half of this century have succumbed to the increased competition of the last quarter century. The legal profession's monopoly has been breached at several places, interstate competition is much more vigorous, explicit price fixing is illegal, and advertising is permitted and vigorously employed to great effect by at least some lawyers. The only hope for reasserting supply control appears to lie in functional specialization, which would further undermine the unity of the legal profession.

HOW SUCCESSFUL WAS THE PROFESSIONAL PROJECT? THE INCOME OF LAWYERS

If it is clear that lawyers engaged in collective action to control supply, that alone does not tell us whether their efforts succeeded. In a later section I analyze the status of lawyers; here I consider whether the professional project has allowed lawyers to extract a monopoly rent for their services. The theory of professionalism as supply control predicts that lawyer income should have fallen between 1900 and the early 1930s as a result of the increased production of lawyers and the decline in demand following the Great Depression; it should have risen until recently as a result of growing control over production and the postwar boom; and it should have started to fall again in the last few years as 'a result of the threefold increase in bar admissions.

There is considerable evidence to confirm all three predictions. Although we have no data on lawyer income prior to the Great Depression, it did fall during the early Depression years. Private practitioners suffered most acutely: their numbers were least controllable and the demand for their services depended most on the strength of the economy. By contrast, physicians suffered less because they had restricted their numbers in the 1920s, and the demand for their services was less closely related to the economy. Although median lawyer income had been greater than that of physicians in 1930, the two were equal in 1940; ten years later lawyer income had fallen to only half that of physicians, and by 1955 median lawyer income was below that of dentists. In the first two postwar decades the legal profession more than recouped these losses, as median lawyer income increased faster than did that of physicians. Since the late 1960s, however, there has been a decline in median lawyer income measured in constant dollars.

Medians can be seriously misleading, however: lawyers at the top of the profession undoubtedly earn more than physicians, whereas those at the bottom earn less. Furthermore, intraprofessional differences also illuminate the success of the professional project. The dispersion of incomes is greater among lawyers than it is within any other profession, suggesting a relatively low level of supply control. At the same time, it has decreased over the years as the profession gained control over supply. Dispersion is greatest among private practitioners, where supply control is least effective. For a long time salaried lawyers earned more than private practitioners—the reverse of the relationship among physicians. The impact of the Great Depression on lawyers varied with their exposure to intraprofessional competition: younger lawyers earned less than both physicians and dentists; older lawyers earned more. Similarly, younger lawyers benefited most from the conjunction of supply control and expanding demand during the 1950s, and older lawyers have held their own during the downward drift of the median income in recent years.

Cross-sectional studies are consistent with these historical trends. The lowest lawyer incomes are found in large cities, where competition is greatest. Rural lawyers, by contrast, seem to have been relatively insulated from the general decline in lawyer incomes during the Depression and again over the last few years. Lawyers' own perceptions mirror this reality: the intensity of complaints about overcrowding varies inversely with the size of the lawyer's firm. Furthermore, comparisons between jurisdictions confirm that the degree of supply control (as measured by the bar examination passage rate or the number of law graduates per year) is correlated with income, although the results are not always statistically significant. It thus seems clear that the professional project of lawyers did succeed in promoting their economic well-being.

DEMAND CREATION: A NEW STRATEGY OF THE PROFESSIONAL PROJECT

We saw that the legal profession's control over the production *of* and *by* lawyers has eroded significantly during the last two decades. The consequent increase in competition coincided with the rise of consumerism as a social movement. At the same time, the profession has displayed heightened concern over its legitimacy, particularly as measured by its contribution to one of the fundamental principles of the liberal state: equal justice under law. The convergence of these events has stimulated interest in another mechanism of market control: demand creation. I survey below a variety of recent public and private initiatives that seek to stimulate and to satisfy the demand for lawyers' services.

THE REDISCOVERY OF LEGAL NEED

The necessary prerequisite to stimulating demand is to identify "needs" that are not being satisfied. This is not a new endeavor. In his classic 1919 study, Reginald Heber Smith thoroughly documented the legal system's neglect of the poor. Although legal aid programs were inaugurated in the late nineteenth century and eventually spread to dozens of American cities, they remained inadequately funded and unambitious. Further studies of lawyer use in the 1940s and 1950s had no visible consequences. The growth of both sociology of law and federal legal aid in the late 1960s led to the most ambitious investigation to date, the American Bar Foundation's (ABF) 1977 report on the legal needs of the public. It revealed that more than a third of the population never had used a lawyer and only a fifth had used a lawyer at least twice. Among those who had ever seen a lawyer, the mean number of consultations was only 2.15 in a lifetime. Additionally, lawyer use varied strongly with age, gender, race, income, and education. These findings would seem to provide an ample foundation for a campaign to provide legal services to the unrepresented; however, the ABF study confirmed other reports that individuals use lawyers largely to obtain, protect, or transfer property. Since most people rarely control any significant amounts of property, the survey respondents encountered a mean of only 4.8 "legal problems" during their lifetimes.

The empirical evidence thus casts considerable doubt on the feasibility of a project of demand creation.

THE LIMITATIONS OF PROFESSIONAL CHARITY

The first response of lawyers to legal needs that were unsatisfied by the market was to provide their services at little or no cost—the charitable obligation known as "pro bono publico." The limitations of this mechanism were immediately apparent, however. The potential recipients of charity made contact with lawyers through a network of intermediaries that tended to exclude many of the neediest: the old and the young, racial minorities, the permanently poor, and the deviant. Lawyers offering charity provided minimal services and almost never engaged in litigation. Surveys revealed that a third of the profession donated no services whatsoever, and the rest averaged three cases, or twenty-seven hours, a year. Although professional associations still devote considerable energy, and even more publicity, to pro bono activities, it is clear that these cannot fulfill the promise of equal justice—and, of course, they generate little or no paying business for lawyers.

INSTITUTIONALIZING THE RIGHT TO CRIMINAL DEFENSE

The first step toward actively involving the state in creating demand was taken by the courts rather than by private practitioners—demonstrating (if any demonstration is needed) that the project of market control is as much a byproduct of adventitious circumstance as it is of conscious planning. The U.S. Supreme Court recognized a constitutional right to legal defense in all federal criminal cases in 1938. It extended this to state court felony defendants in 1963 and nine years later to those accused of misdemeanors punishable by six months' imprisonment. Before these decisions, indigent defendants often were tried without any legal representation. By 1973, state-subsidized lawyers were representing 65 percent of all felony defendants. The new rights stimulated the creation of salaried public defender programs, however, and thus generated little work for private practitioners. Although some courts appointed private counsel, either in lieu of public defenders or when the latter had a conflict of interest, the rate of state reimbursement was low, judicial favoritism gave some lawyers an advantage in appointments, the quality of representation was poor, and abuses (such as overcharging) threatened rather than enhanced the legitimacy of the profession. State involvement thus has tended to diminish the autonomy and altruism of lawyers in the eyes of the public, without producing any significant material benefits for the profession.

THE CONTESTED TERRAIN OF CIVIL LEGAL AID

The entitlement of criminal accused to legal representation is relatively unproblematic, if its implementation has been flawed. There is considerably more controversy over whether the state has any obligation to provide legal aid and advice in civil matters. State and federal supreme courts consistently have rejected claims that the U.S. Constitution guarantees such a right. Until 1965, legal aid programs were locally organized, funded by city and county governments and private philanthropy, restricted in the cases they could bring and the tactics they would use, and trivial in amount—the aggregate budget nationwide was only $4 million. Professional associations opposed any involvement by state or federal governments, recoiling in horror from the 1949 British legal aid program as an example of "creeping socialism."

In light of this history, the expansion of civil legal aid since 1965 has been extraordinary. That year, almost as an afterthought, a legal services program was included in the Office of Economic Opportunity as part of Lyndon Johnson's War on Poverty. The ABA abruptly switched from an implacable foe to a staunch supporter, although many state and local bar associations remained opposed. The budget grew from less than $5 million a year to a high of $321 million, supporting some 6,000 lawyers at the end of the Carter years, before the Reagan Administration cut it by a third. Reagan's efforts to eliminate federal funding for legal aid eventually united virtually every state and local bar association behind the Legal Services Corporation. Nevertheless, the attempt to compensate for reduced federal support by requiring lawyers to donate the interest on their client trust accounts has been only partially successful.

The fundamental contradictions within civil legal aid continue to limit its contribution to either the legitimacy or the material well-being of lawyers. Both conservatives and radicals recognize what liberals would like to deny—that legal aid inevitably is political. This explains the numerous restrictions on tactics, clients, and subject matter contained in the Legal Services Corporation Act of 1974, one of the last statutes Richard Nixon signed before resigning. Moreover, although President Reagan has been unable to persuade Congress to abolish the Corporation, he has gained the confirmation of his appointees to the Board of Governors, whose declared goal is to return the program to the status quo prior to 1965, providing only individual representation in routine matters such as divorce. Because the legal profession initially opposed state payments to private practitioners, fearing that this would compromise their autonomy, the American legal aid program is the only one in the world in which virtually all services are provided by salaried lawyers. In recent years, as the federal budget has grown, bar associations have overcome their earlier scruples and sought to divert government funds to so-called "judicare" programs.

Ironically, however, political conservatives, who normally would favor such schemes as less likely to engage in vigorous, imaginative, partisan advocacy, also are fiscal conservatives, who oppose judicare as a blank check that authorizes practitioners to provide unlimited services in response to an apparently insatiable demand. In any case, the few existing judicare schemes pay so poorly that most lawyers are uninterested in participating, with the result that these programs tend to concentrate their business among a small number of specialists, notwithstanding efforts to distribute clients broadly. The profession thus reaps little symbolic or material benefit from state support for civil legal aid.

THE ROLE OF ORGANIZED PHILANTHROPY

Social activist groups, most notably the American Civil Liberties Union (ACLU) and the National Association for the Advancement of Colored People (NAACP), have been using law as one strategy of change ever since the 1920s. The resources available for public interest law greatly multiplied in the 1970s, as foundations made substantial grants to new firms, vigorous social movements looked to lawyers for advice and assistance, and law graduates eagerly accepted lower pay in exchange for political involvement. Yet, public interest law has suffered even more than legal aid from the impossibility of reconciling explicitly political goals with a legitimacy grounded in the process values of liberalism. Even at its peak, public interest law employed only about 500 to 700 lawyers with a total budget of $35 to $50 million, or little more than 0.1 percent of the profession and the private market for legal services. It always concentrated most of its energies on litigation, at the expense of more explicitly political strategies, because lawyers preferred to use their technical expertise, lacked political contacts and resources, and feared to alienate funding sources. In any case, foundations soon turned away from public interest law, following the internal imperative to find novel projects. Firms have encountered difficulties in replacing foundation grants: their tax-exempt status limits the client fees they can accept; membership dues generate little income; and court awards, always sharply restricted in American practice, are under renewed attack by conservatives. Perhaps the best illustration of the contradictions of liberalism is the fact that the form of public interest law now has been adopted by conservative lawyers, who enjoy tax-exempt status while representing the "public interests" of their corporate donors.

EXPANDING THE MIDDLE-CLASS CLIENTELE

All the programs described above are shaped primarily by the political goal of extending representation and enhancing the legitimacy of the profession and the legal system and only incidentally by the profession's economic interest in creating demand. Lawyers also have devised new delivery mechanisms in pursuit of the latter goal. Many local bar associations sponsor lawyer referral services, in which prospective clients are randomly allocated among the members of the association. Although this may minimize intraprofessional competition, there is no evidence that it generates any additional business. Furthermore, referral services are little used, for clients, like all laypeople seeking professional services, strongly prefer to rely on a friend or relative to recommend a particular lawyer.

Group legal service plans, in which individual clients act collectively to purchase legal services, are not new. Automobile owners needing legal representation while on the road and businesspeople seeking to collect debts both organized such schemes in the 1930s. The profession opposed these initiatives just as it did state subsidization, fearing that the organized clientele (like the public paymaster) would alter the balance of power between lawyer and client. Only when several trade unions and the NAACP persuaded the U.S. Supreme Court to recognize the constitutional right of their members to obtain legal advice from lawyers paid or chosen by the organization did group plans begin to multiply. Even then, the profession continued to enforce "ethical" rules designed to suppress competition by favoring "open" plans, to which any lawyer could belong, while discouraging "closed" plans, in which a limited number of lawyers contracted with the plan membership to provide services at prenegotiated prices. The ABA withdrew this rule only when threatened with an antitrust action by the U.S. Justice Department. Most of the plans subsequently established have been "closed," both because lawyers have greater incentives to form them and because the members themselves prefer to be directed to particular lawyers rather than being forced to "choose" without adequate information about price or quality. Although group plans claimed to enroll seven million members in 1984, their growth has been slowed by the relatively low priority that both individuals and their union bargaining agents place on legal services as a fringe benefit and by the constant erosion of the bargaining power of organized labor in recent years (who now constitute less than 20 percent of the workforce).

Probably the most successful innovation has been the legal clinic, which cuts the cost of legal services by pursuing economies of scale and substituting both capital (word processing equipment and forms) and inexpensive labor (paraprofessionals and secretaries) for legal professionals. In order to do this, clinics must attract a mass clientele through advertising. The organized profession punished them for doing so until the U.S. Supreme Court extended First Amendment protection to some forms of commercial speech by professionals. Then the ABA performed an about-face and tried to design a clinic that would not compete with other practitioners; not surprisingly, the effort failed. Since the first clinic was founded in 1975, the number has grown exponentially to more than 1,000. Within a decade, the two largest clinics had become the second and the forty-first largest law firms in the country, with 550 and 236 lawyers, respectively. Hyatt Legal Services, the largest clinic, spends more than $5 million a year on advertising to attract an estimated 18,000 new clients a month. Yet, despite their claims, it is not clear whether clinics reach a clientele previously unserved by lawyers or simply take clients away from other practitioners, nor is it clear whether they remain cheaper after gaining a substantial share of the market. What does seem certain is that clinics, like closed-panel group plans, contribute to the long-term trend toward concentration within the legal services industry. Also, just as profit-seeking corporations have adopted the forms of public interest law to disguise their pursuit of private material and political advantage, so landlords have been attracted to clinics as a means of achieving economies of scale in evicting tenants.

IS DEMAND CREATION AN EFFECTIVE STRATEGY OF MARKET CONTROL?

Although some commentators on the legal profession feel that the notion of demand creation imputes too much conspiratorial deliberation to the actions of lawyers, it still seems to me the most plausible explanation for the recent dramatic reversal in professional attitudes and behavior. Only when the profession saw an erosion of its control over the production *of* and *by* producers of legal services did it do an abrupt volte-face and embrace legal aid, advertising, organized pro bono activities, and group plans. However, there is reason to believe that this new strategy of market control will be no more effective than the strategies that preceded it. In attempting to enhance public perceptions about the fairness of the legal system, the profession runs the risk of diminishing whatever reputation it may retain for altruism and independence and appearing more obviously commercial and greedy. Nor is the material payoff likely to be worth the cost. Whereas the majority of lawyers serving business clients have enjoyed an extraordinary increase in demand as a result of the simultaneous growth of both the economy and government regulation, the minority serving individual clients have not been so fortunate. The number of lawyers who stand to benefit from demand stimulated by third-party payers is severely limited by the preference of the state for staffed-office programs over judicare legal aid plans and of clients for guidance about which lawyers to choose. The fiscal crisis of the state and the fickleness of philanthropy limit the funding for subsidized demand to a mere 1 or 2 percent of the total market for legal services. Entrepreneurial efforts to cut prices cannot significantly expand middle-class demand, which seems highly inelastic both because individuals rightly fear lawyers and litigation and because the law has evolved to advance property interests that most individuals do not possess.

The danger is not just that demand creation will fail but also that it will undermine professional coherence. Whereas the project of controlling the production of producers tends to unite lawyers, the strategy of demand creation tends to divide them. In each example discussed above, the efforts of the organized profession to maintain internal harmony by spreading business evenly succumbed to the competitive forces that demand creation unleashes. The inevitable result appears to be ever greater concentration among producers. The growth of both criminal and civil legal aid thus pits salaried lawyers against private practitioners and poverty law specialists against generalists. The outcome is large staffed-office programs and judicare mills that may come to resemble the notorious Medicare mills. The rise of public interest law firms divides their members from the bulk of "private interest" firms. Lawyers who join closed-panel group legal service plans gain a competitive advantage over those left outside, notwithstanding the efforts of the profession to favor open-panel plans. Legal clinics take business away from solo and small-firm practitioners, despite the lawyer referral schemes that randomly distribute clients to the latter. Some lawyers compete for prestige by conspicuously donating their time to pro bono projects; others compete economically by repudiating any such obligation. A few lawyers accumulate large clienteles through extensive individual advertising; the profession's efforts to generate nonspecific demand through institutional advertising are a failure. To the extent that the profession responds to the erosion of supply control by seeking to create demand through any of these mechanisms, it is likely to diminish autonomy and altruism, increase internal disharmony, and accelerate concentration.

SELF-REGULATION

THE PROMULGATION OF ETHICAL RULES

One of the hallmarks of a profession most valued by its members is freedom from external, and particularly state, control. As we have seen, the power of lawyers to regulate themselves was an essential foundation for the many restrictive practices that made legal practice a haven from the competitive rigors of the marketplace. The privilege is earned and retained only if it is seen to be exercised, however, and here lawyers, like other professionals, have been patently ineffective. Although the ABA began its professionalizing project in the 1870s, it did not get around to promulgating its first ethical rules for thirty years. Thereafter, revision and refinement of formal rules became a professional preoccupation—almost an obsession—that often seemed a substitute for actually enforcing them. The ABA has engaged in six complete or partial overhauls of its ethical principles in the last seventy-five years. In addition, it has commanded all approved law schools to require instruction in those rules, although numerous studies show that such courses have no perceptible effect on subsequent lawyer behavior.

THE DISCIPLINARY PROCESS

Until well into the twentieth century, professional discipline in most jurisdictions depended entirely on those informal pressures for conformity that inhere in the face-to-face contacts within small local bars. Even after ethical codes were enacted, most lawyers remained ignorant of their contents. One survey revealed that, although fee splitting was illegal in forty-six out of fifty jurisdictions, only 33 percent of a national sample of lawyers knew this, and only 38 percent considered it wrong. As metropolitan bars grew, the influence of informal sanctions declined; indeed, studies revealed that colleagues actually tended to socialize lawyers into unethical behavior during the early years of practice. When disciplinary committees were established, they received few complaints. Clients were unfamiliar with the intricacies of ethical rules and unaware of the mechanisms of professional discipline; furthermore, they often benefited from lawyer "misconduct," such as solicitation or aggressive advocacy. Lawyers, who were better positioned to perceive and report misconduct, were reluctant to "tattle" on their colleagues—for who wished to cast the first stone and possibly invite a retaliatory accusation? Lawyers consistently filed only a tenth of all grievances. A Missouri study revealed that only 11 percent of rural lawyers and 27 percent of urban lawyers *ever* had filed a complaint. Furthermore, lawyer grievances were particularly divisive, because the solo and small firm practitioners who disproportionately were accused knew that the substantive rules outlawed actions, such as ambulance chasing, that only they were under economic pressure to commit.

Formal disciplinary procedures remained thoroughly inadequate until after World War II. The nineteen voluntary state bar associations lacked disciplinary powers and were limited to making recommendations to their state supreme courts; only three jurisdictions kept records of disciplinary decisions. Few lawyers were punished and most of those lightly. The Association of the Bar of the City of New York was one of the most active and best endowed professional bodies. Yet between 1905 and 1920, only

3 percent of its investigations into misconduct led to any penalty; between 1925 and 1935, only 0.7 percent of complaints ended in suspension or disbarment; even in the postwar year 1948/49, the latter proportion remained 0.6 percent. Indeed, the growth of regulatory powers seems to have led to a relaxation of discipline. In California, the number of preliminary investigations per year dropped from more than 1,500 in 1929 to less than 150 in 1948, and only about 2 percent of complaints ended in any sanctions. In Chicago, the number of complaints investigated dropped from 952 in 1933/34 to an annual average of 174 between 1942 and 1948, and the proportion of complaints terminating in significant punishment remained about 1.5 percent throughout the period. When attorneys appealed their disciplinary cases, state supreme courts generally reduced the penalties.

Today, only about 1 percent of lawyers accused of misconduct are suspended from practice or disbarred. Many of them, perhaps most, are readmitted in that jurisdiction or another. Disciplinary bodies still lack adequate resources, with the result that they develop large backlogs and are unable to investigate complaints thoroughly. They also remain solicitous of excuses—such as alcoholism, drug dependence, or compulsive gambling—that would aggravate rather than mitigate misconduct before other forums. They are reluctant to punish lawyers for extraprofessional misconduct: in California, Illinois, and the District of Columbia between 1967 and 1981 there were only 197 such disbarments, 101 of which were the automatic consequence of felony convictions. Although some state bars have coopted laypersons onto their disciplinary committees, they always are outnumbered by, and generally defer to, the lawyer members. Nevertheless, the impatience of the lay public, clients, and legislators with this sorry record is leading to the creation of independent regulatory authorities.

PROTECTING THE CLIENT AGAINST FINANCIAL LOSS

One of the most sensitive problems with which lawyers must deal, the loss or misuse of client funds, has proved singularly intractable. As late as the 1960s, less than half of all jurisdictions had any kind of client security fund. All states have them today, but many place a low ceiling on what will be reimbursed, and others require prior disciplinary action before any payment will be made. The claimant may have no right to a hearing. It still is true that fewer than half of the claims filed are paid, and fewer than two-thirds of those paid are compensated in full. As the number of claims increases, there is mounting pressure to improve both the remedial and the compensatory mechanisms.

ENSURING PROFESSIONAL COMPETENCE

Studies consistently have shown that individual clients are acutely dissatisfied with lawyer performance: their complaints to disciplinary committees
focus far more on delay, discourtesy, and lack of communication than on
ethical violations. Lawyers claim the exclusive right to monitor incompetence, like misconduct, on the ground that they alone possess the necessary technical expertise to ensure that their colleagues attain some minimal level of performance. The profession purports to ensure quality by
monitoring input, process, and outcome. We saw above that lawyers
energetically constructed substantial barriers against entry; however, they
never sought to examine empirically whether those who surmounted the
barriers were any more competent than those who failed. We know that
restrictions on the number of law school places excluded many highly
qualified applicants and that background variables strongly influence who
is accepted. In any case, whatever skills and knowledge a lawyer may have
attained at the time of passing the bar examination are no guarantee of
competence throughout a career that may span fifty years. Lawyers have
been slower than physicians to require continuing education and testing.
The somewhat uncertain progress of specialization could become an additional measure of competence, but thus far it has relied largely on the
meaningless criteria of "experience" and self-certification.

It is much more difficult to use process variables to monitor performance. Larger firms and other bureaucratic settings in government and
industry do supervise the work of younger employed lawyers in a way
that resembles traditional apprenticeship. Judicial clerkships offer a similar
experience. We know almost nothing about the content or quality of such
training, however, and the profession exercises no control over it. Furthermore, it generally is unavailable to those with weaker academic records, presumably more in need of it, who enter private practice on their
own or in office-sharing arrangements. Professional disciplinary bodies
consistently have refused to take jurisdiction over client complaints of
lawyer incompetence. To the extent that lawyers oversee each other's
performance, they do so increasingly across sectors of the profession
rather than within them: house counsel checking on the work of the
outside law firms that their corporate employers retain and judges and
agency administrators scrutinizing the behavior of lawyers appearing
before them. As the profession experiences progressively greater internal
differentiation (a phenomenon I discuss below), these forms of oversight
come to resemble external regulation more than self-regulation.

The outcomes of lawyer effort also elicit forms of feedback, but these
lie outside the profession's control. One is the contingent fee, which proportions the lawyer's reward to the damages recovered by the client.

Although this seems to align the interests of lawyer and client, it actually creates perverse incentives, encouraging the lawyer to accept a settlement that will minimize the amount of effort expended. Of considerably greater importance is the threat of malpractice liability. Until recently lawyers truly were self-regulating in this respect: virtually no claims were made before the 1960s. Now, some estimate, one lawyer in ten is sued every year, although the proportion varies greatly with locality, structure of practice, and specialization. All agree, however, that the number of suits and the probability and size of recoveries have increased; in 1985, for instance, the average jury verdict was over $40,000. Insurance premiums have sky-rocketed as a result, and liability insurance increasingly is compulsory—but this, in turn, amplifies the frequency and size of awards. Yet, if malpractice recoveries undoubtedly benefit injured clients, there is no evidence that they enhance lawyer competence.

THE FUTURE OF SELF-REGULATION

When an occupation is in the process of professionalizing, it both claims the right to regulate its members and promises to exercise this privilege in the public interest. Lawyers, like other professionals, did little to fulfill their pledge, however, beyond engaging in endless debates about the content of ethical rules. This default has stimulated the growth of external regulation. Courts have asserted the right to control the law school curriculum. Courts and agencies police the behavior of lawyers who appear before them. State supreme courts and independent agencies are displacing bar associations as both the source of ethical rules and the mechanism for enforcing them (a more active role than judges have played in the past), and clients are looking to courts to recover mismanaged funds and compensation for malpractice. Just as the profession has watched the erosion of its control over the market for its services, so it is seeing control over conduct and competence slip from its grasp.

HOW SUCCESSFUL WAS THE PROFESSIONAL PROJECT? THE STATUS OF LAWYERS

An occupation professionalizes not just from pecuniary motives but also to elevate its status. Lawyers pursued this goal by seeking to restrict the background characteristics of entrants, promulgating ethical rules and occasionally enforcing them in highly visible moral campaigns, rendering pro bono services in well-publicized test cases, and supporting legal aid programs. Although the legal profession may have enhanced its *self-respect* in these ways, there is little evidence that the public changed its views. A 1973 survey established that the public ranked lawyers below garbage collectors, police, and business firms; five years later they were the equals of Congress, organized labor, and administrative agencies—hardly flattering company. When asked for specific opinions, respondents reply that lawyers are biased in favor of the rich, create unnecessary work for themselves, engage in unethical conduct, frequently are incompetent, show little concern for their clients, and overcharge. Although lawyers deplore this hostility and launch expensive public relations campaigns to dispel it, I am convinced that the problem is structural and thus not remediable by cosmetic changes. The very monopoly that transforms an occupation into a profession also renders lay clients dependent on professionals (breeding mistrust and resentment) and allows and encourages professionals to exploit their clients economically. The cumulative suspicion and hostility this engenders is one explanation for the erosion of professional control over the market for legal services and the curtailment of professional self-regulation. Yet these partial surrenders of professional privilege are likely further to diminish the status of lawyers, at least in the short run.

DIFFERENTIATION WITHIN THE LEGAL PROFESSION

Earlier in this chapter I noted various forms of professional differentiation: the significant degree of economic and social stratification; growing heterogeneity in terms of ethnoreligous background, gender, and race; the emergence of competing professional associations; and the increase in subject-matter specialization. Despite these very important divisions, the American profession has been unusually unitary in one essential respect: the overwhelming majority of lawyers have been private practitioners, and most of these have practiced alone or in association with only a few others. This dominance by private practitioners contrasts sharply to the legal professions of continental Europe, Latin America, and Japan, which tend to be divided into judges and prosecutors, civil servants, lawyers employed in business, and private practitioners—categories that are roughly comparable in size, income, and prestige. Although the core of private practice retains a preeminence in the United States that it enjoys nowhere outside the common law world, its centrality is diminishing, and private practitioners themselves are becoming internally more differentiated (see table 2). These changes are at least as significant as the erosion of professional control over markets and discipline; indeed, the two phenomena are closely related.

THE PROFESSIONAL PERIPHERY: EMPLOYED LAWYERS

Government Lawyers

Despite the myth of excessive government regulation and inflated bureaucracy that conservatives have promoted and the American people seem to have bought in recent years, the proportion of American lawyers employed by government has grown very slowly in the last twenty years (although the absolute number nearly tripled between 1951 and 1980). Furthermore, this growth has been outstripped by the increase in house counsel—confirming, if evidence were needed, that a capitalist society consistently overendows private interests at the expense of public. Moreover, although conservatives have attacked the federal government as a bloated parasite sapping the strength of state and local governments, which are said to be more responsive to their constituencies, the number of lawyers employed by the latter actually has grown more rapidly.

One reason for the relative stasis of this sector is that government lawyers are poorly paid, another example of the relative impoverishment of the public sector. Although I do not mean to slight the idealism of some who choose government employment, it represents a fallback position for many others: lawyers at the bottom of the meritocratic hierarchy (because of their poor grades or the low status of the law school they attended), victims of discrimination on the basis of ethnoreligious background, gender, or race, and those who cannot make a living in private practice at times of overproduction and declining demand, such as the Great Depression. Many take government jobs immediately after law school in order to barter the experience and contacts they acquire for a more lucrative position in the private sector. In a sample of Chicago practitioners in 1975, government had the lowest retention rate of any category: two-thirds of those who began as government lawyers subsequently moved into the private sector. By contrast, there was *no* movement into government from large or medium firms. Although one lawyer in ten is a government employee, the category thus remains low in income and status, internally fragmented, a temporary way station for many, and no threat to the hegemony of private practice.

House Counsel

Whereas corporations in civil law countries often employ large numbers of law graduates to perform a mixture of administrative and legal tasks, American corporations traditionally have purchased most of their legal services from large law firms. This appears to be changing. The number of lawyers employed by commercial enterprises increased fivefold between 1951 and 1980, three times as rapidly as the entire legal profession since 1948. This does *not* seem to be a response to increased government regulation, for the incidence and size of offices of house counsel are greatest in finance, insurance, real estate, transportation, commerce, public utilities, and manufacturing—not sectors in which regulation has intensified in recent years. (Indeed, partial deregulation and increased competition also appear to generate greater demand for legal services.) Rather, greater in-house capacity appears to reflect the economies of scale that can be attained when an enterprise engages in a large number of fairly routine legal transactions. The growth of house counsel thus is a concomitant of the concentration of capital. For the same reason, offices of house counsel are increasing in size: prior to its recent divestiture, American Telephone & Telegraph (AT&T) employed more than 900 lawyers, making its legal staff several times larger than the largest private law firm. In 1980, 7 percent of house counsel were located in offices employing more than 200 lawyers.

This structure of practice has attractions for both employers and employees. Corporations cut costs by as much as half when they transfer work in-house, and house counsel also serve to monitor the cost and quality of services purchased from outside firms. When companies face a stagnant or contracting economy and heightened pressure from international competition, these economies become increasingly significant. Furthermore, the corporation can demand the undivided loyalty of its employees. Together, these factors may explain why house counsel is coming to perform even nonroutine functions, such as litigation. From the point of view of law graduates, corporate employment offers high starting salaries, greater job security than law firms, more control over hours worked, and meritocratic hiring practices. These characteristics are particularly attractive to women and minority lawyers. House counsel also provides a refuge to lawyers who find that large firm practice demands too much time or who fail to obtain partnerships: nearly a quarter of house counsel in Chicago in 1975 began in large or medium firms, and another 17 percent began in small firms or solo practice. Nevertheless, the employment of lawyers in commerce may have reached the saturation point, and their influence within the corporation actually may be declining.

Judges

In civil law systems, judges play a dominant role in litigation, and 15 to 20 percent of law graduates enter the judiciary. The American judiciary, by contrast, has remained a constant 3 percent of the profession since World War II. This underendowment undoubtedly accounts for at least some of the endless delays that plague litigants in American courts. The quality of adjudication in state trial courts also remains unsatisfactory because the judges earn low salaries, enjoy little prestige, frequently owe their jobs to political contacts, and generally cannot aspire to higher judicial office. As litigants have turned to the federal courts for redress, the number of federal judges has increased three times as fast as their state and municipal counterparts, although the latter continue to outnumber the former by six to one. Rather than expand the judiciary, governments have chosen to create a substratum of parajudicial employees (referees, hearing officers) and to hire private practitioners as part-time judges. Although we have seen appellate judges taking strongly independent stands that profoundly affect the legal profession (striking down the limitation on advertising, outlawing price fixing, restraining the campaign against lay competitors, dictating the content of legal education), the majority of judges remain unorganized and without much influence on professional matters.

Law Professors

Law professors emerged as a significant category within the legal profession only at the end of the nineteenth century. At first, most were practitioners or judges who taught only part-time and, at all but the few public institutions, were paid a proportion of student fees. Around the turn of the century a handful of elite schools began hiring full-time academics and paying them about what they would earn in private practice. Other schools followed suit as they adopted the case method of instruction pioneered at Harvard. With the displacement of apprenticeship by formal education, the number of law teachers increased from 293 in 1887 to more than 2,000 in 1948. We can trace the postwar erosion of supply control in the fact that the professoriat grew twice as rapidly as the profession between 1957 and 1970, laying the foundation for the rapid expansion in the number of lawyers during the last two decades. The professoriat also became a more distinct category. Full-time teachers displaced part-time, and faculties gained coherence and collective influence over their members as they expanded from an average of nine full-time instructors in 1948 to an average of twenty-six in 1982. Although salaries steadily have fallen far behind what most teachers could earn in private practice, they still are well above those of most university professors. Like other forms of employment, teaching also attracts those who may fear discrimination elsewhere (29 percent of law teachers at ABA-approved schools in 1969 were Jewish) or want greater control over their time than private practice permits (women were 17 percent of law teachers at ABA-approved schools in 1984). As the professoriat has differentiated itself from the practicing profession, the two have clashed repeatedly over control of the curriculum. However, although law professors jealously guard their formal autonomy, law schools actually devote most of their energies to teaching what is tested on the bar examination.

Lawyer-Politicians

Although this is not the place to examine the impact of lawyers on the political process, the fact that they dominate the political branches of government more strongly in the United States than in any other country also is significant for an understanding of the legal profession. Lawyers consistently have occupied half or more of the seats in Congress and in the upper (if not always the lower) houses of most state legislatures, and they have represented almost as large a proportion of the state and federal executives (governors, presidents and vice presidents, and cabinet members). The fact that a political career beckons both private practitioners and prosecutors may help to explain the extreme politicization of law in America. The presence of lawyers in the political branches also may explain why the legal profession has been able to enjoy so much freedom from state regulation.

Is the Periphery Still Peripheral?

All the categories just discussed have either preserved their proportions of the profession (judges and politicians) or increased them significantly (government lawyers, house counsel, and law professors). Yet, although this has diminished the centrality of private practice, no competing center has emerged. Furthermore, the degree of internal differentiation among American lawyers remains considerably lower than it is within civil law systems, where law students, at graduation, make nearly irrevocable choices among separate career lines leading to the roles of judge and prosecutor, civil servant, employed lawyer, academic, and private practitioner. In the United States, considerable movement between these categories is possible at every point in a lawyer's career. Prosecutors become judges or enter private practice as criminal defense lawyers. Private practitioners and law professors are appointed to the bench at midcareer or later. Government lawyers sell their accumulated expertise to private employers or clients. Private practitioners move to offices of house counsel, serve temporarily in the government (often in high appointive positions), and enter law teaching. Judges return to private practice in order to double or triple their incomes. If the legal profession encounters increasing difficulty in speaking with one voice, each category certainly understands the perspectives of the others. Yet, it is important to remember that several of these "peripheral" categories exercise increasing authority over the core of private practice: state supreme court judges are the ultimate regulators of the profession, legislators represent an alternative and increasingly important focus of state control (particularly through the power of the purse), judges and agency administrators oversee lawyers who appear before them, and professors teach and certify all entrants to the profession.

THE CORE OF THE PROFESSION: PRIVATE PRACTICE

Private practice remains the first choice of the vast majority of American law graduates, an option that they relinquish only under economic pressure. The proportion of the profession in private practice fell during the Great Depression, when insufficient work was available, and rose as the economy recovered and supply control became more effective. In the last few decades, as supply control has eroded and economic growth has been erratic, the proportion has fallen again—from nearly nine lawyers out of ten in 1948 to slightly more than two out of three in 1980. Even greater changes have occurred within private practice.

The Decline of the Independent Professional

Everywhere in the capitalist world lawyers exalt the ideal of the independent professional: the British barrister, the Japanese *bengoshi*, the French *avocat*, the Venezuelan *litigante de prestigio*—and the American solo practitioner. The lawyer who practices alone—responsible to no one and for no one—can be entirely dedicated to the interests of the client and the pursuit of justice (if these two beacons often point in different directions). Yet, although the number of American solo practitioners rose during the Great Depression, when business was too uncertain to permit lawyers to form partnerships or hire employees, their proportion of the profession has dropped by half since the war, from six out of ten lawyers in 1948 to three out of ten in 1980. Furthermore, we can expect the decline to continue, unless other options disappear, since recent graduates show even less inclination to practice alone than did their predecessors. Rather, they strongly prefer to begin their careers as law firm employees: during the same thirty years, the proportion of lawyers who were associates doubled. Consequently, even if we include law firm partners as well as solo practitioners within the category of independent professionals, it has declined from 85 percent of all lawyers in 1948 to 60 percent today. It seems highly likely that half of the profession will be employees in the near future.

Partners do *not* enjoy the same autonomy as solo practitioners, however; they must cooperate with each other and supervise and pay the salaries of their lawyer and lay employees. As law firms grow in size, they depart further and further from the ideal of the independent professional. Such growth also has paralleled the decline of solo practice. In 1947 the average law firm contained only 1.6 lawyers; although current figures are unavailable, the average today must be much larger. The proportion of firm lawyers in two-person firms dropped from 55.8 percent in 1947 to 17.2 percent in 1980; the proportion in two- or three-lawyer firms dropped from three-fourths to less than a third; the proportion in two- to four-lawyer firms from more than four-fifths to just over a third. At the other extreme, whereas fewer than one firm lawyer in twenty practiced with even eight others in 1947, nearly eight out of twenty (38.8 percent) practiced with at least ten others in 1980. Concentration is likely to increase. Recent law graduates show a marked preference for employment in larger firms. Smaller firms are overrepresented in rural areas, where the number of lawyers is relatively static. Nevertheless, it is important to recognize that the proportion of lawyers practicing in what today would be considered just a medium-size firm (more than twenty lawyers) still represents only 13 percent of the profession.

The Rise of Large Firms

Large law firms are a uniquely American phenomenon (although firms of more than 100 have emerged in other common law countries, as well as in Latin America, perhaps reflecting the influence of the United States economy). Even if there are more than six times as many solo practitioners as there are lawyers in firms of fifty or more, large firms enjoy far greater visibility and influence. The growth of the megafirm is a recent phenomenon, which shows no sign of abating. In 1959, only 32 firms in the United States contained more than fifty lawyers; by 1979, the number had increased more than sixfold to 200. In Chicago in 1935, the ten largest firms contained a median of 23 lawyers; in 1979, that median had risen to 148. In 1950, the fifty largest firms in the country contained a median of 44 lawyers; in 1979, they contained a median of 188; six years later, the twenty-five largest firms contained a median of 374 lawyers.

Growth can be attributed to a number of factors: economies of scale (although the largest firms long have passed the point where these are offset by rising administrative costs), the size and internal diversity of clients (reflecting the wave of mergers during the last two decades), the relationship between internal composition and partnership profits (discussed below), the value of name recognition, and perhaps the distinctively American belief in bigness for its own sake. Change and instability have greatly accelerated. Several firms specializing in corporate takeovers have joined the select group of megafirms within twenty years of their founding. Old established firms have shrunk dramatically after losing major clients or suffering the departure of dissatisfied partners or associates. Partners who are thought not to be pulling their weight have been asked to leave. Law firms have split, leaving former partners litigating over clients and the partnership name. Substantial firms simply have dissolved. One quantitative index of the level of such activity is the existence of at least 109 "headhunting" firms in 1984, which earn their living from such lateral mobility.

Firms also have increased their geographic reach by establishing branch offices: pursuing wealthy retirees to the Sun Belt states; representing clients before the federal legislature, executive, and regulatory agencies in Washington, D.C.; accommodating the new activities or newly acquired subsidiaries of corporate clients; or following the expansion of international trade to other world capitals. No law firms had branch offices in the District of Columbia in 1970; ten years later, 178 had them, and seven of these branches were among the twenty-five largest firms in the city. Florida branches were opened by twenty-nine New York City firms between 1974 and 1980. The total number of out-of-state branches nationwide tripled in the five years during 1978 to 1983. By the latter year, 93 of the 100 largest firms had branches, which contained a quarter of their lawyers.

A third change, which has driven the others to a significant extent, is the growth of subordinate personnel within law firms. The number of associates within the profession increased fivefold between 1951 and 1980, while the number of partners increased less than threefold. Although the ratio of associates to partners has been rising throughout private practice, it also varies strongly with firm size. In 1980 firms with fewer than nine lawyers had 0.48 associates per partner, whereas the ratio in firms with at least seventy-five lawyers was more than twice as high (1.11). Some of the larger New York firms have more than three associates for every partner. As firms grow, the ratio for the profession as a whole will increase. The principal explanation for this change is that associates generate profits for partners. Associate work generally is billed to clients at three times the associate's hourly salary; another third of that gross income pays for overhead; and the remaining third enlarges partnership earnings. Although firms understandably are reluctant to disclose these figures, the ratio of associate billings to associate salary may range as high as 5 : 1.

It is clear that the difference between the billing rates of associates and partners is not itself sufficient to explain the difference in their net incomes. Nor do partners work longer hours than associates; rather, the reverse is true, and associate time also is monitored more carefully. Finally, although both associates and partners may work longer hours and bill at higher rates in larger firms, these differences still do not suffice to explain the much higher earnings of partners in the larger firms, which rather are attributable to the higher ratio of associates to partners in those firms. Recently, firms have augmented this ratio by lengthening the period before associates will be considered for partnership, reducing the proportion of associates who are made partners, and retaining more lawyers indefinitely in the status of permanent associate or salaried partner.

Associates are not the only subordinated employees; large firms also contain many nonprofessionals. Because clerical workers represent over-head, law firms have been concerned with keeping salaries down (by resisting unionization, so far very successfully) and replacing labor by capital (through the use of computers and word processing equipment). Recently, however, firms have come to recognize that they can enhance profits by expanding one category of nonprofessional employee, para-legals, whose time can be billed to clients, generally at more than twice the hourly rate at which they are paid. Paralegals not only replace clerical workers but also can substitute for associates in some tasks, cutting costs and making the firm more competitive. It thus is not surprising that partner income varies directly with the ratio of paralegals to lawyers. That ratio also increases with firm size, so that the number of paralegals is likely to grow as the practice of law is concentrated in ever larger productive units. In 1982 there were thought to be 30,000 to 45,000 paralegals. Their continued subordination is facilitated by the fact that almost all are women, and many expect (or are expected) to be in the labor force only temporarily before leaving to raise children. Although paralegals have made several efforts to professionalize in order to enhance their income and status, they have failed to gain the necessary state recognition of their monopoly, partly because lawyers wish to maintain control and partly because the social, political, and economic environment is much less favor-able to the professional project in the late twentieth century than it was a hundred years earlier.

Large firms have begun to employ a third category of subordinated labor: allied professionals. (The rules of professional conduct still protect lawyer dominance by prohibiting lawyers from forming partnerships with nonlawyers if the firm provides legal services.) The goal of such functional diversification is to stimulate demand among corporate clients—the large firm equivalent of group plans and advertising by solo and small firm practitioners seeking to attract individual clients. Law firms have hired nonlawyers to assist clients with lobbying, financial consulting, banking, management, and real estate brokerage. They also have started selling their own expertise to other law firms—both their knowledge of substantive and procedural law and their marketing skills. As profits have accumulated, firms have retained and invested some of them, erecting a building to bear the firm name and then renting out space to other tenants, for instance.

It should be clear that the large law firm differs from the solo and small practitioner in much more than just the size of the unit within which legal services are produced. The use of and reliance on subordinated labor—lawyers, paralegals, clerical workers, and other professionals—will continue to increase. For as competition within corporate practice has intensified (not only among large firms but also with in-house counsel), the firm has no choice but to increase the exploitation of labor in order to compensate for its declining ability to exploit clients. Firms also will continue to diversify—geographically, across substantive fields, and through the provision of nonlegal services—in order to capture and serve new clientele. More firms will have to employ professional managers because of the number and variety of employees, the proliferation of branch offices, the size of the budget, and the complexity of the physical plant. Law firms thus will undergo the same separation of management from control that their corporate clients experienced half a century earlier.

Professional Stratification

Although the extremes within private practice undoubtedly have polarized in recent years, stratification is hardly a new phenomenon. John Heinz and Edward Laumann studied it in detail in Chicago in the 1970s; Jerome Carlin and Jack Ladinsky documented it in Chicago, Detroit, and New York in the 1950s; Adolf Berle and Harlan Fiske Stone deplored it in the 1930s; Alfred Reed argued in the 1920s for formal recognition of the two strata within legal education; and legal historians have identified elites within the larger urban bars throughout the nineteenth century and even before the Revolution. The characteristics that differentiate lawyers are numerous and varied, but they also are sufficiently cumulative to divide the profession into what Heinz and Laumann call "hemispheres." I will refer to the two groups as elite and ordinary lawyers.

Both categories specialize by client: elite lawyers represent only large business clients and extremely wealthy individuals, whereas ordinary lawyers represent small businesses and middle-class individuals. As a result, the increasing urbanization of lawyers and the progressive concentration in the production of legal services also have effected a redistribution of those services from individuals to businesses. In the 1940s more than half the work of lawyers was devoted to individuals. In the 1970s only 18 percent of lawyer effort was devoted to problems involving personal plight. Specialization by client obviously influences the subject matter of practice as well, but here elite lawyers also are far more highly specialized.

Elite lawyers represent and advise a small number of clients, with whom they have ongoing relationships. Ordinary lawyers represent a large number of clients, whom they rarely see again. As a result of both the status differences and the economic relationships between lawyers and clients, ordinary lawyers tend to dominate their one-shot individual clients, whereas large corporations tend to dominate their elite lawyers (particularly now that corporations are using in-house counsel to control and sometimes to displace outside firms). Elite lawyers spend a higher proportion of their time counseling clients; ordinary lawyers devote more energy to litigation. When elite lawyers litigate, they do so in state appellate courts or federal courts or agencies; ordinary lawyers appear before state trial courts and agencies. Elite lawyers belong to larger firms; ordinary lawyers practice alone, in office-sharing suites, or in small firms. Elite lawyers are graduates of private colleges and elite law schools; ordinary lawyers attended public colleges and regional or local law schools.

Who these lawyers are and what they do affect both their prestige and their income. When lawyers are asked to rank their colleagues, they accord higher prestige to office work than to litigation and to specialization than to general practice; rank also varies inversely with the amount of pro bono work the lawyer does. All three factors may reflect the more general proposition that status is tainted by direct contamination with social problems. Rank varies directly with the intellectual challenge of the work and the technical expertise displayed. (Both are functions of what the client can afford.) Rank increases with the stability of clientele and decreases with the number of clients (obviously interdependent variables). Ironically, the less freedom of action a lawyer enjoys, the higher the rank. Status correlates with characteristics of the lawyer as well as of the law practice: Republicans rank higher; Jews, lower. Not surprisingly, prestige and income are closely correlated, and, as we have seen before, income is widely dispersed. In New York City in 1933, law firm partners earned 2.8 times as much as did solo practitioners. In the immediate postwar period, the mean income of salaried lawyers was higher than that of private practitioners because earnings at the base of the pyramid were so low, although earnings at the top were higher. Since the 1960s, however, the median private practitioner has been better off than the median employed lawyer, perhaps because supply control ameliorated the conditions at the base. At the same

time, differences between elite and ordinary lawyers clearly have increased: in 1984 the median income of partners in firms with ten or more
lawyers was $162,400.

It would be a travesty to invoke Disraeli's metaphor of "two nations" to
describe the private practice of law in contemporary America, since there
are very few impoverished lawyers. But lawyers in the two hemispheres
do inhabit different worlds: they perform different functions in different
forums for different clients with respect to different subject matters. They
come from different backgrounds, acquire different educations, practice
within different structures, and enjoy radically different social standing and
income; and there is virtually no movement between the two spheres.

ONE PROFESSION OR MANY? THE PROLIFERATION OF
PROFESSIONAL ASSOCIATIONS

We saw earlier that the unity of the legal profession has been undermined
by its increasing heterogeneity with respect to ascriptive differences of
gender and race, as well as divisions of age. The only institution that
claims to speak for the profession as a whole, the ABA, never has enrolled
even half of all lawyers. In recent years, women, minorities, and younger
lawyers all have formed their own associations rather than relying on the
ABA to represent them. The structural and functional divisions traced
above—between employed lawyers and private practitioners, and within
those categories between government employees, house counsel, judges,
law professors, and politicians, and between the two hemispheres of the
private bar—also threaten the unity of the profession. Judges and professors have their own organizations, the former divided into state and
federal and the latter along ideological lines. Differences within the other
categories sometimes appear in struggles over the governance of state and
local bar associations between younger and older lawyers, solo practitioners and large firm attorneys, private practitioners and employed
lawyers, and lawyers whose backgrounds differ in terms of law school
attended, ethnicity, parental occupation, and social status. Some lawyers
express their alienation from the organized bar by apathy: both membership and activity in bar associations vary directly with income and firm
size (which also provide the material conditions for participation). A third
alternative for dissidents is to form rival associations, either dividing all the
lawyers within a city between two opposed groups (as has occurred in
New York, Chicago, and St. Louis) or creating a national organization for
lawyers defined along functional lines, such as the Association of Trial
Lawyers of America (for plaintiffs' personal injury specialists), the Defense
Research Institute (for defendants' personal injury specialists), or the Amer-

ican Corporate Counsel Association. Finally, bar associations may retreat from controversial activities and positions, such as judicial selection, and adopt the economism of American trade unions, although at the risk of compromising their professional standing. To the extent that lawyers opt for the last three alternatives—apathy, fission, or depoliticization—rather than the first—democratization—professional associations will amplify rather than ameliorate internal divisions.

CONCLUSION

American lawyers have pursued the goal of professionalization with considerable success during the last hundred years. But the very structure of professionalism contains the seeds of its own demise. To begin with, the foundation of the professional project—supply control—inevitably is ephemeral. American lawyers were unique in seeking to gain such control by limiting entry to university law faculties. Although this had the advantage of simultaneously enhancing their status, it necessarily surrendered control to universities, both public and private, which followed their own, often divergent, agendas. In any case, supply control confronts two insoluble problems: one economic, the other political. In a market economy, limitations on supply inexorably amplify the efforts of other producers to enter the market, either legally or illegally. In a liberal polity, such pressures are particularly difficult to resist when those seeking to become professionals also bear ascribed disabilities, such as race and gender.

The response of professions typically is to translate the entry barriers into meritocratic criteria, which purport to reward achievement among producers while simultaneously ensuring quality for consumers. Historically, this has meant a gradual transition: from a relatively free market, which eliminated those qualified producers who could not attract customers, to a bar examination, to attrition through law school examinations, to the present situation of intense competition to enter law school on the basis of earlier academic performance. The irony of this evolution, an irony inherent in liberalism, is that it reduces some ascriptive barriers only by amplifying the advantages of class. It also sorts those who do manage to enter the profession in order to allocate them to strata within the hierarchy—a process that also tends to reproduce class origins. This explains, in part, why ethnoreligious background correlated with professional status in the past and why race still does so today, whereas gender does not determine entry-level positions, although women certainly encounter structural obstacles later in their legal careers. Just as control over the production *of* producers was the necessary antecedent of control over production *by* producers, so erosion of the former appears to have undermined the latter—assisted by the rise of consumer movements, intense competition from other occupations, and the growing dominance of market ideologies. The attempt to control supply and to justify such control thus seems doomed to failure.

In the last two decades, American lawyers have looked to demand creation as an alternative mechanism of market control. This strategy also contains unresolvable contradictions. From an economic perspective, efforts to stimulate demand pit one professional against another, redistributing business among lawyers but not necessarily expanding the pie. To the extent that the profession presents a convincing case for unsatisfied demand, the public may turn against lawyers and insist that they satisfy such demand at little or no cost. From a political perspective, the profession may solidify its reputation for greed at the expense of any residual claim to altruism and suffer further reductions in its autonomy through increased dependence on the state and on private third-party payers. From a political perspective, liberalism cannot offer a coherent justification for redistributing legal services. If the inspiration is formal equality, capital can take greater advantage of the new institutions, as it has by establishing conservative "public interest" law firms. To the extent that the goal is substantive equality, legal aid programs must become openly partisan, rendering them vulnerable to attack by political opponents. Therefore, demand creation cannot remedy the failures of supply control.

The project of supply control has so dominated the history of American lawyers partly because, in sharp contrast to civil law professions, the private practitioner long was the principal character in the American drama; and within that category the sole practitioner, who is particularly exposed to market forces, was even more prominent than in other common law professions. Yet, many of the same forces that have transformed the professional project also fundamentally have altered the social organization of the profession. Nearly half of all American lawyers now are employed. Virtually all law graduates begin their careers as employees. Moreover, even the minority who ultimately become partners in private firms depend increasingly on lawyer and nonlawyer employees, both to perform the work and to generate profits for partners. The erosion of supply control has made it more difficult to extract monopoly rents from clients; however, it has allowed, indeed, compelled, some lawyers to turn to a strategy of demand creation, which relies on the extraction of surplus value from subordinates and accelerates the trend toward concentration in both large firms serving business and clinics serving individuals. As productive units expand and grow more dependent on both salaried workers and specialized managers, they come to resemble capitalist enterprises far more than autonomous professionals.

The heightened competition accompanying the erosion of supply control also produces greater functional differentiation, the contemporary counterpart of that geographic dispersion earlier permitted by the American frontier. However, because the American population is so heterogeneous, and because ethnoreligious minorites gained entry to the profession in the 1920s in the absence of effective supply control and women and racial minorites gained entry in the 1970s as part of the feminist and civil rights movements, structural and functional differentiation within the profession has been imbued with ascriptive differences. Inequalities in the larger society inevitably are mirrored in professional stratification.

Although self-governance is the principal impetus behind the professional project, it is theoretically contradictory and hopelessly flawed in practice. Justified in terms of "independence," it ultimately depends on state power to enforce its rules and often to compel membership. Claiming to promote the public interest, it inevitably pursues parochial advantages. Purporting to answer the question "quis custodes custodiet," it frequently responds "nemo." The professional association occupies the unenviable role of the traditional chief or council of elders under colonial rule: simultaneously responsible to the superordinate state and to the fellow professionals whom it purports to govern. Not surprisingly, it never fully satisfies the expectations of either. In recent years, self-governance has faced increasing challenges from both within and outside the profession. Professional associations operated by and for independent private practitioners command decreasing loyalty within the growing sectors of the judiciary, the professoriat, government lawyers, house counsel, and associates. Voluntary bodies dominated by elderly white males can attract neither membership nor participation from lawyers who are young, members of racial minorities, or women—categories that soon will include a majority of the profession. External observers—consumers and the general public—are even less contented with the performance of professional associations. Expressing this dissatisfaction, courts strike down restrictive practices, legislatures create independent regulatory bodies, and clients sue for malpractice. Professional associations will survive, but with impaired legitimacy and diminished authority.

The hallmarks of professionalism are becoming vestigial. Lawyers exercise little control over their markets. The university (and the state, which often funds both it and its students) determines the number of entrants. Efforts to stimulate demand cannot compensate for this loss of supply control and carry the risk of displaying the commercialism of lawyers while simultaneously increasing their dependence on public and private third-party payers. Lawyers have little choice but to embrace bureaucratic and capitalist relations of production, both as employees and as employers. Social heterogeneity, structural and functional differentiation, and professional stratification undermine the collegiality necessary for self-governance. Furthermore, both clientele and public, long quiescent and deferential, are becoming aroused and even hostile. Despite this transformation, many American lawyers will continue to enjoy substantial incomes, if not always the status that usually accompanies wealth in American society. However, they will do so either as entrepreneurs selling the services of others or as highly educated employees selling their credentials in markets dominated by organized consumers and employers—not as professionals.

NOTE

I present and document the data on which this chapter is based in my forthcoming book on American lawyers, to be published by Oxford University Press in 1988. Consequently, I have omitted citations and references here. Philip Lewis, Murray Schwartz, and William Simon made valuable comments on an earlier draft. I am grateful for financial support from both the Academic Senate and the Law School Dean's Fund of The University of California, Los Angeles and from the National Science Foundation (Grants SES 81 10380, SES 83 10162, and SES 84 20295).

Tables

5.1. Law School Enrollment, Bar Admissions, Practitioners, and Population per Lawyer

Year	Law school enrollment Total[a]	ABA approved	Unapproved[a]	Bar admissions[b]	Number of lawyers	Population per lawyer
1840	345					
1850	400				23,939[c]	969
1860	1,200				34,839[c]	903
1870	1,653				40,736[c]	947
1878	3,012					
1879	3,019					
1880	3,134				60,626	827
1881	3,227					
1882/83	3,079					
1883/84	2,686					
1884/85	2,744					
1885/86	3,054					
1886/87	3,185					
1887/88	3,667					
1888/89	3,906					
1889/90	3,517					
1889	4,486					
1890	4,518				85,224	739
1899	12,408					
	12,384					
1900	12,516			2,750	109,140	696
1904	15,000					
1909	19,498					
1910	19,567			4,125	114,704	802

239

5.1. *Continued*

Year	Law school enrollment Total[a]	ABA approved	Unapproved[a]	Bar admissions[b]	Number of lawyers	Population per lawyer
1915/16	22,993					
1919	24,503					
1920	20,992			6,004	122,519	863
1920/21	27,313					
1921	27,100			5,777		
1922	32,111			7,068		
1923	36,211			7,106		
1924	39,782 / 36,639			7,846		
1925	42,743 / 38,412			8,211		
1926	44,273 / 42,042			9,576		
1927	44,341			10,026		
1928	42,323	15,384	31,103	10,685		
1929	43,876			10,397		
1930	41,426 / 39,013			10,012	160,605	764
1931	39,868	17,483	21,934	9,676		
1932	37,259			9,340		
1933	37,057			9,258		
1934	37,872			9,099		
1935	41,418	20,430	21,490	8,971		
1936	40,529	22,094	18,124	8,591		
1937	38,056	24,029	15,226	8,934		
1938	37,406[d] / 35,755	23,827	13,579	8,797		
1939	34,539[d] / 33,508	22,661[d] / 25,578	11,878[d] / 8,961	8,531		
1940	30,830	24,047	5,989	7,942	179,567	733
1941	21,943[e] / 22,033	17,274[e] / 18,394	4,669	7,706		
1942	17,671[f] / 9,839	13,768[f] / 7,871	3,903[f] / 2,148	6,591		
1943	6,332[d] / 6,428	4,797[d] / 4,803	1,535[d] / 1,625	2,973		
1944	7,465	5,619	1,874	1,853		
1945	10,752	9,466	2,134	2,142		

5.1. *Continued*

Year	Law school enrollment Total[a]	ABA approved	Unapproved[a]	Bar admissions[b]	Number of lawyers	Population per lawyer
1946	38,331	33,904	5,871	4,815		
1947			8,674	6,782		
	51,015	43,719	7,296			
1948	56,914	46,647	10,267	11,299	169,489	
1949	57,759	46,645	11,114	13,344		
1950	53,025	43,685	9,340	13,641	212,605	709
1951	47,610	39,626	7,984	13,141	221,605	696
1952	41,276	35,634	5,642	11,900		
1953	39,339	34,423	4,916	10,976		
1954	39,565	35,015	4,550	9,928	241,514	672
1955	40,347	35,792	4,555	9,587		
1956	41,888	37,949	3,939	9,450		
1957	42,271	38,883	3,438	9,592	262,320	653
1958	42,645	39,144	3,502	10,465		
1959	43,507	39,631	3,876	10,744		
1960	43,695	40,381	3,314	10,505	285,933	632
1961	45,012	41,499	3,513	10,729		
1962	48,663	44,805	3,858	10,784		
1963	54,433	49,552	4,881	10,788	296,069	637
1964	59,813	54,625	5,548	12,023		
1965	65,057	59,744	5,313	13,109		
1966	68,121	62,556	5,565	14,637		
1967	70,332	64,406	5,926	16,007	316,856	621
1968	68,562	62,779	5,783	17,764		
1969	72,032	68,386	3,646	19,123		
1970	86,028	82,041	3,987	17,922	355,242	572
1971	95,943	93,118	2,825	20,510		
1972	105,245	101,664	3,581	25,086	358,920	
1973	114,800	106,102	8,698	30,707		
1974	116,517	110,713	5,804	33,358		
1975	122,542	116,991	5,551	34,930		
1976	125,010	117,451	7,559	35,741		
1977	126,085	118,557	7,528	37,302	462,000	
1978	126,937	121,606	5,331	39,086		
1979	126,915	122,860	4,055	42,756		
1980	128,983	125,397	3,586	41,997	542,205	418
1981	129,739	127,312	2,427	42,382	569,000[g]	403[g]
1982	129,124	127,828	1,296	42,905	595,107[g]	390[g]

5.1. *Continued*

| | Law school enrollment | | | | | |
Year	Total[a]	ABA approved	Unapproved[a]	Bar admissions[b]	Number of lawyers	Population per lawyer
1983	128,742	127,195	1,547	41,684	622,000[g]	377[g]
1984	NA	125,698	NA	42,630	649,000[g]	364[g]

[a] Enrollment figures for unaccredited law schools incomplete.

[b] Excludes admission of out-of-state attorneys on motion.

[c] Includes abstractors, notaries, and justices of the peace.

[d] May be inflated because it includes graduate and other studies.

[e] Second figure from Committee on Trend of Bar Admissions, 1942.

[f] Spring 1942.

[g] Estimates.

5.2. Distribution (in Percent) of Lawyers Among Practice Settings

	1948	1951	1954	1957	1960	1963	1966	1970	1980	Percent change of absolute numbers within category 1951–1980
Private practice										
Total	89.2	86.8	85.5	80.1	76.2	74.7	73.5	72.7	68.3	109
Solo practitioners	61.2	59.0	57.5	51.9	46.3	42.1	39.1	36.6	33.2	50
Partners	23.6	23.2	23.3	23.3	24.1	26.1	27.1	28.5	26.3	205
Associates	4.4	4.6	4.7	4.9	5.8	6.5	7.2	7.6	8.8	391
Private employ (excluding education)	3.2[a]	5.7	6.9	8.3	9.2	10.2	10.6	11.3	10.9	401
Education	—	0.6	0.6	0.6	0.7	0.8	0.9	1.1	1.2	445
Government (excluding judicial)										
Total	8.3	9.8	9.6	10.3	10.2	10.9	10.8	11.1	10.8	195
Local	4.7	3.9	3.9	3.3	3.3	2.9	2.6	2.4	5.6	78[b]
State	3.6	1.8	1.6	1.7	1.7	2.4	2.6	2.9	3.7	
Federal	3.6	4.1	4.1	5.3	5.2	5.6	5.6	5.8	1.5	192[b]
Judicial	4.2	3.6	3.6	3.3	3.2	3.3	3.4	3.2	3.6	156
Retired or inactive	3.5	3.4	3.0	3.2	4.3	4.5	5.1	5.2	5.3	310
Total										166

[a] Includes education.

[b] Legal aid–public defender treated as half state-local and half federal.

6

The Australian Legal Profession

From Provincial Family Firms to Multinationals

DAVID WEISBROT

The Australian legal profession is structurally diverse, geographically dispersed, and unintegrated. Regulation is localized in each state and territory. Lawyers are concentrated in capital cities separated by hundreds or thousands of miles and dependent on relatively poor and expensive transportation and communications. Local professions traditionally saw themselves as self-contained: most matters involved state rather than federal laws, procedures, and officials; the mass media tended to be local; rivalries developed between the states; there were impediments to interstate law practice, and there were no significant national professional associations.

The legal profession has experienced substantial change since the early 1970s. The number of lawyers greatly increased following the establishment of more degree-granting institutions. The number of women law students and lawyers grew dramatically. The "minerals boom," the massive inflow of capital from transnational corporations, and a general upsurge in Australian business activity led to the emergence of large American-style corporate law firms (Mendelsohn & Lippman, 1979: 78–83), which have continued to expand through mergers and the establishment of branch offices in other capital cities. Residential conveyancing, once the bread and butter of solicitor incomes, declined substantially, and the profession has had to look for new sources of work. Most of these changes were occasioned by external circumstance. Although the New South Wales Law Reform Commission has had a reference on the legal profession since 1976 and produced a great deal of interesting literature, its basic recommendations still have not been considered by the New South Wales Parliament.

In New South Wales and Queensland, lawyers are admitted as either barristers or solicitors. The Victorian profession is fused de jure but divided de facto by function and professional association. Practitioners who act in both capacities sometimes are called "amalgams." They are relatively rare in Melbourne, where they practice mainly criminal and family law, but are more common in the countryside (Disney et al., 1977: 24). In the other states and territories, the composite "barrister and solicitor" is used in legislation, admission formalities, and practice, although some practitioners voluntarily act as barristers would in a divided profession. Others simply call themselves "solicitors" to indicate that they generally do not act as advocates in litigation (New South Wales Law Reform Commission [NSWLRC], 1981a: 173). Solicitors now have rights of audience in virtually all Australian courts that permit lawyers to appear.

If we aggregate the figures supplied by all the professional associations, there were about 22,000 practicing lawyers in Australia in 1985, about 10 percent of whom practiced exclusively as barristers. About 72 percent of these lawyers were located in the two most populous states, New South Wales and Victoria (see table 1).

Whereas the legal profession did not grow as fast as the general population for several decades after the Great Depression, the ratio of population to lawyers has fallen significantly in all states and territories in the past 15 years (see table 1). In 1985 the population per lawyer was about 700—higher than in the United States (400) and Canada (580) but far lower than in England and Wales (1,165) (Disney et al., 1986: 50) and Japan (11,000).

The number of law schools has increased significantly in the past twenty years, especially in the larger states. Before 1960, New South Wales contained only the University of Sydney Law Faculty. Since then faculties granting LL.B. degrees have been established at the Australian National University (in the enclave of Canberra), the University of New South Wales, Macquarie University, and the New South Wales Institute of Technology (Bowen Report, 1979: 47–50, 101–103). New South Wales admitted 167 lawyers in 1960, 443 in 1970, 789 in 1980, and 1,229 in 1984—more than a sevenfold increase (Disney et al., 1986: 49). Admissions of Queensland solicitors jumped from 19 in 1960 to 252 in 1984 (ibid.).

In 1984, there were 8,762 students studying for LL.B. degrees at an Australian university, 6.5 percent of all university undergraduates (Commonwealth Tertiary Education Commission [CTEC], 1984: 12). Nearly three-fourths were enrolled in New South Wales, Victoria, and the Australian Capital Territory (see table 2). A further 550 students were enrolled in nondegree university law courses leading to diplomas or certificates (CTEC, 1984: 13). Undergraduate law enrollments in 1984 were similar to those in medicine (8,907) and education (7,282); very much greater than those in agriculture (1,829), architecture (3,157), dentistry (1,221), and veterinary science (1,187); and very much smaller than those in arts

(48,258), economics and commerce (18,980), engineering (11,493), and science (23,883) (ibid., 12).

The number of law students doubled between 1950 and 1965 and tripled between 1965 and 1980 (see table 2). The most rapid increase occurred during the brief life of the reformist Labor federal government (1972–1975), when heavy demand for tertiary places combined with a massive increase in federal funding for education contributed to the expansion of existing law schools, the launching of new ones, the abolition of tuition and the establishment of the Tertiary Education Assistance Scheme (see below, section on education for the profession). This period also saw the politicization of youth by Australia's controversial involvement in the Vietnam War, the optimism engendered by economic growth, the establishment of national legal aid and health insurance schemes, a national commission of inquiry on poverty (including law and poverty), increased public funding for social welfare programs, expansion of the public service and the regulatory commissions, and the founding of the Aboriginal Legal Service and the beginning of the community legal centers movement (Basten et al., 1985: 116–125).

Despite occasional expressions of concern about the "oversupply" of law graduates (Bowen Report, 1979: 42–44, 58–61), the legal profession has not pressed the universities to reduce student numbers, and the small decline in the past few years reflects general university funding problems. However, the New South Wales legal profession has attempted some supply control by limiting the number of places at the College of Law (the locus of mandatory postgraduate professional training for solicitors) and by making unrestricted practicing certificates more difficult to obtain (see below, section on education for the profession). Occasional publicity about the scarcity of legal jobs for new admittees (see, e.g., *Sydney Morning Herald* 11 [May 28, 1985]) certainly has not diminished the demand for places in the law faculties; and, notwithstanding the increased anxiety among law graduates, 96 percent of the Class of 1983 were employed by April 1984—only medical and health science graduates fared better (Australian Mathematical Society, 1985: 4).

The figures provided by the professional associations understate the number of people in Australia with legal training and the number who use this training in their work. For example, many law graduates employed in commerce and industry, government lawyers, and academic lawyers do not maintain current practicing certificates or join professional associations. The federal Department of Employment and Industrial Relations (DEIR, 1983: 89) estimates that 10–15 percent of lawyers are employed by state and commonwealth governments, while "surplus" law graduates "appear to be absorbed relatively easily into generalist administrative positions."

As in other common law countries, the number of judicial officers is relatively small. For example, New South Wales has seventy-two judges, evenly divided between the district and supreme courts. Victoria has twenty-two supreme court judges and thirty-seven country court judges. Queensland has fifteen supreme court judges and nineteen district court judges. South Australia has fourteen supreme court judges and ten district court judges. The total is about 1,000, including federal and specialist courts and the magistracy.

Public attitudes toward lawyers and the legal profession in Australia appear to be ambivalent. Few people reject the view that lawyers are more interested in making money than in helping their clients, and equally few believe that solicitors will work as hard for a poor client as they will for one who can pay (Tomasic, 1978: 223, 250). A strong plurality believe that consultation with a lawyer is a last resort (ibid., 226). On the other hand, many accept the need for professional expertise in dealing with "legal problems" and believe that the ethical standards of lawyers are high and that they may be trusted with clients' money and confidences (ibid., 228–229, 287–289). Few seem to know what to do in the event of a problem with their lawyers or what role a professional association plays with respect to complaints and discipline (ibid., 290–295).

The Morgan Gallup Poll (1984: 1) found that the Australian public rated lawyers exactly in the middle of seventeen occupations with respect to honesty and ethical standards, below physicians, dentists, bank managers, school teachers, engineers, police officers, university academics, and accountants but considerably above business executives, politicians, journalists, real estate agents, advertising people, union officials, and car salespeople (in order). The ratings for lawyers changed little between 1976 and 1984. Women rated lawyers more highly than men did, and young people rated lawyers more highly than older people did (ibid., 2).

Daniel's very comprehensive survey of occupational prestige in Australia (1983: 118) revealed that judges, who combine professional identity with state authority, headed the list, followed by medical specialists and barristers. Solicitors trailed church leaders, professors, general medical practitioners, generals, architects, and dentists. A rough aggregation of the various branches of the professions would seem to place law and medicine together at the top (ibid., 140). Daniel found considerable consensus among various demographic groups.

This chapter will examine the factors that have contributed to the unique character of the Australian legal profession: its geographic fragmentation, the long and unresolved debate about division and fusion, the significant splits between different branches of the profession, the elite social backgrounds of Australian lawyers, the shift from apprenticeship to university training, the changing nature of lawyers' work, the rise of the corporate law firm, the maintenance of self-regulation, and the relationship between lawyers and the state.

THE DEVELOPMENT OF A FRAGMENTED PROFESSION

HISTORY

Colonial Australia received its beliefs about the legal profession, as well as its personnel, from Britain. The earliest legal history was shaped by two key issues: the admission to practice of emancipated convict lawyers and the question of division or fusion. In early nineteenth century New South Wales (which included what is now Victoria, Tasmania, and Queensland) there were several former solicitors from England or Ireland who had been convicted of offenses (such as fraud or forgery), transported to the then penal colony, and subsequently pardoned or granted a "ticket of leave" from further penal servitude. Some were acting as "agents," handling commercial matters and engaging in advocacy before (lay) magistrates. There also were a number of "bush lawyers" in the colony. For example, Samuel Terry, an emancipated convict turned merchant, possessed the only up-to-date copy of Blackstone's Commentaries and was a major source of legal advice. Because neither the governor, the military judge-advocates, nor the lay magistrates were lawyers, these exconvicts had considerable influence.

In 1814 the Home Office sent Letters Patent, or the "Second Charter of Justice," which reconstituted the colonial court system and established a supreme court, empowered to make rules of practice, appoint court officials, and promulgate fee schedules subject to approval by the governor (Bennett, 1969: 17).

One of the earliest issues facing Jeffrey Bent, an English barrister appointed the first judge of the Supreme Court, was whether to allow the former convicts to practice. Bent was strongly opposed to admission, which brought him into conflict with Governor Macquarie, who believed that emancipated convicts should, as far as possible, return to society without continuing disabilities (ibid., 18). This dispute mirrored a more general struggle by emancipists for full civil rights, which was opposed by the "exclusives," who had no convict taint and sought commercial and other advantages at the expense of the emancipists, many of whom had become influential and prosperous. The exclusives went so far as to seek to bar the emancipists from entering contracts or holding property, which would have thrown the colonial economy into chaos.

When Bent first opened the Supreme Court, he found that the two magistrates who would be sitting with him favored admitting the emancipist lawyers. Bent adjourned the Court after several sittings and refused to reconvene it for two years, rather than admit the emancipists. He finally was recalled and replaced in 1817 (Castles, 1971: 106—108). The home authorities notified Macquarie in 1816 that former convicts would be permitted to practice law only if there were less than two "free" lawyers in the colony, and the British Government soon sent two salaried solicitors from England (ibid., 110).

In 1823 England promulgated the Third Charter of Justice, still in force, which moved the colony toward civil administration, separated Tasmania from New South Wales, and provided for the establishment of supreme courts in each colony, with the power to admit lawyers to practice unless they had been convicted of any crime that would have disqualified them from practicing in England (Bennett, 1969: 33). This sealed the fate of the convict lawyers but generated another controversy by referring to the admission of people "in the character of Barristers and Advocates, as of Proctors, Attorneys and Solicitors," thereby suggesting that the profession might be divided. At the same time, English barristers were appointed as attorneys-general of the two colonies and allowed to practice privately only as barristers, observing the restrictions that obtained at home (ibid., 33—34). The court proceeded to grant equal rights of audience to all practitioners but maintained separate rolls for the two branches of the profession. Some newly admitted barristers petitioned the Court to order all solicitors "to retire from the Bar—confining themselves to their own province in the profession"; the court refused but expressed the hope that, in time, the profession would be divided (ibid., 34—36).

In 1828 new legislation conferred on the Supreme Court the power to regulate the admission of legal practitioners. After spirited debate, the Court promulgated rules that divided the legal profession "in like manner as the same is divided in England" if the Crown so approved, which it did six years later. Notwithstanding the small population of the colony, the scarcity of qualified lawyers, and the legal and economic disabilities of many residents, the Supreme Court thus chose to fragment existing legal resources. This decision doubtless was influenced by the judges' adherence to tradition and their own background as barristers, their belief that the colonial administration should be modeled on British customs and institutions, and their hope that a separate bar might reduce litigiousness by limiting speculative actions and promoting "restraint and decorum in advocacy" (ibid., 45). Numerous efforts were made to end the division of the profession in the nineteenth century and again in 1931, but all failed in the face of strong, organized opposition from the legal profession, which complained of governmental "interference" with the "independence" of the profession (ibid., 50—66, 132). In 1892, however, solicitors obtained rights of audience in the Supreme Court in cases originating in their own firms (ibid., 61).

The separate colony of Victoria was created in 1851, inheriting New South Wales law and practice, including the divided legal profession. In 1860 a cross-practice bill narrowly was defeated. Over the next thirty years seven fusion bills were introduced in Parliament, and *all* were passed by the lower house, some with very large majorities, owing to several factors: the strong support of businesspeople, who sought a less complicated and expensive system, the larger number of Irish and North American lawyers less wedded to English traditions, and the free-wheeling nature of the Gold Rush period. After each of these was defeated in the upper house (where lawyers and conservative interests were more strongly represented)—the last by a single vote in 1884—fusion finally was approved in 1891 (Disney et al., 1977: 21; Forbes, 1979: part IV and 93–112).

The Victorian Bar Association, formed largely to combat the 1884 bill, moved to undercut this legislation, with great success. Before it could be tested, the barristers engaged in a boycott of all amalgams and amalgam firms and nonmembers of the association. As a result, "division was regaining its normal primacy" within a year after the fusion legislation was enacted, and division was even more strictly enforced in the provincial towns where the position had been more flexible. The boycott had the active support of most prominent barristers, and its leader later became Chief Justice. The judiciary encouraged division by insisting on special court dress, awarding higher costs to "pure" barristers, and otherwise discriminating against amalgam advocates. De facto division received de jure recognition in 1936, when amendments to the Legal Profession Practice Act, requiring practitioners to keep trust accounts, contribute to a fidelity fund, and possess annual practicing certificates, expressly exempted "pure" barristers (ibid., 121–130). Victorian lawyers who choose to practice as barristers sign a formal undertaking to that effect and are placed on the unofficial Roll of Barristers kept by the Victorian Bar.

The separate colony of Queensland, created in 1859, also inherited the divided profession from New South Wales. Cross-practice bills in the 1870s eventually led to the Legal Practitioner's Act of 1881, with unrestricted rights of cross-practice. Queensland barristers immediately met and instructed those who planned to work as amalgam "legal practitioners" to notify the Bar, which would deny the barrister briefs from solicitors, ensure ostracism by fellow barristers, and jeopardize future judicial appointment. Solicitors who sought to exercise rights of advocacy were met with judicial rules about court dress and harsh treatment from the bench. In 1938 the de facto position was codified in a new act, which formally restored division and effectively denied solicitors rights of audience in the

Supreme Court. These were restored in 1973, but their exercise is discouraged (ibid., 153—161, 172).

The Charter of Justice, which created Tasmania in 1823, provided for the admission of all lawyers without reference to division, and Tasmania was not affected by subsequent developments in New South Wales. Given the small size of the colony, the shortage of qualified lawyers, and the fact that only one of the first forty-five lawyers admitted was a "pure" barrister, there were fewer internal pressures for mitosis (Ross, 1975: 1). Admission as a "pure" barrister has been possible since 1952, mainly to accommodate visiting counsel from Melbourne, who have not faced the restrictive residence rules placed on visiting counsel in other states (Forbes, 1979: 178). In 1985, only 9 out of 310 Tasmanian lawyers held themselves out as pure barristers (Disney et al., 1986: 48).

The colony of South Australia was formed in 1837 and received its laws and practices directly from England (rather than New South Wales). From the beginning, the very small legal profession practiced in an amalgamated fashion, and its main energies were devoted to opposing (unsuccessfully) the Torrens title reforms, which allowed "land agents" to handle domestic conveyancing (ibid., 179). In the late 1920s and in 1959/60 the bench promoted division, but before exercising rule-making powers the South Australian judges (unlike their counterparts in New South Wales) sought a mandate from the profession, which was not forthcoming. In the early 1960s a small "voluntary Bar" developed in Adelaide (70 out of 1,080 lawyers in 1985), fortified by a strict residence rule protecting it from competition with the larger and more established Bars in the eastern states (Disney et al., 1986: 48). Because solicitors do not enjoy a monopoly over conveyancing, however, full division has not been viable (Forbes, 1979: 179—184). The Northern Territory was transferred from South Australia to Commonwealth administration in 1910, and the small profession developed in the fused tradition. In recent years, however, a small separate bar has emerged in Darwin and, with it, some efforts at restricting the inflow of visiting counsel (Ditton, 1980: 123).

The Swan River colony was founded in 1829 in what is now Western Australia. Because it was a small, isolated, agricultural outpost, fusion always was likely. Unlike the profession in Tasmania, however, most early lawyers in Western Australia were barristers, and, while they did not object to a fused profession, they asserted that it should be exclusively composed of barristers. Given the fact that land agents handled conveyancing matters, as they did in South Australia, it was not wholly outlandish to profess no need for solicitors. In 1861 the Chief Justice promulgated an ordinance without reference to attorneys. This was disallowed by the Legislative Council, and a fused profession subsequently developed (Forbes, 1979: 185—186). The first "voluntary Bar" was es-

tablished in 1959, encouraged by the judiciary and unopposed by the Law
Society. In 1985 it numbered 50 out of 945 (Disney et al. 1986: 48).

Given the diversity of local structures, federal practice has had to be
flexible. Rights of audience in all federal courts are guaranteed to all
admitted lawyers (Commonwealth Judiciary Act of 1903, s. 49). In the
Australian Capital Territory itself, the Legal Practitioners Ordinance 1970
provides for admission of barristers and solicitors, although a small separate "voluntary Bar" also developed contemporaneous with those in South
Australia and Western Australia.

PRESENT DIVISIONS

Even in the formally divided professions in the eastern states it no longer is
particularly accurate to characterize solicitors as office lawyers and barristers as courtroom lawyers. Solicitors handle a very large proportion of
lower court litigation, and many, particularly in the larger city firms, have
developed the sort of specialized expertise (in such areas as commercial
and company law, administrative law, and taxation) that once was thought
to be the preserve of the Bar. For their part, barristers do an increasing
amount of noncontentious counseling ("chamber work"). Further, in the
divided professions it is common for a lawyer to work for a number of
years as a solicitor in a large city firm (more rarely in a suburban firm),
acquiring the necessary expertise, reputation, and contacts, before "making
the jump" to the bar. Hetherton (1981a: 77) found that as much as 96
percent of the commercial bar, 84 percent of the criminal bar, and 82
percent of the personal injury bar in Melbourne had followed this route.
While less common, some barristers—even Queen's Counsel—become
solicitors. In recent years, a number of prominent barristers specializing in
the regulatory areas have joined big city solicitors' firms, lured by better
remuneration, tax advantages that are unavailable to barristers as sole
practitioners, the greater support services, and the benefits of direct client
contact (17 *Justinian* 6 [May 1981]).

The divided profession is best understood in terms of what barristers
are restrained from doing, whether formally or voluntarily. Barristers must
be "independent" sole practitioners. They cannot enter partnerships with
solicitors or other barristers (although they may, and generally do, arrange
themselves into "floors" of chambers) or be employed (rather than merely
"retained") by a company (New South Wales Bar Association rule 16).
With a few limited exceptions (patent matters, courts-martial, voluntary
assistance to community legal aid centers, and "dock defences") criminal
matters are handled on short notice at the request of the court). Barristers
cannot provide their services without the intervention of an instructing

solicitor (idem., rule 26). Barristers may not sue for fees or handle a client's money or property. While not expressly prohibited from doing so, barristers refrain from conveying property and probating wills, which are the staple diet of solicitors. As a consequence of these restraints, barristers generally are freed from the obligations imposed on solicitors to keep audited trust accounts, contribute to a fidelity fund, maintain liability insurance, and hold a practicing certificate.

By way of compensation for the trade restraints, a number of very important advantages attach to practice as a barrister. While solicitors constitute up to 90 percent of the large, divided professions in the eastern states, it is a common view, inside and out (Daniel, 1983: 118), that barristers form the "top ten percent," with Queen's Counsel at the apex. Partners in the major city firms sometimes are included in this elite (Meagher, 1983: 173). Solicitors generally must travel to barristers' chambers for conferences (New South Wales Bar Association rules 34−35). Queen's Counsel and judges are chosen almost exclusively from the ranks of practicing barristers. Indeed, when two solicitors unexpectedly were appointed to the Queensland Supreme Court in the late nineteenth century, barristers boycotted the swearing-in ceremony and attacked the appointments in the local legal journal (Forbes, 1979: 163−165). Few such appointments have been made to the superior courts of general jurisdiction in this century (although solicitors have been appointed to the federal Family Court and industrial courts). Further, the two-tiered scales of costs maintained in most jurisdictions markedly favor barristers. Barristers' bills of cost are not subject to review by court officers. Barristers are immune from liability for negligence as advocates. Barristers enjoy rights of preaudience (their matters are heard by the court before those in which clients are represented by solicitors) and rights of precedence on ceremonial occasions (NSWLRC, 1981a: 74). Most solicitors believe that judges (as former barristers) favor barristers over solicitor-advocates (ibid.). In most superior courts barristers must wear special court dress, including wigs and gowns (NSWLRC, 1981a: 279−289; 1981b: 448−449). Solicitors may not wear special court dress even when appearing as advocates.

While a small number of lawyers in the nominally fused professions voluntarily have differentiated themselves into a separate bar, the much larger number of solicitors have moved the "lower branch" of the profession into new specializations (tax, trade practices and other business regulation, administrative law, resources exploitation, company takeovers, securities and financial regulation, etc.) with higher status and income. The history of the Australian legal professions suggests that division will not flourish in the absence of routinized but lucrative office work to sustain a lower branch. Since this sort of work is certain to diminish in the next decade or two, the lower branch will have to find new areas and forms of practice, producing divisions based on subject-matter specialization (see below, section on lawyers and the state). There also appears to be greater acceptance of the idea of appointing judges from outside the practicing bar, although this remains rare.

The Australian legal profession is further fragmented by the division of the bar into Queen's Counsel and "junior counsel." Queen's Counsel, who make up about 8 percent to 10 percent of the bar, wear distinctive silk gowns, are expected to (and do) charge considerably higher fees, almost always must appear with a junior counsel (the latter traditionally charging two-thirds of the Queen's Counsel's fee), and may not undertake certain types of work (such as drafting or settling pleadings or affidavits). In the fused professions, appointments as Queen's Counsel are also made but generally are restricted to those lawyers who have been practicing solely as barristers or undertake to do so after the appointment (NSWLRC, 1981a: 69, 249–256, 259–260). It is not uncommon for barristers to be appointed Queen's Counsel in their late thirties, somewhat younger than in England, because the greater number of judges in Australia's federal system results in senior counsel being selected for the Bench at a greater rate (*Australian Financial Review* 2 [June 13, 1975]). The state government generally appoints on the recommendation of the attorney-general or the Chief Justice, who seek advice from the local bar association. Most appointments are relatively uncontroversial, but in 1969 a South Australian barrister who was an active Communist party member had his nomination rejected by the conservative state government. Six months later the government changed, and the new Labor government approved the appointment (Fisse & Kelly, 1970). (This Queen's Counsel was appointed to the South Australia Supreme Court in 1986.) In 1981 the New South Wales attorney-general broke with tradition and appointed two public lawyers—the head of the Anti-Discrimination Board and a senior lawyer in the state attorney-general's department—in order to broaden the base of appointments (*Sydney Morning Herald* 2 [September 19, 1981]). The following year he appointed the distinguished law professor Julius Stone as the first and only legal academic Queen's Counsel (*Sydney Morning Herald* 2 [March 6, 1982]).

Although some legal academics engage in practice, and some practitioners teach, the noticeable antipathy and mutual lack of respect between academic lawyers and practitioners is "the most significant division within the profession" (Halliday, 1981: 26). A large percentage of legal academics have only limited practice experience, although most are admitted to practice (ibid., 31). Because practitioners do not regard academic skills and expertise as transferable to practice they rarely consult academics (ibid., 27). Perhaps the most extreme view was expressed by a former president of the New South Wales Bar Association (Meagher, 1983: 175):

In the whole of Australia ... there are only one or two academic teachers of any real value in real property, in contracts or in torts, yet there are about seventeen law schools [sic]. There are, to be sure, multitudes of academic homunculi who scribble and prattle relentlessly about such non-subjects as criminology, bail, poverty, consumerism, computers and racism. These may be dismissed from calculation: they possess neither practical skills nor legal learning. They are failed sociologists.

Legal academics have been equally outspoken in their criticism of practitioners and professional associations, particularly with respect to self-regulation and the delivery of legal services (Halliday, 1981: 27–28, 30; Basten et al., 1985: 113). As a consequence, Australian academic lawyers find it difficult to move back and forth between the different segments of the profession (Halliday, 1981: 31) and are effectively excluded from appointment as judges.

The dominance of the private profession in Australia also has left the large number of public lawyers isolated. The federal and state attorney-general and justice departments contain the main concentration of lawyers, but others are found in departments or commissions dealing with foreign affairs and trade, finance and taxation, consumer affairs, corporate affairs, commerce, land and environment, law reform, human rights, and oversight (ombudsman's offices). Many private practitioners and judges view government lawyers as "an inferior caste" because they have "but one master and [are] subject to public service discipline, [which] is inimical to professional independence" (Sexton & Maher, 1982: 99–101).

GEOGRAPHIC FRAGMENTATION

Of all the political and social institutions in Australian society, the legal profession may be the most decentralized, with each state and territory having its own, powerful professional associations. This reflects the fragmentation throughout Australian society, in which history, problems of travel and communications, interstate rivalries, and resource imbalances (both human and physical) have contributed to a strong emphasis on states' rights. Differentiation within the legal profession, the exclusionary membership policies of some professional associations, and the disparities in the sizes of state and territory professions (which engender controversies over supply control and reciprocity) accentuate localism.

These factors combine to severely inhibit collective action and influence, especially on a national level (Halliday, 1981: 13; Basten, 1982: 260–261). Australian professional associations have operated under an "antivoluntaristic assumption," reacting to initiatives proposed by gov-

256 David Weisbrot

ernmental or publicly appointed agencies, such as law reform commissions (Halliday, 1982b: 229–234; Ross, 1982: 58–59). In the past decade, however, the resurgence of the Australian Labor party at the federal and state levels and its promotion of legal and social change have stirred the profession to greater political mobilization (Halliday, 1982b: 246).

The Law Council of Australia was founded in 1933, but it was not until 1974 that it established a permanent secretariat in response to the federal Labor government's law reform agenda, which included ominous proposals to enact a national no-fault accident compensation scheme and to establish a large, salaried legal aid service (Sexton & Maher, 1982: 36, 163–165; Higley et al., 1979: 56). Although the council admitted individuals as members in 1985, it is essentially a loose confederation of eleven constituent state and territory associations. The member associations are the Law Societies of all eight jurisdictions (in Victoria it is called the Law Institute) and the Bar Associations of the three states with divided professions. The secretary-general has attempted to coax reformist splinter groups back into the fold (4 *Legal Service Bulletin* 213 [1979]), but the Law Council still is seen as the corporate voice of the state legal establishments.

The Law Council of Australia sponsors the annual Australian Legal Convention, organizes occasional conferences, and sometimes coordinates submissions to governmental bodies. Its numerous committees do not meet frequently and have not produced any significant or influential research or publications (Ross, 1982: 58) or had much impact on debates over legal issues. For example, the Law Council's delegate to a national workshop on legal aid research in 1981 felt unable to "represent" the Law Council since its nature made it "impossible to outline a consensus of views of the private profession in Australia on the subject" (Boer, 1981: 20). However, the council actively campaigned against the elimination of automatic rights of appeal to the High Court in certain cases in 1984 and against the institution of a national identity card in 1986. The council has allowed constituent associations to veto discussion of the division-fusion issue and reciprocity of admissions (Queensland lawyers fear being swamped by lawyers from New South Wales and Victoria). In 1981 the Victoria Law Institute threatened to withdraw if the veto power were not removed, at least with respect to "vital interests" (*Sydney Morning Herald* 3 [July 10, 1981]). A compromise was engineered to allow discussions without a decision that would bind the minority states.

The Australian Bar Association was founded in 1962, largely through the efforts of the New South Wales Bar Association, which was frustrated by the numerical superiority of the Law Societies in the Law Council. The Bar Association was influential in fostering the development of the separate Bars in South Australia and Western Australia, which are fused de jure (Disney et al., 1977: 36; Clarkson Report, 1983: 13). Although it claims to represent 2,600 barristers, it has not been particularly active in recent years (*Sydney Morning Herald* 15 [October 6, 1983]).

Both national associations tend to restrict their activities to matters involving federal or uniform law or interstate interests (Ross, 1982: 58), but state associations generally make their own submissions even on such issues (Halliday, 1981: 22). National associations of lawyers play a more limited role in national affairs than the Australian Medical Association (Higley et al., 1979: 57) or national lawyers, groups in England, Canada, or the United States.

There also are a number of other professional groups that operate across state and territory boundaries, such as the Australian Legal Workers Group (Ross, 1982: 43–53), the Society of Labor Lawyers, the Women Lawyers Association, the Environmental Law Association, the Commerical Law Association, and the Communications Law Association. Hetherton (1978: 174–175) found that only "a tiny minority" of Victorian lawyers were active in such organizations, and fewer than a fourth of the "active" lawyers were under thirty-five years of age (Tomasic & Bullard, 1978: 190; Tomasic, 1983b: 59).

Another factor severely inhibiting national professional identity is the relative lack of interstate mobility. Whereas it is common for American students to grow up in one state, study law in a second, and practice in a third, this is fairly unusual in Australia. Anderson and Western (1967: 68) found that 71 percent of Australian law students come from the city in which they attend university. This figure would be even higher but for the presence of overseas students and the fact that the Australian National University in Canberra (an enclave in New South Wales) draws students from the neighboring states. Of the 4,460 undergraduate law students in New South Wales in 1985, only 134 (3 percent) were from out of state and 91 (2 percent) from overseas (mainly Asia).

There is equally little mobility in professional practice. In 1975, 93.5 percent of solicitors and 94.7 percent of barristers practicing in New South Wales received their legal education in that state, and another 3 percent in each category were educated in Canberra (Beed & Campbell, 1977: 55). Lawyers not in private practice were only marginally more likely to have received their legal education outside the state (ibid.). Law firms, even the leading firms, traditionally have restricted their operations to one capital city, although this has begun to change (see below, section on the changing face of legal practice).

Barriers to reciprocal admission reinforce geographic fragmentation. Most jurisdictions automatically admit practitioners from the United Kingdom and New Zealand (New South Wales Supreme Court, *Solicitors Admission Rules*, rule 4). Virtually all states and territories admit a practitioner from another jurisdiction that grants reciprocity. While New South Wales,

Victoria, and the Australian Capital Territory long have received out-of-state lawyers as a matter of course, some of the smaller professions have sought to limit external competition by means of a residence requirement or similar device. Queensland requires solicitors to have an intention to practice in that state for at least nine months after admission; South Australia requires "adequate knowledge of South Australian law and practice," which ordinarily requires a residence of at least three months (Disney et al., 1977: 170). The courts also have been reluctant to allow out-of-state lawyers to appear in individual matters, particularly on a regular basis (ibid., 166).

New South Wales and Victorian lawyers correctly perceive these measures as restrictive trade practices rather than controls on competence or honesty, and the issue has threatened the Law Council of Australia. The Northern Territory traditionally received barristers from Victoria (and to a lesser extent New South Wales and South Australia), many of whom have provided their services to the Aboriginal Legal Service at reduced costs. In 1980, however, after the Darwin Bar rapidly expanded from three barristers to nine, the Northern Territory Law Society (with statutory power over the de jure fused profession) began to take a tougher stand and considered a number of devices, such as reducing the number of admission ceremonies from twelve to four per year (Ditton, 1980: 123).

The Australian Constitution (s. 117) prohibits any state from discriminating against the citizens of another state. Nevertheless, the High Court has upheld the validity of South Australia's residency rule (*Henry* v. *Boehm* [1973] 128 C.L.R. 482; cf. Re Sweeney [1976] Qd.R. 296; see also Forbes, 1979: 168–171). At the federal level, reciprocity operates simply and inclusively. A lawyer admitted in any state or territory may, by registration with the High Court, practice in every federal court. However, federal courts only recently began to supplant state courts exercising delegated federal powers.

Australia is a highly urbanized country in which the capital cities are not only major population centers but also centers of government, commerce, industry, and higher education. Most superior courts are located in the metropolitan areas. Consequently, virtually all barristers, academic lawyers and government lawyers, and most solicitors work in the major metropolitan centers.

Vinson and his colleagues (1974: 6) found that solicitors were highly concentrated in the metropolitan areas of the capital cities in ways similar to the distribution of physicians and dentists. In all states except Queensland and Tasmania between 78 percent and 86 percent of solicitors were located in the capital. Those two states, which have the most even distribution of population between capital city and elsewhere, show a slightly lower concentration (56 percent to 58 percent) but still a substantial imbalance. Throughout Australia, 56 percent of solicitors practiced in the central business districts of the state capitals, 22 percent in the suburbs of the capital cities, 8 percent in other cities, and 14 percent in the country (ibid., 7–8).

The major change in the distribution of the legal profession since World War II has been the growth of suburban solicitors, following a general demographic trend. Between 1954 and 1973, the population per solicitor in the Sydney suburbs fell from 9,700 to 3,200, although this ratio still was much higher than in the city (see table 3). Given the centrality of conveyancing to solicitors, it is not surprising that legal services followed population and homebuilding into the suburbs. Both the Gaskin Report (1974: 8) and Beed and Campbell (1977: 117) found that the number of solicitors increased more rapidly along the coast than in inland areas, suggesting that solicitors are affected by quality of life considerations. The distribution of solicitors was correlated with the volume of retail sales and other commercial indicators, but there was a slight negative association with a general index of status and income (the proportion of the population in upper-status occupations and tertiary industry, per capita income, and private rent levels), which is associated with the distribution of doctors and dentists (Vinson et al., 1974: 10, 12–14). Centralization of the superior courts and the chambers system have resulted in the concentration of almost all barristers in the capital city centers (NSWLRC, 1981c: 86; Disney et al., 1977: 175; Sexton & Maher, 1982: 16). Barristers do travel on circuit to the country towns, and barristers from the larger states also appear in the smaller states and territories (Ross, 1975: 3).

New South Wales and Victoria not only contain three-fourths of all Australian lawyers but also have low ratios of population per lawyer (see table 1). This imbalance is likely to increase given that the larger states have more law students and there is very little interstate movement of lawyers (Beed & Campbell, 1977: 55). In December 1984 there were 3,804 full-time and part-time university law students in New South Wales, 2,024 in Victoria, 842 in Queensland, 740 in South Australia, 397 in Western Australia, 286 in Tasmania, and 669 in the Australian Capital Territory (CTEC, 1984: 12). In New South Wales, another 724 students were studying for an LL.B. at the New South Wales Institute of Technology, and others were qualifying through the Admission Board system (see below, next section). The production of lawyers in New South Wales is thus likely to be two to three times higher than in Western Australia over the next five years, even in proportion to population, although this may be counterbalanced somewhat by the disinclination of Western Australian law graduates to take jobs outside private practice (Yorke, 1983: 278).

The low population per lawyer ratio of the Australian Capital Territory and its rapid fall from 1,367 in 1973 (Tomasic, 1983a: 449) to 509 in 1985 owe much to the presence of the Australian National University Law Faculty and the increasing importance of Canberra and the federal government in national affairs. In the past fifteen years, the number of government lawyers has grown (Sexton & Maher, 1982: 98), the number, size, and influence of regulatory commissions have expanded, and the High Court has been based permanently in Canberra, although it still undertakes a limited number of circuits, particularly to the smaller states.

These interstate and urban-rural differences suggest that the rural regions of states with high ratios of population per lawyer (such as South Australia, Queensland, and Western Australia) are poorly served by the legal profession. Many of those regions are without a single lawyer (Vinson et al., 1974: appendix C). Even New South Wales, with the largest pool of lawyers, has few in the rural North West Statistical Division (containing a relatively high proportion of Aboriginal inhabitants) and in many of the working-class outer suburbs (ibid., 8 and appendix C).

All university law schools are situated in metropolitan areas. The older schools are found mainly in or near the central business districts. Many of the newer law schools are located in the metropolitan suburbs, but none is rural. Ziegert (1983: 12) found that 91.6 percent of Sydney University law students were born in an urban setting. Many of the most prestigious private secondary schools also are located in metropolitan areas, so that affluent students from rural backgrounds are accustomed to boarding at city schools.

The law schools at Queensland and Macquarie Universities offer external or correspondence courses aimed at country students (Bowen Report, 1979: 33, 107–108). The Admission Boards, particularly in New South Wales and Queensland, also have offered correspondence courses for country students (ibid., 175–176). The external degree program at Macquarie University gives a preference to country applicants, but they represented only about 1 out of every 6.5 applicants in 1976. Similarly, the New South Wales Admission Board correspondence course is reserved mainly for country students but does not fill its annual quota (ibid., 51–52, 160).

EDUCATION FOR THE PROFESSION

The legal profession in colonial Australia initially was composed of people who had been admitted in Great Britain or Ireland or had taken their articles in Australia and passed a professional examination (Bowen Report, 1979: 6–9; Martin, 1983: 35–39). Law faculties emerged in the second half of the nineteenth century at Melbourne University in 1857 (Derham, 1962: 209–211) and Adelaide University in 1876. Apprenticeship remained a major mode of qualification well into the second half of the twentieth century, however, particularly in New South Wales and Queensland. In 1964 the Martin Committee (1964: 70) found that, although the great majority of lawyers in most jurisdictions were university graduates, only 50 percent of barristers and 59 percent of solicitors in New South Wales and 71 percent of solicitors in Queensland were graduates. It was not until 1968 that yearly admissions to practice throughout Australia tipped in favor of university graduates, and even in 1978 nearly one-third of admittees lacked university degrees (Bowen Report, 1979: 184). It probably was not until the late 1970s that the number of lawyers with degrees in New South Wales outweighed the number admitted by apprenticeship (Halliday, 1982a: 20).

Australia generally is undereducated by the standards of developed countries. Only 35 percent of Australian secondary-school graduates proceed to tertiary studies of any kind, compared to 65 percent in the United States and 68 percent in Japan. Apprenticeship thus has been the main route of entry to most occupations, but law was alone among the professions in retaining this path.

Australia's first university was established in Sydney in 1850, with chairs in classics, mathematics, chemistry, and philosophy. Even though judges and barristers were instrumental in creating and governing it, no law faculty was organized. Indeed, the first head of the university (a professor of classics) was disdainful of professional education and reaffirmed the traditions of British amateurism: "The soundest lawyers come forth from schools in which law is never taught, the most accomplished physicians are nurtured where medicine is but a name" (Martin, 1983: 56). After a number of false starts and "experimental" programs, a law faculty opened in 1890 as part of a major expansion of the university facilitated by the largest bequest to date (ibid., 59–78, 81, 95–98).

Because the profession has been less active in providing legal education in Australia than in England, the universities have had to offer both practical and theoretical instruction (McGarvie, 1978: 226). Law schools tended to have one full-time professor, but the rest of the teaching was done part time by legal practitioners. Until the 1930s, only Sydney University had more than one full-time legal academic; there were only fifteen throughout the country in 1946 (Derham, 1978: 9). In 1950 there were twenty-one full-time law teachers and ninety-three part-timers (Commonwealth Bureau of Census and Statistics [CBCS], 1952: 4). By 1984, the six original law schools (one in each state) had been joined by six more, as well as by several legal studies departments. The number of full-time legal academics had risen to 380, including 67 at Monash and 56 at the University of New South Wales, the largest faculties (CTEC, 1984: 30), to which must be added more than 100 legal studies teachers (Ross, 1982: 62). While student numbers increased sixfold between 1950 and 1984 (see table 2), therefore, full-time staff increased more than twenty times. As long as law teaching remained a part-time activity, legal research was very limited (Halliday, 1982a: 45–46), inhibiting what Weber called "a far-reaching emancipation of legal thinking from the everyday needs of the public" (ibid., 6). The widespread perception that law schools were adjuncts to the legal profession rather than academic faculties dedicated to liberal education was accompanied by limited recurrent funding, low staff ceilings, small libraries, scant research funds and assistance, and poor infrastructural facilities (ibid., 41–42). Although the law schools looked to the United States and England (Derham, 1978: 8) and invoked Blackstone and Langdell (Brown, 1908: 5; Martin, 1983: 5, 93), Australian law courses remained fairly uniform through the 1950s, dominated by the perceived need to reproduce legal practitioners (Lucke, 1978: 201). Having won the right to be the primary locus of legal education and socialization, law schools also inherited the empiricist tradition of English legal training, with its emphasis on the practical, inductive reasoning, and the absence of any sociological jurisprudence. Thus a Harvard Law School dean visiting in 1952 observed that Australian legal education was at once more rigidly theoretical and more narrowly practical than in the United States (Griswold, 1952: 145–146).

By the early 1960s, there was movement away from this position in both the writing of leading academics (Derham; 1962, 1969) and the recommendations of consultative bodies. The Committee on the Future of Tertiary Education in Australia of the Australian Universities Commission (now CTEC) released a 1964 report, which "encouraged, or perhaps even generated" significant change (Lucke, 1978: 203).

> It is very desirable that lawyers seeking admission to independent practice ... have an education founded upon full-time studies at university level. Before they become immersed in the day-to-day routines and demands of law offices, lawyers bearing the responsibilities of independent practice should have had at least three years of university education designed not so much to train them as legal practitioners as to provide them with the background intellectual training necessary for leaders in the highly complex society of the future. (Martin Report, 1964: vol. 2, p. 49)

The report called for the establishment of more university law schools (with an urgent need for a second one in New South Wales), "first class facilities" for legal teaching and research, and diversity in legal education. It also recommended that the training of a professional lawyer be divided into three relatively discrete stages: (1) academic training at a university; (2) subsequent practical training, with both institutional and in-service components; and (3) continuing education (ibid., 52–56). This later was echoed in reports on legal education in England (Ormrod Report, 1971: 100), Victoria (Freadman Report, 1969: 395), and Tasmania (Cosgrove, 1970) and was accepted as policy by the New South Wales Law Society (Peden, 1972: 8). The establishment of practical legal training courses controlled by the profession reduced the pressure on the university law schools to engage in professional training.

By 1976, Lucke (1978: 202) identified at least ten different styles of degree programs, including three-year undergraduate, three-year postgraduate, four-year undergraduate, five-year combined, and six-year part-time or external courses. A large percentage of students now do combined degrees where these are available (Halliday, 1982a: 28), and combined degrees are compulsory at New South Wales and Macquarie and effectively so at Monash.

The "second" law schools at the University of New South Wales and Monash University in Victoria and the third generation at Macquarie and the Legal Studies Department at LaTrobe were established not only to accommodate increased demand for student places but also to stimulate diversity and dynamism in legal education and scholarship.

There has been considerable discussion about, but no approval of, the establishment of the first law school (and university) in the Northern Territory, a third law school in Queensland at Griffith University, a second law school in South Australia at Flinders University, and a second law school in Western Australia at Murdoch University (*Western Australian* 1 [October 23, 1984]).

The new law schools, and some of the older ones, have limited the number of compulsory core subjects, as recommended by both the Ormrod Report (1971: 48) and a convocation of Australian law school deans (Lucke & Wallace, 1978: 192). Mandatory courses range from 36 percent of the curriculum at the University of Tasmania to 76 percent at Sydney in 1976 (Lucke & Wallace, 1978: 140; Lucke, 1978: 221 n. 52). At the University of New South Wales, for example, there were 64 elective subjects as well as a number of research options available in 1985. Only Monash and New South Wales offer full-fledged clinical programs, with students working in community legal centers dealing with real clients under faculty (and adjunct) supervision supplemented by seminar work, although law students at other institutions do work as volunteers (Basten et al., 1985: 127). In many fundamental areas, such as criminal law and procedure, there still is a paucity of research and literature, both empirical and analytic. Law still is compartmentalized in the traditional but arbitrary way, with contracts, torts, procedure, and so on taught in discrete and unintegrated units. At most law schools, instructors lecture on black letter law to large groups of students with whom they have little interaction and whom they evaluate only through examinations (Derham, 1969: 536). One commentator thus could say of Sydney University Law School in 1983 that the "curriculum and expository, formalist style of legal discourse have remained remarkably constant since 1890" (Martin [1983: 5]; for critiques of legal formalism and advocacy of a social theory of law, see Kavanagh [1986], Cranston [1978], and Wallace & Fiocco [1981]).

A longitudinal study of students who entered law schools in four Australian universities in three states (Victoria, Queensland, and Western Australia) in 1965 found significant if contradictory changes in student attitudes as their education progressed (Anderson et al., 1978: 189–190). On one hand, law students

> who are initially conservative and somewhat closed-minded in intellectual style, tend to become more engaged with the problems of their society, more committed to social reform and more open in their approach to intellectual matters.

On the other hand, there was a striking shift from

> a community centred orientation to one which was profession centred: judgments about the effectiveness of professional services should be made by the profession; the profession should discipline professional misbehaviour; professional training is best carried out in institutions run by the profession; government control over professional activity is a retrograde step; client's interest and the public's interest are secondary to the profession's interest.

Legal education is principally the responsibility of the states. The Australasian Universities Law Schools Association (AULSA), which draws its membership from legal academics in Australia, New Zealand, and Papua New Guinea, occasionally makes recommendations on educational, industrial, and other matters. In 1977, the Australian Legal Education Council (ALEC) was established by representatives of the practicing profession, the judiciary, legal academics, teachers of practical training courses, law students, and government lawyers (Bowen Report, 1979: 229–231). It meets semiannually and serves as a forum but has no prescriptive powers.

In all jurisdictions except the Australian Capital Territory and Western Australia, supreme court judges determine the educational requirements for admission. In the Australian Capital Territory and Western Australia the admission boards also contain lawyers and, in Western Australia, all *retired* judges. These admitting authorities can approve or reject a particular law school's degree as satisfying the educational requirement for admission, stipulate particular compulsory subjects, require additional examinations, and conduct their own courses, as happens in New South Wales (Samuels, 1978: 673, 681). While law schools generally have been allowed to shape their own curricula, there have been some instances of judicial intervention. When the Adelaide University Law Faculty decided to remove procedure from the list of compulsory subjects in 1973, the Supreme Court judges responded by making it an admission requirement (Lucke & Wallace, 1978: 194). The South Australian admission rules require a graduate who has not studied either jurisprudence, comparative law, Roman law, or legal history to serve an extra year of articles (Lucke, 1978: 214). A 1983 meeting of the New South Wales Admission Board, attended by only a few judges, ruled that the University of New South Wales Law School's subject entitled "Law, Lawyers and Society" no longer satisfied the legal ethics requirement. This apparently was retribution for the mildly critical approach and the involvement of some of the teachers in law reform activities. The decision was rescinded shortly thereafter, at the urging of the Chief Justice and others.

Instead of obtaining a law degree, approximately 3,000 people are enrolled in the Admission Board system in New South Wales, which requires attendance at weekly lectures and periodic examinations. Progress through this course is slow and haphazard, taking four to thirty-eight years. Only about 60 percent of enrolled students appear to be "active" (i.e., sitting examinations) at any given time; only 22 percent proceed through the course with the minimum number of examination attempts; and "a very large proportion who enter the system are never admitted to practice" (Bowen Report, 1979: 158–159, 307). The expansion of university courses has overwhelmed the relatively steady production of Admission Board students (an average of 141 admissions per year between 1960 and 1978). Whereas Admission Board students were 72 percent of all New South Wales admissions to practice in 1960 and 88 percent in 1962, the proportion remained below 50 percent from 1968 and was 29 percent in 1978 (Bowen Report, 1979: 184 and table 7-A).

The New South Wales Admission Board course is poorly conceived, poorly administered, poorly taught, and poorly examined. There are no separate library facilities for board students, and they have no borrowing privileges at other law libraries. Lecturers, most of whom are full-time practitioners, keep no office hours and offer no tutorials, study groups, academic counseling, or remedial programs. The nature of the lectures and exams encourages rote learning and discourages independent inquiry or research. The board program is virtually open admission, although there is a numerical quota; it is virtually tuition free, although there is a small fee for examinations; and it offers its courses at night and by extension. Approximately 25 percent of board students are New South Wales public servants, and the board traditionally has been a very important vehicle for qualification by those in the magisterial bureaucracy (Bowen Report, 1979: 158, 166–170). A 1975 survey indicates that most board admittees work as employed lawyers, rather than at the Bar (Beed & Campbell, 1977: 69). Another raison d'être was service to country students via extension courses (ibid., 160–161, 175); however, examination sittings in the country have declined dramatically in recent years. With the advent of the extension program at Macquarie University and the exclusively part-time program at New South Wales Institute of Technology, many thought the Admission Board program would be phased out. This has not happened, largely because the Supreme Court has protected the program it supervises, but the board is unlikely to receive sufficient resources to upgrade its program.

Some states still admit through apprenticeship (Trumble, 1978: 570). In Tasmania, a person who has articled for five years may be admitted after examination (Tasmania Legal Practitioners Act of 1959, s. 13[a] [iv]; see also Ross [1975: 4]. In Western Australia there is an equivalent admission procedure for articled clerks (Western Australia Legal Practitioners Act of 1893, s. 15[2] [b]; see also Clarkson [1983: 149, 184–185]), as well as an admission procedure for experienced articled clerks (ss. 16 and 19). New South Wales limited entry through articles in 1968 and effectively closed it in 1975 (New South Wales Supreme Court, *Solicitors Admission Rules* 4[ddd] and [di]).

A number of tertiary institutions in Australia also offer "legal studies" courses, which usually accommodate commercial and business studies or social science students who wish to acquire a complementary legal background but are not seeking a professional qualification, as well as students who are potential teachers of legal studies at the secondary level. All states and territories offer legal studies courses for senior secondary students. In Victoria, legal studies has the third highest enrollment (out of over forty subjects), behind only English (which is compulsory) and biology (Harley, 1985: 33; Lindgren, 1980: 400–401, passim).

Entry into law school is second in difficulty only to entry into medical school, and most of those admitted in New South Wales are in the top 5 percent on statewide matriculation examinations. The Institutes of Technology in New South Wales and Queensland do accept some students on this basis but cater mainly to students with work experience. The University of New South Wales and Monash University law schools have small special admission programs for Aborigines. In accordance with government equal opportunity policies, a number of universities are beginning to consider special admissions for students from "disadvantaged" backgrounds (*Sydney Morning Herald* 4 [March 9, 1985]).

Australian, like British, higher education is stratified into technical colleges at the bottom, colleges of advanced education and institutes of technology in the middle, and universities at the top. The two institute law schools are the newest, catering largely (Queensland) or exclusively (New South Wales) to part-time students. For several reasons, however, there is relatively little stratification among university law schools, particularly when compared to the United States. First, there is very little interstate mobility of students or practitioners. Second, all Australian universities are public (statutory) institutions, although there has been some discussion of allowing the establishment of private universities, particularly for students from nearby Asian countries (*The Australian* 13 [November 20 1985]. Academic salaries are effectively fixed by the federal Academic Salaries Tribunal, and all university academics of equivalent rank earn the same salary regardless of subject area, except for special loadings for additional responsibilities or clinical duties. Third, the trend toward combined courses means that potential law students choose universities on the basis of the perceived quality or reputation of both the law school and the *other* school or faculty involved.

Nevertheless, there is some stratification between older and newer law schools. In New South Wales, all judges and senior counsel and most senior partners in solicitors' firms, senior government lawyers, and legal academics are graduates of Sydney University (or qualified through the Admission Board examinations). Now, however, public and private sector employers recruit graduates equally from the various law schools. The older law schools have taken a conservative approach to research, curriculum development, assessment, student choice of electives, teaching methods, interdisciplinary approaches, and other matters of pedagogy and philosophy. The newer law schools have been more dynamic and innovative, parlaying their concern for teaching into better resources. In 1984, Sydney and Melbourne Universities had the highest student-faculty ratios among university law schools (32.6 and 23.4, respectively), and the University of New South Wales and Macquarie and Monash Universities had the lowest (13, 17.8, and 17.9).

In 1974 all tertiary tuition fees were abolished with the stated purpose of opening higher education to working-class students (but see Anderson et al., 1980; Linke et al., 1985). Fees have been reintroduced for overseas students, and an A$250 "administrative charge" has been levied on most students. Although there are other expenses (books, transportation, and housing), few Australian students find themselves deeply in debt when they graduate. At the same time that tuition fees were abolished the government also introduced the Tertiary Education Assistance Scheme (TEAS) for full-time students in approved tertiary courses who are citizens or permanent residents. The allowance is means-tested (by parental income if the student is not "independent") but not competitive, and there are no age restrictions. When first instituted, the allowances were reasonably related to maintenance costs, but unlike other social welfare benefits, the TEAS allowance is not indexed and has not kept pace with inflation, particularly in the cost of rental accommodation. A significant number of full-time students now work part time to make up the shortfall. In 1984, the maximum yearly allowance for university students was A$3,355 (Department of Education and Youth Affairs, 1984: 4), excluding allowances for dependents. There also is a federal Aboriginal Study Grants Scheme, which assists Aboriginal and Islander students (ibid., 6). Most law schools allow students to pursue their degrees part time.

The strong trend in Australia since the 1970s has been away from articles as the main method of postuniversity practical legal training and toward the recommendations of the Ormrod Report (1971: para. 100) and Martin Report (1964: vol. 2, paras. 52–56): six to nine months of professional education in an institutional setting followed by a period of in-service training as an admitted, but restricted, practitioner. All states (and the Australian Capital Territory) except Western Australia now have established postgraduate practical legal training courses (Bowen Report, 1979: 204–205; Clarkson Report, 1983: 171–172; Balmford & Hutchison, 1978: 483–489), and Western Australia is likely to do so soon (Clarkson Report, 1983: 179–184). In New South Wales articles have been abolished, and in South Australia articles are available only for people who cannot obtain a place in the practical legal training course or are granted an exemption by the Supreme Court in "exceptional circumstances." In Victoria, Queensland, and the Australian Capital Territory articles remain an infrequently used alternative to the courses. In Tasmania, a period of articles is required *after* completion of the training course (Disney et al., 1986: 263). Most courses are independent, facilitating control by the local legal profession (Balmford, 1978: 495) but also are affiliated with tertiary institutions, facilitating eligibility for Commonwealth funding (ibid., 498). Most courses are practical but not clinical, relying on simulation exercises to develop such professional skills as interviewing, taking instructions, legal drafting, negotiation, conveyancing, advocacy, keeping files, office organization and procedures, law office and trust accounting, and litigation and administrative procedures (Bowen Report, 1979: 193; Balmford & Hutchinson, 1978: 490).

In all states except South Australia, new admittees hold a restricted practicing certificate for a period of six months to three years, during which they cannot practice on their own. Although described as in-service training, it really is more like a period of probation, given the absence of any formal program of study, supervision, or assessment. In New South Wales and Queensland, the only jurisdictions with de jure divided professions and no common admission, an aspiring barrister need not attend the practical legal training course. The New South Wales Bar Association does require one year of pupillage or "reading" under a senior barrister, but membership in the association is not a prerequisite for admission; pupillage also is customary in Queensland (Disney et al., 1977: 132).

Continuing legal education programs are not mandatory for periodic recertification of practitioners, nor are they used to define specialists or as a form of probation for those guilty of ethical violations. Nevertheless, there is a wide range of programs available (Stewart & Balmford, 1978: 696–700; Bowen Report, 1979: appendix J), and participation is encouraged by the professional associations (Clarkson Report, 1983: 190). In 1984 there were 787 higher-degree (LL.M. and Ph.D.) students in law in Australia, (3.3 percent of all graduate students), 85 percent of whom were in Sydney, Canberra, or Melbourne (CTEC, 1984; 11). Law had by far the smallest proportion of graduate students relative to undergraduate enrollment, even compared to other professional subjects such as medicine, veterinary science, and dentistry.

LAWYERS AND THE SOCIOECONOMIC ELITE

The shift from the "white Australia policy" to "multiculturalism" and the large influx of migrants from other than Anglo-Celtic backgrounds after World War II has significantly affected Australian society and culture (Altman, 1980: 61–63; Wilton & Bosworth, 1984). The effect on the legal profession, thus far small, doubtless will increase as the second generation of migrants comes of age. University law students tend to come from homes that are more affluent than the norm; most attended select (and expensive) private secondary schools; and their parents generally are professionals or managers. The legal profession has allowed entrants to qualify by means other than full-time university study, however.

AGE

Students who enter university directly from high school at eighteen or nineteen years of age account for the majority of law students. Most Australian law students are required, or choose, to do a "combined law degree" program (usually arts-law, commerce-law, or science-law), which normally takes at least five years. If we add six months for the postgraduate practical legal training course or a year or two of articles, the typical entrant is twenty-three to twenty-seven years old.

With the increase in the number of law schools, and thus of law graduates, since the 1960s as well as the decline of the Admission Board programs, the average age of the profession has fallen steadily for the past two decades. Currently, about half of all solicitors in New South Wales are under thirty-five (Bowen, 1978: 15). About two-thirds of city solicitors, corporate lawyers, and country solicitors and three-fourths of suburban solicitors are under forty (Tomasic & Bullard, 1978: 21–22). The Bar is somewhat older, with only 8.5 percent under thirty and 52.8 percent under forty.

There appears to be some correlation between age and attitudes toward the profession and professional associations. Among a sample of New South Wales solicitors, 67 percent of those over fifty were satisfied that the self-regulating Law Society adequately represented the interests of the general public, compared to only 35 percent of those between thirty-five and forty-nine and 43 percent of those under thirty-five (Australian National Opinion Poll [ANOP], 1979: 14—18). Younger respondents were concerned that the Law Society was not sufficiently diligent or vigorous in exercising its disciplinary powers.

The judiciary, of course, is older than the practicing profession. One profile of the judges of the Supreme Courts of Victoria and New South Wales found that most judges were appointed after twenty-five years of practice, "usually at the age of about fifty" (Sexton & Maher, 1982: 5). The retirement age for all state and federal judges is seventy, except in Victoria, where it is seventy-two (ibid., 78 n. 7; Crawford, 1982: 30—31).

GENDER

Until the early part of the twentieth century, women were prohibited from practicing. Victoria removed the legal barrier in 1903, followed by Tasmania (1904), Queensland (1905), South Australia (1911), New South Wales (1918), and Western Australia (1923). In New South Wales, the first woman was admitted to practice in 1921 (she had been the first woman law graduate in 1902); in Victoria, the first woman was admitted in 1923 (she was appointed Victoria's first and only woman Queen's Counsel in 1965) (Disney et al., 1977: 188).

Only a few women were admitted to practice before the 1960s. Women constituted 1 percent of solicitors in New South Wales in 1950, 6 percent in 1975, and nearly 14 percent in 1984 (see table 4). Women made up only 11.4 percent of all Australian university law students in 1960, 12.4 percent in 1968, 22.1 percent in 1974, and 29.1 percent in 1977 (Tomasic, 1983a: 451). By the mid-1980s, they almost certainly exceeded 40 percent (Kirby, 1982: 11). In New South Wales in 1983, 40.3 percent of law students were women, which closely parallels the representation of women in university studies generally (41.4 percent) (Australian Bureau of Statistics [ABS], 1984: 15). At the University of New South Wales Law Faculty, women constituted 45.6 percent of all students in 1985, a much higher proportion than in engineering (5 percent), architecture (26.5 percent), applied science (27 percent), and medicine (34 percent). While these figures indicate a continuing change in the gender composition of the Australian legal profession, the increased entry of women apparently will not affect the class composition. Both the Ziegert survey in Sydney (1983: 9) and the Hetherton survey in Victoria (1981a: 116) revealed that there was no significant difference between men and women lawyers in terms of social background (i.e., schooling, parents' education and occupation). Hetherton's survey of the Victorian legal profession found that the median income of women was just over half that of men, and the upper quartile of women was well below the male median (Hetherton, 1981a: 126; 1981b: 300). There were relatively few women barristers or partners in law firms and relatively more women practicing as employed solicitors (Hetherton, 1981a: 116–119; 1981b: 300). Women were markedly concentrated in family law and probate; strongly underrepresented in commercial law, company law, and criminal law; and somewhat underrepresented in tax and estate planning, personal injury, and litigation (outside the Family Court) (Hetherton, 1981a: 131–137; 1981b: 301, 307).

Recent statistics from the New South Wales Law Society (Hunt, 1984: 739–740) also bear out the differences in the occupational profile (and, perforce, income) of men and women lawyers (see table 5). In New South Wales in 1984, women constituted only 3.9 percent of partners in solicitors' firms and 8 percent of sole practitioners but 26.5 percent of employed solicitors. Stated another way, while 48.9 percent of male solicitors in private practice were partners and only 27.4 percent were employed, only 14.2 percent of women were partners and fully 70.8 percent were employed. According to figures supplied by the Women Lawyers Association of New South Wales, only about 78 of the 1,100 active barristers in that state in 1985 were women. Because women entered the Bar late and in small numbers, few have reached the bench. There are a handful of women judges at the district court level, but there has been only one Supreme Court judge (in South Australia) and no women on the Federal Court. The first woman was appointed to the High Court in February 1987. As of the end of 1984, six of the forty-six judges of the Family Court, including the Chief Judge, were women.

RELIGION

Australia is reputed to have one of the lowest rates of church attendance (or the equivalent) in the Western world, and there are few formal links between legal and religious institutions or personnel. One recent survey of New South Wales lawyers indicated that the religious profile of the legal profession closely followed that of the general community (see table 6). Figures are not available on the judiciary generally, but studies of past and present justices of the High Court of Australia show an underrepresentation of Catholics and an overrepresentation of Protestants (Baxter, 1983: 6; Neumann, 1973). This may be because more Catholics have supported the Australian Labor party, which has not had the opportunity to make many High Court appointments.

ETHNICITY

Australian lawyers overwhelmingly are Australian born (84 percent in Victoria, 88.4 percent in New South Wales), with most of the immigrant lawyers coming from the United Kingdom, Ireland, New Zealand, or other English-speaking countries (Tomasic & Bullard, 1978: 21–23; Hetherton, 1978: 15–17). Suburban solicitors in New South Wales were most likely to be foreign born (17.5 percent), while country solicitors were almost all Australian born (97.8 percent) (Tomasic & Bullard, 1978: 173). Until 1975, all Australian jurisdictions admitted only Australian and British citizens. South Australia removed this requirement in 1975, and most jurisdictions have followed suit in the past few years; however, the Commonwealth Public Service Act now requires that most Commonwealth employees— including government lawyers—be Australian citizens (Bowen Report, 1979: 95–96).

Hetherton (1981a: 34–35) found a correlation between ethnicity and the types of work performed by lawyers in Victoria. Virtually all lawyers practicing company and commercial law were Australian born. In the relatively newer (and thus more open) area of taxation, 25 percent of lawyers (and 41.7 percent of their fathers) were foreign born. As Ziegert (1983: 24) noted, this sort of correlation may reflect socioeconomic factors to a greater extent than sociocultural considerations. Law students whose parents were born overseas were less likely to attend elite private schools, and their fathers had less formal education and lower occupational status (ibid., 22–23). Although immigrant participation in university education tends to increase with length of residence (Anderson & Western, 1970: 22), law schools had among the highest proportions of Australian-born students of any tertiary faculty (Anderson et al., 1980: 93). At the University of New South Wales in 1985, Australian-born students constituted a higher proportion in law (81 percent) than in any other faculty.

A small number of Aboriginal lawyers have qualified in the past decade, assisted somewhat by special admission programs at the University of New South Wales and Monash University. Six Aborigines have been admitted to practice in New South Wales, two each in Victoria and Tasmania, and one each in South Australia and the Northern Territory.

Even the small number of lawyers whose origins lie outside the British Isles has caused concern among the most conservative elements of the profession. In a submission to the New South Wales Law Reform Commission, the late Francis C. Hutley, then a Supreme Court judge, wrote:

> The immediate effect of World War II was to open up the legal profession to groups who had no historical connection with the professions. [This resulted in] the flooding of the profession by persons who, without either professional family association or adequate indoctrination, have acquired the often dangerous skills put into the hands of lawyers.
>
> If the maintenance of professional standards, particularly of integrity, which need to be above those of the general community, is of fundamental importance and it is desired to greatly increase the number of lawyers and to draw the increase from largely represented classes such as the aboriginals and migrants, an elaborate course of indoctrination will be necessary. The clan type loyalty which I understand is the basis of such aboriginal and migrant morality is fundamentally inconsistent with the individual integrity which is required of a lawyer. (Hutley, 1977: 11)

SOCIOECONOMIC CLASS

The decline of apprenticeships and part-time evening courses (the Admission Board programs) in favor of university training inevitably operated against the interests of those from lower socioeconomic backgrounds (O'Malley, 1983: 76). The abolition of tuition and the introduction of government allowances in 1974 failed to increase the enrollments of (or even applications from) disadvantaged students, indicating that the main problems lie at earlier stages in the education and socialization of working-class children (Linke et al., 1985: 139).

Even within the elite world of the university, "medicine and law reflect by far the most extreme [socioeconomic] discrimination levels, not only for student enrolments but also applications" (ibid., 138). Social background also plays a part in predisposing some students toward legal studies. Anderson and Western (1970: 24) found that "students in the science and humanities streams choose medicine and law respectively if they are from high status families, engineering or teaching if they are from lower status families."

Law students' fathers overwhelmingly are professionals or managers; the proportion of blue-collar workers is only about a fourth as high as it is in the general population (Tomasic & Bullard, 1978: 178–179; Hetherton, 1978: 12–14; Anderson & Western, 1967: 69; Ziegert, 1983: 27–28). Law students also come from relatively affluent families and have relatively highly educated parents (Anderson et al., 1980: 77, 87). Indeed, law students have the most elite social backgrounds of all university students in Australia (ibid., 81–82).

A striking feature of the Australian legal profession is its "hereditary and tribal aspects" (Sexton & Maher, 1982: 8). Tomasic and Bullard (1978: 23, 177) found that about 40 percent of barristers and 50 percent of solicitors in New South Wales had close relatives who were legally qualified and that this varied with type of practice: country solicitors (53.6 percent), city solicitors (49.9 percent), suburban solicitors (46.2 percent), barristers (41.4 percent), corporate lawyers (34.2 percent), and government lawyers (32.3 percent).

Hetherton found a similar pattern in Victoria (1978: 15). Almost 40 percent of practicing lawyers had another lawyer in the family, and about 13 percent had two or more (mainly spouses, brothers, and uncles). Over 15 percent had lawyer fathers, even though lawyers accounted for only about 0.3 percent of the male workforce in Victoria at that time.

The type of secondary schooling is strongly associated with both background and future career. Among the Western democracies, only Ireland has a greater proportion of children attending private schools—for obvious religious reasons (Smark & Whelan, 1985: 4). Australia also has a sizable systemic Catholic school population, but most elites are alumni of Protestant private schools (and some independent Catholic private schools). Among those members of the national elite who were educated in Australia, 38 percent came from private non-Catholic schools, even though those schools accounted for only 9 percent of the national secondary enrollment (Higley, 1979: 86). The figure would have been substantially higher except for the fact that only a small percentage of trade union officials (6 percent) and Labor party leaders (8 percent) attended these schools. By comparison, 56 percent of business leaders, 47 percent of the conservative political leaders, 45 percent of media executives, and 64 percent of academic leaders attended private non-Catholic schools. State (public) schools educated 73 percent of secondary students but provided only 48 percent of the national elite (and 83 percent of trade union leaders). Catholic school graduates (18 percent of the national secondary enrollment) were marginally underrepresented among the elite (14 percent).

Attendance at one of the elite private schools not only reflects privilege but also strongly enhances the chance to go on to university (ibid., 87) and activates the old school tie network, particularly in a country where all the universities are public and relatively equal. All twelve directors of BHP, Australia's largest company, are graduates of Protestant private schools, as are all the directors of AMP, the largest insurance company, and all but one director of Westpac, the largest banking corporation (Smark & Whelan, 1985: 4).

Among university students, law students have the highest proportion of private secondary-school education (Anderson et al., 1980: 124); only about one-third attend state schools (which educate about three-fourths of all secondary students) (see table 7). When the few selective state schools are added to private secondary schools, only about 12 percent to 20 percent of law students remain who attended ordinary state secondary schools. Among New South Wales lawyers, alumni of state schools were least likely to be barristers (28.8 percent) and city solicitors (37.7 percent) and most likely to be employed corporate (45.8 percent) or government lawyers (44.9 percent) (Tomasic & Bullard, 1978: 181). Only 11 percent of barristers attended nonselective state schools.

Nearly two-thirds of judges who have served or are serving on the High Court of Australia attended independent schools in Australia or the United Kingdom, while only 6 percent attended Catholic schools and 26.5 percent attended state schools (one-third of whom attended selective state schools) (Baxter, 1983: 12–13). Of the thirty-four judges on the New South Wales Supreme Court in 1977, 90 percent had been to private secondary school, and the same was true of the twenty-two judges of the Victorian Supreme Court in 1978 (Sexton & Maher, 1982: 5).

Hetherton's study of the Victorian profession (1981a: 34) indicated that commercial solicitors, with the highest status and income, had the most establishment backgrounds—the greatest proportion of high-status secondary schooling (61 percent) and the lowest percentage of working-class fathers (2.3 percent)—and virtually all were from Australian or British families. Taxation law, by contrast, had the greatest proportion of "ethnic" practitioners and state-school graduates but still only a very small proportion of working-class fathers (8 percent). This suggests that upwardly mobile lawyers without establishment connections find easier access to the newer, more innovative areas of taxation law and planning. Lawyers working in the area of "personal plight" (criminal law, family law, personal injury, and workers' compensation), which offers the lowest status and least remuneration, were most likely to have working-class fathers (20 percent) and least likely to have other lawyers in the family. Victorian barristers were somewhat less likely than solicitors to come from a working-class background, an ethnic family, or a state secondary school, but there was no significant correlation between their social background and their specialization (ibid., 73).

In New South Wales, Tomasic (1983a: 458) found no significant correlation between father's occupation, lawyer's schooling or religion, and most types of practices. A more detailed study of criminal lawyers—who rank twenty-fourth out of twenty-eight legal work categories in terms of prestige and twenty-first in terms of income (Tomasic & Bullard, 1978: 38)—revealed them considerably less likely to be Protestant, to have gone to a high-status secondary school, or to have university qualifications

(Tomasic, 1981: 147, 150—151 and table 1). There was a high correlation between the size and location of the first law firm in which a solicitor worked and the last (Tomasic, 1983a: 453).

As O'Malley pointed out (1983: 91), however, internal differentiation and stratification have not caused significant disunity within the profession. Rather, the high degree of social homogeneity, the need to preserve common benefits (such as self-regulation and certain monopolies), and the overarching ideology of the rule of law all serve to unify lawyers.

Starting from a position of relative privilege, lawyers acquire further status, affluence, and influence by virtue of their professional membership. In a study of occupational status in Australia (Broom et al., 1977: 89, 103), physicians ranked first by a significant margin, followed by industrial efficiency engineers, dentists, judges, and lawyers and legal officers (see also Higley et al., 1979: 55). The 1984 survey by the Graduate Careers Council of Australia (Australian Mathematical Society, 1985: 4) ranked law third out of thirty-four groups (behind only medicine and health sciences) in terms of the employment prospects of graduates. Only 4.1 percent of law graduates still were seeking work four months after completing their studies. Law graduates, who earned an average of A$27,400 (40 percent above the national average) five years after graduation, ranked behind only dentists (A$33,050) and physicians (A$34,994) (Walker, 1985: 49). Income would increase rapidly with experience for private practitioners who become barristers or partners in a firm of solicitors.

LAWYERS AND THE STATE

LAWYERS IN THE STATE

The ideology of the rule of law is strong in Australia, as in most Western democracies. The "myth of neutrality" of the law (Sexton & Maher, 1982: 13—14) is sufficiently durable to survive the active participation of lawyers in partisan politics, the political appointment of judges, and the use of judges in policy-making inquiries.

Tomasic and Bullard (1978: 26, 188) found that New South Wales lawyers strongly identified with the conservative political parties, although this also is true of all professionals and managers in Australia (Western, 1983: 76—78). Nearly three-fourths of city and country solicitors, 67 percent of corporation lawyers, and 62 percent of suburban solicitors stated that the conservative parties best served their political orientation, while only 13.5 percent of all solicitors identified with the Labor party. A majority of suburban solicitors, corporation lawyers, government lawyers, and barristers believed that "lawyers are mainly interested in preserving the status quo" (ibid., 314). Only government lawyers (30.8 percent) and barristers (30.1 percent) showed any significant support for the Labor party (ibid., 188). Anderson and Western (1970: 3) found that law students were politically the most conservative (but socially the most radical) of all professional students. Political orientation does not necessarily translate into political affiliation, however, since few lawyers belong to political parties (Tomasic & Bullard, 1978: 191; Tomasic, 1983b: 57).

The proportion of practicing lawyers actively involved in electoral politics appears to be small, at least in New South Wales. With the exception of country solicitors, of whom about 16 percent have been candidates in local elections and 7 percent in state elections, very few lawyers report having stood for political office (Tomasic & Bullard, 1978: 189). Perhaps the majority have heeded the warning of a former chief justice, Sir Owen Dixon: "once a politician, never again a good lawyer" (quoted in Evans [1981: 15]). Compared to the United States and Great Britain, the proportion of Australian politicians with legal backgrounds is small. In federal Parliament in 1979, 18 percent of the House of Representatives were lawyers (mainly from the conservative coalition parties), as were 14 percent of the Senate. Less than 10 percent of state MPs in Queensland and Western Australia were lawyers, and in no state did the figure exceed about 15 percent (of both houses) (Sexton & Maher, 1982: 139). It still is a common belief, however, that "a career at the Bar remains the best passport to a safe Liberal [i.e., conservative] seat and to a ministerial office" (Ford, 1965: 104).

Yet the influence of lawyer-politicians in Australia is considerably greater than these figures would suggest. About half of all prime ministers have been lawyers, and lawyers have occupied the office for twenty-five of the last thirty-five years, including the long reign of Sir Robert Menzies (1939–1941 and 1949–1966) (ibid., 138). Disproportionate numbers of lawyers also have been opposition leaders, state premiers, and federal and state ministers (Disney et al., 1977: 197). In 1983, five of the eight heads of federal and state governments were lawyers; four of these were Labor party politicians, which was unusual. In Australia's major modern political crisis, the sacking of the Labor government by the governor-general in November 1975, almost all major protagonists were lawyers (as they were in America's Watergate scandal) (Sexton & Maher, 1982: 143–144). Active involvement in party politics also is associated with leadership in the legal profession (Higley et al., 1979: 57–58).

Judges are simultaneously state officials and leaders of the legal profession. Federal and state governments actually make appointments to the bench, although the governor-general or the state governor formally may have that authority. The conservative parties have dominated since Federation and thus have made the great bulk of judicial appointments. Consequently, judicial conservatism has come to be seen as natural and "apolitical" (Brown, 1984: 23), notwithstanding the fact that during the eighty-five-year history of the Australian High Court thirteen of the thirty-three justices and five of the seven chief justices were expoliticians. In the past fifty-six years, Labor governments have made only five appointments to the High Court. With some notable exceptions, Labor also has appointed judicial conservatives (Sexton, 1979: 109; Evans, 1981: 13).

The power of the judiciary in Australia goes beyond its traditional role of applying the law. Judges regularly have been appointed to head a wide range of nonjudicial bodies, such as the Prices Justification Tribunal, the Family Law Council, the Stevedoring Industry Council, the Student Assistance Tribunal, the Academic Salaries Tribunal (Sexton & Maher, 1982: 2), the Parliamentary Salaries Tribunal, the Commonwealth Grants Commission (which recommends Commonwealth funding for the states) (Kirby, 1983: 9), and the Press Council (which reviews complaints about unfair reporting). Judges often are appointed chancellors of universities.

Another very significant expansion of the legal/judicial role has been the extensive use of extraparliamentary commissions of inquiry presided over by judges or senior counsel and charged with examining broad political, social, economic, and cultural matters, as well as legal issues. Some inquiries concentrate on fact-finding, paralleling the ordinary investigative and judicial processes. Others are "wide-ranging [canvasses] of mixed fact and policy questions resulting in a series of policy recommendations to the government of the day" (Sexton, 1984: 3). These have covered a huge range of topics, including film censorship, control of communism, petroleum exploration on the Great Barrier Reef, uranium mining and export, drugs, gambling and prostitution, "human relationships," and poverty in Australia (Sexton, 1984: 4; McInerney, 1978: 548; Sallmann & Willis, 1984: 17−18). They allow governments to circumvent difficult issues by referring them and then invoking the experience, prestige, and putative neutrality of judges and senior counsel to legitimate those recommendations the governments ultimately choose to accept (Sexton, 1984: 5; McInerney, 1978: 551). The characteristics of Australian legislatures—limited sitting days, party solidarity, inexpert ministers, the concentration of power in an executive cabinet, and the inadequate committee system—are further impetus for the delegation of policymaking.

Although the proliferation of commissions of inquiry sometimes has occasioned outcries of "judicial imperialism" (Reid, 1980: 5), judges in Victoria long ago stopped making themselves available (McInerney, 1978: 541−549), and judges in other states are becoming increasingly reluctant to accept such assignments, fearing that they (properly) will be perceived as making policy and thus will be drawn out of the shelter afforded by the rule of law ideology and into the political fray (Brennan, 1978: 14).

REGULATION OF THE PROFESSION

In all jurisdictions except Western Australia, the principal professional associations regulate admission and discipline. The Law Societies have power over both solicitors and barristers in the fused professions but only over solicitors in the divided professions. Since Law Societies have statutory responsibility for issuing annual practicing certificates to solicitors and amalgam practitioners (except in Western Australia), and the fee includes membership in the Law Society, all practicing lawyers are members (NSWLRC, 1982a: para. 2.2).

Most privately practicing barristers belong to the bar associations in the divided jurisdictions. The bar associations do not exercise statutory powers in any state, but their rules of conduct are recognized by the courts, which allow the bar associations to bring disciplinary proceedings (NSWLRC, 1981b: 461–463). The executive bar councils may fine, reprimand, or expel members, but they have no compulsory powers of investigation (ibid., 462–464). The requirement of twelve months' pupillage has inhibited academics, government lawyers, and corporation lawyers from joining bar associations, and the Queensland Bar Association actively discourages membership by barristers who are not practicing privately (Halliday, 1981: 12).

The leaders of the professional associations were an average of forty-eight years old and had practiced more than twenty years; none ever had held a significant position outside the profession (Higley et al., 1979: 103). Active involvement in party politics also appeared to be associated with leadership in the legal profession (ibid., 57–58). Now, however, there is a trend toward a younger, more active leadership. In 1979, members of the Council of the Victorian Law Institute averaged only thirty-nine years of age (Halliday, 1981: 19). The bar associations have required seniority in the leadership positions. The Council of the New South Wales Bar Association must be composed of five Queen's Counsel and fourteen others, of whom three must be of less than ten years' standing and two of less than five years' standing. The Victorian Bar Council is composed of eleven barristers of at least twelve years' standing, four barristers of six to fifteen years' standing, and three of at least six years' standing (Sexton & Maher, 1982: 35).

The nature of the leadership may be one cause for the "significant level of dissatisfaction on the part of lawyers with their professional associations" (Tomasic & Bullard, 1978: 33). In New South Wales, 56 percent of lawyers agreed that "the Council of the Law Society is not really in touch with the needs of its members"; 50 percent felt the same way about the Bar Council; and 68 percent agreed that "the Law Society is more concerned with lawyers who are employers than with lawyers who are employees" (ibid., 270). A 1979 survey found that 51 percent of solicitors believed that the Law Society Council was representative of the legal profession as a whole, but younger lawyers and those who practiced outside the city were less content (ANOP, 1979: 24; Hetherton, 1978: 175—177).

The major controversy surrounding the professional associations, however, involves their dual role as self-interested lobbyists and guardians of the public interest. When the New South Wales Law Reform Commission proposed to end the profession's exclusive control over its own affairs (by adding a minority of lay persons to governing councils, for instance), the responses from the professional associations ranged from "scorn and derision [to] palpable alarm" (*Sydney Morning Herald* 7 [April 8, 1982]). The then president of the bar typified the proposals as "a threat to traditional values ... a great step towards the attainment of anarchy.... The Bar which to any extent is controlled by the government is a Bar which must be by definition unacceptable to the public" (Meagher, 1980: 11—12). Lawyers themselves are skeptical about the "service ideal" as a justification for self-regulation. Tomasic and Bullard (1978: 275) found that only 46 percent of New South Wales lawyers felt that "lawyers are primarily motivated by a desire to serve the community," while 45 percent agreed that "most solicitors are more interested in making money than in helping their clients." Nor was altruism cited as a principal motivation for becoming a lawyer or a major contribution to success as a lawyer (ibid., 5; Tomasic, 1983a: 452—453; Anderson & Western, 1970: 25).

Because of the fragmented nature of the Australian legal profession, there has been no attempt to develop a national code of professional responsibility. A comparison of the positions of the various jurisdictions reveals that "there is a marked lack of actual conflict on matters of substance although numerous differences of detail occur" (1[2] *Australian Bar Gazette* 15 [1964]).

While ethical rules may be more hortatory than regulatory, they help to reaffirm legal culture (Tomasic, 1983a: 464), enforce professional solidarity, and secure legitimacy for self-regulation (O'Malley, 1983: 78). New South Wales Bar Association Rule 2 enunciates the so-called cab-rank principle that barristers must take any work that comes their way. There are fourteen express exceptions, however, including field of practice, complexity, other professional or personal commitments, conflicts of interest, and insufficient fee. Thus the rule serves to reinforce the profession's service ideal while offering such a comprehensive list of exemptions that no barrister would have difficulty refusing work "properly."

The profession frequently has fallen back on "historical" justifications for self-regulation, although there is an embarrassing gap of some centuries since the medieval guilds and the Star Chamber (Sexton & Maher, 1982: 174). Lawyers also have offered rather inapt—or disingenuous—analogies to other professions and occupations. To quote a past president of the

New South Wales Bar Association again:

> All major activities should be fundamentally self-governing. Trade unions are run by the members of those trade unions not by consumers. Doctors manage their own affairs, as do chemists and accountants. Why should barristers have to endure a regime which no respectable trade union would tolerate for one moment. (Meagher, 1980: 12)

Of course, this statement fails to acknowledge that none of these bodies also claims to act in a public capacity and yet remain free from all public regulation and accountability. Indeed, the Medical Disciplinary Board in New South Wales (and most other jurisdictions) is presided over by a medical lay person—a judge.

Governments do have considerable power over lawyers' fees. At the 1983 Australian Legal Convention, the then federal attorney-general, Senator Gareth Evans, warned lawyers to reduce fees voluntarily or face the threat of government action. Senator Evans referred to "a significant range of powers" available, including the power to (1) legislate regarding fees in the various federal courts and tribunals, (2) determine how the Commonwealth Crown Solicitor's office will brief the private profession (work that represented A$3.4 million in the 1982/83 financial year), (3) establish legal aid policies (federal government contributions accounted for about A$36 million in payments to the private profession in 1982/83), and (4) legislate to bring the legal profession under the jurisdiction of the Trade Practices Act and the Trade Practices Commission with respect to restrictive practices that increase fees (*Sydney Morning Herald* 1 [July 14, 1983]).

Although the federal Trade Practices Act probably does not apply to the legal profession generally (Heydon, 1976; cf. Nieuwenhuysen & Williams-Wynn, 1982: 62–66, 72), it has led to the abandonment of fee scales in the Australian Capital Territory, which is governed by the federal Parliament (*Sydney Morning Herald* 3 [December 10, 1983]). The Family Court of Australia also has imposed fee scales and ruled that charges above scale are ineffective unless the client has agreed to them after being expressly advised to seek independent legal advice on the question (NSWLRC, 1981a: 76).

State governments have the power to fix the prices of goods and services but have not regulated legal fees. Because some fee scales must be proclaimed by statute, the government has the right to disapprove them. In late 1983, 20-percent to 48-percent increases in the New South Wales fee scales for conveyancing were gazetted after consideration by a committee of judges (including the Chief Justice) and solicitors. However, the attorney-general announced that the public should ignore the increases, undertook to have Parliament disallow them, and referred the matter to the Law Reform Commission (*Sydney Morning Herald* 6 [January 4, 1984]). The increases subsequently were reduced. While solicitors and clients may set fees by agreement, the Commonwealth Attorney-General estimated that "somewhere between about 85 and 90 per cent of the work done by the legal profession around Australia is done on scales of fees ..." (*Sydney Morning Herald* 13 [July 5, 1983]). The committee in Victoria that sets the scales for noncontentious matters (such as conveyancing, probate, and administration) usually includes the government statistician, the only non-lawyer involved in this process in any state or territory (Disney et al., 1977: 305). In half of the jurisdictions, the Law Society itself sets the scales, in the other half there is some judicial involvement. Courts usually set the fee scales in contentious matters. Scales sometimes are "suggested" for barristers, but since they do not have a direct relationship with clients, they are far less subject to regulation, and many charge above the scale (NSWLRC, 1981a: 81). The lesser restraint on barristers' fees has meant that they have increased faster than those of solicitors in recent years (Disney et al., 1977: 309). A former Chief Justice of the High Court of Australia, Sir Garfield Barwick, cited (apparently without irony) the unrestrained nature of barristers' fees as an important occupational health measure: "The Bar itself is a place where the only protection against being overworked a man gets in the long run is the level of his fee" (12 *Justinian* 10 [May 30, 1980]).

Costs almost invariably are awarded against unsuccessful civil litigants in Australia. They may be determined by the court, agreed on between the parties, or left to the court's taxing officers. In practice, solicitors' fees in most contentious matters are effectively constrained by scales of so-called party and party costs, for it is unlikely that a solicitor will seek to recover from a successful client more than the legal costs awarded, and the unsuccessful client already will be paying the legal costs of *both* sides. Barristers' fees are not similarly constrained, for the briefing solicitor is obligated to pay the full amount agreed regardless of result or costs awarded. Indeed, New South Wales Bar Association Rule 82 actually prohibits any agreement between a barrister and a solicitor to remit any portion of the fees in the event that the costs awarded or the taxation of the solicitor's bill of costs limits the client's obligation to pay full solicitor and client costs. Even in the event of a settlement, 75 percent of New South Wales barristers report that they always or almost always demand full payment (NSWLRC, 1981a: 83). The New South Wales Bar Association and the Law Society have established a voluntary arbitration system for settling fee disputes between barristers and solicitors, but it has handled only about four matters a year (ibid., 77–78).

Any client may request formal taxation by court officials of a solicitor's bill of costs. Taxation officers are reputed to be strict in assessing costs and to err on the side of the client. Nevertheless, the taxation process is not wholly satisfactory (Disney et al., 1977: 331–332). The very existence of taxation is unknown to the vast majority of clients, and solicitors are not obliged to inform them. The process is formal, legalistic, and somewhat unpredictable. The bill actually can be *increased* by taxation, although this is uncommon (see *Florence Investments Pty. Ltd.* v. *H. G. Slater & Co.* [1975] 2 N.S.W.L.R. 398, 400), and the "loser" in the process bears the full costs of taxation. In most jurisdictions, if the taxation officer reduces the bill by at least one-sixth, the client has "won" and the solicitor bears the costs of taxation.

Formal power to admit is vested in the supreme courts, but day-to-day responsibility is delegated to bodies such as the Admission Boards in New South Wales and Queensland and the Council of Legal Education in Victoria, which usually include a number of Supreme Court judges and practitioners. The evaluation of educational requirements usually is straightforward except when overseas qualifications are offered; for instance, the Supreme Court admitted a South African solicitor over the objection of the New South Wales Law Society (*Sydney Morning Herald* 10 [September 8, 1983]). Most character evaluations also have been uncontroversial, although the applicant's political views appear to have been a factor in the decision to refuse admission in a few celebrated cases (*Re B*, [1981] 2 N.S.W.L.R. 372; see generally Basten & Redmond [1979]).

The supreme courts also have inherent power to discipline lawyers; they generally exercise this power concurrently with statutory disciplinary tribunals. The system generally reacts to complaints to the relevant professional association. Most are received from aggrieved (present or former) clients, although lawyers, judges, and magistrates sometimes complain (NSWLRC, 1980: 51). Lawyers occasionally are obliged to disclose unprofessional behavior: a solicitor who has reasonable suspicion that the trust accounts of another are not in order must report that to the Law Society (New South Wales Supreme Court, Solicitors' Practice Rule 4). (Such provisions are engagingly referred to as "pimp rules" in the legal profession.) Complaints from the public usually must be in writing (often in the form of a statutory declaration) (NSWLRC, 1979a: 30–32, 56–57). The Law Society generally takes action on its own initiative only when trust account inspections reveal irregularities (ibid., 30; see New South Wales Legal Practitioners Act 1893, s. 42).

The Law Society's Legal Department investigates complaints and has discretion to decide whether to proceed. If trust account irregularities are alleged, an inspector or special investigator may be appointed (NSWLRC, 1979a: 33–34; see New South Wales Legal Practitioners Act 1893, ss. 42, 82A). Otherwise the normal procedure is to ask the accused solicitor for comments. If the Legal Department concludes the complaint is valid, it refers the matter to the Complaints Committee of the Law Society Council, which reviews the investigation and, where appropriate (in most cases) (ibid., 36), refers it to the full council. The council usually adopts the recommendation of the Complaints Committee, which can censure the solicitor, appoint an investigator or receiver, request undertakings from the solicitor, find no misconduct, suspend or revoke the solicitor's practicing certificate, or refer the matter to the statutory disciplinary tribunal (or, more rarely, the Supreme Court) (ibid., 36–37). Disciplinary proceedings are "protective" of the public interest rather than punitive (*Weaver* [1977] 1 N.S.W.L.R. 67), so that the practitioner is not entitled to the safeguards available in other adversary proceedings, although natural justice (due process) must be respected. The onus of proving misconduct lies on the professional association, generally on the balance of probabilities, although the quantum of proof must increase with the seriousness of the charges and the consequences for the respondent (*Briginshaw* v. *Briginshaw* [1938] 60 C.L.R. 336; *New South Wales Bar Association* v. *Livesey* [1982] 2 N.S.W.L.R. 231).

Because the Law Society has the power to issue practicing certificates, it also may suspend or terminate them or impose conditions or restrictions (subject to appeal to the Supreme Court) when a solicitor is medically unfit, bankrupt, or in jail; when there is a question about trust accounts; or when there is a statutory breach or professional misconduct.

The elaborate bureaucracy protects practitioners. The New South Wales Law Reform Commission analyzed a large sample of complaints against solicitors handled by the New South Wales Law Society between 1974 and 1976. It found that 95.3 percent of complaints did not go beyond the first step. Of the 4.7 percent referred to the Complaints Committee, only one in four went as far as the disciplinary tribunal. Only 2 percent of all complaints resulted in the imposition of any sanction against the solicitor involved (NSWLRC, 1979a: 40).

The commission found that "a significant number of complaints against lawyers are not dealt with fairly and effectively" because of the Law Society's "excessive reluctance" to consider complaints of negligence, incompetence, and delay and its "unhelpful attitude to complainants"; the unduly limited reference to prior complaints against the same solicitor; the Law Society's "perfunctory investigation of many complaints" and its "excessive sympathy for, and leniency to, solicitors under investigation"; and the "excessive reluctance" to refer matters to the disciplinary tribunal (ibid., 7–8).

Far fewer complaints are received about barristers, probably because of their different relationship to clients. Barristers do not hold or deal with client money or bill clients directly, and they are less accessible to clients (ibid., 100). After analyzing three years of complaints against barristers, however, the New South Wales Law Reform Commission concluded that the bar's disciplinary procedures were as ineffective as those of the Law Society, for similar reasons (ibid., 107).

Negligence and delay were the two most common sources of client dissatisfaction (NSWLRC, 1980: 12–13). Disciplinary action focused mainly on dishonesty, however, even though the proportion of such complaints was only about 2 percent (ibid., 37). Of the fifty-five solicitors struck off the Roll in New South Wales between 1968 and 1978, fifty-four had committed trust account offenses (NSWLRC, 1979a: 40). Since then both the Law Society (1979) and the courts (Re Moulton [1981] 2 N.S.W.L.R. 736; Re Johns [1982] N.S.W.L.R. 1) have asserted that negligence, incompetence, or delay may amount to professional misconduct.

Among solicitors against whom complaints were filed, sole practitioners were overrepresented (47.4 percent of complaints but 28.3 percent of practitioners) and larger firms underrepresented: those with four to nine partners contained 23 percent of solicitors but received 12 percent of complaints; those with more than nine partners contained 10 percent to 11 percent of solicitors but received less than 1 percent of complaints (NSWLRC, 1980: 112). Of the eighty-two solicitors struck off between 1968 and 1982, sixty-seven (82 percent) were sole practitioners, and seven (9 percent) were in two-partner firms (Sydney Morning Herald 4 [December 5, 1981]; almost all had committed breaches of trust accounts. Fully 87 percent of complaints about large firms related to billing (NSWLRC, 1980: 45). Experience was no guarantee of probity: 85 percent of trust account complaints were made against solicitors with more than fifteen years' standing, although less than 40 percent of all solicitors had practiced that long (ibid., 41). Fewer complaints were filed against city solicitors in proportion to their numbers than against suburban and country solicitors (ibid., 13). Conveyancing (21.4 percent), probate (16.7 percent), family law (11.9 percent), other litigation (11.4 percent), and nonlitigious commercial matters (9.3 percent) accounted for the bulk of complaints, but it must be remembered that conveyancing and probate account for as much as 60 percent of solicitors' work (ibid., 11, 107). Delay (28.6 percent), negligence (13.1 percent), various aspects of billing (12.6 percent), and poor communications (8.3 percent) were the primary reasons for client dissatisfaction (ibid., 109).

In the last ten years all jurisdictions have required both solicitors and amalgams to purchase professional indemnity insurance, and all maintain fidelity funds, which reimburse the clients of defaulting solicitors for money or other property held in trust. There have been very few claims in the Australian Capital Territory, Tasmania, South Australia, Western Australia, and Queensland in the past ten years (NSWLRC, 1981c: 138). There have been a sizable number in Victoria, but they involve only three or four solicitors a year (out of about 4,000). One massive defalcation in 1976 accounted for most of the A$11.5 million the Victorian fund had to pay (ibid., 137). In New South Wales, however, there are many claims against solicitors for large amounts of money (see table 8). Indeed, the Law Reform Commission believes that New South Wales has the worst defalcation record in the English-speaking world (36 *Justinian* 7 [November 28, 1984]). The Law Society has noted, however, that the A$16 million paid out in claims between 1975 and 1982 is only 0.09 percent of the estimated A$20 billion handled by solicitors' trust accounts during that period (Garling, 1983: 127). Money placed with solicitors for investment on long-term mortgages was by far the most common source of problems, because clients do not make frequent inquiries about the funds and do not expect a regular accounting. The jump in claims since 1978 coincided with a slump in real property values compounded by high interest rates, making it difficult for solicitors to "pay back" funds improperly used for personal investments or expenditures. Defaulting solicitors usually had a very successful practice but often encountered personal problems, such as gambling or drinking (ibid., 128–129).

The fidelity funds are generated by compulsory payments from solicitors holding current practicing certificates (which contribute about 10 percent of the total) and the Solicitors Statutory Interest Accounts operated by the Law Society, into which solicitors must deposit a proportion of their trust funds based on their annual turnover (NSWLRC, 1981c: 167–173; Legal Practitioners Act 1983, s. 42A). Since 1980 the annual net income from these accounts in New South Wales has been about A$10 million (21 *Law Society Journal* 434.47 [1983]).

Clients or exclients with a grievance against a solicitor also may sue for negligence or breach of contract. Negligence requires more than a mere error of judgment; the solicitor's work must have fallen below that of the reasonably well informed and competent member of the profession (*Saif Ali* v. *Sydney Mitchell & Co.* [1978] 3 W.L.R. 849, 861). The solicitor also may owe a duty of care to third parties—for example, a beneficiary who suffers a loss as a result of a negligently prepared will (*Vulic* v. *Bilinsky* [1983] 2 N.S.W.L.R. 472).

Unlike Canada and New Zealand, Australia has not yet abandoned the House of Lords decision in *Rondel* v. *Worsley* ([1967] 3 W.L.R. 1666), which retained the common law immunity for barristers in the course of litigation and extended it to solicitors doing advocacy work, although the scope of the immunity has been limited somewhat with respect to preparatory work (*Saif Ali*, supra).

Aggrieved clients also may be able to invoke consumer protection legislation. The New South Wales Supreme Court held that a solicitor, although carrying on a business, could not be a "trader" within the meaning of consumer protection legislation (nor could physicians or dentists)

(*Holman* v. *Deol* [1979] 1 N.S.W.L.R. 640, 651). Subsequent amendments now permit a client or former client to sue a solicitor in the Consumer Claims Tribunal for up to A$1,500 in lieu of seeking common law damages (*Sydney Morning Herald 2* [October 26, 1979]).

PUBLIC FUNDING FOR LEGAL SERVICES: LEGAL AID

There is no constitutional right to counsel in Australia, and the courts have not developed common law doctrine sufficiently to find such a right either. In *McInnis* v. *R.* ([1979] 143 C.L.R. 575), an accused charged with rape, kidnapping, and assault was tried without benefit of counsel, who had withdrawn at the last moment when legal aid was refused by the Western Australian Legal Services Commission on the ground that the accused did not have a meritorious defence. Denied an adjournment, the accused represented himself and was convicted. On appeal, the High Court, over a lone stinging dissent, found that while "it is in the best interests of the administration of justice that an accused be ... represented," there is "no absolute right to legal aid" and no breach of natural justice if an accused is unable to obtain legal representation. While the *McInnis* decision has been "almost universally condemned" (Sallmann & Willis, 1984: 147), it remains the legal position in Australia.

Prior to the establishment of the Australian Legal Aid Office (ALAO) by the federal Labor government in 1973, legal aid was entirely the responsibility of the states except in the Australian Capital Territory, for which the federal government is responsible (see table 9). Legal aid at the state level was based on notions of charity rather than right; professional associations organized judicare schemes utilizing private practitioners. A small salaried staff in some states provided "public solicitor" and "public defender" representation of indigent defendants in criminal trials (Sackville, 1975: chaps. 2–3). Legal aid was funded primarily by interest on solictors' trust accounts, client contributions, and costs paid by losing litigants, although government was a major source in some of the smaller states (Western Australia—34.8 percent of the budget; South Australia—43.1 percent; Tasmania—76.1 percent). In 1972/73 about A$3.1 million was spent on Law Society legal aid schemes, less than 10 percent of which was contributed by state treasuries (ibid., 160–162).

Representation was unavailable for summary offenses in the magistrates' courts (where most criminal matters are heard) and for committal hearings, juvenile court hearings, and bail applications (ibid., 119–120). Legal aid was available for litigation but not for the many other services lawyers render to fee-paying clients (ibid., 122–123). The schemes provided no community education about legal rights or, indeed, about what legal services were available (ibid., 124–125). The legal aid schemes did not protect clients against the ruinous prospect of having costs awarded against them if they lost (Basten et al., 1985: 115). Even today, only New South Wales (Legal Assistance Act, s. 47) shields legally aided clients from costs and hosts a Public Interest Advocacy Centre. Finally, eligibility for legal aid was severely restricted by merit and means tests. Because the means test was not adjusted for inflation, 75 percent of the population of New South Wales were eligible for assistance in 1943, when the Public Solicitor's Office was established, but only 12.9 percent in 1973 (Sackville, 1975: 79, 140–141).

In mid-1973, a Labor government executive directive established the ALAO—a national program involving federal funding and using salaried lawyers (indeed, its control was overly centralized in the federal Attorney-General's Department) (Basten et al., 1985: 117; Armstrong, 1980: 221) The ALAO always was constitutionally suspect (Basten et al., 1985: 118; McMillan, 1975: 165), so that its services were restricted to those "for whom the federal government has a special responsibility," such as recipients of federal welfare pensions and those involved in proceedings before the (federal) Family Court.

The ALAO consciously was modeled on the U.S. Legal Services Program. Apart from providing individual legal advice and representation, it was supposed to engage in social activism by practicing "preventive law," pursuing "impact litigation," becoming involved in community organization and education, and lobbying for law reform (Chamberlain, 1981: 25; Basten et al., 1985: 117; Armstrong, 1980: 220–221). In fact, political controversy over the ALAO resulted in a "very orthodox legal aid service" resembling the British judicare model (Armstrong, 1980: 221). Salaried lawyers often became mere "high level clerical officers" responsible for assessing eligibility and assigning cases to private practitioners (ibid., 233–234).

Even the limited involvement of salaried lawyers provoked powerful attacks from the private profession and the judiciary. The Australian Capital Territory Supreme Court ruled that salaried lawyers were not entitled to act on behalf of legal aid clients because of the inherent conflict of interest when a lawyer is paid by one entity (the government) to represent another person (*Re Bannister; ex parte Hartstein* [1975] 5 A.C.T.R. 100). The Court also expressed concern about the threat to the "independent" status of the lawyers involved (and the profession generally) and the conflicts that would arise when legal aid lawyers proceeded against government agencies. The decision subsequently was nullified by legislation. The Victorian Law Institute challenged the ALAO's very existence in the High Court (McMillan, 1975: 165) but dropped the case when a conservative government came to power in 1975, which highlighted the political nature of the opposition (Basten et al., 1985: 118).

Prominent members of the judiciary remain hostile to legal aid. For example, the former Chief Justice of the High Court, Sir Garfield Barwick, has stated that legal aid

> imposes a serious threat to the administration of the law. When the profession is not restrained by the cost to the client the tendency is to explore every alley, however unprofitable and however blind ... what legal aid is doing is alerting men to legal rights which they would not otherwise have been bothered about. (*Justinian* 11 [June 1980]).

Similarly, Justice Rogers of the New South Wales Supreme Court has written that legal aid hinders the administration of justice by encouraging aided litigants to refuse to settle civil claims, to take "unmeritorious or unrealistic points," and to refuse to plead guilty (Rogers, 1981: 67). Justice Yeldham of the same court also has cautioned against any "deviation of legal aid funds from the private profession to salaried legal aid officers" lest there be created "a giant bureaucratic octopus employing hundreds of salaried legal advisers and promoting a breed of second and third class lawyers" (Yeldham, 1985: 16—17).

Federal expenditures on legal aid have increased from virtually nothing in 1972/73 to over A\$70 million in 1983/84, and total government funding has increased from about A\$3 million to over A\$100 million in the same period (see table 9), of which the private profession received 65 percent (Basten et al., 1985: 132). It is questionable whether governments can afford to maintain such generous levels of support to the private profession. Since 1979/80, federal payments for private lawyers have increased 80.2 percent in real terms, while the corresponding caseload increased only 27.1 percent (Attorney-General Evans in Commonwealth Senate, *Hansard* 928 [May 26, 1983]). In New South Wales the position is even worse and has prompted charges of "over-servicing" and "milking the system" (*Sydney Morning Herald* 2 [July 11, 1983]. Between 1979/80 and 1981/82, payments by the New South Wales Legal Services Commission to private lawyers in civil cases rose by 280 percent, while the caseload increased by only 11.5 percent (ibid.). At least one study (Meredith, 1983) purports to demonstrate that there is no significant difference in cost per case between legal assistance provided by salaried and private lawyers, but grave doubts have been expressed regarding the study's methodology and counterintuitive conclusions (Attorney-General Evans in Commonwealth Senate, *Hansard* 929—933 [May 26, 1983]).

After the governor-general sacked the Labor government in 1975, the caretaker conservative coalition government campaigned on a platform that included the abolition of the ALAO. With months of their electoral victory, however, the coalition parties responded to the strong public support for the ALAO and pledged not to disband it (Armstrong, 1980: 240—241). Instead, the ALAO became a part of the government's "New

Federalism" policy of returning to the states powers and responsibilities that had been centralized during the previous administration. The Commonwealth's involvement was restricted to distributing the funds and creating a national monitoring body (the Commonwealth Legal Aid Council [CLAC]) to coordinate the eight local commissions. The New Federalism's maintenance of constant funding levels during a period of sharply rising costs starved legal aid after 1975 (ibid., 249), and the Labor government had to double the federal contribution in its first full year in office (1983/84) (see table 9).

The Commonwealth government's original model for the states, contained in an Australian Capital Territory ordinance proposed in 1977, would have given the private profession at least seven representatives on an eleven-member body, compared to only one for consumers of legal aid. The proposal drew strong criticism in the media and from community legal centers and social welfare and public employee groups, and the Law Society's representation was reduced to a minority (Armstrong, 1980: 244). Queensland and Western Australia gave the profession effective control of their legal services commissions, reserving only one of seven places for a consumer representative (Khan & Hackett, 1977: 274). In Victoria, New South Wales, and South Australia the professional associations control fewer positions, but two-thirds of the commissioners still are lawyers.

Eligibility for assistance remains very limited, with the means test close to the poverty line (CLAC, 1984: 16–18, 24; 5[5] *Legal Aid Clearinghouse Bulletin* 160 [September–October 1984]). Legal assistance at reduced rates is available to some through membership in a trade union or other organization, but prepaid legal services have not yet captured the interest of the Australian public, although lawyers appear to favor such schemes (Evans, 1982: 4, 40). The ALAO devoted 80 percent of its time to family law matters (6 *Justinian* 12 [September 30, 1979]); public solicitor–public defender schemes focus on criminal law; and the judicare schemes also have concentrated in these areas (see table 10).

The mainstream legal services have continued to focus on individual litigation rather than activist lawyering and to utilize private practitioners instead of building up a corps of salaried lawyers. Two alternatives have been more innovative, however. The federally funded Aboriginal Legal Service (ALS) began in Sydney in the early 1970s as a result of initiatives by the Aboriginal community (rather than the government) and now is a network of seventeen bodies across Australia (Lyons, 1984: 138).

Although it operates as an orthodox legal aid agency, using white lawyers and a large number of Aboriginal paralegal field officers to provide representation in individual (mainly criminal) cases and welfare matters, ALS also has engaged in lobbying, community organization, and test-case litigation, particularly in support of the campaign for the recognition of Aboriginal land rights (Lyons, 1984: 145; Tatz, 1980: 91).

The community legal centers evolved as a result of the social activism and politicization of the late 1960s and early 1970s. They consciously embraced the political ideology and strategy of the welfare movement: "a commitment to 'grass-roots level activity, community control, empowering the recipient, deprofessionalization, assertion of rights, demystification and free access to services'" (Basten et al., 1975: 129). From the founding of the first center in Fitzroy, Victoria, in late 1972, the movement has expanded considerably, particularly in Victoria, New South Wales, and South Australia. There are about forty-five centers in Australia receiving funding from the federal government (about 2 percent of all legal aid expenditures) or states, but many others operate on a voluntary basis or with some private or local government support—twenty-eight in Victoria alone (Neal, 1984: 25). Reliance on volunteers—lawyers, students, counselors, and others—has been a distinguishing characteristic of *all* centers (Basten et al., 1985: 122).

The legal centers also have collected statistics, prepared submissions to governments and inquiries, engaged in community legal education and publications, planned campaigns, and lobbied (Basten et al., 1985: 126; Neal, 1984). They have developed expertise in areas other lawyers have ignored almost entirely, such as welfare rights (including representation at hearings), children, mental health, prisoners' rights, landlord-tenant law, consumer credit, and antidiscrimination. The centers have attacked (or ignored) traditional notions of professionalism by advertising, using paralegals and lay persons, and blurring the distinction between barristers and solicitors. They also have affected legal education by promoting clinical programs and "poverty law" electives, such as welfare, housing, and antidiscrimination law (Basten et al., 1985: 135). The legal centers have played an important political role by campaigning for increased funding for legal services independent of both the profession and the government, lobbying for broader representation on the legal aid commissions (and participating themselves), and supporting particular law reform efforts. Perhaps most important is the fact that they have been accepted by governments and the media as alternative voices on issues of law reform, legal aid, and social welfare, supplementing and occasionally supplanting the traditional conservative voice of the professional associations (ibid., 132).

THE CHANGING FACE OF LEGAL PRACTICE

For over a century, legal practice in Australia has been organized around the legal profession's monopoly over certain lucrative kinds of work, particularly conveyancing. That monopoly persists except in two states, whose vast territory, small population, isolation, and limited number of lawyers were key factors in the advent of paraprofessional land agents. In a country reputed to have the highest rate of private home ownership in the industrialized world, domestic conveyancing is not only the public's main point of contact with the legal profession but also a prime source of legal fees. A 1974 survey of Victorian solicitors revealed that 37 percent of the time and 47 percent of the income of solicitors' firms related to conveyancing (Hetherton, 1978: 80). In New South Wales, Tomasic and Bullard also found that conveyancing occupied much of the time of solicitors (over eleven hours per week for city solicitors, over fifteen hours per week for suburban and country solicitors) and accounted for a large part of their incomes (Tomasic & Bullard, 1978: 171, 215). A report commissioned by the New South Wales profession disclosed that in 1976, conveyancing and probate together accounted for 56 percent of the income of the average Sydney solicitor and 70 percent to 80 percent of the income of suburban and country solicitors (see table 11). Conveyancing accounts for as much as 80 percent of solicitor–client contact in New South Wales (Bowen, 1978: 24).

Australia is one of the pioneers of simplified land registration, and most conveyancing of registered title is routine work often handled by paralegal staff within the solicitor's office. With conveyancing fees generally determined by ad valorem scales, the work provides lawyers with "professional fees for clerical services" (Forbes, 1979: 227) and with windfall profits during property booms. Although sometimes justified as a means of subsidizing other important but less lucrative work (17 *Justinian* 14 [May 1981]), there is little evidence that this actually occurs and no argument why it should.

Although conveyancing is sufficiently widespread that most solicitors have an interest in protecting the monopoly, a few firms have captured much of the work. Fifteen firms in Sydney and about ten in Melbourne each handle upward of 2,000 conveyances per week. These firms have cultivated relationships with the main real estate agencies, banks, building societies, and credit unions and often have located their offices nearby. The solicitors' firms complete the conveyance very quickly, ensuring that the real estate agents' commissions are released promptly.

Comparisons of conveyancing costs dramatically demonstrate the effect of the legal monopoly. For example, an A$80,000 house conveyed in 1980 would have cost the purchaser A$757 in Victoria, A$612 in New South Wales, A$590 in Queensland, and A$424 in Western Australia, but A$244 when performed by a South Australian landbroker and A$162 by a Western Australian settlement agent (Nieuwenhuysen & Williams-Wynn, 1982: 30). South Australian lawyers have matched the fees of local landbrokers but still have captured only about 20 percent of the market (Forbes, 1979: 179 n. 27). Given the importance of the conveyancing monopoly to solicitors, it is not surprising that the Law Societies have aggressively prosecuted alleged breaches by nonlawyers (Forbes, 1979: 227) and that judicial interpretation of the often ambiguous or awkward provisions of the Legal Practitioners Acts has been favorable to the profession (see, e.g., *Law Society of N.S.W.* v. *Newlands* [1964] 81 W.N. 341).

In recent years, "cut-price conveyancing companies" have sprung up in New South Wales and Victoria, seeking loopholes in the monopoly by encouraging clients to do some of the work themselves (with advice or a kit) and paying friendly solicitors (more rarely barristers) by the hour to perform those acts reserved for qualified persons, such as drawing up the contracts of sale and engrossing documents. The Law Institute of Victoria proceeded against the cooperating solicitors for professional misconduct, such as touting and splitting fees with unauthorized persons (14 *Justinian* 12 [October 1980]; 16 *Justinian* 2 [March 1981]). In New South Wales the Law Society has prosecuted the cut-price conveyancers summarily under the Legal Practitioners Act and sought injunctive and other relief in the Supreme Court. One conveyancing entrepreneur, who also complained about the difficulty of finding a solicitor to represent him against the Law Society, stated that the Law Society's "technique is to bleed the companies to death with protracted and unnecessary litigation" (21 *Justinian* 4 [February 1982]).

The success of the conveyancing companies, as well as that of do-it-yourself kits for probate, name changes, simple divorces, company formation, and other relatively routine matters, has prompted the professional associations to engage in public relations campaigns, advertising in the mass media to extol both the greater competence and professionalism of solicitors and (paradoxically) the security against incompetence and fraud provided by fidelity funds and compulsory liability insurance, but this is unlikely to stem the tide. The task of establishing a computerized central register of all land records is well under way; proposals have been made to require vendor disclosures about title and restrictions and to standardize and simplify requisitions and inquiries of local and statutory authorities (29 *Justinian* 8 [February 29, 1984]; Cribb, 1985: 2). These measures would further undercut the justification for the solicitors' monopoly.

In 1980 a Ministerial Council on Housing Costs, composed of housing ministers from all Australian governments, called for "greater competition in the supply of conveyancing services" (29 *Justinian* 6 [February 29, 1984]). In 1981 the Victorian Consumer Affairs Council recommended that a system of conveyancing agents be established similar to that in South Australia and Western Australia (ibid.). In 1984 the New South Wales Law Reform Commission considered (without recommending) the relaxation of the monopoly to allow conveyancing by financial institutions, licensed law conveyancers, and government offices (ibid., 6–7).

Further pressure on fees for conveyancing and other services also will come from the competition stimulated by the recent liberalization in the rules regarding advertising by solicitors in Western Australia, Victoria, and New South Wales. No Australian jurisdiction has a specialization scheme, and solicitors may not claim superior expertise, although they may list fields of practice. Most advertisements have been placed by small firms in suburban newspapers, although there have been some on late-night television as well (*Sydney Morning Herald* 6 [October 5, 1985]). The larger firms have tended to be more subtle, placing notices about seminars and staff recruitment in the major newspapers. The Victorian Law Institute already has set up a Marketing Committee to assist solicitors with advertising (59 *Victoria Law Institute Journal* 1036 [1985]).

Another significant area of legal work under threat is personal injury. Hetherton found that 17.4 percent of the work done by Melbourne solicitors involved workers' compensation (5.5 percent), automobile accidents (9.5 percent), and other personal injury matters (2.4 percent) (Hetherton, 1978: 86). These areas were almost equally important to New South Wales lawyers (Tomasic & Bullard, 1978: table 89; Tomasic, 1983a: 445). Much of the workers' compensation and industrial accident work is channeled to a limited number of firms by the trade unions (NSWLRC, 1980: 43). Such cases are easily routinized, allowing personal injury lawyers (both solicitors and barristers) to carry large caseloads. Because liability may be strict or presumed and the overwhelming proportion of cases are settled, and because most defendants are insured, this area pays well, if it is not particularly prestigious (Tomasic & Bullard, 1978: 38).

Australia prohibits contingent fees (*Re Veron, ex parte Law Society of N.S.W.* [1966] 84 W.N. 136; *Re Evatt* [1967] 67 S.R. [New South Wales] 236, [1968] 117 C.L.R. 177; *Clyne* v. *N.S.W. Bar Association* [1960] 104 C.L.R. 186, 202). Although some solicitors will handle a matter "on spec," it is much less common for a barrister to risk earning no fee if the case is lost (*National Times* 42 [March 1, 1985]). Recently, however, the New South Wales Law Society questioned the prohibition, citing the problems of middle-income earners who neither can afford the costs of litigation nor are eligible for legal aid (ibid.).

At the same time, new areas of lawyering have emerged. The explosion of administrative and regulatory law in the past decade has created a "veritable bonanza" for lawyers in such areas as trade practices (antitrust) (Mendelsohn & Lippman, 1979: 89), finance and securities, industrial and intellectual property, media, and natural resources and the environment. In the 1970s, lawyers began to compete aggressively with accountants and tax avoidance entrepreneurs in such areas as tax advising and business planning (Ross, 1976: 66). The prevalence of combined degree programs at universities and the popularity of the law–accounting combination mean that an increasing proportion of lawyers will have accounting qualifications (and vice versa). At the University of New South Wales, for example, over one-third (34.2 percent) of all combined law degree students in 1985 were studying accounting, and more than half (53 percent) combined law with some commerce discipline. There still is considerable room for growth in these areas. For example, while lawyers have been intimately involved in the recent corporate takeover fever, most of the leading advisers in New South Wales are merchant bankers. The loss of income from conveyancing, probate, and personal injury—which together may account for some 80 percent of the average solicitor's earnings in the large eastern states—threatens the continued viability of solo and small firm practice, particularly in the suburbs and the country. Ethical and legal restrictions on solicitors' mortgage finance companies and nominee companies, which are very profitable spin-offs from conveyancing, have further eroded the incomes of general practitioners, particularly in the country (Ackland, 1983: 38).

This is not to suggest that the forms of private practice have changed radically or are likely to do so soon. Sole practitioners still make up 63 percent of all law firms in Australia (see table 12). Ninety percent of all law firms have fewer than four partners, and only eighty-five firms have more than nine. Fifty-seven of those larger firms are in Melbourne and Sydney (see table 12), and almost all the rest are in other capital cities (Meredith, 1978: 349). Solicitors rely heavily on subordinate labor. In the average New South Wales firm there was one employed solicitor and three office staff for every principal (ibid., 350). Sole practitioners' firms contained an average of six people, while firms with more than four principals averaged forty-eight. Employed solicitors have been increasing as a proportion of the profession during the last forty years, especially in states dominated by capital cities; in 1985 they constituted 28 percent of all solicitors (Disney et al., 1986: 56–57). Small firms are struggling, with overheads rising faster than fees (Meredith, 1978: 358). The New South Wales Law Society has established a scheme to assist lawyers in trouble, which expects to handle hundreds of inquiries (Angly, 1983: 41). Hetherton (1978: 141) found that Melbourne solicitors were more likely to fear competition from lay organizations of accountants, financial advisers, tax consultants, and lay conveyancers than from specialist solicitors, large firms, or salaried lawyers in corporations or legal aid. In recent years in the Sydney metropolitan area there have been attempts to promote group legal services (33 *Justinian* 2 [August 20, 1984]) and "legal clinics," which have advertised on television and opened offices within major department stores for "one stop shopping" (*Sydney Morning Herald* 6 [October 5, 1985]).

The large corporate law firm also has emerged in Australia in the past two decades. Until well into the 1950s, solicitors' firms were essentially small family concerns. Even the "leading firms" consisted of only a few partners and a large body of law clerks (Mendelsohn & Lippman, 1979: 79–82). The clerk system began breaking down as better-paying white-collar jobs lured away potential applicants. The permanent clerks were replaced by articled clerks seeking admission as solicitors, and a large proportion were retained once they qualified, increasing the cost of legal services. The large firms steadily shed family law, criminal law, and conveyancing in favor of work from corporations and governments (ibid., 90). These firms also corporatized their own personalities, replacing "the character of a partnership of individuated legal practitioners" with a body of increasingly specialized "organization men" who handle only a discrete portion of a complex legal problem (ibid., 93–95). The large corporate law firms initially were limited to a single capital city (usually the main centers of commerce and finance, Sydney and Melbourne), referring work to law firms in other cities when necessary.

After a period of growth and consolidation, however, the big firms began to seek mergers and other linking arrangements in order to achieve economies of scale, offer a broader range of specialist services, establish national coverage and sometimes overseas offices, compete with accountants and merchant bankers, and attract or keep corporate clients that are increasingly willing to "shop around" (Crisp, 1985: 20; Bowne, 1984: 25; 21 Justinian 11 [February 1982]). The first significant interstate merger occurred in 1974, between one of the largest law firms in Sydney and a Canberra firm, giving the former access to the burgeoning work in trade practices and other areas of federal business regulation. In 1979 another large Sydney firm joined with a leading commercial firm in Perth, establishing a precedent that has been followed often.

In the 1980s virtually all the leading firms in Sydney and Melbourne expanded in size and number of locations through merger or confederation, and medium-sized firms engaged in an "enormous amount of merger activity" in order to keep pace (Crisp, 1985: 20). Partnerships are limited to 20 by the companies legislation in the various jurisdictions. After submissions from the profession, the Ministerial Council for Companies and Securities, which is composed of the state and federal attorneys-general, raised the ceiling for solicitors' firms to 50 in New South Wales and Victoria in 1965, then to 100, and finally to 200 in 1985 (Disney et al., 1986: 60 n. 40). In 1984, leading Sydney, Melbourne, and Perth firms (with a Canberra branch and a Brisbane agency) created what probably is Australia's largest law firm, with over 90 partners and 150 other solicitors. The linkage was described as a "federation" rather than a merger. A joint partnership is run by a national committee, but the constituent firms retain their local identities, at least for the time being, and profits are not pooled (*Sydney Morning Herald* 17 [July 19, 1984]; 32 *Justinian* 3 [August 1984]). Intrastate mergers also are very common. In 1984 one of Sydney's leading commercial law firms merged with two medium-sized firms possessing special expertise in planning and environmental law, family law, insurance, and taxation, creating the fifth largest practice in Sydney (30 *Justinian* 2 [April 1984]). In the same year, four of the leading firms in Melbourne merged two-by-two, and one of the new firms—Melbourne's largest— now has established a Sydney office (*Sydney Morning Herald* 21 [June 18, 1984]; 17 [July 19, 1984]).

Because commercial work has been more concentrated in Sydney than in Melbourne (Crisp, 1985: 20), the largest firms in Sydney are considerably larger than those in Melbourne (Wilson, 1983: 36). The enduring Sydney–Melbourne rivalry has meant that leading firms in each city are more interested in linking with firms in other capital cities, particularly Canberra and Perth, than with each other (ibid.). In late 1983 one of the leading Melbourne commerical law firms sent three of its senior partners to establish an office in Sydney—the first time one of the large firms attempted to tackle the rivalry head on, rather than relying on the traditional referral and agency arrangements (*Sydney Morning Herald* 32 [October 15, 1983]). A number of more aggresive medium-sized firms have effected Sydney–Melbourne mergers in the past few years as well, and the barriers appear to be falling.

The larger firms also have sought to expand their international connections. One leading Sydney firm has established a network of associated firms in Singapore, Papua New Guinea, Japan, France, Israel, and Holland (32 *Justinian* 3 [August 1984]). A Melbourne firm opened the first London office in 1974, followed by two Perth firms in 1979, and a Sydney firm opened the first New York office in 1979 (*Sydney Morning Herald* 13 [December 18, 1979]). Offices in these international financial centers are more common now, as are offices in the regionally important centers of Singapore and Hong Kong. Two leading American law firms established offices in Australia—one in Sydney (in the late 1970s) and one in Melbourne (in 1983) (Wilson, 1983: 36).

The emergence of the megafirm probably poses a greater threat to the survival of a separate Bar than any political action. Until the growth of the large corporate law firms in the late 1960s, "the bar continued to attract the lion's share of talented university graduates in law" (Mendelsohn & Lippman, 1979: 82). Today the leading solicitors' firms hire the top graduates and can provide the prestige, varied and challenging work, and level of remuneration and perquisites to keep them. The large firms all have litigation departments but still brief counsel for advocacy in the higher courts. Less advice is sought from barristers, however, and the Bar no longer has a monopoly on specialized knowledge (ibid., 97). Large firms have the advantages that flow from size as well as direct client contact. At the other end of the spectrum, many small firms of solicitors are hanging on to advocacy work, for which they previously would have briefed junior barristers, in order to compensate for the downturn in conveyancing and other traditional solicitors' work (Bowne, 1983: 11).

The stratification of the Australian legal profession compels caution in interpreting "average" income data. Nevertheless, the mean income of barristers is considerably higher than that of the other categories of private practitioners, and it is followed by city solicitors, country solicitors, and suburban solicitors (whether measured by the income of principals or that of employed solicitors) (NSWLRC, 1981a: 86; Tomasic & Bullard, 1978: 49, 53; Hetherton, 1978: 41–47; 17 *Justinian* 4 [May 1981]).

Of course, there is a great deal of variation within the bar, with the "high-flying"20 percent getting 80 percent of the work while "the very junior bar is starving" (Bowne, 1983: 11). Leading Sydney Queen's Counsel were commanding A$3,000 to A$5,000 per day in 1985 for commercial matters, and even the Commonwealth government paid A$1,250 per day to senior counsel. According to the Chief Judge of the Federal Court, a "reasonably successful" New South Wales Queen's Counsel earns A$250,000 per year (net before tax) and the most successful senior counsel, considerably more (*Sydney Morning Herald* 3 [March 8, 1984]). As a result, senior counsel have been reluctant to accept appointments to the bench, even to the prestigious state supreme courts and the Federal Court, where salaries are A$75,000 to $A90,000 (ibid.). Well-established junior barristers in the main capital cities gross between A$50,000 and A$100,000 (Bowne, 1983: 11–12; *Sydney Morning Herald* 1 [August 12, 1983]). A large proportion of barristers, however, particularly those with less than six years' experience, are grossing only A$20,000 to A$30,000 (ibid.). Overheads can be substantial, averaging 30 percent (NSWLRC, 1981b: 435). In Sydney, barristers' chambers traditionally have been purchased rather than rented (as they are in Melbourne), and chambers on a "good floor" (i.e., one that attracts a large amount of business) cost as much as A$200,000 to A$300,000 (*Sydney Morning Herald* 28 [December 2, 1985]). In the newer chambers, rooms rent for A$800 to A$1,000 per month, although some cost as much as A$2,000 (Bowne, 1983: 11).

The spread of solicitors' incomes is at least as great. Partners in the four leading Sydney firms earn A$250,000 or more per year, and those in the other medium to large corporate firms earn about A$150,000 (Bowne, 1984: 25). Some large firms divide the profits equally among all partners, but most allocate on the basis of performance, such as business brought in or billable hours. One of the largest Sydney firms recently disclosed that its forty-three partners divided over A$8 million in profits on A$23 million

of annual billings, for a profit margin of 35 percent. Surplus value undoubtedly accounted for much of the profit: employed solicitors earned an
average of A$26,000, while most bill at least three times their salaries
(ibid.).

Most solicitors, however, have relatively modest incomes—perhaps
A$25,000 for a principal in a small firm in New South Wales (Meredith,
1978: 69–70; Tomasic & Bullard, 1978: 48–49; *National Times* 48 [July 26,
1981]). Overheads are higher for solicitors than barristers—60 percent to
70 percent of fees (NSWLRC, 1981*b*: 435) and as much as 75 percent in the
big city firms (Angly, 1983: 41)—mainly because of greater client contact
and fiduciary responsibilities. The Law Council of Australia has calculated
that the profitability of solicitor's practices in Victoria recently has been
declining by 15 percent a year (*National Times* 48 [July 26, 1981]), with the
smaller firms suffering more (Bowne, 1983: 13).

Over the past thirty years, the real incomes of Australian lawyers have
declined rapidly against average male earnings, while incomes in medicine
have kept pace, and those in architecture, accounting, and dentistry have
increased substantially (Disney et al., 1977: 372). The declining profitability of small solicitors' practices coincided with the increasing output of
law school graduates, and it is young lawyers who have borne the brunt of
the economic difficulties. A 1983 survey by the Young Lawyers' Committee of the New South Wales Law Society revealed that the average annual
salary of solicitors under thirty-six in private practice less than five years
was A$14,015, which is just under the average male income in that state
(New South Wales *Law Society Journal* 360 [June 1985]). In Western Australia, by contrast, law firms have been complaining about a shortage of
graduates, and the University of Western Australia Law School has increased its student intake.

CONCLUSION

Twenty-five years ago, the Australian legal profession was composed
of numerous small firms and, in the divided jurisdictions, a small separate bar. Even the "leading firms" contained only a few solicitors supported by a large cast of law clerks, and they maintained a presence in
only one city. Solicitors' work consisted mainly of conveyancing, probate, and personal injury, protected by statutory monopolies rigorously
enforced by the professional associations and courts. Only a small
proportion of lawyers were salaried. The division of the profession was
relatively rigid, and in the early 1960s separate bars were established
even in the formally fused jurisdictions.

The profession also was highly fragmented geographically, with little interstate mobility. There were no significant national professional associations and little Commonwealth involvement in or funding of legal services. The court system was organized around the states, until the Federal Court and the Family Court of Australia were established.

Each state had one university law faculty, none of which could claim to be a "national" school. A few full-time academics were supported by many more part-time teachers who practiced full time. In New South Wales and Queensland, a large proportion of lawyers had qualified for admission through articled clerkships or Admission Board programs without taking university law degrees. Law students and lawyers were overwhelmingly male and drawn from privileged backgrounds.

The profession maintained substantial control over admissions, discipline and regulation, fee setting, and restrictive practices. Legal aid was organized by the law societies and funded mostly from the interest on solicitors' trust accounts.

In some respects the legal profession has not changed greatly in the last quarter century. While the profession has been substantially feminized (in composition, if not philosophy), most lawyers still come from elite social backgrounds. Given the ascendance of university law schools, the balance is likely to tip even further in favor of privilege. Governments have not sought to redress this situation, beyond providing some financial assistance to students from disadvantaged backgrounds who are able to obtain admission to law school in a very competitive environment. In a 1978 submission to the New South Wales Law Reform Commission, the New South Wales Law Society stated that it did not maintain records of the socioeconomic backgrounds of its members, nor did it regard this as relevant information, since "the socio-economic background of the members of the profession does not affect the ability of the legal profession to render legal services for all sectors of the community and does not make the profession unsympathetic to the needs of the disadvantaged sectors" (Law Society of New South Wales, 1978: 14–15). Fitzgerald has found a link between social background and willingness to do poverty law work (1977: 28), however, and Tomasic (1983a: 453) found that a New South Wales lawyer's first job was affected by "type of schooling and parental occupations" and that there are "significant correlations between last and first law offices in terms of their size and location."

The Australian legal profession remains geographically divided. Most legal services are concentrated in the capital cities, and there is little linkage between the professions in the various states and territories. The Law Council of Australia is only a loose confederation of autonomous state associations. Interstate mobility still is very limited, both because of obstacles to reciprocal admission and because the larger population is relatively immobile. Some of the smaller jurisdictions, such as Tasmania and the Northern Territory, which traditionally have permitted appearances by out-of-state lawyers in individual cases, appear to be tightening up. Perhaps the most significant trend toward a national identity is the emergence of large corporate law firms, which rapidly are expanding across state and national boundaries.

The Australian legal profession also remains remarkably autonomous, having weathered the attacks of the 1960s and 1970s. State and territorial associations control admission, discipline, and many aspects of practice. Salaried legal aid services have grown, but the private profession still provides the bulk of legal aid, receives most of the government funds allocated to this area, and has a major (often majority) representation on the state legal services commissions.

Legal practice has become somewhat more varied in the past few decades, however. While the great majority of law graduates still enter private practice (80 percent of the New South Wales College of Law's 1984 graduates who reported having secured employment within six months of completion), there now are more alternatives. Salaried legal services—in both government offices and independent community legal centers—have expanded significantly, and many more lawyers work for the state and Commonwealth governments. Government lawyers now represent 10 percent to 15 percent of the profession (DEIR, 1983: 89). There also are more lawyers working as in-house counsel for corporations and in other capacities in the commercial and financial sectors (Hoskins, 1978: 9).

The legal academy also has grown considerably in the past twenty-five years, although it has become more differentiated from the practicing profession as full-time academics replaced practitioners teaching part time (Halliday, 1981). Academics have begun to create a descriptive and critical legal literature and have broadened the curriculum. The number of faculties granting LL.B. degrees has doubled, which greatly increased the number of law students and young lawyers.

The Australian legal profession always has asserted its "professional" status and demanded the appropriate income even when most lawyers qualified through apprenticeship and much of the work (conveyancing and probate) was routine. Now, when large numbers of lawyers with academic training are being produced, the economic base of the small firm is under threat. The professional associations have been dominated by elite lawyers and have not, until recently, devoted much attention to the problems of young inexperienced lawyers, small firms, or employed solicitors. One of the major challenges facing professional associations today is to accommodate the large numbers of young lawyers whose disaffection could threaten the unity that has helped to preserve professional autonomy.

The solicitor's traditional staples of conveyancing, probate, and personal injury will continue to decline. Increased competition among lawyers and with nonlawyers, as well as law reform initiatives and advances in information technology, will result in lower fees and will deprive lawyers of some of the work that has been secured by statutory monopolies. The sole practitioner or small firm will either have to increase volume or acquire new areas of expertise. Pursuit of the latter course is likely to result in larger firms.

The traditional justification for the divided profession has been to provide specialist advice and advocacy work on behalf of a large mass of general practitioners (solicitors). When separate bars emerged in the fused professions in South Australia and Western Australia in the 1960s, it appeared that division was the dominant trend. While the separate bar is not immediately threatened, the trend of the 1980s appears to be division of a very different sort. Solicitors are likely to bifurcate into high-volume legal clinics for the routine representation of individuals and large corporate firms able to offer a wide variety of specialist services. The latter category already has begun to challenge the Bar's prestige, expertise, and income. The ultimate outcome will be a unitary legal profession—albeit one that is highly stratified and differentiated.

Tables

6.1. Population per Lawyer, by State and Territory,[a] 1938/39–1985

Year	ACT	NSW	Vic	Tas	Qld	SA	WA	NT	Total Australia
1938/39	—	1,500	1,900	1,800	2,300	1,900	2,300	—	1,340
1954	—	1,400	1,900	2,300	2,650	2,500	3,250	—	—
1968	950[b]	300[b]	1,700	2,400	2,570	2,700	2,900	—	1,600
1977	597	794	846	1,346	1,422	1,606	2,126	—	1,000[b]
1985	509	573	658	1,030	989	974	1,102	840	693
(N)[c]	(464)	(9,347)	(6,134)	(420)	(2,500)	(1,377)	(1,238)	(160)	(21,640)

[a] *Abbreviations:* ACT—Australian Capital Territory; NSW—New South Wales; Vic—Victoria; Tas—Tasmania; Qld—Queensland; SA—South Australia; WA–Western Australia; NT—Northern Territory.

[b] Estimated.

[c] Number of lawyers in 1985.

Sources: 1938–1968—Disney et al. (1986: 49); 1977—Tomasic (1983a: 449); 1985—lawyer figures supplied by the various professional associations; general population figures from Cameron (1985: 77).

6.2. LL.B. Students by State, 1950–1984

State	1950	1960	1965	1975	1980	1984
NSW	750	769	792	2,798	3,876	3,804
Vic	419	1,005	1,299	2,431	2,232	2,024
Qld	66	147	144	891	903	842
SA	109	130	315	607	666	740
WA	74	95	176	390	394	397
Tas	33	71	107	169	270	286
ACT	15	40	206	631	640	669
Total	1,466	2,257	3,039	7,917	8,981	8,762

Sources: CBCS (1952: 6–7; 1960: 10; 1965: 12); Universities Commission (1975: 6); CTEC (1981: 11; 1984: 12)

6.3. Population per Solicitor in New South Wales, 1954–1973

Year	NSW	Sydney city	Sydney suburbs	Total metropolitan	Country
1954	1,400	140	9,700	1,250	1,700
1961	1,300	110	6,300	1,200	1,550
1966	1,350	40	5,250	1,100	2,100
1971	1,200	30	3,400	900	2,100
1973	1,100	20	3,200	860	1,800

Source: Law Society of New South Wales (1978: 2).

6.4. Active Women Solicitors in New South Wales

Year	Number	Percent of all active solicitors
1950	15	1.0
1958	65	3.0
1969	161	5.0
1975	304	6.0
1984	1,056	13.7
1986	1,419	16.1

Sources: 1950–1975—Disney et al. (1977: 188); 1984 —Hunt (1984: 739–740); 1986—24 *New South Wales Law Society Journal* 50 (May 1986).

6.5. Distribution of Active Women Solicitors in New South Wales by
Type of Work, 1977, 1984

Type of work	Percent women	
	1977	1984
City solicitor	6.6	16.5
Suburban solicitor	3.2	11.6
Country solicitor	5.6	6.5
Corporation lawyer	4.2	20.6
Government lawyer	3.8	23.8
Barrister	4.1	7.1

Sources: 1977—Tomasic & Bullard (1978: 172); 1984—Hunt (1984: 739–740).

6.6. Religion of New South Wales Lawyers, 1978

Religious grouping	Percent lawyers	Percent in community
Church of England or Anglican	33.0	33.9
Catholic	30.0	30.7
Methodist, Uniting, or Presbyterian	15.0	12.8
Jewish	3.1	0.9
No religion	11.0	9.6
Other	6.9	12.5

Sources: Lawyers—Tomasic (1980: 187, table 1); population—Skinner (1985: 53).

6.7. Type of Secondary Schooling of Lawyers and Population (in Percent)

Group	State schools	Independent	Catholic
Australian university law students 1965[a]	32.0	33.0	29.0
Victorian lawyers 1976[b]	27.7	44.9	24.8
New South Wales lawyers 1977[b]	40.6	32.8	17.3
University of New South Wales law student intake 1985[c]	40.0	26.0	31.0

Sources: [a]Anderson & Western (1967: 70); [b]Tomasic (1983a: 451–452); [c]University of New South Wales Registrar.

6.8. New South Wales Fidelity Fund Claims Experience, 1973–1982

Year	Claims admitted	Number of solicitors involved	Amount paid, A$
1973	NA	NA	498,000
1975	NA	NA	773,544
1976	55	19	1,461,213
1977	145	18	1,130,971
1978	245	28	1,716,253
1979	203	32	1,866,576
1980	446	36	4,506,325
1981	231	23	2,964,251
1982	NA	NA	2,155,006

Sources: Claims admitted and number of solicitors involved—NSWLRC (1981c: 136); amounts paid out on claims—Garling (1983: 127).

6.9. Expenditures on Civil and Criminal Legal Aid in Australia, 1971–1984

Year[a]		NSW	Vic	Qld	SA	WA	Tas	ACT	NT	Other	Total	Commonwealth and state total
						State or Territory						
1971/72	C	0	0	0	0	0	0	14	0	257	271	
1972/73	S	616	1,187	239	338	173	82	0	0		2,645	2,916
	C	0	0	0	0	0	0	108	0	258	366	
1973/74	C	731	558	296	187	166	62	120	60	368	2,547	
1974/75	C	1,444	1,023	567	569	397	336	349	175	767	5,627	
1975/76	C	3,882	2,783	1,648	747	968	737	923	336	503	12,528	
1976/77	C	6,808	4,282	3,380	1,583	2,290	918	980	1,016	580	21,837	
1977/78	C	6,908	4,789	3,749	1,856	3,085	1,041	1,087	1,016	538	24,067	
1978/79	C	6,917	5,327	4,126	2,363	3,007	1,128	1,289	1,156	885	26,198	
1979/80	C	6,923	5,487	4,922	2,414	3,816	1,217	1,397	1,597	913	28,685	
1980/81	S	12,913	7,254	4,109	1,376	1,206	250	179	33		27,320	
	C	7,437	6,779	3,844	2,721	3,289	1,763	1,511	818		28,162	55,482
1981/82	S	17,272	9,139	5,023	1,126	1,502	210				34,272	
	C	9,515	9,182	4,162	3,695	5,005	2,225	1,796	996		36,576	70,848
1983/84	C	13,510	17,879	8,449	7,711	5,153	2,840	1,942	1,239	11,300	70,023	

[a] Abbreviations: C—Commonwealth; S—state and other.

Source: Abel (1985: 632).

6.10. Subject Matter of Legal Aid Cases in Australia, %

	Family	Housing	Employment	Welfare	Consumer or personal injury	Other civil	Criminal	Number of cases
Law Society schemes								
1971/72								
Victoria	61					29	10	5,553
Queensland	79					21	0.3	4,017
South Australia	42					11	32	4,079
Western Australia	67					19	15	1,173
Tasmania	64					15	21	1,625
1972/73								
Victoria	61					29	11	8,546
Queensland	80					0.6	20	4,623
South Australia	44					22	34	4,264
Western Australia	76					16	8	2,197
Tasmania	62					17	22	NA
1973/74								
New South Wales	75						25	2,420
Victoria	60					25	15	9,158
Queensland	75					25	0.6	6,149
South Australia	43					23	34	5,214
Western Australia	79					12	9	2,773
Tasmania	68					11	21	NA

Victoria Legal Aid Committee 1978	52	—	2.2	—	15	27		
Fitzroy legal services								
1978	21.6	10.6	4.3	1.3	30	13	22.9	
1982	18	6	2	1	34	15	27	187
Redfern Legal Centre 1982	22	12	2	3	33	15	17	175
Caxton St. Legal Centre 1982	20	9	2	3	25	25	16	3,096

Source: Abel (1985:636).

6.11. Percentage of Total Income New South Wales Solicitors Derive from
Conveyancing and Probate, by Location of Practice, 1973 and 1976

Type of work	Sydney city		Sydney suburbs		NSW country	
	1973	1976	1973	1976	1973	1976
Conveyancing	48	45	61	69	60	57
Probate	12	11	11	11	14	13
Total	60	56	72	80	74	70

Source: G. G. Meredith, *Report to the Profession* (University of New England, 1977) as quoted in NSWLRC (1980: 43).

6.12. Distribution of Solicitors' Firms by Size, 1985

Size	NSW	Vic	Qld	SA	WA	Tas	ACT	NT	Total Australia
Sole practitioner (%)	59	69	60	60	67	44	58	75	63
2–3 partners (%)	32	21	30	21	23	32	31	13	27
4–9 partners (%)	8	8	9	9	7	22	10	13	8
10–19 partners (no.)	8	31	5	11	5	1	—	—	61
20 or more partners (no.)	11	7	2	1	3	—	—	—	24

Note: Law firms with ten or more partners are not reported in percentages because of the small numbers involved.
Source: Disney et al. (1986: 58–59).

REFERENCES

Abel, Richard. 1985. "Law Without Politics: Legal Aid Under Advanced Capitalism," 32 *UCLA Law Review* 474.

Ackland, Richard. 1983. "The Easy Days Are Ending for Fringe Financiers," *National Times* 38 (December 16).

Altman, Dennis. 1980. *Rehearsals for Change—Politics and Culture in Australia.* Melbourne: Fontana Books.

Anderson, D. S., R. Boven, P. J. Fensham, and J. P. Powell. 1980. *Students in Australian Higher Education: A Study of Their Social Composition Since the Abolition of Fees.* Canberra: Australian Government Publishing Service.

Anderson, D. S., and J. S. Western. 1967. "Notes on a Study of Professional Socialization," 3 *Australian and New Zealand Journal of Sociology* 67.

————. 1970. "Social Profiles of Students in Four Professions," 3(4) *Quarterly Review of Australian Education* 1.

Anderson, D. S., J. S. Western, and P. R. Boreham. 1978. "Law and the Making of Legal Practitioners," in R. Tomasic, ed., *Understanding Lawyers*. Sydney: The Law Foundation of New South Wales and George Allen & Unwin.

Angly, Patricia. 1983. "No Justice for Lawyers as Recession Cuts Profit Margins," *National Times* 41 (April 15).

Armstrong, Susan. 1980. "Labor's Legal Aid Scheme: The Light that Failed," in R. B. Scotton and Helen Ferber, eds., *Public Expenditures and Social Policy in Australia*, vol. II. Melbourne: Longman Cheshire.

Australian Bureau of Statistics (ABS). 1984. *Tertiary Education, New South Wales 1983*. Sydney: ABS.

Australian Mathematical Society. 1985. "Mathematics Graduates Are Highly Employable." Sydney: Australian Mathematical Society (Information Bulletin).

Australian National Opinion Poll (ANOP). 1979. "An Attitude Study Amongst N.S.W. Solicitors." Unpublished paper prepared for the Law Society of New South Wales.

Balmford, Rosemary, and W. B. Hutchinson. 1978. "Australian Legal Practice Courses," in R. Balmford, ed., *Legal Education in Australia*. Melbourne: Australian Law Council Foundation.

Basten, John. 1982. "Control of the Legal Profession," in *Power in Australia: Directions of Change*. Canberra: Centre for Continuing Education, Australian National University.

Basten, John, Regina Graycar, and David Neal. 1985. "Legal Centres in Australia," 7 *Law & Policy* 113.

Basten, John, and Paul Redmond. 1979. "Character Review of Intending Lawyers," 3 *University of New South Wales Law Journal* 117.

Baxter, Stephen. 1983. "An Analysis of the Social Backgrounds of the Justices of the High Court of Australia." Unpublished paper, Sydney University.

Beed, T. W., and I. G. Campbell. 1977. "Supply and Demand Factors Associated with the Legal Profession of New South Wales." University of Sydney Sample Survey Centre (Occasional Paper No. 1).

Bennett, J. M., ed. 1969. *A History of the New South Wales Bar*. Sydney: Law Book Company.

Boer, Ben, ed. 1981. *Legal Aid Research in Australia: Workshop Proceedings*. Canberra: Commonwealth Legal Aid Council.

Bowen, Jan, ed. 1978. *The Legal Labour Market*. Sydney: New South Wales Foundation.

Bowen Report. 1979. *Legal Education in N.S.W.: Report of Committee of Inquiry*. Sydney: Government Printer, New South Wales.

Bowne, Angela. 1983. "Where the Fees Will Fall," *Business Review Weekly* 11 (August 20).

————. 1984. "Top Law Firm Learns to Live with the 80s," *Business Review Weekly* 25 (August 4).

Brennan, F. G. 1978. "Limits on the Use of Judges," 9 *Federal Law Review* 1.

Broom, Leonard, P. Duncan-Jones, F. Lancaster Jones, and Patrick McDonnell. 1977. *Investigating Social Mobility*. Canberra: Australian National University Research School of Social Sciences, Department of Sociology (Departmental Monograph No. 1).

Brown, David. 1984. "Judging the Judges," *Australian Society* 21 (April 1).

Brown, W. Jethro. 1908. "Law Schools and the Legal Profession," 6 *Commonwealth Law Review* 3.

Cameron, R. J. 1985. *Year Book Australia 1985*. Canberra: Australian Bureau of Statistics.

Castles, Alex. 1971. *An Introduction to Australian Legal History*. Sydney: Law Book Company.

Chamberlain, Edna R. 1981. *Legal Services for Low Income Persons in the United States and Britain*. Canberra: Commonwealth Legal Aid Council.

Clarkson Report. 1983. *Report of the Committee of Inquiry into the Future Organisation of the Legal Profession of Western Australia*. Perth: Government Printer, Western Australia.

Commonwealth Bureau of Census and Statistics (CBCS). 1952. *University Statistics 1950*. Canberra: CBCS.

————. 1960. *University Statistics 1960*. Canberra: CBCS.

————. 1965. *University Statistics 1965*. Canberra: CBCS.

Commonwealth Legal Aid Council (CLAC). 1984. *Summary of Eligibility Criteria of the A.L.A.O. and Legal Aid Commissions Throughout Australia*. Canberra: CLAC.

Commonwealth Tertiary Education Commission (CTEC). 1981. *Selected University Statistics 1980*. Canberra: CTEC.

————. 1984. *Selected University Statistics 1984*. Canberra: CTEC.

Cosgrove, H. E. 1970. *The Teaching of Law Students or Graduates the Techniques of Practical Application to Real Problems of Learned Law*. Hobart: Winston Churchill Memorial Trust (Report No. 9).

Cranston, Ross. 1978. "Law and Society: A Different Approach to Legal Education," 5 *Monash University Law Review* 54.

Crawford, James. 1982. *Australian Courts of Law*. Melbourne: Oxford University Press.

Cribb, Tim. 1985. "Seller Beware In Land Deals," *Sydney Morning Herald* 2 (August 20).

Crisp, Lyndall. 1985. "Fewer but Bigger Law Firms Ahead," *National Times* 20 (March 22).

Daniel, Ann. 1983. *Power, Privilege and Prestige—Occupations in Australia*. Melbourne: Longman Cheshire.

Department of Education and Youth Affairs. 1984. *Directory of Higher Education Courses 1985*. Canberra: Australian Government Publishing Service.

Department of Employment and Industrial Relations (DEIR). 1983. *Employment Prospects by Industry and Occupation*. Canberra: Australian Government Publishing Service.

Derham, David. 1962. "Legal Education—University Education and Professional Training," 36 *Australian Law Journal* 212.

———. 1969. "Legal Education—A Challenge to the Profession," 43 *Australian Law Journal* 530.

———. 1978. "An Overview of Legal Education in Australia," in R. Balmford, ed., *Legal Education in Australia*. Melbourne: Australian Law Council Foundation.

Disney, Julian, John Basten, Paul Redmond, and Stan Ross. 1977. *Lawyers*. Sydney: Law Book Company.

———. 1986. *Lawyers*, 2d ed. Sydney: Law Book Company.

Ditton, Pam. 1980. "Northern Territory Legal Profession—Closed Shop?," 5 *Legal Service Bulletin* 123.

Evans, Gareth. 1981. "The Politics of Justice." Melbourne: Victorian Fabian Society (Pamphlet No. 33).

Evans, John A. 1982. *Group Legal Services in Australia*. Canberra: Australian Government Publishing Service.

Fisse, W. B., and D. St. L. Kelly. 1970. "Political Influence in the Appointment of Queen's Counsel," 44 *Australian Law Journal* 318.

Fitzgerald, Jeffrey. 1977. *Poverty and the Legal Profession in Victoria*. Canberra: Australian Government Printing Service.

Forbes, J. R. 1979. *The Divided Legal Profession in Australia*. Sydney: Law Book Company.

Ford, G. W. 1965. "Work," in A. F. Davies and S. Encel, eds., *Australian Society: A Sociological Introduction*. Melbourne: Cheshire.

Freadman Report. 1969. "Service Under Articles," 43 *Victorian Law Institute Journal* 395.

Garling, Kim. 1983. "Case Histories of Trust Account Cheats," 21 *Law Society Journal* 126.

Gaskin Report. 1974. "Solicitors in New South Wales." Unpublished paper prepared for the New South Wales Law Foundation.

Griswold, Erwin N. 1952. "Observations on Legal Education in Australia," 5 *Journal of Legal Education* 139.

Halliday, Terence C. 1981. "The Fractured Profession: Structural Impediments to Collective Action by the Australian Legal Profession." Presented at the American Sociological Association Annual Meeting, Toronto.

———. 1982a. "Legal Education and the Rationalization of Law: A Tale of Two Countries." Presented at the Tenth World Congress of Sociology, Mexico City (August).

———. 1982b. "Prospects of Power: Legal Associations and Government 1970–1990," in *Power in Australia: Directions of Change*. Canberra: Centre for Continuing Education, Australian National University.

Harley, Peter. 1985. "Legal Studies ... A Bicentennial Subject?," 16 *Independent Education* 33.

Hetherton, Margaret. 1978. *Victoria's Lawyers*. Melbourne: Victoria Law Foundation.

————. 1981*a*. *Victoria's Lawyers—Second Report*. Melbourne: Victoria Law Foundation.

————. 1981*b*. "Practising Women Lawyers in Victoria—Some Survey Findings and Unanswered Questons," in P. Cashman, ed., *Research and the Delivery of Legal Services*. Sydney: Law Foundation of New South Wales.

Heydon, J. Dyson. 1976. "Lawyers' Fees and the Trade Practices Act, s. 45," *Australian Current Law Digest* DT 27.

Higley, John, Desley Deacon, and Don Smart. 1979. *Elites in Australia*. London: Routledge & Kegan Paul.

Hoskins, Rosemary. 1978. *Lawyers in Commerce? Employer Attitudes Towards the Employment of Law Graduates*. Sydney: Law Foundation of New South Wales.

Hunt, John. 1984. "Law Society Computer Statistics," 22 *New South Wales Law Society Journal* 738 (November).

Hutley, Francis C. 1977. Submission to New South Wales Law Reform Commission (April 29, unpublished).

Kavanagh, Patrick. 1986. "The Future for Legal Education," 11 *Legal Service Bulletin* 55.

Khan, A. N., and J. Hackett. 1977. "Legal Aid: The Western Australian Commission," 2 *Legal Service Bulletin* 274.

Kirby, Michael D. 1982. "The Women Are Coming," *Australian Law News* 11 (June).

————. 1983. "Recession, Law Reform and Education," 13 *Queensland Law Society Journal* 62.

Law Society of New South Wales. 1978. *Composition of the Profession*. Sydney: Law Society of New South Wales (submission to New South Wales Law Reform Commission).

————. 1979. "Professional Misconduct and the Establishment of a Lay Review Tribunal." Special Bulletin No. 1 of 1979.

————. 1985. "Law and Employment: A Statement of Employment Prospects for Law Graduates." Annual Bulletin.

Lindgren, Kevin E. 1980. "Legal Studies in Australian Schools—An Account and Some Issues," 54 *Australian Law Journal* 399.

Linke, R. D., L. M. Oertel, and N. J. M. Kelsey. 1985. "Participation and Equity in Higher Education: A Preliminary Report on the Socioeconomic Profile of Higher Education Students in South Australia, 1974–1984," 11(3) *Australian Bulletin of Labour* 124.

Lucke, Horst K. 1978. "University Training of Lawyers: Contents of the Curriculum, Number of Courses, Electives and Non-law Subjects," in R. Balmford, ed., *Legal Education in Australia*. Melbourne: Australian Law Council Foundation.

Lucke, Horst K., and R. J. Wallace. 1978. "Law Courses in Australia," in R. Balmford, ed., *Legal Education in Australia*. Melbourne: Australian Law Council Foundation.

Lyons, G. 1984. "Aboriginal Legal Services," in P. Hanks and B. Keon-Cohen, eds., *Aborigines and the Law*. Sydney: George Allen and Unwin.

McGarvie, R. E. 1978. "Mechanics of Curriculum Planning," in R. Balmford, ed., *Legal Education in Australia*. Melbourne: Australian Law Council Foundation.

McInerney, Murray. 1978. "The Appointment of Judges to Commissions of Inquiry and Other Extra-Judicial Activities," 52 *Australian Law Journal* 540.

McMillan, C. K. 1975. "Constitutional Challenge to A.L.A.O.," 1 *Legal Service Bulletin* 165.

Martin, Linda. 1983. "From Apprenticeship to University Law School: Legal Education and the New South Wales Legal Profession 1815–1890." LL.B. honours thesis, School of Law, Macquarie University.

Martin Report. 1964. *Report of the Committee on the Future of Tertiary Education in Australia*. Canberra: Australian Universities Commission.

Meagher, Rod. 1980. "A Step toward Anarchy," 15 (2) *Australian Law News* 11.

———. 1983. "How Can You Learn Practice in Theory?" *Proceedings and Papers of the 7th Commonwealth Law Conference*. Hong Kong: Seventh Commonwealth Law Conference Ltd.

Mendelsohn, Oliver, and Matthew Lippman. 1979. "The Emergence of the Corporate Law Firm in Australia," 3 *University of New South Wales Law Journal* 78.

Meredith, G. G. 1978. "Structure and Financial Performance of Legal Practices in New South Wales," in R. Tomasic, ed., *Understanding Lawyers*. Sydney: New South Wales Law Foundation.

———. 1983. *Legal Aid: Cost Comparison—Salaried and Private Lawyers*. Canberra: Australian Government Publishing Service.

Morgan Gallup Poll. 1984. "Doctors, Dentists, Bankers Tops for Honesty, Ethics," *Finding No. 1182, Published Bulletin* (May 22). Sydney: Morgan Gallup Poll.

Neal, David, ed. 1984. *On Tap, Not on Top: Legal Centres in Australia 1972–1982*. Melbourne: Legal Service Bulletin.

Neumann, Edward. 1973. *The High Court of Australia*. Sydney: Sydney University Press.

New South Wales Law Reform Commission. 1979a. *Complaints, Discipline and Professional Standards—Part 1*. Sydney: NSWLRC (Legal Profession Discussion Paper No. 2).

———. 1979b. *Professional Indemnity Insurance*. Sydney: NSWLRC (Legal Profession Discussion Paper No. 3).

———. 1980. *The Legal Profession—Background Paper III*. Sydney: NSWLRC.

———. 1981a. *The Structure of the Profession*. Sydney: NSWLRC (Legal Profession Discussion Paper No. 4[1]).

———. 1981b. *The Structure of the Profession—Part 2*. Sydney: NSWLRC (Legal Profession Discussion Paper No. 4(2)).

————. 1981c. *Solicitor's Trust Accounts and the Solicitors' Fidelity Fund.* Sydney: NSWLRC (Legal Profession Discussion Paper No. 6).

————. 1981d. *Advertising and Specialisation.* Sydney: NSWLRC (Discussion Paper No. 5).

————. 1981e. *The Legal Profession—Background Paper IV.* Sydney: NSWLRC.

————. 1982a. *First Report on the Legal Profession—General Regulation and Structure.* Sydney: NSWLRC.

————. 1982b. *Second Report on the Legal Profession—Complaints, Discipline and Professional Standards.* Sydney: NSWLRC.

————. 1982c. *Third Report on the Legal Profession—Advertising and Specialisation.* Sydney: NSWLRC.

————. 1983. *The Magistracy—Interim Report: First Appointments as Magistrates Under the Local Courts Act, 1982.* Sydney: NSWLRC.

Nieuwenhuysen, John, and Marina Williams-Wynn. 1982. *Professions in the Marketplace—An Australian Study of Lawyers, Doctors, Accountants and Dentists.* Melbourne: Melbourne University Press.

O'Malley, Pat. 1983. *Law, Capitalism and Democracy.* Sydney: George Allen & Unwin.

Ormrod Report. 1971. *Report of the Committee on Legal Education.* London: HMSO (Cmnd. 4594).

Peden, John R. 1972. *Professional Legal Education and Skills Training for Australian Lawyers.* Sydney: Law Book Company.

Reid, G. S. 1980. "The Changing Political Framework," *Quadrant* 1 (January–February).

Rogers, Justice. 1981. "Early Disposition of Cases and the Containment of Costs in Court Proceedings," in Ben Boer, ed., *Legal Aid Research in Australia.* Canberra: Commonwealth Legal Aid Council.

Ross, Stan. 1975. "The Legal Profession in Tasmania," 5 *University of Tasmania Law Review* 1.

————. 1976. "The Role of Lawyers in Society," *Australian Quarterly* 61 (March).

————. 1982. *Politics of Law Reform.* Sydney: Penguin Books.

Sackville, Ronald. 1975. *Legal Aid in Australia.* Canberra: Australian Government Publishing Service.

Sallmann, Peter, and John Willis. 1984. *Criminal Justice in Australia.* Melbourne: Oxford University Press.

Samuels, Gordon. 1978. "Control of Admission to Practice—Its Effect on Legal Education," in R. Balmford, ed., *Legal Education in Australia.* Melbourne: Australian Law Council Foundation.

Sexton, Michael. 1984. "Royal Commissions and the Australian Political Process." Unpublished paper, University of New South Wales.

Sexton, Michael, and Laurence W. Maher. 1982. *The Legal Mystique: The Role of Lawyers in Australian Society.* Sydney: Angus & Robertson.

Skinner, T. J. 1985. *New South Wales Year Book No. 69.* Sydney: Australian Bureau of Statistics.

Smark, Peter, and Judith Whelan. 1985. "A Middle-Class Dilemma: How to Educate Kate and James," *Sydney Morning Herald* 4 (July 22).

Stewart, R. A. F., and Rosemary Balmford. 1978. "Further Legal Education—Professional Continuing Legal Education," in R. Balmford, ed., *Legal Education in Australia*. Melbourne: Australian Law Council Foundation.

Tatz, Colin. 1980. "Aborigines: Legal Aid and Law Reform," 5 *Legal Service Bulletin* 91.

Tomasic, Roman, ed. 1978. *Understanding Lawyers*. Sydney: Law Foundation of New South Wales and George Allen & Unwin.

———. 1980. "Typifying Lawyers: A Sociological Study of the Legal Profession in New South Wales." Ph.D. thesis, University of New South Wales.

———. 1981. "Criminal Lawyers and Their Clients," 14 *Australian and New Zealand Journal of Criminology* 147.

———. 1983a. "Social Organisation Amongst Australian Lawyers," 19 *Australian and New Zealand Journal of Sociology* 447.

———. 1983b. "Lawyers and Social Control—A Preliminary Inquiry," 3 *Windsor Yearbook of Access to Justice* 20.

Tomasic, Roman, and Cedric Bullard. 1978. *Lawyers and Their Work in New South Wales*. Sydney: Law Foundation of New South Wales.

Trumble, P. C. 1978. "In-Service Training for Practice as a Solicitor," in R. Balmford, ed., *Legal Education in Australia*. Melbourne: Australian Law Council Foundation.

Universities Commission. 1975. *Selected University Statistics 1975*. Canberra: Universities Commission.

Vinson, T., R. Homel, and R. Bonney. 1974. *Territorial Justice in Australia*. Sydney: New South Wales Bureau of Crime Statistics and Research (Statistical Report No. 20).

Walker, Frank. 1985. "Out There in the Job Market, a Degree Still Pays Off," *The National Times* 49 (September 13).

Wallace, Jude, and John Fiocco. 1981. "Recent Criticisms of Formalism in Legal Theory and Legal Education," 7 *Adelaide Law Review* 309.

Western, John S. 1983. *Social Inequality in Australia*. Melbourne: Macmillan.

Wilson, Malcolm. 1983. "The Mohammed Ali of the Legal Firms," *Sydney Morning Herald* 36 (October 1).

Wilton, Janis, and Richard Bosworth. 1984. *Old Worlds and New Australia: The Post-War Migration Experience*. Melbourne: Penguin Books.

Yeldham, David A. 1985. "A Judicial View of the System of Legal Aid," 15 *Queensland Law Society Journal* 9.

Yorke, Douglas. 1983. "Lawyers in the West: Tighter Controls Ahead," 8 *Legal Service Bulletin* 275.

Ziegert, Klaus. 1983. "Students in Law School: Some Data on the Accumulation of Advantage." Unpublished paper, Sydney University Department of Jurisprudence.

7

New Zealand Lawyers

From Colonial GPs
to the Servants of Capital

GEORGINA MURRAY

The social role of lawyering is similar to that of any other craft: the artisan is the legal professional, the tools are the legal form and ideology, and the dominant client is capital (McBarnet, 1984: 238). This description of the internal structure of the New Zealand legal profession and its social environment is informed by the fact that law and lawyers are a strategic part of the national economy. Although law enjoys a symbiotic relationship with both the state and the economy, lawyers are not mere instruments, however, for they sometimes act against the interests of capital (e.g., in environmental matters) and those of the state (e.g., with respect to employment). The legal form can offer individuals some protection, but the fact that legal expertise is marketed as a commodity limits this protection and makes it impossible to view law as fully autonomous. Lawyers sell their services to those (mainly capitalists) who can buy this ability to manipulate the "rule of law."

The other resource of the legal profession is legal ideology. Law sustains the dominant ideology of New Zealand society, defining and legitimating institutions of property and power and thereby allowing capitalism to operate within the appearances of liberal democracy and free enterprise. There is a contradiction between ideal and reality, however. Because law largely mediates between different capitalist fractions, which oppose each other as well as the working class, lawyers (potentially) have difficulty maintaining their image of impartiality and fairness. Yet it is this picture of professional detachment and objectivity that ensures continued public support for the entire legal system.

In developing the historical background for this sociological overview, I have had to utilize the meager secondary literature,[1] while supplementing it with my own empirical research (Murray, 1984)[2] and other surveys (Heylen Research Centre, 1978; 1980; Auckland District Law Society, 1981). I begin by presenting the public's image of the law. Following a short account of New Zealand legal institutions, which differ sharply in some respects from those of other common law countries, I describe the legal profession, presenting demographic and sociographic data, outlining the division of rewards, and narrating the changes in the rules concerning admission to the profession and in its internal organization. Then I portray lawyers' functions and career choices, the provision of legal aid, and the utilization of lawyers' services. I conclude by returning to the public's image of the law and contrasting it with the data presented concerning the actual operation of the legal system.

The New Zealand public have a very positive image of lawyers, seeing them as highly qualified, intelligent, approachable, trustworthy, competent, and concerned about the community (see table 1). The public accord lawyers considerable prestige and perceive their work as complex, difficult, necessary, and rewarding. There are some reservations, however: a bare majority of the public consider lawyers to be overpaid; many think that they are wealthy and earn a considerable amount of money; and a not insignificant minority regard them as tricky or sharp. This generally positive public evaluation is consistent with the ideological view that the legal system offers equal access to justice regardless of the individual's class, sex, religion, or age.

Lawyers' self-perceptions largely parallel the favorable public image. Writings by lawyers constantly invoke the concepts of objectivity, homogeneity, professionalism, and community; for instance:

> We are a nation of three million, no two of whom are completely alike. Collectively, we have many interests in common. Indeed, in the last analysis we sink or swim together. Equally we belong to numerous small common interest groups within the nation, e.g. regional, social, economic, political and others, the interests of which inevitably conflict.... As life becomes more complex, so we all become more inter-dependent and at many points each of us needs help and protection. That is what the rule of law is all about— protecting us from others, which we all applaud, and protecting others from us. (Castle, 1977: 10)

This is "righteous" law (Cain, 1976: 230), presenting the case for collective justice through the rule of law.

THE HISTORICAL DEVELOPMENT OF LEGAL INSTITUTIONS

INTRODUCTION

New Zealand first was settled by the Maori, who had their own dispute resolution procedures, and it was not discovered by the British until 1789.

In 1840 the Treaty of Waitangi was signed by fifty "friendly" chiefs, who accepted sovereignty in the person of the governor, Captain Hobson. The moral and legal status of the treaty always have been controversial (Kelsey, 1983: 24—29), but it paved the way for the establishment of a British legislature and courts the following year and the creation of a legal system that accorded only marginal recognition to Maori customs in its special provisions for Maori land.

British courts were adapted to suit the new colony's needs. There were few judges and many magistrates, the latter often legally unqualified. Today the system is structured in the familiar hierarchy: a Court of Appeal, twenty-eight High Court judges divided among 10 judicial districts, and eighty-seven district court judges (previously called magistrates). All courts exercise criminal and civil jurisdiction, and district courts also have family court divisions. Judges in the lower courts are recruited from the entire legal profession; higher court judges are drawn from barristers, barristers sole, and Queen's Counsel. New Zealand has pioneered several important legal innovations, which are described below.

OMBUDSMAN

There is no separate system of administrative courts in New Zealand, but in 1962 the Scandinavian ombudsman was adopted in a common law jurisdiction for the first time in the form of a Parliamentary Commissioner. The ombudsman is empowered to examine the administrative decisions of government departments and local authorities. He has no influence over the private sector, since his decisions cannot be admitted in subsequent judicial proceedings. The nine lawyers employed in the ombudsman's office constitute 45 percent of the staff. Because the ombudsman conducts his own investigations, there is little scope for private legal representation. For the public the process is inexpensive and quick. We do not know whether the ombudsman's activities have reduced the number of judicial challenges to administrative actions. Although the public is said to see the ombudsman as a "system defender"—an officer of the state who preserves the status quo (Jones, 1973: 249)—there is no evidence to substantiate this.

LABOR DISPUTES

New Zealand has had an Arbitration Court for labor disputes ever since 1894. Disputes of interest are dealt with by collective bargaining, but processes of conciliation and ultimately arbitration are available to the parties. The Arbitration Court, which has representatives from the Employers' Federation and the Federation of Labour as well as legal professionals, registers collective agreements, whether concluded consensually or by award; thereupon they become binding on the industry and not just the immediate parties. Disputes of right pass through a series of committees chaired by an independent person; if the parties continue to disagree, the matter is referred to the Arbitration Court for a decision. Personal grievances pass directly to the court when the parties fail to agree.

Lawyers have come to play an increasing role in the working of this machinery, primarily as advocates before the Arbitration Court. However, they cannot appear before the Conciliation Council and can participate in arbitration proceedings only with the consent of all the parties (Industrial Relations Act of 1977, ss. 54[4], 78[3]).

In the preliminary stages, the parties are heard by either a conciliator from the Industrial Conciliation Service or a mediator from the Industrial Mediation Service. These "impartial" persons need not be legally qualified. The final stage takes place inside the Arbitration Court under the jurisdiction of a judge and is formal in comparison to the ongoing industrial relations process and labor-intervention schemes abroad (Howells, 1977: 7). Arbitration court judges are barristers or solicitors with at least seven years of experience. The full Arbitration Court includes the judge and four members, half nominated by the Employers' Federation and half by the Federation of Labour. It is limited to hearing disputes of interest at the request of one or both parties. The Federation of Labour employs one lawyer; the Employers' Federation employs four in each of its regional offices. Because these lawyers do not hold practicing certificates, they can participate freely at all stages of the arbitration process. The Arbitration Court has been a major force since its inception. Its ostensible purpose is to advance the interests of workers, but many workers are skeptical, regarding it as a means by which the state controls the working class in the interests of business (Bedggood, 1981: 75–76). Perry (1985: 13) makes a similar point:

> Any discussion of corporatist tendencies in New Zealand should therefore begin not with 1984 but with 1894 and the passing of the Industrial Conciliation and Arbitration Act. What the act ensured is that the trajectory of trade union development in New Zealand, almost from the outset, was closely tied to the development of the New Zealand state.

ACCIDENT COMPENSATION

New Zealand has moved compensation for personal injuries from the private law to the public law. This novel legislation provides insurance for all injuries. Enacted in 1972 and updated in 1982, the Accident Compensation Act has dispensed with the fault principle and sought to render lawyers superfluous. The injured person is compensated for both permanent physical disability and income loss, with regular adjustments for inflation.

The Accident Compensation Act is administered by the Accident Compensation Commission, whose decisions are subject to a right of appeal to the High Court and the Court of Appeal. The profession was divided at the introduction of the system but did not oppose it (Ison, 1980: 184). Nevertheless, some lawyers did object on a variety of grounds: the loss of civil rights, less generous benefits, extra costs, the abandonment of the fault principle, implementation problems, greater bureaucracy, and a decline in the national character created by greater reliance on the state (Sandford, 1974: 5). The latent cause of their dissatisfaction—fear of losing clients—seems to have diminished over the years, perhaps because lawyers do represent claimants at reconsideration hearings and may charge them considerably more than the costs usually awarded (Ison, 1980: 111–112). In general, the legal profession now is reconciled to accident compensation and views it as a significant contribution to the security of all accident victims, who previously had to take their chances in a "forensic lottery" (Blair, 1983: 6).

Another view attributes accident compensation not to welfare state altruism but to the need of monopoly capital to socialize the costs of workers' injuries (Shannon, 1982: 172). It does seem that international pharmaceutical companies are coming to New Zealand for trial runs of some of their products because they will not be liable for damages.

LAND LAW

The Torrens system of land registration was introduced into New Zealand in 1870; its principal features are the registration of land title and the subsequent guarantee of that title by the state. Lawyers conduct conveyancing according to a fixed scale of fees. The Royal Commission on Legal Services (1979: vol. 2, pp. 156–157) found that New Zealand domestic conveyancing costs were a smaller proportion of the sale price than in any jurisdiction they surveyed. Landbrokers as well as lawyers can convey property (Land Transfer Act of 1952, s. 229; Legal Practitioners Act of 1982, s. 65). Real estate agents also can draw up preliminary agreements. The Minister of Housing has declared his intention to allow the Housing Corporation to provide a conveyancing service for its own clients.

MAORI LAND

New Zealand was, until very recently, a British Commonwealth colonial farm. Land is and was among its prime resources and the base for its main exports. The colonial settlers (called *Pakeha* by the Maori) needed Maori land to realize the agricultural profitability of their new country. Maori land traditionally was owned collectively. By the terms of the Treaty of Waitangi (1840), Maori could sell their "customary land" only through the Crown. Land had vital sentimental and spiritual importance to the Maori. Furthermore, they were quick to recognize its economic value and their increasing numerical vulnerability (the 1858 census showed Maori already outnumbered by Pakeha). Consequently, they were extremely reluctant to sell their land. This reluctance, coupled with the rapacious demands of the Pakeha, led to the Land Wars of 1860 to 1870. When the fighting ended, the government felt free to undertake widespread confiscation of land from both the "unfriendly" Maori (the guerilla fighters) and the "friendly" tribes (those Maori who fought with the Pakeha against their own people). The profits from sales of confiscated land were used to pay war costs.

War and the subsequent land confiscation considerably demoralized the Maori, but it was during the subsequent peace that most land was alienated, for with it "came the Native land court, a veritable engine of destruction for any tribe's tenure of land anywhere" (Kawaharu, 1977: 15). The Native Lands Act of 1862 established the Native Land Court (later the Maori Land Court) under the presidency of a Pakeha magistrate. The *New Zealand Herald*, an extremely conservative daily newspaper, reported in 1883: "The working of the Native Land Court has been a scandal for many years past, but as the main sufferers were the Maoris, nobody troubled themselves very much" (quoted in Williams [1983: 319]). It was the zeal of this Native Land Court and its "'free trade' in the alienation of Maori land from 1865 to the 1890s which effectively undermined and dissolved the material basis of Maori social existence" (ibid., 266). Maori customary land now has been converted largely to freehold.

Today, the Maori Land Court consists of a chief judge and any other judges that the governor-general believes a particular situation may warrant. It deals with problems surrounding multiple land ownership, partitioning and combining titles for better land utilization, effecting exchanges, directing owners' meetings, confirming sales, and administering decedents' estates. A Maori Appellate Court consists of any three or more judges of the Maori Land Court. Few lawyers today still specialize in Maori land matters.

LAWYERS IN NEW ZEALAND

INTRODUCTION

In its broadest sense, the term "lawyer" covers not only those registered and practicing as barristers and/or solicitors but also judges (defined by the census as jurists) and those with law degrees working in the public sector, for corporations, or as law teachers. The Law Practitioners Act of 1982, s. 54 limits rights of audience to those enrolled as barristers or solicitors. In this chapter, I will use the term "legal profession" to refer to private practitioners, although numerical data will include lawyers in the broader sense.

New Zealand traditionally has had a fused profession. The first Supreme Court Ordinance provided separately for the admission of barristers and solicitors; however, each was allowed to perform both roles for a period of five years unless the Supreme Court decided otherwise. The first Law Practitioners Act (1861) still allowed the Supreme Court to direct that no barrister could act as a solicitor and vice versa, but no such direction was given. Although there were separate rolls for barristers and solicitors, a lawyer could be inscribed on each. Now a lawyer is admitted as "a barrister and solicitor of the Court," and there is a common roll, but a practitioner must obtain a current practicing certificate as either a barrister, a solicitor, or a barrister and a solicitor (although the choice does not limit the lawyer's competence). The work of a solicitor revolves around commercial transactions and conveyancing. If these break down and the client needs to go to court, the solicitor usually will put the matter into the hands of a barrister or barrister sole (defined below), or if the matter is very important and the client has sufficient resources, the solicitor will brief a Queen's Counsel. Barristers have all the powers and responsibilities of their English counterparts (Law Practitioners Act of 1982, s. 61). Their work centers around criminal and civil litigation. A barrister who only accepts instructions from a solicitor on behalf of a client and practices individually rather than in a firm is known as a *barrister sole* and generally charges a higher fee than does a barrister. Although there were only one or two barristers sole listed as practicing in Auckland in 1920, 1940, and 1960, their numbers had increased to forty-one in 1980 (Crothers, 1985). In 1986 the Law Society Register for the greater Auckland region included ninety-three barristers sole and twelve Queen's Counsel. Queen's Counsel charge the highest fees, which are prescribed by the governor general through an Order in Council. A Queen's Counsel may not practice as a solicitor and must hold a practicing certificate as a barrister. Because Queen's Counsel require impeccable reputations, they tend to avoid serious criminal cases (e.g., the defense of drug charges) and hence concentrate on major civil matters. These categories also differ in prestige. Because barristers sole work only when instructed by another lawyer, their income depends more on personal reputation than does that of a barrister working in a firm or even a sole practitioner. Hence a barrister usually enjoys considerable popularity and prestige among other lawyers before assuming the status of a barrister sole.

The professional monopoly in New Zealand dates from the colonial era. The first Supreme Court Ordinance (1841) admitted to practice only those qualified in Britain. The Conveyancing Act of 1841, which followed two months later, allowed solicitors of the (English) Supreme Court to practice as attorneys or solicitors and permitted both solicitors and barristers to perform conveyances. The virtual monopoly of conveyancing persists, although its continuation has been questioned by the Consumers Council and others (Charters, 1982), and the government is seriously considering competing with the private sector by offering its own conveyancing service. Barristers and solicitors continue to enjoy exclusive rights of audience in the higher courts, although litigants may represent themselves or be advised by a layperson.

Nonlawyers are not prohibited from doing most forms of legal work, however, as long as they do not pretend to be lawyers. The functions of accountants and tax consultants overlap with those of lawyers. There are no restrictions on paraprofessionals employed by lawyers as legal executives (outside the courtroom). They do such "nonskilled" work as preparing documents and registering land transactions and also are involved in highly skilled legal research, interviewing clients and preparing opinions.

NUMBER OF LAWYERS

In 1981 there were approximately 4,149 lawyers in New Zealand, of whom 3,915 were barristers and/or solicitors and 234 were judges or legal executives (Crothers, 1985). The number of lawyers increased steadily from 229 at the first census in 1871 to 1,945 in 1956 (see table 4). Although there was substantial growth between 1871 and 1891 (149 percent) and between 1901 and 1921 (94 percent), this was primarily a function of population increases. Since 1956 the increase has been dramatic. In the twenty-year period from 1961 to 1981, the number of lawyers increased 98 percent (from 2,091 to 4,149). During this period the tight supply control previously exercised by the profession broke down; the law schools appropriated the qualification process from the profession through compulsory university credentials and restrictions on part-time university courses (see the section on legal education, the qualification process, following). This opened entry not merely to greater numbers but also to women and non-Pakeha. The ratio of population to lawyers now is at its lowest level ever: 783 : 1.

LEGAL OCCUPATIONS

An occupational profile compiled from census data shows the distribution of lawyers among occupations in 1971 and 1981 (see table 2). The great majority of New Zealand lawyers still are in private practice, as they always have been. They work as sole practitioners, in partnership (as either principals or employees), and as barristers sole. The number of judges and magistrates (now district court judges) increased from 13 in 1878 to 96 in 1981; there were 115 such positions in 1986. This has permitted a substantial increase in litigation. The category of "other lawyers" (not specifically defined in the census but understood to be legal executives) also rose rapidly from 26 in 1971 to 126 in 1981 (Crothers, 1985).

In addition to those practicing privately, lawyers also are employed as house counsel for large corporations, in government departments, and in universities. The numbers in these categories are comparatively small, although they have increased recently (see table 3).[3] Two main trends are apparent. First, the proportion of those who define themselves as self-employed has declined from a peak of a third of the profession in 1891 to a mere 9 percent at the end of the 1930s. Second, until the mid-1950s, 70 percent to 85 percent of the profession were "entrepreneurs"—lawyers in practice on their own or principals in firms—and only a small minority were employed. Since then the proportions have changed steadily, so that by 1981 over 40 percent of the profession was employed. (The number of entrepreneurs and salaried lawyers do not equal the total of all lawyers. The discrepancy of 14 percent in the 1891 census could be attributable to pupils, who were neither entrepreneurs nor salaried. The small discrepancies since pupillage ended in 1900 probably represent unemployed lawyers.)

The increased "proletarianization" of lawyers could reflect the influx of younger lawyers; the average age of the profession declined from 42.6 years old in 1971 to 38.1 in 1981 (Crothers, 1985). More lawyers are becoming employees as the economic climate for small business worsens. Yet, although the average Auckland law firm has expanded from 1.6 lawyers in 1920 to 4.1 in 1985, a third of all firms still contain only one lawyer (see table 4). At the same time, large firms continue to grow. In 1985 the largest contained 57 partners and employees. Then, in June 1986, "Law Link" united nineteen firms from Whangarei to Invercagill, containing 128 partners and 140 other legal staff. Law Link will practice as a network of independent law firms providing a coordinated nationwide legal service with uniform costs and standards and shared expertise and information (*Auckland Star* [May 27, 1986]). Paradoxically, although more lawyers are becoming employees (and thus less entrepreneurial), they increasingly see their work as resembling that of financiers and bankers (Heylen Research Centre, 1978: 38).

GEOGRAPHIC DISTRIBUTION OF LAWYERS

There is a very uneven distribution of lawyers in New Zealand (see map). One would expect low concentrations of lawyers in rural areas, but this does not explain the differences in the ratios of lawyers to population. The simple explanation is that lawyers set up practice where they can maximize their incomes: in highly centralized capitalist economies this means major urban areas. In 1978, 41 percent of the New Zealand legal profession was located in the Auckland Law Society District, compared to 35 percent of the population (Heylen Research Centre, 1978). This helps to explain the differences between adjacent counties with urban populations, such as Rodney (602 inhabitants per lawyer) and Franklin (2,422 per lawyer); the former is wealthy North and the latter, poor South Auckland.

Even among those urban areas found by Sloper (1981: 506) to be best served by lawyers, there were considerable variations based on differences in wealth, for example, between Christchurch City in the South Island (564 people per lawyer), and the mainly urbanized Tauranga County in the North Island (929).

Although my own work deals only with the Auckland Law Society District, it gives information about the geographic distribution of lawyers by employment status (see table 4). This indicates that employees and employers are concentrated in inner-city Auckland, while sole practitioners are found predominantly in the suburbs. Disproportionate numbers of sole practitioners are women and/or from working-class backgrounds, and most earn considerably less than law firm partners (see section on division and stratification within the profession, hardcore discrimination, following). The eighty-seven barristers sole in the greater Auckland region in 1982 were found overwhelmingly in the inner-city area.

AGE

The shifts in the age distribution of lawyers illustrate the impact of World War II and the erosion of supply control in the 1960s (see table 5). Before

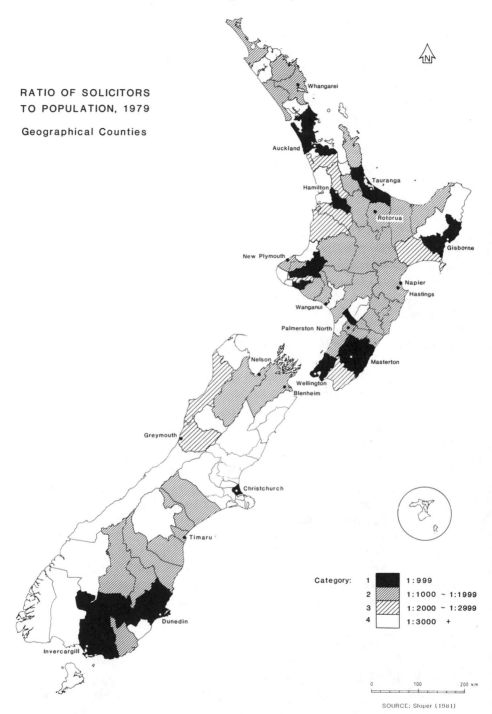

RATIO OF SOLICITORS
TO POPULATION, 1979

Geographical Counties

Category:
1   1:999
2   1:1000 – 1:1999
3   1:2000 – 1:2999
4   1:3000 +

0   100   200 km

SOURCE: Sloper (1981)

the 1960s, the profession was becoming progressively older. In 1961, a third of all lawyers were at least sixty-four years old, and less than a third were under thirty-five. In 1981 only 12 percent were over sixty-four and more than half were under thirty-five. Although the proportion of lawyers between thirty-five and sixty-four has remained roughly the same in absolute terms, this cohort has been overwhelmed by the young.

GENDER

Law always has been an androcentric profession in New Zealand; all that has varied is the degree of male dominance; however, the number of women has increased substantially since 1966 (see table 6). There was no woman lawyer in New Zealand until 1901. The first to practice law independently was Ellen Melville, who opened her office in Auckland in 1909 (Bush, 1972: 537). Nevertheless, less than 0.5 percent of the profession was female until 1945, and few women entered the profession before the 1960s. One result is that none of the twenty-eight High Court judges and only two of the eighty-seven district court judges are women. Once the profession lost partial control of recruitment, however, women entered in large numbers. The earlier process of entry through law clerking may have discouraged many women, for this mode of entry required (male) sponsorship. Even in 1981, women were only 9 percent of the profession. The law never prohibited women from entering the profession, as it did in other countries; rather, the barriers that they confronted were attitudinal. The women who overcame the ideology that "a woman's place is in the home" and entered practice then were faced with further variants of the superordinate male and subordinate female roles. This is the view of a young woman lawyer, who had just set up a successful partnership with her husband and another man:

> The predominant source of discrimination has been colleagues. The source of their discrimination has been firstly verbal sexual harassment and belittlement and secondly attitudinal. Until recently I didn't cope very well at all. I sublimated my anger. I did not confront it. You need a practised response. You can be accused of lacking humour and you want to remain popular. (Murray, 1984: 191)

A regional law society report expressed concern about the status of women lawyers (Auckland District Law Society, 1981). Although this working group was convened by a man, the report apparently was motivated and largely written by women. Nevertheless, women still face problems based on their actual or presumed relationship to their families; child-rearing is considered women's work in New Zealand. In practical terms this often means that women must choose between a family and a career in law.

Women lawyers complained about the demands of this dual role as domestic workers and wage workers, with no concessions being made on either side (Murray, 1984). The problem is exacerbated by the inflexibility of the legal profession: there are no crèche (day care) facilities within firms, glide time (flexible scheduling of work hours), or job sharing (ibid.). A woman lawyer who was contemplating having children expressed this point:

> Law is so inflexible that it seriously disadvantages women against men. In my first job there was glide time for the secretaries but not for the lawyers. It was thought unprofessional. There is no physical problem to working at home. The problem is the professional image. Maternity leave is totally inadequate. There is no guarantee of return or promotion to former status level. (Murray, 1984: 198)

The situation of women is improving, however, at least quantitatively. In 1985, 59 percent of entering law students at the University of Auckland were women. In September 1983, for the first time in New Zealand, more women than men were admitted to the Bar. The *New Zealand Herald* referred to this as a "ladies' day." Things may change as the profession recognizes the potential of cheap female labor; women are seen as being at the bottom because they cannot legitimately demand an equal share of the rewards in view of their dual role commitments.

In a survey of practitioners in 1978, 81 percent disliked the idea that any concessions should be made to women lawyers to allow them to have a family and continue working (Heylen Research Centre, 1978: 3). Women now are coming up with their own solutions. Some are going into sole practice (to avoid blocked mobility in firms) or starting their own partnerships (*Auckland Star* [April 16, 1985]). Conservative attitudes not only prevent women from achieving personal success in a well-paid and prestigious profession but also obstruct legal progress for all women in New Zealand (Murray, 1985):

> There is, of course, a basic delusion in expecting any statute to be an effective tool in the development and promotion of self-determination for women. Even when the principles of the statute seem a laudable attempt, we must never lose sight of the fact that its working, enactment, enforcement, interpretation and application to women's lives is in the hands of the patriarchy. Statutory lip-service costs little when brethren in the police, courts, law firms and other institutions can be relied on to render it ineffective. (Charters, 1985: 12–14)

PARENTAL OCCUPATION

There is no general information about the occupational background of the parents of New Zealand lawyers. My own survey shows that lawyers were disproportionately the children of parents (especially fathers) who held high-status occupations (see table 8).[4] Eighty-three percent of lawyers have parents in the three highest socioeconomic categories, compared to only 38 percent of the general working population. Thirty-nine percent of lawyers come from the highest category, compared to only 6 percent of the general working population.

The employment status of the lawyer related very strongly to father's occupation (see table 7). Indeed, 22 percent of successful partners and barristers sole were the children of lawyers. Higher proportions of partners (39 percent) and employees (49 percent) than sole practitioners (16 percent) had fathers in the "professional" rank. Individual respondents recognized their class advantages (Murray, 1984: 188). The class origins of lawyers and law students seem to have risen (ibid., 106). A survey at Auckland University revealed that the occupations of law students' fathers are somewhat higher than those of other students (31 percent vs. 27 percent in the second highest category) (Jones, 1983).

Interestingly, women lawyers have a larger proportion of fathers in the highest category than do men lawyers and a slightly smaller proportion in the lowest (see table 8). When legal role was analyzed by occupation, it was found that the relatively low rank of sole practitioner was being populated by the daughters of high-status fathers and the sons of lower-status fathers. These women, relegated to the margins of the profession because of blocked mobility within the firms where they had been trained, were most likely to complain about discrimination in the profession. The men in this role from working-class backgrounds (18 percent of the male sample) did not attribute their marginal positions to class origin. Most lawyers' mothers were housewives (39 percent) (Murray, 1984: 112). The general status of female employment in New Zealand is poor (Bedggood, 1981; Crothers, 1977), so it is not surprising that the employed mothers of the respondents commonly were between the second and fourth status categories, lower than those of their husbands.

ETHNICITY

Ethnic minorities always have been underrepresented in the legal profession (see table 9). They constitute 13 percent of the total population but never have been more than 2.6 percent of lawyers (New Zealand Department of Statistics, 1985: 91). There were no non-Pakeha lawyers until 1926, twenty-five years after the first woman became a lawyer.

The 1981 census figures show that 97 percent of the profession are Pakeha, 0.7 percent Maori, 0.21 percent Pacific Islander, 0.65 percent Chinese, 0.57 percent Indian, and 0.2 percent other ethnic groups. The entire working population is 88 percent Pakeha (Crothers, 1985).

There are several reasons why non-Pakeha entered the legal profession so late and remain so few. First, ethnic minorites tend to have low class positions (Murray, 1984: 110), limiting their social aspirations and material opportunities; we have seen that most lawyers have high-status backgrounds. Second, the racism prevalent in New Zealand is bound to influence those controlling recruitment into the profession. My respondents recognized the existence of such views and had experienced them personally. Law schools, by contrast, have introduced an affirmative action program (the Polynesian preference). Finally, Polynesians from outside New Zealand often took a law degree in New Zealand and then returned home to practice in the Islands (MacPherson, 1977; 1984).

FAMILY TIES

Family also plays a part in patterns of recruitment (Murray, 1984: 145). My respondents thought relatives were important—even (or particularly) those lawyers who had none. Law firm partners and barristers sole were most likely to have had a relative precede them (half had relatives in the profession). It turned out that two-thirds of these relatives were principals themselves, indicating that even position within the legal hierarchy was transmitted intergenerationally. After fathers, most of the relatives were brothers, although a few were uncles or grandfathers. There were no mothers or sisters, although there was one grandmother. The impression of a tracery of family networks is confirmed by a description of a number of male legal dynasties that span as many as four generations, which defines an old Pakeha family in a colonial society that is only 150 years old (Cooke, 1969: 219).

SECONDARY EDUCATION

Although no information is available on the preuniversity schooling of all New Zealand lawyers, my own survey of Auckland lawyers suggests that it reflects the status of lawyers' fathers. In describing schooling opportunities in Auckland, we can distinguish between (1) costly private and elite public schools, which are located in expensive neighborhoods and have a reputation for scholarship, and (2) nonelite public and private schools, which generally are coeducational and located in poorer neighborhoods. Among private schools there also is a religious difference: the elite schools are predominately Protestant, while the nonelite are overwhelmingly Catholic. Most lawyers (75 percent) were educated in elite schools and over half (52 percent) in elite public schools (see table 11). Nearly 90 percent of partners and barristers sole were educated in elite schools, particularly private schools. Sole practitioners typically were drawn from elite public schools (69 percent). Nearly three-fourths of those lawyers from nonelite public schools were employees, although a substantial majority of the latter came from elite schools.

DIVISION AND STRATIFICATION WITHIN THE PROFESSION

INTRODUCTION

The New Zealand public view the legal profession as homogeneous (Heylen Research Centre, 1978: 30–33), which is consistent with the image that the profession likes to project. Some practitioners recognize the internal divisions, however (Murray, 1984: 195–199). Writers in the United States have seen their profession as stratified (see chapter 2; Carlin, 1962; Auerbach, 1976). This is equally true in New Zealand. Internal distinctions are based on the lawyer's class origin, gender, and ethnicity; but the law school attended is not as significant as it seems to be in the United States. Stratification also is linked to the economic cycle; there are fewer employers and more employees when the economy is contracting, forcing firms to merge in order to survive (Giddens & Held, 1982: 6). Nevertheless, the status range within the profession mirrors the total range of social statuses no more closely in New Zealand than it does in other countries.

The distribution of rewards described in the following section reflects the heterogeneity within the legal profession. Unfortunately, the New Zealand Department of Statistics gives only average annual gross and net income figures for self-employed lawyers. My own research on Auckland lawyers offers a fuller description of the range of incomes obtained at various levels: by partners, self-employed lawyers, and employees; and by gender and ethnicity.

According to the Department of Statistics, the gross average income of partners rose 36 percent between 1978 and 1980. Whether by cutting overheads or using more low-paid employees, partners increased their net incomes 57 percent in the same period. Figures for firms were very similar. In 1980, the average net income per partner was NZ$31,099, which was then the U.S. equivalent of $79,800 (New Zealand Department of Justice, 1981: 479). Between 1975 and 1985, the average annual rate of inflation was 11.8 percent in New Zealand.

INCOME BY ELITE STATUS

Partnership in a large law firm is associated with high income and status elsewhere in the common law world, and the association holds good in New Zealand as well. To test this, I defined an elite lawyer as a partner in an inner-city Auckland firm with at least six lawyers. Cross-tabulating income with elite versus nonelite status, I found a very strong gamma of 0.70, suggesting that a lawyer's status is a crucial factor in the income that that lawyer will earn (see table 11).[5] Practically all elite lawyers earn NZ$30,000 or more, and almost half earn over NZ$50,000. Only 37 percent of nonelite lawyers earn over NZ$30,000, and only 20 percent more than NZ$50,000, while just under 40 percent earn under NZ$20,000. Some barristers sole, who also enjoy high prestige, have the most lucrative practices. A leading criminal barrister sole was reported to earn NZ$10,000 a case in 1982 and to average two cases a week. Although there were only forty-one barristers sole in Auckland in 1980, seven of whom were university lecturers (Crothers, 1985), the role is well-recognized step in the career of the ambitious and talented lawyer seeking to become a Queen's Counsel. An interesting anomaly is that some young women I interviewed, described by all as talented lawyers, had chosen to assume this role rather than become sole practitioners or undergo what they saw as continued humiliation in a firm. These women, although acknowledged as exceptional lawyers, were felt by others to be demeaning an honored and esteemed position traditionally reserved for the learned middle-aged male.

INCOME BY GENDER

Gender is strongly correlated with earnings (see table 13). Twenty-six percent of men lawyers earn more than NZ$50,000, compared to only 2 percent of women lawyers. Half of all men lawyers earn NZ$30,000 or more, but only 5 percent of women lawyers earn this amount. At the other end of scale, 7 percent of the women but none of the men in my sample earn less than NZ$10,000.

This is not merely a matter of differences in status. At each level, gender is a crucial variable (see table 13). A woman partner or barrister sole earns NZ$17,000 less than her male counterpart; a women employee earns

NZ$9,000 less. Gender even overrides employment status. For example, a woman sole practitioner earns much less than a male employee does (NZ$21,500 vs. NZ$26,521), while even a woman partner or barrister sole earns only NZ$27,678—just NZ$1,000 more than a male employee. Such income discrepancies remain even when allowance is made for the effects of class, ethnicity, and length of service, as we will see from the multivariate analysis below.

HARDCORE DISCRIMINATION

Hardcore discrimination against women lawyers cannot be shown until we control for their comparatively limited experience. Further analysis of the data shows that the association between gender and income cannot be explained by other factors (see table 14). The 1982 average income of Auckland Law Society District lawyers was NZ$35,007. Those lawyers whose fathers were in the top socioeconomic rank earned NZ$1,170 more than the average. When this is adjusted for the other variables, they earned only NZ$930 more than the average. There is a postive but weak correlation between the father's occupation and a lawyer's income (eta = 0.24). When we control for all other variables, the relationship is stronger (beta = 0.36). The multiple classification analysis thus shows that the father's high socioeconomic status is a fairly strong predictor of higher income. The data on ethnicity indicate that non-Pakeha have higher income, although this is not statistically significant (and attributable to an anomalous sample). Other variables significantly influence the relationship between gender and income (the eta of 0.28 declines to a beta of 0.18), for there is a strong relationship between income and both years of service and employment status. Yet even when we allow for all the other variables, women still earn NZ$10,000 less than the average and thus earn less for equal (if less desirable) work (Murray, 1984: 159). The analysis shows the desirability of being a barrister sole or a partner; the two categories average NZ$43,500. When the other variables are taken into account, the predicted income of a partner or barrister sole is reduced to NZ$41,000, while a sole practitioner approaches the mean (rising from NZ$34,000 to NZ$35,000), and employees also rise slightly (from NZ$27,000 to NZ$28,000). This correlation between status and income is the strongest in the table, although it also weakens when other factors are considered. Income generally increases with service except for an apparently anomalous dip in the predicted income of middle-aged lawyers, which is even more marked when allowance is made for other variables. There are several possible explanations for this. First, some middle-aged women are returning to the profession after taking time off to raise a family. Because they often find it difficult to reenter firms, they are among the most poorly paid in the profession, working as part-time adjuncts to family practices or establishing solo practices (in one case as a barrister sole). Second, the group with middling experience included lawyers embarking on sole practice and becoming barristers sole. Their incomes were very low at the beginning of these new careers. Third, some lawyers in this group were working part time because they had family commitments or were developing other sources of income (one man also was a potter).

Hardcore discrimination still occurs in the practice of law. Class affects admission to the profession (see table 8), the status a lawyer is likely to attain within it (see table 7), and, as we have just seen, the income the lawyer will earn. Class is importantly crosscut by two variables. Ethnicity limits the chance of entering law school, although its effect on income after entry to the profession is unclear. Also, while women now are entering the profession in numbers comparable to those of men and even obtaining partnerships as quickly, they are still disadvantaged in the kind of practice they can expect and, as we have seen, the rewards they gain. It is possible to deduce from this that those least likely to succeed as lawyers are non-Pakeha women from poor backgrounds, few of whom even enter the profession.

LEGAL EDUCATION

INTRODUCTION

The profession has undergone dramatic change since the 1960s. There has been enormous growth in numbers, a substantial and accelerating increase in the entry of women, and even greater improvement in access for ethnic minorities. These are the result not of conscious policies but of the loss of the supply control previously exercised by the profession when entry occurred through clerkship. Such control has passed to law schools, which have broadened access in every respect except class background. In other disciplines, the increase in the proportion of women was nowhere as marked has it has been in law (see table 15).

THE QUALIFICATION PROCESS

In the 1870s, entry to the profession was dependent on "a competent knowledge of the Latin tongue" (Northey, 1962: 9–10). Academic legal education was strongly criticized by the Royal Commission on Education (1925) as "inappropriate for entrants to a profession of the first rank." No degree was required to become a solicitor, and after five years of practice a solicitor could become a barrister.

As a result of the report of the Royal Commission on University Education in New Zealand (1925), the University of New Zealand was authorized to examine entrants but could not require any course to be taken by a candidate residing more than ten miles away or who would be prevented from attending by "being engaged in acquiring a profession or trade or earning a livelihood" (ibid.). The University established the Council of Legal Education to advise it. In 1961 the Council was reconstituted to consist of the following: two High Court judges appointed by the Chief Justice; a district court judge appointed by the chief district court judge; four people appointed by the Council of the New Zealand Law Society; the deans of the law faculties of the Universities of Otago, Canterbury, and Auckland and Victoria University of Wellington; and one person appointed by the Council of the New Zealand Law Students Association (Law Practitioners Act of 1982, s. 31). The Council prescribes the courses of study to be followed by those who wish to enter the profession. It was not until 1965 that the Council required an LL.B. degree (Northey, 1970: 19). As the number of full-time law teachers has increased, they gradually have seized the initiative in shaping educational change (Northey, 1962: 11), although they have not been pleased that universities had to teach the courses required by the Council. After graduation, a lawyer now must practice for three years within an eight-year period before establishing an independent practice.

In 1951 the dozen full-time law students constituted only 6 percent of the 200 law students at the University of Auckland. The rest were evening students pursuing their practical qualifications during the day as law clerks. In 1959 full-time students were 25 percent of enrollment. By 1971, the original proportions had reversed: 600 out of the 800 law students were studying full time (75 percent), and eight years later the proportion still was 71 percent (Northey, 1970: 16–17; Sinclair, 1983: 256). One stimulus for the change was the law teachers, who sought to enhance their own status by divesting themselves of the more practical courses. The dean of the Auckland Law School stated in 1970: "The universities cannot accept as their function or duty the provision of purely vocational training" (Northey, 1970: 19).

The combination of the degree requirement (imposed in 1965) and the deliberate elimination of lectures offered outside of traditional law clerk hours made entry more difficult. This did not affect the wealthy student, who always had been able to shortcut the system, not being dependent on law clerk's wages. It did place pressure on those working-class law students who relied on wages, bursaries, and scholarships, however. The profession strongly objected to the change, not because of concern for the working-class student, but because it eliminated law clerks as a source of cheap labor (Sinclair, 1983: 258) and reduced the profession's control over entry.

WHICH LAW SCHOOL?

There are four law schools in New Zealand, but the choice of a school has much less impact on the lawyer's career than it does in the United States or England or even in Canada or Australia. All schools are organized and financed entirely by the state and follow a fairly standard program. In theory, and probably in practice, they are equal in academic quality. Some are more desirable than others, but only because of geographic proximity to markets. Geographic location is an important determinant of future occupational success. Median lawyer incomes in the three major cities in 1978 were NZ$18,614 in Christchurch, NZ$18,175 in Auckland, and NZ$14,191 in Wellington (New Zealand Department of Justice, 1981: 482).

LAW SCHOOL ADMISSIONS

Students seeking to become lawyers must be admitted to a university and obtain high grades during the first year of general education (the "inter-mediate" year) in order to gain entry to the law faculty. Competition for admission to the latter is becoming more intense; more than 500 intermediate-year students have indicated their intent to read law in recent years, but only 8 percent of the students at Auckland University in 1985 were enrolled in the law faculty. The law degree requires a minimum of three years of study. Graduates must pass a professional examination, given twice a year. Although 97 percent of those sitting the examination pass it, students who wish to work in a top-ranking inner-city firm must perform outstandingly.

The greatest change in law school admissions in recent years has been the increase in women. Hopkins (1983: 5) suggests that women entrants have higher qualifications than do men. Sargisson (1982: 159) argues that women get higher grades in law school. The Auckland Law School in-stituted a Polynesian preference scheme in 1976/77, under which 5 Poly-nesian students were accepted in 1986; another 12 Polynesians also were accepted that year, for a total of 17 out of 200 (8.5 percent). Although this is less than the 11.7 percent of the general population who were Poly-nesian in 1985 (New Zealand Department of Statistics, 1985: 91), it represents an increase over the present 3 percent of practicing lawyers who are non-Pakeha.

MOTIVES FOR ATTENDING LAW SCHOOL

Rathjen (1976) suggests that law students in the United States are motivated by the values of the marketplace: they view the law as a mechanism for resolving disputes among private interests and see the profession as advancing their own social mobility. This could be applied equally to the New Zealand lawyers whom I interviewed. I asked them to recall their motives for attending law school. Pragmatism (the elimination of other occupational options) was a major factor for 57 percent, altruism influenced only 8 percent, and very few believed in justice. Only a small minority referred explicitly to financial prospects. A fifth (20 percent) were influenced by peers, and slightly less found law intrinsically interesting.

FINANCIAL ASSISTANCE AT LAW SCHOOL

Students, especially those from working-class backgrounds, have increasing difficulty finding the means to attend tertiary institutions. I asked my respondents how they had managed while they were students. Their main source of financial aid had been university bursaries and scholarships provided by the state (54 percent of respondents) and holiday earnings (33 percent). Parents were most important primarily to those who became partners and barristers sole (11 percent of respondents). Women students are particularly vulnerable to the problems of cyclical employment, for, unlike men, they cannot earn large sums of money at holiday times in laboring jobs. Most of the older lawyers sampled had received income from their firms, presumably while serving as law clerks. More than half of sole practitioners had depended primarily on their own resources, compared to less than a quarter of partners and barristers sole.

THE LAW SOCIETY

The attempt in 1869 to create a national law society by an act of Parliament successfully was opposed by staunch regionalist sentiment. In 1878 the District Law Societies Act recognized fourteen district associations. At first their functions were limited: they could oppose admissions, bring disciplinary proceedings before the Supreme Court, and prosecute unquali-

fied people who were practicing law. Most of their energies were devoted
to maintaining libraries and answering complaints (Dugdale, 1979: 5).

In the 1890s the fierce regionalism that had led to the formation of local
law societies dissipated somewhat, and regional delegates were sent to
form a national council. The New Zealand Law Society was established in
1896. Membership by those holding practicing certificates became compulsory in 1935. The New Zealand Law Society is responsible for discipline and is empowered to fine or suspend practitioners or strike them
from the roll, subject to appeal to the High Court and the Court of Appeal.
The 1978 survey revealed that 32 percent of the lawyer respondents had
been the object of complaints; 48 percent of the complaints were directed
at sole practitioners (Heylen Research Centre, 1978: 22). The lawyer respondents asserted that the number of complaints had grown because the
public were becoming more "vociferous and demanding" (ibid.).

Protection for client funds is derived from the compulsory audit of trust
accounts by the Law Society. Since 1929, the statutory Fidelity Guarantee
Fund has ensured against any shortfall. Until 1983 the public were protected against excessive charges for lawyers' services by the power of the
court to review bills of costs to determine whether they were reasonable
and in accordance with the recommended scale of fees. This scale now has
been abolished, and fees are set competitively on a piece-rate basis,
although the Law Society has retained the power to deal with fee
complaints.

Ethical standards are defined in the Rules Governing the Conduct of
Practitioners (New Zealand Law Society, 1970). Five sections deal with the
management of a legal business, two with professional property, one with
the society's general policy decisions, and the last with the prohibition on
advertising, which was repealed on April 1, 1985.

Law Societies today perform various functions in addition to discipline
and control of legal education. The Auckland Law Society, for example,
has six council committees, twenty-seven subcommittees, and a number of
standing committees. One of the functions most popular among members
is continuing education: 93 percent of the 1978 sample had attended at
least one lecture in the previous twelve months (Heylen Research Centre,
1978: 4). Some of the women in my sample felt that the Law Society's
seminars and conferences were chauvinistic, however, since they were
scheduled at times when women with children could not attend; and
worse, some events, such as the Waitangi Conference of 1982, specifically
excluded women.

I found a strong relationship between a lawyer's status and the degree
of involvement in the Law Society. Thirty percent of partners and barristers sole participated, compared to only 20 percent of employees and 19
percent of sole practitioners (Murray, 1984: 140).

PRIVATE PRACTICE

Although the public view the lawyer as functioning inside the courtroom, this image is incorrect. Although all certified lawyers can appear in court in New Zealand, as elsewhere, few do so regularly. A national survey revealed that conveyancing, not litigation, was by far the most common activity among lawyers, followed by company and commercial law (see table 17). When these transactions break down, the brief usually is placed into the hands of a barrister or litigator within the firm or an outside barrister sole. Whereas the Heylen Research Centre (1978: 9) queried a national sample about specialties in which they had "ever worked," I asked Auckland Law Society District lawyers about the areas they had "been practising [in] since [they] graduated." In descending order, they were as follows: conveyancing (75 percent of respondents), matrimonial (71 percent), commercial (67 percent), nonmatrimonial litigation (65 percent), general (60 percent), and criminal (58 percent) (multiple responses permitted) (Murray, 1984: 157). John Marshall, a senior commercial partner in an inner-city Auckland firm, reported an explosion in the amount of commercial law work available and a general shortage of lawyers to handle it because law firms are competing for lawyer employees with commercial and industrial employers (*Auckland Star* 20 [May 20, 1986]). Lawyers rarely mentioned other areas of work, such as estates (9 percent), town planning (7 percent), administration (6 percent), and tax (4 percent). A factor analysis of my data suggested an association between criminal law and other litigation, on one hand, and conveyancing and commercial law and general practice on the other hand (Murray, 1984). We thus see that the work of solicitors centers around the preparation, negotiation, and drafting of documents. Nearly 80 percent of the respondents to the 1978 survey reported that they were acting increasingly as financiers and bankers, and 56 percent disapproved of this trend (Heylen Research Centre, 1978: 38).

LEGAL AID

THE LEGAL PROFESSION AND THE GOVERNMENT

Both the New Zealand Law Society and the District Law Societies have been concerned with legal aid. Criminal legal aid was introduced in 1912 and gradually extended. Until recently, the legal profession opposed proposals for civil legal aid:

> Rather than support an organized scheme the Law Society gave an undertaking that no person with a reasonable cause would be prevented from bringing

or defending legal proceedings because he could not afford to pay for them. By 1969 [the year of the Legal Aid Act] this developed into a "partnership between the Government and the legal profession." (New Zealand Department of Justice, 1981: 9)

When the duty solicitor scheme was introduced in 1974, it, too, "was heralded as yet another example of a partnership between the government and the legal profession" (ibid., 65). This "partnership" was threatened with dissolution in 1981, when the Law Society "indicated that they could not continue to encourage support for the scheme" (ibid., 65). Lawyers and lay activists persuaded the Auckland District Law Society and the New Zealand Law Society to support a Neighbourhood Law Office, which opened in 1977 in Grey Lynn, a working-class areas with a very high Polynesian population (40 percent). After initial grants of NZ$20,000 for each of the first two years, the government gave the office nothing in 1979, 1980, 1982, and 1983 and only NZ$3,000 in 1981. With the election of a Labour government in July 1984, the grants returned to their earlier levels.

Total government expenditure on legal aid in 1981/82 was estimated at NZ$5,000,000, of which half or more was for civil legal aid, about a tenth for the duty solicitor scheme, and a fifth for criminal legal aid. There also was considerable expenditure on the representation of children (New Zealand Department of Justice, 1981: 11, 65, 75, 150). Legal aid makes a substantial contribution to the income of comparatively few firms, and the median income from legal aid is only a few hundred dollars. New Zealand has no statutory scheme for legal advice and assistance outside of court, although this can be provided through the civil legal aid scheme for matrimonial property problems. Most matrimonial cases now are settled outside of court. A special parliamentary review committee is considering amalgamating both types of legal aid, but it is not contemplating subsidizing legal advice.

LEGAL AID IN THE COURTS

Although any criminal accused may apply for legal aid at any stage of the proceedings, the applicant's means and the gravity of the offence influence the decision as to whether assistance will be granted. Civil legal aid, which also depends on financial eligibility and the merits of the case, is rendered almost exclusively in domestic proceedings (94 percent of the expenditure in 1981). It is estimated that 80 percent of all domestic proceedings are assisted by legal aid. The duty solicitor scheme, in which New Zealand was a pioneer, pays private lawyers to attend district courts and interview, advise, and represent criminal accused who do not already have a lawyer. At least 37 percent of defendants in 1979 used a duty solicitor (New

Zealand Department of Justice, 1981:66), and 35.6 percent of lawyers interviewed in 1978 had acted as duty solicitors or represented an accused under the legal aid scheme within the previous twelve months (Heylen Research Centre, 1978:11). Criminal defense is disproportionately in the hands of solicitors under the age of thirty-six, who are relatively inexperienced (ibid., 12).

LEGAL AID IN THE COMMUNITY

The development of community legal aid represents an increasing recognition that private law firms "cannot provide readily accessible advice and representation for all the legal needs in society" (New Zealand Department of Justice, 1981:77). The Grey Lynn Neighbourhood Law Office has greatly expanded its services since it was opened in August 1977 (see table 17). Two other community law centers have been opened: at Dunedin in June 1980 and in Wellington in June 1981. They differ from Grey Lynn in that they are operated by volunteer law students rather than paid qualified staff and offer part-time advice and legal referral services similar to those of a Citizens' Advice Bureau, although students can continue to assist with cases when they are referred to a barrister. In 1980 there were fifty-four Citizens' Advice Bureaux with sixty full-time employees throughout New Zealand. The first office was opened in 1970 in Ponsonby, then a working-class area. Citizen's Advice Bureaus offer advice and act as referral agencies for law firms; forty-four of the bureaus have legal advice services.

EVALUATIONS OF LEGAL SERVICES

Although there is widespread usage of legal aid, ethnic minorities (who are overrepresented among accused), the physically and mentally disabled, and those in institutions lack adequate access to law (New Zealand Department of Justice, 1981:38–46). Furthermore, the various schemes are poorly coordinated and underdeveloped; there was widespread ignorance and bewilderment about the legal system generally, particularly about the assistance to which people are entitled, and low-income wage earners often were ineligible.

ATTITUDES TOWARD LEGAL SERVICES

CLIENTS

A 1978 survey revealed that 74 percent of the public had obtained legal advice at some point during their lives (Heylen Research Centre, 1978:10), compared to 57 percent of the English population in 1977 (Royal Commission, 1979: vol. 2, p. 184). Members of the managerial and professional classes used lawyers most (83.2 percent); laborers and the semiskilled used them least (60.5 percent) (Heylen Research Centre, 1978: 10). Most clients (80 percent of respondents) used lawyers in connection with economic matters: to transfer property (39 percent), for financial transactions (16 percent), to invest money (8 percent), and for general business purposes (17 percent) (ibid., 55). Women used lawyers less than did men (70 percent vs. 78.2 percent) (ibid., 10).

Those who had used lawyers generally were quite pleased with the experience (ibid., 55). On the whole, they were satisfied that lawyers had their interests at heart, gave sufficient explanations, did not pass their cases off to juniors, and devoted sufficient time to the matter. They were, however, less satisfied that lawyers were knowledgable and even more inclined to think that lawyers were too cautious and did not provide their best services. Their greatest grievance was that lawyers were so expensive. Those who had visited a lawyer to defend a criminal charge or pursue a matrimonial matter (and thus probably received legal aid) had the worst impressions of the lawyer's concern and involvement. On the other hand, those who had seen a lawyer about a business or investment matter (25 percent of the respondents) were most likely to feel that the lawyer was approachable and involved. Few of these, if any, were recipients of legal aid.

LAWYERS

When asked to identify the important issues facing the legal profession, lawyers ranked business problems high (see table 18). Among the respondents, 59 percent considered the cost of running a legal practice to be a serious concern. Issues of supply control also were prominent, as were questions of demand creation. Few saw the possible range of demand creation, however; lawyer respondents were not eager to enter new markets. Lawyers expressed little concern that the profession was providing insufficient community service or that legal rights were not being enforced, but Auckland lawyers were more aware of these problems, perhaps because of the presence of a neighborhood law office (Heylen Research Centre, 1978: 26).

CONCLUSION

New Zealand is a class society (Bedggood, 1981: 72), and in any class society the law always must be an unjust exchange between unequal combatants (Pashukanis, 1978). We saw that the New Zealand public believe that the law is in the responsible hands of a homogeneous profession that provides a fair service and can mitigate the consequences of unequal access to law. Are they right? We have no real evidence concerning the quality of lawyer's services, although we have seen that those likely to be served by legal aid also are more likely to be dissatisfied with their experiences with lawyers. We can draw definite conclusions about some things, however. The legal profession is an inegalitarian institution. Lawyers are either principals (and thus capitalists, because they exploit labor), employees (workers), or sole practitioners (petty bourgeois). They come overwhelmingly from the upper status groups; within the profession, those with higher status backgrounds are advantaged occupationally. Thus class divisions outside the profession are reproduced within it.

Education plays a powerful role in recruiting people into and excluding them from social elites. In New Zealand the mechanism is elite public and private secondary schools. Further selection occurs at entrance to universities and, within them, to law faculties. The limitations on social mobility—both entry to the profession and position within it—work against the long-term interests of the profession by inhibiting meritocracy. Status rather than talent will surface. On the other hand, it is useful to have lower-status workers content to do the profession's menial work without demanding the same rewards. These positions increasingly are going to middle-class women, who are displacing working-class men. Thus far, the main factor inhibiting the entry and promotion of women has been patriarchy—a male-centered orientation expressing a paternal but basically antagonistic attitude toward women. Its effect is manifest in women lawyers' unequal access to rewards (income, prestige, and types of work). Even when women become partners, they earn much less than do men. Some women are responding to these pressures by forming self-help groups. There are two such groups in Auckland: the Women's Subcommittee of the Law Society and the Auckland Women Lawyers Association. They also are forming their own law practices. Membership within a gender status does not necessarily mean identification with the collective interests of that status, however (Murray, 1984: 187). Such identification requires a level of feminist consciousness that is difficult for women to acquire or maintain in a hostile male environment. New practitioners (which includes most women) usually are overworked and seldom have the energy to invest in anything but their own survival. Just by being there, women are doing something positive for other women. Not all women lawyers see the parallels between their own experiences of inequality and class or ethnic discrimination, however (ibid., 183).

The third main division within the legal profession reflects racism. It overlaps with class divisions, since Polynesian lawyers generally are from working-class backgrounds (ibid., 110). The small number of non-Pakeha in the profession is being remedied somewhat by the Polynesian preference in university recruitment. There also are a few Polynesian law firms in predominantly Polynesian areas, so that minority admissions also have strengthened the representation of minority interests.

Although there have been changes, the law remains a profoundly inegalitarian profession: that white middle-class men have been joined by some white working-class men and middle-class women in subordinate positions is not a great improvement. What is the profession doing to equalize access to law practice? Almost nothing. Few lawyers recognize that there is unequal access; those who do may not see it as a problem. Feminist lawyers are a notable exception; they have put pressure on the Law Societies to change; however, nothing comparable has been done about the class and ethnic inequalities within the profession. Of course, the problem is too profound to be overcome by any remedial affirmative action program, although this is an essential short-term response.

Although the profession is elitist, it can be a force for change. One in four of the lawyers I interviewed described their political views as ranging from "barely left" to "radical left." New Zealand lawyers often have taken leading roles in actions such as the injunction against the Rugby Union's tour of South Africa. The legal profession has not approached legal aid in the same spirit, however; instead, it has seen legal aid as a means of satisfying the profession's needs for both symbolic capital and income. Now that the profession has lost much of its control over supply, and greater numbers of lawyers are seeking work, there is pressure to expand areas of competence and to enhance professional prestige. The professional project is not only expansive but also is defensive. The profession fights to protect its territory from incursions by the public, who increasingly are using legal do-it-yourself manuals, such as "divorce kits" and "how to buy your own house kits." Lawyers even have to resist the state, which is preparing to perform conveyances for its clients. The last word on the professional project appropriately can be left to Don Dugdale (1985), Vice President of the New Zealand Law Society:

> Some of the silly people who say that conveyancing is easy go on to complain that lawyers have a "conveyancing monopoly." Monopoly is a loaded word. It is used to make what is a wide provision enacted by Parliament to protect the public from quacks and charlatans look like an economic conspiracy. It would I suppose be possible to get rid of these prohibitions and let any witch doctor practise as a surgeon or dentist or a lawyer or electrician, at the expense of the gullible. Or it would be possible to do what has been done in other countries, to establish a tribe of half lawyers who make a living out of the less complicated aspects of conveyancing. But in this event it would be necessary to set up a whole new structure to establish educational qualifications, protection against negligence and peculation. Experience abroad suggests that the service

provided is less good, the costs are no less and all you have achieved is to have satisfied the Walter Mitty fantasies of some failed land agent or disgruntled legal executive.

An even more chilling prospect, from the point of the public, is a proposal currently being peddled by ambitious functionairies employed by the [State] Housing Corporation to act as a solicitor to those purchasers who are buying their homes with the assistance of Housing Corporation loans. Why chilling? Because if the Housing Corporation is allowed to fill this role it will be difficult to resist similar claims by some finance companies. But everyone with any experience knows that members of the public need to be protected from these finance companies, not delivered trussed and bound into their clutches.

Tables

7.1. How New Zealanders Perceive Their Lawyers

	Public image as perceived by lawyers, % (N = 243)	Lawyers' self-image, % (N = 243)	Actual public image, % (N = 1,000)
Lawyers are highly qualified professional people			
Yes, very much so	15.2	16.9	70.8
Yes, quite a lot	72.4	60.7	24.2
No, not really	12.4	21.5	4.7
No, not at all	—	0.9	0.2
Lawyers are intelligent people			
Yes, very much so	11.5	10.7	58.6
Yes, quite a lot	78.6	78.1	35.3
No, not really	9.9	10.7	5.3
No, not at all	—	0.5	0.3
Lawyers are honest, trust-worthy people			
Yes, very much so	3.7	17.7	47.7
Yes, quite a lot	64.6	76.1	36.1
No, not really	29.2	6.2	13.6
No, not at all	2.5	—	1.0
Lawyers are wealthy people who earn a lot of money			
Yes, very much so	44.2	4.5	38.4
Yes, quite a lot	45.0	19.9	35.9
No, not really	9.9	69.3	22.7
No, not at all	0.9	6.3	1.9

7.1. *Continued*

	Public image as perceived by lawyers, % (N = 243)	Lawyers' self-image, % (N = 243)	Actual public image, % (N = 1,000)
Lawyers are conservative and old-fashioned people			
Yes, very much so	5.3	4.1	4.7
Yes, quite a lot	45.3	21.5	29.6
No, not really	46.1	60.7	52.0
No, not at all	3.3	13.7	12.8
Lawyers are serious and unapproachable people			
Yes, very much so	4.1	1.6	4.8
Yes, quite a lot	40.7	10.3	18.2
No, not really	49.4	58.7	51.4
No, not at all	5.8	29.4	25.2
Lawyers are tricky or sharp people			
Yes, very much so	3.2	0.8	9.7
Yes, quite a lot	47.8	12.4	28.1
No, not really	45.9	62.0	40.3
No, not at all	3.3	24.8	21.0
Lawyers are competent at the job that they do			
Yes, very much so	4.9	6.1	53.5
Yes, quite a lot	81.4	86.8	38.8
No, not really	13.7	6.2	5.9
No, not at all		0.9	1.4
Lawyers are flashy and trendy people			
Yes, very much so	0.8	0.4	2.3
Yes, quite a lot	4.1	2.0	13.5
No, not really	56.8	50.9	57.2
No, not at all	38.3	46.7	26.3
Lawyers are concerned about the needs of the community			
Yes, very much so	—	6.6	26.6
Yes, quite a lot	26.3	61.4	41.6
No, not really	64.6	28.2	24.4
No, not at all	9.1	3.8	5.4

7.1. *Continued*

	Public image as perceived by lawyers, % (N = 243)	Lawyers' self-image, % (N = 243)	Actual public image, % (N = 1,000)
Lawyers are hardworking people			
Yes, very much so	7.4	36.9	44.4
Yes, quite a lot	60.7	60.6	39.6
No, not really	28.5	2.0	13.2
No, not at all	3.4	0.5	1.8
Lawyers are overpaid for the work that they do			
Yes, very much so	23.0	3.3	20.8
Yes, quite a lot	54.7	8.7	34.7
No, not really	21.4	57.7	34.6
No, not at all	0.9	30.3	8.9
Lawyers have too much influence in the community			
Yes, very much so	5.3	—	6.6
Yes, quite a lot	25.5	5.7	18.7
No, not really	57.6	59.5	60.4
No, not at all	11.6	34.8	12.7
The job that lawyers do has a lot of prestige			
Yes, very much so	28.0	12.8	47.9
Yes, quite a lot	61.2	56.4	36.9
No, not really	9.9	28.7	12.9
No, not at all	0.9	2.1	1.5
The job that lawyers do is boring and uninteresting			
Yes, very much so	1.6	—	3.6
Yes, quite a lot	19.5	7.4	17.5
No, not really	57.7	41.3	53.6
No, not at all	21.2	51.3	24.5
The job that lawyers do is complex and difficult			
Yes, very much so	12.8	16.9	34.7
Yes, quite a lot	76.0	64.9	43.5
No, not really	11.2	16.9	17.0
No, not at all	—	1.3	4.3

7.1. *Continued*

	Public image as perceived by lawyers, % (N = 243)	Lawyers' self-image, % (N = 243)	Actual public image, % (N = 1,000)
The job that lawyers do is rewarding and satisfying			
Yes, very much so	7.0	29.7	45.2
Yes, quite a lot	65.9	64.1	44.9
No, not really	24.1	5.7	7.6
No, not at all	3.0	0.5	1.1
The job that lawyers do is a necessary one			
Yes, very much so	12.0	56.6	80.5
Yes, quite a lot	68.4	41.7	15.8
No, not really	17.9	1.7	2.4
No, not at all	1.7	—	1.2

Source: Heylen Research Centre (1978: 30–33).

7.2. Occupational Profile

	Average age		Percent male		Percent wage worker		Percent unemployed		Number	
	1971	1981	1971	1981	1971	1981	1971	1981	1971	1981
Barristers or solicitors	42.6	38.1	98.2	91.1	28.5	40.5	0.3	0.7	2,634	3,915
Employees: corporate or law teachers	40.9	36.4	92.3	69.0	80.7	85.0	3.8	0	26	126
Judges or magistrates	56.9	54.4	98.6	100	100	100	0	0	73	99
Other judges	0	60.8	0	66.6	0	100	0	0	0	9
All lawyers	41.5	38.3	98.1	90.5	30.8	43.3	0.3	0.7	2,733	4,149

Source: Crothers (1985).

7.3. Size of Law Firms and Other Law Offices in the Auckland Metropolitan Area, 1920–1985

Number of lawyers	1920		1940		1960		1980		1985	
	No. of offices	%	No. of offices	%	No. of offices	%	No. of offices	%	No. of offices	%
1	48	50.5	138	63.0	77	41.2	113	46.9	96	33.3
2	29	21.5	47	21.5	50	26.7	21	8.7	68	23.6
3	13	13.7	16	7.3	25	13.4	22	9.1	38	13.2
4	5	5.3	5	2.3	15	8.0	20	8.3	19	6.6
5	—	—	6	2.7	7	3.7	16	6.6	15	5.2
6	—	—	2	0.9	7	3.7	10	4.1	5	1.7
7	—	—	—	—	1	0.5	5	2.1	12	4.2
8	—	—	3	1.4	1	0.5	6	2.5	8	2.8
9	—	—	2	0.9	2	1.1	7	2.9	—	—
10	—	—	—	—	1	0.5	2	0.8	3	1.0
11–19	—	—	—	—	1	0.5	17	7.1	15	5.2
20–29	—	—	—	—	—	—	—	—	7	2.6
30+	—	—	—	—	—	—	2	0.8	2	0.7
Totals	95	100	219	100	187	100	241	100	288	100
Total no. of lawyers	155		384		443		911		1,172	

7.3. Continued

Number of lawyers	1920 No. of offices	1920 %	1940 No. of offices	1940 %	1960 No. of offices	1960 %	1980 No. of offices	1980 %	1985 No. of offices	1985 %
Average no. of lawyers per firm	1.63		1.75		2.4		3.8		4.1	
Companies										
1	—		11		5		10		NA	
2	—		1		—		2		NA	
3+	—		—		2		1		NA	
Total	—		12		7		13		NA	
Public sector										
1			4		5		7		—	
2			—		1		3		—	
3+			—		1		4		—	
Total			4		7		14		—	
University			—		1		13		—	

Source: Crothers (1985).

7.4. Distribution of New Zealand Lawyers by Practice Situation, 1871–1981

Year	Number of lawyers	Population per lawyer[a]	Percent employers	Percent self-employed	Total % entre-preneurs	Percent employed	Number of judges
1871	229	1,120	NA[b]	NA	NA	NA	NA
1874	230	1,500	NA	NA	NA	NA	NA
1878	285	1,607	NA	NA	NA	NA	13
1881	362	1,475	NA	NA	NA	NA	15
1886	511	1,214	NA	NA	NA	NA	13
1891	571	1,171	41.3	32.9	74.2	12.4	51
1896	604	1,230	45.2	39.4	84.6	11.3	36
1901	636	1,283	57.4	28.5	85.9	13.7	50
1906	785	1,193	60.3	20.4	80.7	17.7	43
1911	950	1,114	67.1	16.0	83.1	14.8	40
1916	1,125	1,022	61.9	10.3	72.2	26.1	51
1921	1,234	1,031	70.5	12.0	82.5	16.8	51
1926	1,635	861	68.5	9.5	78.0	21.5	47
1931	NA	NA	NA	NA	NA	NA	NA
1936	1,762	893	68.3	8.9	77.2	20.9	45
1941	NA	NA	NA	NA	NA	NA	NA
1945	1,455	1,201	81.3	6.0	86.3	11.4	NA
1951	NA	NA	NA	NA	NA	NA	NA
1956	1,945	1,119	NA	NA	84.4	15.6	54
1961	2,091	1,156	NA	NA	76.1	23.9	57
1966	2,366	1,132	NA	NA	73.8	26.1	67
1971	2,660	1,077	NA	NA	71.5	28.5	73
1976	3,525	888	NA	NA	63.9	36.1	87
1981	4,149	783	NA	NA	59.5	40.5	108

[a] Excludes Maori, 1871–1945.
[b] Not available or reclassified.
Source: Crothers (1985).

7.5. Age Distribution of Lawyers, 1896–1981

Year	Under 20	20–24	Age 25–44	45–64	65+
1896	0.8	3.5	62.3	29.6	3.8
1901	0	4.7	60.3	31.2	3.6
1906	0	7.4	59.4	29.4	3.3

Year	Under 25	25–34	35–44	45–54	55–64	65+
1916	5.6	4.5	53.4	30.7		5.8
1921	0	2.1	33.7	29.5	15.4	15.6
1926	0.3	9.1	34.4	27.8	15.6	12.9
1931	0.1	1.7	27.8	32.0	21.2	17.2
1936	0.1	0.1	18.8	28.9	32.3	29.7
1956	0.3	3.1	38.6	24.7	20.5	12.3
1961	0	6.3	25.5	17.9	17.3	33.0
1966	0	6.3	29.3	21.6	13.0	29.5
1971	8.2	32.5	20.4	14.0	12.0	11.6
1976	8.2	41.2	20.7	7.3	8.6	8.6
1981	7.5	45.2	23.4	12.1	6.9	4.6

Source: Crothers (1985).

7.6. Gender of Lawyers, 1871—1981

Year	Total	Men	Women	Percent women
1871	229	229	0	0
1874	230	230	0	0
1878	285	285	0	0
1881	362	362	0	0
1886	511	511	0	0
1891	571	571	0	0
1896	604	604	0	0
1901	636	635	1	0.16
1906	785	783	2	0.25
1911	950	947	3	0.32
1916	1,125	1,122	3	0.3
1921	1,234	1,130	4	0.3
1926	1,635	1,631	4	0.24
1936	1,762	1,755	7	0.4
1945	1,455	1,426	19	1.3
1956	1,945	1,917	28	1.4
1961	2,091	2,058	33	1.6
1966	2,366	2,335	31	1.3
1971	2,660	2,613	47	1.8
1976	3,525	3,380	145	4.2
1981	4,149	3,693	348	8.9

Source: Crothers (1985).

7.7. Practice Situation of Lawyers by Father's Occupation

Father's occupation	Law firm partners and barristers sole No.	%	Sole practitioners No.	%	Employees No.	%	All lawyers No.	%
Lawyer	161	21.7	4	1.2	47	7.4	211	12.6
Other profession	129	17.3	45	15.1	266	42.2	440	26.3
Farmer	2	0.2	123	41.2	53	8.4	178	10.6
Executive—government	2	0.2	0	0	0	0	2	0.1
Executive—other	206	27.8	40	13.3	85	13.4	331	19.8
Business proprietor	81	11.0	2	0.6	58	9.2	141	8.5
Clerical	0	0	80	26.7	48	7.6	128	7.6
Tradesperson	161	21.7	5	1.8	74	11.8	241	14.4
Total	742	100	299	100	631	100	1,672	100

Number of missing observations = 15.
Source: Murray (1984).

7.8. Occupation of Fathers of Members of Auckland District Law Society

Father's status	Percent male lawyers in 1982	Percent female lawyers in 1982	Percent all lawyers in 1982	Percent New Zealand population in 1966
SES 1	32.5	44.4	33.6	5.8
SES 2	28.4	23.4	27.9	19.3
SES 3	21.5	15.7	21.0	13.3
SES 4				28.2
SES 5	} 17.6	} 16.6	} 17.5	21.3
SES 6				12.1

Sources: Murray (1984: 106); New Zealand Census 1966.

7.9. Ethnic Minorities in the Legal Profession, 1871–1981

Year	Number of lawyers	Number of Maori	Number of Pacific Island Polynesian	Other ethnics	Percent non-Pakeha
1926	1,635	3	0	2	0.3
1936	1,762	0	2	3	0.3
1945	1,455	1	0	0	0.06
1956	1,945	6	0	0	0.3
1961	2,091	5	0	0	0.23
1966	2,366	6	0	0	0.25
1971	2,660	11	0	0	0.4
1976	3,525	16	9	33	1.6
1981	4,149	29	9	70	2.6

Source: Crothers (1985).

7.10. Practice Situation of Lawyers by Secondary School Education

	Elite public	Other public	Elite private	Other private	Row total
Partner or barrister sole	409 (46.5%)	40 (13.0%)	253 (63.7%)	40 (39.2%)	742 (44.0%)
Sole practitioner	206 (23.4%)	43 (14.2%)	7 (1.8%)	42 (41.0%)	299 (17.7%)
Employee	265 (30.1%)	223 (72.8%)	138 (34.5%)	20 (19.8%)	646 (38.3%)
Column total	881 (52.2%)	307 (18.2%)	398 (23.6%)	102 (6.0%)	1,687 (100.0%)

Missing cases = 0.
Source: Murray (1984).

7.11. Lawyer Income by Elite versus Nonelite Practice

Income, NZ$	Not elite	Elite	Row total
Under 10,000	12 (0.9%)	0 (0.0%)	12 (0.8%)
10,000–15,999	173 (12.5%)	0 (0.0%)	173 (10.6%)
16,000–19,999	349 (25.3%)	2 (0.7%)	351 (21.6%)
20,000–29,999	333 (24.1%)	2 (0.7%)	335 (20.6%)
30,000–39,999	80 (5.8%)	42 (17.0%)	121 (7.5%)
40,000–49,999	166 (12.0%)	80 (32.6%)	246 (15.1%)
50,000 or more	267 (19.4%)	120 (48.9%)	387 (23.8%)
Column total	1,379 (84.9%)	244 (15.1%)	1,624 (100.0%)

Gamma = 0.70; missing cases = 63.
Source: Murray (1984).

7.12. Lawyer Income by Gender

Income, NZ$	Men	Women	Row total
Under 10,000	0 (0.0%)	12 (7.0%)	12 (0.8%)
10,000–15,999	126 (8.7%)	47 (27.1%)	173 (10.6%)
16,000–19,999	291 (20.1%)	59 (34.1%)	351 (21.6%)
20,000–29,999	288 (19.9%)	46 (26.7%)	335 (20.6%)
30,000–39,999	120 (8.2%)	2 (1.0%)	121 (7.5%)
40,000–49,999	242 (16.7%)	4 (2.1%)	246 (15.1%)
50,000 or more	383 (26.4%)	4 (2.1%)	387 (23.8%)
Column total	1,450 (89.3%)	174 (10.7%)	1,624 (100.0%)

Gamma = −0.67; missing cases = 63.
Source: Murray (1984).

7.13. Mean Lawyer Income by Gender and Practice Situation (NZ$)

	All	Men	Women
Barristers sole and law firm partners	43,528	44,117	27,678
Sole practitioners	31,482	32,142	21,250
Employees	24,548	26,521	17,115

Source: Murray (1984).

7.14. Lawyer Income by Father's Occupation, Ethnicity, Gender, Practice Situation, and Continuous Experience, NZ$ (Grand Mean Income NZ$35,007)

Variable + category	Percent cases	Unadjusted deviation	Eta	Deviation adjusted for independents	Beta
Father's occupation					
SES 1	929	1,170		930	
SES 2	465	4,670		7,300	
SES 3	283	−6,450		−10,580	
SES 4−6	252	−3,820		−3,550	
			0.24		0.36
Ethnicity					
Non-Pakeha	212	2,490		5,240	
Pakeha	1,316	−0,400		−840	
			0.06		0.12
Gender					
Male	1,388	1,570		1,010	
Female	140	−15,490		−9,950	
			0.28		0.18
Practice situation					
Partners and barristers sole	701	8,550		6,010	
Sole practitioners	255	−1,300		0,060	
Employees	573	−9,880		−7,380	
			0.48		0.35
Length of service					
0−4 years	279	−12,660		−6,690	
5−9 years	322	−0,070		4,750	
10−14 years	435	4,410		−50	
15−19 years	101	−3,780		−13,110	
20−24 years	103	−1,710		−3,280	
Over 24 years	289	7,570		7,000	
			0.39		0.33

Multiple r squared 0.398
Multiple r 0.631

Source: Murray (1984: 165).

7.15. Enrollment in Selected Faculties of Auckland University, 1965–1985

	Law			Architecture			Commerce			Medicine		
Years	M	F	%F	M	F	%F	M	F	%F	M	F	%F
1965	448	17	3.6	291	5	1.6	646	51	7.3	—	—	—
1966	513	23	4.2	312	6	1.8	690	42	5.7	—	—	—
1967	538	27	4.7	324	5	1.5	722	57	7.3	—	—	—
1968	629	42	6.2	400	10	2.4	849	59	6.4	—	—	—
1969	669	59	8.1	405	9	2.1	935	68	6.7	—	—	—
1970	715	84	11.1	422	17	3.8	1,044	96	8.4	—	—	—
1971	683	109	13.7	444	23	4.9	1,049	102	8.8	35	10	22.0
1972	699	143	16.9	409	34	7.6	978	139	12.4	77	24	23.7
1973	596	149	20.0	436	45	9.3	967	164	14.5	119	39	24.6
1974	597	195	24.6	436	74	14.5	1,004	174	14.7	129	52	28.7
1975	564	213	27.4	426	80	15.8	1,005	223	18.1	135	52	27.8
1976	548	245	30.8	449	127	22.0	1,132	277	19.6	300	153	33.7
1977	522	260	33.2	432	122	22.0	1,134	287	20.1	331	191	36.5
1978	548	271	33.0	433	123	22.0	1,216	306	20.1	377	222	37.0
1979	526	298	36.1	386	107	21.7	1,250	348	21.7	411	233	36.1
1980	532	321	37.6	386	106	21.5	1,223	355	22.4	420	249	37.2
1981	539	336	38.4	372	110	22.8	1,266	454	26.3	418	271	39.3
1982	521	371	41.5	366	115	23.9	1,302	525	28.7	403	269	40.0
1983	520	376	41.9	374	128	25.4	1,362	607	30.8	399	270	40.3
1984	604	481	44.3	364	144	28.3	1,381	690	33.3	401	262	39.5
1985	562	467	45.3	368	156	29.7	1,290	649	33.4	389	261	40.0

Source: John Clark, Assistant Registrar, Auckland University.

7.16. Lawyers' Work Specialties (in Percent)

Type of work	Ever worked[a]	Worked in last 12 months[a]	Most time spent at present
Conveyancing	96.8	83.9	34.5
Company and commercial	89.4	79.4	8.7
Estate	85.2	62.1	2.8
Family law	78.2	57.2	10.3
Criminal law	67.1	39.5	3.7
Other litigation	79.1	50.6	9.1
Tribunals	72.1	52.6	1.2
Other	18.4	17.7	4.6
None of the above	NA	NA	25.1

N = 243.
Note: a Multiple responses permitted
Source: Heylen Research Centre (1978: 9).

7.17. Caseload of Grey Lynn Neighbourhood Law Office, 1978–1980

Period	Inquiries	Files opened
8/1/77–7/31/78	2,126	518
8/1/78–7/31/79	5,703	585
8/1/79–7/31/80	8,710	634
8/1/80–9/30/80	1,925	125
Total	18,464	1,862

Source: New Zealand Department of Justice (1981: 95).

7.18. Lawyers' Views Concerning the Importance (in Percent) of Issues Facing the Legal Profession (N = 243)

Issues facing the profession	Serious	Minor	None
Continuing education	49.3	44.9	4.9
Cost of legal services to public	35.8	45.2	17.7
Poor communication between lawyer and client	28.3	57.7	13.1
Insufficient student training	61.7	32.5	4.9
Maintaining professional standards	34.5	52.8	12.3
Public image of lawyers	43.2	44.4	11.5
Poor communication between profession and public	36.6	48.1	14.4
Costs of running a practice	58.8	33.7	6.6
Insufficient job prospects for new graduates	50.2	39.5	9.4
Number of complaints received by Law Society	33.7	52.3	12.7
Too many legal executives	5.3	14.8	78.2
Increasing specialization	6.5	26.4	27.2
Government inroads into traditional fields	30.4	40.7	65.4
Insufficient work available	13.9	45.3	39.5
Unequal access of public to the law	13.9	45.3	39.5
Lawyers with sideline	26.7	50.2	21.8
Business interests	23.8	49.4	25.5
Sole practitioners inadequately prepared	38.2	47.3	12.8
Legal profession not providing sufficient community service	5.3	37.4	56.0
Areas neglected by skilled people (e.g., some parts of common law)	8.6	36.2	53.9
Practitioners involved in unethical conduct	22.6	59.7	16.4

Source: Heylen Research Centre (1978: 26).

7.19. Members of the Auckland District Law Society, 1982

Barristers sole		87
Principals		
Solicitor principal	26	
Barrister and solicitor principal	928	
Total		954
Employees		
Barrister and solicitor (private)	598	
Solicitor (private)	10	
Barrister and solicitor (government)	36	
Solicitor only (government)	2	
Total		646
Grand total		1,687

Source: Auckland District Law Society (1982).

7.20. Division of the Lawyer Sample

	Women	Men
Entrepreneurs	24	23
Employees	26	27

NOTES

I wish to thank John Hannan, Dave Bedggood, and Cluny MacPherson for their original assessment of the material and especially Charles Crothers for allowing me to use his data and for his criticisms throughout. I also am grateful for information from the following: Joan Bowring, Don Farr, Colin Hutchinson, Kay McKelvie, Shane Martin, Colin Q. Nicholson, Q.C., Shirley Potaka, Deborah Tohill, Margaret Vennell, Catherine West-Newmann, David Williams, and John Wood.

1. Although the New Zealand Department of Justice has commissioned studies on legal aid (1981), and the *Report* of the Royal Commisision on the Courts (1978) contains a section on the legal profession, there has been no systematic official or academic study of New Zealand lawyers other than my own thesis (1984) and Patrick Shannon's M.A. thesis (1974).

2. Some of the material used in this chapter was based on a December 1982 stratified random sample of the Auckland Law Society District, whose distribution is shown in table 19. In February 1982, the Auckland Law Society contained 1,687

members, 1,536 of whom were men. There was no problem in selecting thirty entrepreneurial and thirty nonentrepreneurial men. The methodological problem lay in sampling the small number of women employees (117) and the entrepreneurial women (34). I took a saturated sample of the women entrepreneurs and a substantial sample of nonentrepreneurial women. The responses subsequently were weighted to reflect the total membership of the Auckland Law Society (39.84 for male entrepreneurs, 21.45 for male employees, 1.8 for female entrepreneurs, and 5.03 for female employees). The finished structure of the sample design and the roles of the eventual respondents (out of a target sample of 120) are shown in table 20. The measure of association used is a gamma coefficient, where the data were ordinally or dichotomously grouped.

3. The public sector might also be said to include those who defend criminal accused under the legal aid system, even though they are in private practice (Heylen Research Centre, 1978: 10). There is no public defender in New Zealand. Similarly, criminal prosecutions are conducted by private practitioners, mostly by Crown solicitors appointed by warrant. When the Crown Solicitor's Office cannot handle the work because of a conflict of interest, it is assigned to other firms. There are Crown solicitors in every major city.

4. Table 8 uses the standard New Zealand occupational scale, which contains six categories (Elley & Irving, 1972). For statistical reasons, the lawyers' fathers were placed in only four groupings, the last of which contained the bottom three categories. The 1966 census figures for the general population were chosen because they most closely resembled the age cohort of the fathers of my respondents.

5. Gamma $= (P - Q)/(P + Q)$; it is an ordinal measure of association varying between $+1$ and -1. It has a very intuitive interpretation (Nie et al., 1975).

6. The multiple correlation ratio is a nonlinear measure of relationships between the predictor variable and the dependent variable. The square of the multiple correlation ratio equals the proportion of variance in the dependent variable that statistically is explained by the set of predictor variables.

REFERENCES

Auckland District Law Society. 1981. "Report of the Working Party on Women in the Legal Profession." Auckland: Auckland District Law Society.

———. 1982. *Auckland Law Society Register.* Auckland: Auckland District Law Society.

Auerbach, Jerold. 1976. *Unequal Justice.* New York: Oxford University Press.

Bedggood, David. 1981. *Rich and Poor in New Zealand.* Sydney: George Allen and Unwin.

Blair, A. P. 1983. *Accident Compensation in New Zealand.* Wellington: Butterworths.

Bush, Graham. 1972. *Decently and in Order.* Auckland: Collins.

Cain, Maureen. 1976. "Necessarily Out of Touch: Thoughts on the Social Organisation of the Bar," in Pat Carlen, ed., *The Sociology of Law*. Keele: University of Keele.

Carlin, Jerome. 1962. *Lawyers on Their Own*. New Brunswick, N.J.: Rutgers University Press.

Castle, Lester. 1977. "The Contemporary Lawyer," 1977 *New Zealand Law Journal* 10–16.

Charters, Ruth. 1982. "The Conveyancing Monopoly and the Public Interest," 1982 *New Zealand Law Journal* 162–163.

———. 1985. "Letter of the Law," 12–14 *Broadsheet* 131 (July/August).

Cooke, Robin, ed. 1969. *Portrait of a Profession: The Centennial Book of the New Zealand Law Society*. Auckland: H. J. Reed.

Crothers, Charles. 1976. "Occupational Status and the Social Arithmetic of Class in New Zealand." Paper presented to the Annual Conference of the New Zealand Sociological Association.

———. 1977. "Sample Size Selection for Exploratory Surveys," 12(2) *New Zealand Statistician* 10–16.

———. 1985. "Census Occupational Datafile." Unpublished paper.

Dugdale, D. F. 1979. *Lawful Occasions*. Auckland: Auckland Law Society.

———. 1985. "Conveyancing not for Amateurs," *New Zealand Times* (July 7).

Elley, W. B., and J. C. Irving. 1972. "A Socio-economic Index for New Zealand Based on Levels of Education and Income from the 1966 Census," 7 *New Zealand Journal of Education* 153–167.

Giddens, Anthony, and David Held. 1982. "Introduction," in Anthony Giddens and David Held, eds., *Classes, Power and Conflict*. Berkeley: University of California Press.

Heylen Research Centre. 1978. *The Legal Profession: A Survey of Lawyers and Members of the Public*. Auckland: Heylen Research Centre and New Zealand Law Society.

———. 1980. *New Zealand Law Society Survey of Professional Incomes*. Auckland: Heylen Research Centre and New Zealand Law Society.

Hopkins, Robyn. 1983. Untitled memorandum. Auckland: Auckland Law School.

Howells, John. 1977. *Industrial Mediation in New Zealand: The First Two Years*. Wellington: Industrial Relations Centre (Victoria University Research Monograph 3).

Ison, T. G. 1980. *Accident Compensation*. London: Croom Helm.

Jones, John. 1983. *The Socio-economic Backgrounds of Students at Auckland University*. Auckland: Higher Education Office, University of Auckland.

Jones, P. E. R. 1973. "A Sociological Note on the Role of the Ombudsman," in S. Webb and J. Collette, eds., *New Zealand Society: Contemporary Perspectives*, pp. 242–252. Sydney: John Wiley.

Kawaharu, Hugh. 1977. *Maori Land Tenure: Studies of a Changing Situation*. Oxford: Clarendon Press.

Kelsey, Jane. 1983. "The 'Rule of Law' as a Tool of Colonisation of Aoteroa,

1840–1983." Paper presented at the Annual Conference of the New Zealand Sociological Association.

McBarnet, Doreen. 1984. "Law and Capital: The Role of Legal Form and Legal Actors," 12 *International Journal of the Sociology of Law* 231–238.

MacPherson, Cluny. 1977. "Polynesians in New Zealand: An Emerging Ethnic Class," in David Pitt, ed., *Social Class in New Zealand.* Auckland: Longman Paul.

———. 1984. "On the Future of Samoan Ethnicity in New Zealand," in Paul Spoonley, Cluny MacPherson, David Pearson, and Charles Sedgwick, eds., *Tauiwi: Racism and Ethnicity in New Zealand.* Auckland: The Dunmore Press.

Murray, Georgina. 1984. Sharing in the Shingles. M.A. thesis, sociology, University of Auckland.

———. 1985. "Access to Law." Paper presented at the Annual Conference of the Research Committee on Sociology of Law, International Sociological Association, Aix-en-Provence.

New Zealand Department of Justice. 1981. *Access to the Law Report: A Research and Discussion Paper.* Wellington: Planning and Development Division, Department of Justice.

New Zealand Department of Statistics. 1985. *New Zealand Official Year Book,* 90th ed. Wellington: Government Printer.

New Zealand Law Society. 1970. *Rules Governing the Conduct of Practitioners.* Wellington: New Zealand Law Society.

Nie, Norman H., C. Hadlai Hull, Jean G. Jenkins, Karin Steinbrenner, and Dale H. Bent. 1975. *SPSS: Statistical Package for the Social Sciences.* New York: McGraw-Hill.

Northey, J. F. 1962. "Legal Education and the Universities," 1962 *New Zealand Law Journal* 9.

———. 1970. "Trends in Legal Education," in *Legal Education in the Seventies.* Auckland: Legal Research Foundation (Occasional Pamphlet No. 6).

Pashukanis, Evgeny. 1978. *Law and Marxism.* London: Ink Links.

Perry, Nick. 1985. "Corporatist Tendencies in Context: The New Zealand Case." Paper presented to the Australian and New Zealand Sociological Conference, Brisbane, Queensland.

Rathjen, Gregory. 1976. "The Impact of Legal Education on the Beliefs, Attitudes and Values of Law Students," 44 *Tennessee Law Review* 85.

Royal Commission on University Education in New Zealand (Reichell-Tate Commission). 1925. *Report.*

Royal Commission on Legal Services (Benson Commission). 1979. *Final Report* (2 vols.) (Cmnd. 7648/1). London: HMSO.

Royal Commission on the Courts (Beattie Commission). 1978. *Report.* Wellington: Government Printer.

Sandford, Kenneth. 1974. *Personal Injury by Accident and the Accident Compensation Commission Act: A Commentary.* Wellington: Accident Compensation Commission.

Sargisson, Hannah. 1982. *Women in the Legal Profession: A Discussion of Their*

Changing Profile. LL.B. (honours) dissertation, Auckland Law School.

Shannon, Patrick. 1974. *Professing the Law.* M.A. thesis, sociology, University of Auckland.

————. 1982. "Bureaucratic Initiative in Capitalist New Zealand: A Case Study of the Accident Compensation Act of 1972," 88 *American Journal of Sociology* 154–175.

Sinclair, Keith. 1983. *A History of the University of Auckland, 1883–1983.* Auckland: University of Auckland Press and Oxford University Press.

Sloper, Geoff. 1981. "Geographical Distribution of Law Services throughout New Zealand," in *New Zealand Department of Justice, Access to the Law* (Report No. 6), Appendix 14. Wellington: Planning and Development Division, Department of Justice.

Williams, David. 1983. *The Use of Law in the Process of Colonisation: An Historical and Comparative Study with Reference to Tanzania (Mainland) and New Zealand.* Ph.D. dissertation, law, University of Dar es Salaam.

8

Past and Present

A Sociological Portrait of the Indian Legal Profession

J. S. GANDHI

My effort in this chapter is to construct, within a sociological framework, a collective picture of the legal profession in contemporary Indian society. To do so, I explore the available historical evidence concerning its genesis and evolution in the last 200 years. India's legal profession is an important case for those who argue, as I do, against the assumption that professions emerge as a uniform response to the universal demands of complex modern societies. Rather, their form is shaped by their history. The distinctive feature of the contemporary Indian legal profession is that it has no roots in Indian cultural history. Instead, its origins lie in the entry and entrenchment of the British in India and the superimposition of their own legal system on the traditional institutions of caste, family, and village *panchayat* (an assembly of elders who administer justice). I trace this history from the beginning, describe the profession's current organization and functioning, and discuss its social concerns and its potential for facilitating social change.

THE GENESIS OF THE PROFESSION

THE EARLIEST BRITISH ADMINISTRATION

Although this matter has been debated (Rocher, 1968/69; Sarkar, 1958), there is practically no evidence that lawyers were found in either Hindu or in Mughal India. The literature about both eras emphasizes the active role of the judges. In addition, although the Mughals boasted a multi-tiered judicial and revenue system, they respected the autonomy of the local traditional judicial system composed of village and caste panchayats. Lawyers as a category of experts representing the claims of litigants scarcely could have existed as a functional specialty, therefore, and they certainly never evolved into a profession in the modern sense. Nothing in the political system, the judicial institutions, or the fabric of social relations was conducive to such a development. Just as secularization and the rise of centralized monarchies were necessary prerequisites to the development of legal professions in the West, so the onset of a new form of rule had the same effect in India. The legal profession emerged as a necessary concomitant of the inception and evolution of the British administration.

The entry of the British into India ushered in a fundamental change in the political order, replacing the independent monarchical states with an overarching political authority. For the first time in Indian history a unified ruling elite had appeared, with the will and ability to establish comprehensive control over the whole subcontinent. To succeed in this task, the British had to enact uniform codes, which could apply equally to an ethnically diverse society and yet be effective. The ultimate product was the series of codes and acts drafted by the first Indian Law Commission (established in 1834) and its successors and passed between 1859 and 1882 (Lindsay, 1941). The enactment of uniform law made allowances for some local rules and customs so as not to offend the sensibilities of certain caste groups and turn them against the state. This did not prevent the passage of legislation abolishing cruel and discriminatory practices from the past, such as the laws against *suttee* (the burning of a widow on her husband's funeral pyre) and slavery, the Caste Disabilities Removal Act of 1850, and an act allowing Hindu widows to remarry (Singh, 1973).

In this legislation, the British were "acting out" in an alien setting practices that could have meaning only in a system of rational legal administration, based on adversary proceedings in which each party is represented by a legal expert. Yet the British attempted to establish a Western legal system without ensuring that the parties would have the benefit of legal expertise.

The creation of the first British court in Bombay in 1672 established the foundation for the legal profession in India; however, the British East India Company refused to send out either a legally trained judge or any attorney or law clerk. For a century they held the view that they had a choice as to whether or not to introduce a legal profession. They plainly were apprehensive that the members of such a profession might lead the struggle for independence, an apprehension that was not unwarranted, as we shall see. It is puzzling, however, that even a profit-seeking organization could think it possible to have a rational, court-based, adversarial system without a legal profession.

Mayor's courts were established early in the eighteenth century in the presidency towns of Bombay, Calcutta, and Madras, the seats of the Company's government; however, the mayors and aldermen who sat in them had no legal knowledge and were in no position to question the assertions of those who practiced before the courts as attorneys. In the late eighteenth century the impossibility of the situation eventually was recognized. A Supreme Court was set up at Calcutta in 1774, empowered by charter to admit both advocates and attorneys, to remove them from the roll for reasonable cause, and to prevent those not duly enrolled from practicing in the court (Morley, 1849). The court applied mainly English law, although it recognized Hindu and Muslim law in family matters. It had broad jurisdiction in Calcutta but a much more limited competence in the *mofussil* (countryside). The establishment of this court allowed English barristers to practice as advocates and become judges, and thereafter English barristers also were to be found in Madras and Bombay (although Supreme Courts were not established in these cities until 1801 and 1823, respectively). The attorneys practicing in the mayor's courts ceased pleading and became solicitors (Schmitthener, 1968/69).

After this the legal profession expanded steadily. The professionals at the Supreme Courts enjoyed great prestige and handsome earnings, which they displayed in their lordly style of living (ibid.). These lawyers charged fees two to five times as high as those in England and actively resisted attempts by the courts to regulate them. This is understandable in light of the great prosperity of the presidency towns. Indians used these courts and sometimes interpreted or advised on Hindu and Muslim law; however, no Indian lawyers practiced before them until the middle of the nineteenth century, when there were a handful of Indian solicitors in Calcutta.

DISCREPANT STRUCTURES

Although the profession in the presidency towns was not formally organized, it was controlled by the judges, who were qualified lawyers. The position in the mofussil was very different. The British allowed two discrepant professional structures to emerge and coexist in the first half of the nineteenth century, unifying them only gradually. Starting in 1772, civil and criminal courts were established in all district headquarters in the mofussil, with a *sudder* (provincial court) at the apex. These courts applied mainly Hindu and Muslim law. Although the sudder courts were staffed by British civil servants, most other judges were Indian, as were all those representing the parties, until 1846.

For the first twenty years, there were no forms of pleading and no limitations on who could draft pleadings or the fees they could charge. Bengal Regulation VII of 1793 empowered the sudder *dewanee adalat* (provincial civil court) to appoint *vakeels* (pleaders: sometimes spelled "vakīls") and control their conduct; it also required that vakeels be trained at Hindu and Muslim religious schools at Benares and Calcutta.

The British approach to the profession in the mofussil was no more than a series of ad hoc responses to obvious problems. Since the mofussil system was isolated from the courts in the presidency towns, its practitioners could not interact with or be influenced by the barristers and solicitors in the latter. *Mukhtars*, who functioned as attorneys and could appear in the criminal courts in the mofussil, were not regulated at all until 1865. British administrators justified the dual legal system as a way of maintaining the indigenous character and lifestyle of the people; however, this was no reason for failing to deal with the obvious oddities and irregularities of practice in these courts. A more cogent explanation for their neglect was the primacy of their interests in the presidencies, the industrial and mercantile nerve centers of their still fragile economic empire.

UNIFICATION OF THE LEGAL SYSTEM

While this dual system persisted, the only breach in the wall between British and Indian practitioners was the admission of barristers to practice in the sudder courts in 1846. However, in 1858 the government superseded the East India Company and took direct charge. As a result, in 1862, the courts were consolidated into a unified system in each of the three presidencies, with High Courts in Calcutta, Bombay, and Madras at the apices. This allowed a professional ethos gradually to diffuse throughout the legal community. Indian lawyers could practice alongside their British counterparts, absorbing norms of professional conduct derived from the British legal system. The profession quickly became Indianized, secularized, and homogenized.

Although some British resisted the idea of appointing Indians as judges or allowing them to plead in the new High Courts, a more liberal view prevailed. The High Courts could admit the vakeels who had pleaded at the Sudder courts, although they had to demonstrate additional qualifications, and a distinction arose between vakeel and pleader. The functional distinction between barrister (now advocate) and solicitor (or attorney: the terms were used interchangeably) was maintained only for those High Court cases that would have been heard in the old Supreme Courts, not for appellate matters. Indian vakeels also could be promoted to the rank of advocate. The Pleaders, Mukhtars and Revenue Agents Act of 1865 and the Legal Practitioners Act of 1879 defined the grades of practitioners more clearly.

Another element in the Indianization of the profession occurred when Indians began to qualify as barristers in the English Inns of Court and return to practice in India. This qualification carried considerable prestige, but it was open only to those whose families could support them, not only during their education but also during the early years of practice. Among the fathers of the 108 Indian barristers known to be practicing in 1885, 11 percent were titled and official, 18 percent were landowners, 17 percent were lawyers, 18 percent were civil servants and other professionals, and 16 percent were businessmen (Duman, 1983). Nevertheless, the proportion of Indians rose rapidly. In 1871 the Bombay High Court had 38 solicitors (28 British and 10 Indian) and 24 advocates (17 British and 7 Indian). In 1911 there were 150 solicitors (20 British and 130 Indian) and 250 advocates (16 British and 234 Indian). For years Indian advocates encountered racial prejudice by British solicitors and skepticism among some Indian litigants, who feared that Indians lacked the competence to conduct cases in English; however, this prejudice diminished as Indian advocates began to win notable successes against British opponents (Setalvad, 1946).

Legal professions in the West underwent a lengthy process of universalization (gradually admitting all who could complete the formal legal training) and secularization (abandoning tests of adherence to and knowledge of religious rules). In India, these changes were compressed into fifty years. Not only did they open the profession to properly qualified Indians, who achieved formal and substantive parity with the British, but they also eliminated religious discrimination. Secular legal education displaced the requirement of education in a Hindu or Muslim college, and legislation such as the Punjab Chief Court Act of 1886 dispensed with religious qualifications for practice.

Nevertheless, the pre-1862 division of the court system had a lasting effect on the profession. The Legal Practitioners Act of 1879 preserved the existing divisions of advocates, attorneys, and vakeels in the High Courts and pleaders, mukhtars, and revenue agents in the lower courts, while defining the qualifications of each and procedures for promotion. These occupations had no power of self-government; they were under the jurisdiction of the High Court. Not until 1926 did the Indian Bar Councils Act put the regulation and control of the profession into the hands of newly established provincial bar councils. These had fifteen members: the advocate general, 10 elected by the High Court bars, and four nominated by the High Court bench. These councils regulated legal education, admission to the profession, and discipline of misconduct.

Although this was a major step toward autonomy, the profession remained divided by grades and regions. National Independence in 1947, followed by proliferation of reform legislation and codification, generated strong pressure for a unified bar (Mahajan, 1963). The All-India Bar Committee, established in 1951 to consider this and related questions, led to passage of the Advocates Act of 1961. Practicing pleaders who were law graduates could become advocates on payment of a fee; the rest could continue to practice as pleaders, but no more pleaders were to be enrolled. Subject to such historical survivals, there was to be only one class of legal practitioners, the advocates, who would be admitted by state bar associations on examination and then be entitled to practice anywhere in India. This has completed the process of homogenizing and unifying the bar in India.

THE INDIAN LEGAL PROFESSION TODAY

SIZE AND ORGANIZATION

The Indian legal profession is very large in absolute terms compared to those in other countries; in 1983, the Bar Council of India reported a total of 247,373 advocates.[1] In proportion to population the picture is very different, however: 2,770 people per advocate (1981 census). This varies regionally, from 747 in Delhi to 4,731 in Andhra Pradesh and 8,373 in the outlying states of Assam, Nagaland, Meghalaya, Manipur, and Tripaya. Delhi is the capital city and the seat of the Indian Supreme Court and a host of other courts and tribunals (e.g., income tax and labor tribunals). The states following in rank order are noted for food production and industry and also include two of the earliest High Courts in the country. Thus the population-lawyer ratio appears to vary with the size and growth of the economy, the extent of metropolitan social life, and the length of the tradition of professional activity in the British courts.

Indian advocates practice in a three-tiered court system, with appeals from district court to High Court and Supreme Court, as well as in other courts and tribunals. The 1971 census reported the distribution of legal occupations (see table 1). The last two categories in table 1 are paralegals, who may or may not have a law degree. The strongly "male" image of the legal profession is consistent with the absence of women, while its predominantly urban character results from the location of courts.

The Indian legal profession is unusual in the disparity between the number of students enrolled in law courses and the number who enter the legal profession. Menon (1979) reports that even in leading universities, such as Delhi, only 10 percent of the law students enrolled intend to go into practice. Kidder (1974) found that only 2 percent of Bangalore law students intended to go into practice. There was an intake of 200,000 students in all law schools in 1978/79, while only 10,000 new lawyers registered with the country's bar councils. We can understand this disproportion by placing it in the context of the massive unemployment among educated Indians. A degree in law improves the holder's prospects of employment or promotion in both the private and the public sectors.

Manufacturing companies, in particular, employ law graduates to draft legal documents and to advise about employment matters, especially those arising from labor legislation on wages, bonuses, medical facilities, and working conditions. Employers can hire these graduates at the same salary as clerical employees.

This huge output of law graduates also contributes to the generally low level of education within the profession. The standard of teaching varies from indifferent to deplorable. Many students work full time during the day, studying part time in the evening. Most take their studies casually, leaving their preparation to the end of term and relying on cheap course notes and guides. This combination of poor teaching, mass production of law graduates, the low proportion of graduates intending to practice, and acute unemployment among the educated produces a vicious circle. The system of professional education increasingly, although unintentionally, is directed toward enhancing employment prospects of any kind. Despite the small proportion of law students who become practitioners, lawyers often talk of overcrowding in the profession (Gandhi, 1982) and blame it for unprofessional practices, such as touting, overcharging, and professional rivalry. There is ample evidence (Morrison, 1972; Sharma, 1984; Gandhi, 1982) that lawyers in the lower courts procure business through touts. I also found the practice in higher courts. The popular perception of the Indian legal profession as highly exploitative and unscrupulous is not unfounded (Gandhi, 1982). Although the Bar Council of India can promulgate standards for professional education and rules for professional conduct, such anecdotal information as we have suggests that few complaints are filed, they take an extremely long time to process, and substantial penalties are rare.

SOCIAL BACKGROUND

The legal profession in India has always been and still is elitist. The traditional stratification of Indian society, in which caste and class have broadly corresponded, persists today; nearly half the population still lives below the poverty line. The high cost of legal education confines the profession to high castes and upper classes. During British rule, law was the most remunerative profession in India, and a successful lawyer earned far more than his British counterpart (Schmitthener, 1968/69; Morrison, 1972). For the affluent, expenditure on legal education was the soundest investment. In addition, the independence movement offered a successful lawyer a chance of elevation to the bench.

The few studies available support these speculations. The high social standing of the earliest Indian barristers already has been mentioned. Of

162 Hindu lawyers who played an important part in the independence movement, at least a third were Brahmins and probably substantially more, and the rest came from landed or business families (Bhasin, 1985). Similarly, out of the 31 Hindu supreme court judges during 1950 to 1967, nearly half were from Brahmin families and the rest from professional and business families (Gadbois, 1968/69). Similarly, half of the Hindus currently on the Indian Supreme Court are Brahmins (judging by caste titles).

Empirical studies of lawyers practicing at the district court level indicate a virtually total monopoly of the bar by the locally dominant castes (Morrison, 1968/69; Rowe, 1968/69; Kidder, 1974; Sharma, 1984). I discovered that a district court bar in the Punjab was dominated by the urban merchant castes, even though the rural areas accounted for the largest single category of litigants. The combination of caste with social networks produces a highly stratified profession. Those with intimate connections to the police, the surrounding rural areas, the judiciary, or the profession prosper much faster than do those without connections or touts. It is not technical excellence but rather network connections and professional deviance that produces profits. As one respondent said, "Ten per cent of the Bar monopolises ninety per cent of the total business." The composition of the profession thus is elitist, and its functioning is particularistic. It does not fulfill the ideal of a profession serving all but mirrors the basic inequalities of Indian society.

INDIAN LAWYERS IN POLITICS AND SOCIAL CHANGE

GROWTH OF SOCIOPOLITICAL SENSITIVITY

The ability of lawyers to use their legal expertise to further their own interests or those of clients always has placed them close to the centers of political power. The increase in the sociopolitical sensitivity of the Indian profession during the sixty years prior to Independence in 1947 is an unusual illustration of this proposition. They were central participants in the political affairs of the country and still are today. A barrister was the first president of the Indian National Congress, which led the struggle, and practitioners at the Bombay High Court also were important party leaders at that time. Some lawyers gave up their careers to assist Mahatma Gandhi in his Champaran project for investigating the exploitation of Indian peasants by the British indigo planters (Schmitthener, 1968/69). I have described elsewhere (Gandhi, 1982) the participation of lawyers in the Punjab who protested against repressive legislation and were subject to specially vindictive measures after the Amritsar massacre. Although there was disagreement as to whether to cooperate with British institutions, some lawyers pursued equality in the courts, and others gained experience in provincial and municipal councils, thereby acquiring political and administrative realism.

This deep involvement of lawyers in the independence movement may be explained partly by the fact that, as members of a class accustomed to respect, they were able to elicit continuing respect from both Indians and the British by invoking British law. It also is clear that many who later became leaders of free India foresaw the British withdrawal and the chance of occupying high office. For instance, the correspondence between Jawaharlal Nehru, the first prime minister, and his father, a leading lawyer, shows that the latter was willing to use his professional earnings to support his son in politics. Nearly half of the 184 lawyers who participated in the independence movement ultimately occupied important political positions in free India (Bhasin, 1985). There seems to have been an element of conscious career building, especially when one considers the development of the profession since Independence.

INDEPENDENCE AND SOCIAL CHANGE

Lawyers played a central role in drafting of the Constitution. Nearly all those who made the most substantial contributions in the Constituent Assembly were lawyers, notably Pandit Jawaharlal Nehru, Sardar Patel (Home Minister), Dr. B. R. Ambedkar (later Law Minister), and Dr. R. Prasad (the first president). The proceedings clearly show the part played by lawyers in elaborating basic concepts of secularism, democracy, and egalitarianism. Because lawyers understood Indian social reality in formal rather than substantive terms, they also introduced some well-known ambiguities into the Constitution, such as the uncertainty about whether fundamental rights or the directive principles of state policy were primary (Rao, 1968).

Even after the Constitution was adopted, lawyers continued to play a substantial role in national politics. They represented 35.3 percent, 31.4 percent, 30 percent, and 26.9 percent of the first four *Lok Sabhas* (national legislature; lower house of Parliament). Although Galanter (1968/69) argues that the participation of lawyers in post-Independence politics has declined, table 2 shows that the proportion of lawyers in the Seventh and Eighth Lok Sabhas has remained high. They are appreciably more strongly represented in Congress-I (the government party), and two-thirds of the senior ministers in the last two cabinets have been lawyers. The *Rajya Sabha* (the council of states; upper house of Parliament) has a similar proportion of lawyers.

Recent figures show that Indian lawyers still successfully seek positions of political power; however, the pattern of the profession's political participation has changed. During the independence movement, the mass of the profession were collectively involved in politics (Prasad, 1957); now lawyers participate individually, seeking personal gains by aligning themselves with a particular party. The parties also benefit by using lawyers' forensic capabilities, both inside and outside the legislature. One can hardly exaggerate their role in selling party policies to the illiterate and semiliterate masses.

THE PROFESSION FOR SALE?

The maintenance of a legal system that is independent of politics and can protect the rights of all requires a disinterested legal profession that will defend due process and equality against the narrowly instrumental views of the political process. Lawyers in Indian politics instead have become mere advocates for the interests of the party or group they have joined. A content analysis of lawyers' public pronouncements about the contemporary legal system during the period 1976 to 1981 clearly confirms this.[2] Lawyers associated with the government (most of whom belonged to the Congress-I party) tried to persuade the judiciary and the rest of the profession to accept constitutional departures favored by the government, such as giving it greater authority over the administration of justice and removing the constitutional power of the courts to invalidate legislation infringing fundamental rights. Lawyers from both the Congress-I and Janata parties indulged in legal populism, asserting their party's commitment to making justice inexpensive and accessible and establishing visible (and ineffective) committees to propose reforms. When practitioners organized meetings on contemporary issues, they would invite leaders of the governing party to speak, thus enhancing the legitimacy of both politicians and lawyers by expressing their shared concern for the common good and giving the lawyers entry into the inner circles of the party in power.

These activities are symptomatic of a decline in professional autonomy, which can infect even the judiciary. Less social distance between lawyers, politicians, and the judiciary (Mahajan, 1983) exposes judges to the temptation to seek preferment on political grounds. The absence of any effective professional disciplinary process can only foster the general ethos of opportunism. For all the schemes of legal reform and legal aid that have been advanced, only a strong legal profession could overcome the many inadequacies of the Indian legal system as an instrument of social change (Gandhi, 1985). Instead, it not only engages in the unprofessional practices I have described but also lacks any critical sense of its own deficiencies. It confines itself to congratulatory rhetoric regarding its central place in the past and future of Indian society, whereas its actual attitudes are selfish and profit-oriented.

CONCLUSION

Let me recapitulate the argument briefly. Because the legal profession emerged during the colonization process, it has no roots in Indian society. It came to be regarded as a means of social mobility, disconnected from traditional society. It grew as a result of the country's economic development and urbanization. It was an important element in the struggle for independence and thus became an avenue of sociopolitical advancement. In the post-Independence period, lawyers have pursued power and advantage for themselves and their parties and have failed to develop any sense of a professionalism that would control deviant practices or promote legal values or the public interest. The outlook for the profession is bleak, unless it changes radically.

Tables

8.1. Distribution of Legal Professionals in India, 1971

Category	Total (No.)	Male (%)	Female (%)	Urban (%)	Rural (%)
Judges and magistrates	5,949	98.9	1.1	87.0	13.0
Legal practitioners and advisors	90,906	99.0	1.0	89.7	10.3
Legal assistants[a]	5,695	99.96	0.04	47.3	52.7
Jurists and legal technicians (including petition writers)[a]	45,118	98.3	1.7	67.5	32.5
Total	147,662	99	1	81	19

[a] Unqualified (no law degree).

Source: Census.

8.2. Lawyers in Politics

Category	Seventh Lok Sabha (1980–1984)	Eighth Lok Sabha (1985–)
Members of Parliament	527	512
Law graduates		
Number	168	149
Proportion of members	31.8%	29.1%
Law graduates—ruling parties		
Number	121	123
Proportion of ruling parties	34.4%	NA
Law graduates—opposition party		
Number	47	24
Proportion of opposition party	26.7%	NA
Cabinet members	41	50
Law graduates		
Number	19	25
Proportion of cabinet	46.3%	50%
Ministers	19	15
Law graduates		
Number	12	10
Proportion of ministers	63%	67%

NOTES

1. Advocates must register with their regional bar councils in order to practice; this figure is the sum of those contained in the lists submitted to the Bar Council of India by the regional bar councils. Because these lists are not always submitted regularly, the figures may not be current. In addition, it includes lawyers who leave practice for other employment without informing the regional bar council (7 percent to 10 percent of the total).

2. My analysis is based on statements reported in both the national media and some of the more important regional newspapers.

REFERENCES

Bhasin, Lalit. 1985. *Lawyers in the Freedom Struggle of India.* Delhi: Delhi Art Press.
Duman, Daniel. 1983. *The English and Colonial Bars in the Nineteenth Century.* London: Croom Helm.

Gadbois, George H. 1968/69. "Indian Supreme Court Judges: A Portrait," 3 *Law & Society Review* 317.

Galanter, Marc. 1968/69. "Introduction: The Study of the Indian Legal Profession," 3 *Law & Society Review* 201.

Gandhi, J. S. 1982. *Lawyers and Touts: A Study in the Sociology of the Legal Profession.* New Delhi: Hindustan Publishing Corporation.

———. 1985. "Potentials and Parameters of Social Change Through Law in the Contemporary Indian Society: A Sociological Assessment," in Adam Podgorecki, Christopher Whelan, and Dinesh Khosla, eds., *Legal Systems and Social Systems.* London: Croom Helm.

Kidder, Robert L. 1974. "Formal Litigation and Professional Insecurity: Legal Entrepreneurship in South India," 9 *Law & Society Review* 11.

Lindsay, Benjamin. 1941. "Law," in L. S. S. O'Malley, ed., *Modern India and the West.* London: Oxford University Press.

Mahajan, Krishan. 1983. "Dinner Lawyering," *The Hindustan Times* (October 10).

Mahajan, Mehr Chand. 1963. *Looking Back.* Bombay: Asia Publishing House.

Menon, Madhav N. R. 1979, "Reforming Legal Education: Issues, Priorities and Proposals," in *Report of the Committee on Reforms in Legal Education in the 1980s.* New Delhi: AILTA.

Morley, William H. 1849. *An Analytical Digest of all the Reported Cases Decided in the Supreme Court of Judicature etc.* London: W. H. Allen.

Morrison Charles. 1968/69. "Social Organization at the District Courts: Colleague Relationships among Indian Lawyers," 3 *Law & Society Review* 251.

———. 1972. "Munshis and their Masters: The Organization of an Occupational Relationship in the Indian Legal System," 31 *Journal of Asian Studies* 309.

Prasad, Rajendra. 1957. *Autobiography.* Bombay: Asia Publishing House.

Rao, B. Shiva. 1968. *The Framing of India's Constitution* (5 vols.). New Delhi: Indian Institute of Public Administration.

Rocher, Ludo. 1968/69 "'Lawyers' in Classical Hindu Law," 3 *Law & Society Review* 383.

Rowe, Peter. 1968/69. "Indian Lawyers and Political Modernization: Observations in Four District Towns," 3 *Law & Society Review* 219.

Sarkar, U. C. 1958. *Epochs in Hindu Legal History.* Hoshiarpur: Vishveshvaranand Vedic Research Institute.

Schmitthener, Samuel. 1968/69. "A Sketch of the Development of the Legal Profession in India," 3 *Law & Society Review* 337.

Setalvad, C. H. 1946. *Recollections and Reflections: An Autobiography.* Bombay: Padma Publications.

Sharma, K. L. 1984. *Sociology of Law and Legal Profession.* Jaipur: Rawat Publications.

———. 1982. *Indian Social Problems.* Horsham, England: JK Publishers.

Singh, Yogendra. 1973. "Legal System, Legitimation and Social Change in India," *Working Paper for the Seminar on Law and Social Change*, organized by the Indian Council of Social Research, New Delhi, March 21–29.

Contributors

Richard L. Abel is Professor of Law at the University of California, Los Angeles. He has written widely about the legal profession, torts, and dispute processes and has been editor of the *Law & Society Review* and *African Law Studies*. He edited *The Politics of Informal Justice* (2 volumes) (Academic Press, 1982). His forthcoming books are *The Legal Profession in England and Wales* (Basil Blackwell, 1987) and *American Lawyers* (Oxford University Press, 1988).

Harry Arthurs is Professor of Law at Osgoode Hall Law School and President of York University. He has written extensively on the legal profession, legal education, labor relations, and administrative law. His most recent book is *"Without the Law": Legal Pluralism and Administrative Justice in Nineteenth Century England* (University of Toronto Press, 1985).

J. S. Gandhi is Associate Professor of Sociology of Law at the Jawaharlal Nehru University, New Delhi. He is the author of *Lawyers and Touts: A Study in the Sociology of the Legal Profession* (Hindustan Publishing Corporation, 1982) and senior author of *"Socio-Economic Study of Village Mithepur"* and has contributed articles to professional journals.

Philip S. C. Lewis is Senior Research Fellow at All Souls College, Oxford. He founded the Working Group for Comparative Study of Legal Professions and edited (with Robert Dingwall) *The Sociology of Professions: Lawyers, Doctors and Others* (Macmillan, 1983). He has written about the legal profession and legal aid and the sociology of law and is coauthor of *Social Needs and Legal Action* (Martin Robertson, 1973) and author of the eighth edition of *Gatley on Libel and Slander* (Sweet & Maxwell, 1981).

Georgina Murray is a junior lecturer in sociology at Auckland University. Her M.A. thesis, "Sharing in the Shingles," was the basis for her contribution to the present volume. She is completing her Ph.D. thesis on interlocking company directorships and their relationship to economic patterns in New Zealand.

Alan Paterson is Professor of Law at the University of Strathclyde. He has written about the legal profession and legal aid and is the author of *The Law Lords* (Macmillan, 1982) and *The Legal System of Scotland* (W. Green, 1983).

David Weisbrot teaches law at the University of New South Wales and formerly was Dean of Law at the University of Papua New Guinea. He is the author or coauthor of *Criminal Law and Practice of Papua New Guinea* (1979; 2d ed., 1985), *Law and Social Change in Papua New Guinea* (1982), *Australian Criminal Law and Process* (in press), and *Australian Lawyers* (in press).

Richard Weisman is Associate Professor of Sociology, Glendon College, York University. His recent book, *Witchcraft, Magic, and Religion in Seventeenth Century Massachusetts* (University of Massachusetts Press, 1984), dealt with changes in legal, popular, and theological conceptions of witchcraft.

Frederick H. Zemans is Professor of Law at Osgoode Hall Law School. He is a fellow of the International Society of Procedural Law and has written extensively on legal aid and the provision of the legal services, the legal profession, and family law and is editor of *Perspectives on Legal Aid* (Greenwood Press, 1979).

Index

Designer: U.C. Press Staff
Compositor: Asco Trade Typesetting Limited
Text: 11 Palatino
Display: Palatino
Printer: Edwards Bros., Inc.
Binder: Edwards Bros., Inc.